ARMENIAN APOCRYPHA

RELATING TO ABRAHAM

Society of Biblical Literature

Early Judaism and Its Literature

Rodney A. Werline, Series Editor

Editorial Board

Mark J. Boda
George J. Brooke
Esther Glickler Chazon
Steven D. Fraade
Martha Himmelfarb
James S. McLaren
Jacques van Ruiten

Number 37

ARMENIAN APOCRYPHA

RELATING TO ABRAHAM

Armenian Apocrypha

Relating to Abraham

Michael E. Stone

Society of Biblical Literature
Atlanta

ARMENIAN APOCRYPHA
Relating to Abraham

Copyright © 2012 by the Society of Biblical Literature

All rights reserved. No part of this work may be reproduced or transmitted in any form or by any means, electronic or mechanical, including photocopying and recording, or by means of any information storage or retrieval system, except as may be expressly permitted by the 1976 Copyright Act or in writing from the publisher. Requests for permission should be addressed in writing to the Rights and Permissions Office, Society of Biblical Literature, 825 Houston Mill Road, Atlanta, GA 30329 USA.

Library of Congress Cataloging-in-Publication Data

Stone, Michael E., 1938-
 Armenian apocrypha relating to Abraham / by Michael E. Stone.
   pages cm. — (Early Judaism and its literature ; no. 37)
 Includes bibliographical references.
 ISBN 978-1-58983-715-7 (paper binding : alk. paper) — ISBN 978-1-58983-716-4 (electronic format)
 1. Testament of Abraham—Criticism, interpretation, etc. 2. Abraham (Biblical patriarch) I. Title.
 BS1830.T32S76 2012
 229'.9140.1667—dc23

2012041815

Printed on acid-free, recycled paper conforming to
ANSI/NISO Z39.48-1992 (R1997) and ISO 9706:1994
standards for paper permanence.

Contents

Preface ix
Abbreviations xi
List of Works Published Here by Date xv
List of Manuscripts Published Here xvi
List of Manuscripts Consulted in Appendix 1 xvii

GENERAL INTRODUCTION 1
    Character of the Armenian Abraham Traditions 1
    Specific Exegetic and Narrative Traditions 2
    Structure and Discussion of Selected Elements 3
    Biblical and Nonbiblical Episodes in the Abraham Saga 15
    Date of the Abraham Saga 16
    Sources of the Abraham Saga: The Ravens 18
    Sources of the Abraham Saga: Early Armenian Commentaries
        on Genesis 20
    Affinities of Armenian 24
    Editorial Procedures 24

TEXTS AND TRANSLATIONS

1. LISTS AND CHRONOLOGY (M2769) 29
    Text 1 32
    Text 2 33

2. STORY OF FATHER ABRAHAM 36
    Պատմութիւն Հայր Աբրահամու 37
    Story of Father Abraham 41

3. BIBLICAL PARAPHRASES ON ABRAHAM 51
    Text and Translation 51

4. THE MEMORIAL OF THE FOREFATHERS ABRAHAM,
    ISAAC, AND JACOB 55
    The Character of the Document 56
    Remarks on the Text, Collations, and Apparatus 57

Ի սմին աւուր յիշատակ նախահարցն. Աբրահամու.
Իսահակայ եւ Յակոբայ.................................. 58
Variant Readings.. 62
On This Day Is the Memorial of the Forefathers, Abraham,
Isaac, and Jacob...................................... 64
Appendix: Continuation of M1665 down to Jacob.................. 71

5. GENEALOGY OF ABRAHAM............................... 78
Ազզաբանութիւն Աբրահամու............................ 78
Genealogy of Abraham.................................. 81

6. POEM ON ABRAHAM, ISAAC, MELCHIZEDEK, LOT 86
Ոտանաւոր Աբրահամու Սահակայ Մելքիսեթեկի Ղովտա 87
Poem on Abraham, Sahak, Melchizedek, Lot................... 89

7. THE TREE OF SABEK AND MELCHIZEDEK 94
Պատմութիւն վասն ծառոյն Սաբեկայ....................... 95
Story Concerning the Tree of Sabek........................ 97

8. STORY OF THE HOLY FATHER ABRAHAM AND
OF ISAAC, HIS SON, AND OF MAMRĒ, HIS SERVANT 101
Recension A 101
Պատմութիւն սուրբ հօրն Աբրահամայ եւ Սահակայ
որդոյ նորա, եւ Մամբրէի ծառայի իւրոյ.................. 103
Վասն Սահակայ որդոյ Աբրահամու 106
Variant Readings...................................... 110
Story of the Holy Father Abraham and of Isaac, His Son,
and of Mamrē, His Servant 112
Concerning Mamrē, Who Was Abraham's Servant and
Pastured Sheep on the Mountain....................... 116
Concerning Sahak, Son of Abraham........................ 120

9. STORY OF FATHER ABRAHAM: RECENSION B 122
Story of Father Abraham – Text............................ 122
Story of Father Abraham – Translation 123

10. ABRAHAM IN AN ELENCHIC TEXT 125
Elenchic Text (M10200) – Text 125
Elenchic Text (M10200) – Translation....................... 126

11. THE STORY OF TERAH AND OF FATHER ABRAHAM 127
Manuscripts of Text 11 127
Պատմութիւն Թարայ եւ հօրն Աբրահամու 128

CONTENTS vii

    This Is the Story of Terah, and of Father Abraham 146
    Concerning the Birth of Sahak 160

11A. CONCERNING ABRAHAM'S HOSPITALITY 166
    վասն Հիւրընկալութեան Աբրահամու ի վերայ
        Ճանապարհին. 166
    Concerning Abraham's Hospitality on the Way 169
    Վասն Ծնընդեան Իսահակայ. 172
    Concerning Isaac's Birth. 174

12. SERMON CONCERNING THE SODOMITES. 178
    /fol. 206v / Քարոզ ի բան վասն Սոդոմացւոցն ի բանն
        որ ասէ աղաղակ Սոդոմացւոց ելաւ առաջի իմ. 180
    Variant Readings. 188
    Sermon on the Word Concerning the Sodomites, in the Verse
        That Says, "The cry of the Sodomites went forth before me". 192

13. THE TEN TRIALS OF ABRAHAM, MS M717. 204
    Տասն փորձութիւնք Աբրահամու 205
    Ten Trials of Abraham 205

14. SYNAXARIUM, CONSTANTINOPLE 1730 206
    Synaxarium 1730 – Text. 207
    Synaxarium 1730 – Translation 209

15. SERMON CONCERNING HOSPITALITY. 213
    Քարոզ վասն հիւրընկալութեան. 213
    Sermon Concerning Hospitality 223
    Concerning the Birth of Sahak 230

Appendix 1: Other Abraham Works and Fragments 235

Appendix 2: Further Abraham Notes: Literary and Iconographic. 241

Bibliography 243

Index of Sources 253

Index of Names and Select Subjects 263

Preface

Nearly all of the texts published in this volume are seeing the light for the first time. Two of them, however, are extant in eighteenth-century Armenian printings, texts nos. 11A and 14. In this volume, they too are translated for the first time into a modern language. This book is a sequel to two earlier volumes, *Armenian Apocrypha: Relating to Patriarchs and Prophets* (Jerusalem: Israel Academy of Sciences and Humanities, 1982) and *Armenian Apocrypha: Relating to Adam and Eve* (SVTP 14; Leiden/New York: Brill, 1996). In view of the wealth of still unpublished Armenian apocryphal literature, further sequels can be envisaged.

Not all the apocryphal Armenian Abraham texts are included in this volume. I have chosen to publish those that seem to be of particular interest. Additional texts have been examined in manuscripts, and some indication of their character and content is included in the Appendix at the end of this work. Even then, more unpublished texts still live on in manuscripts.

I acknowledge the permission of the librarians and curators of the various collections to publish the texts from manuscripts in their collections: the Matenadaran in Erevan, the Armenian Patriarch of Constantinople, the Director of the Oriental Division of the Staatsbibliothek in Berlin, the Bibliothèque nationale de France, and the British Library. At various points the librarians and their staffs were most helpful. Permission to reprint the section of Biblical Paraphrases (text no. 2 here) from *Armenian Apocrypha: Relating to Patriarchs and Prophets* was granted by the Israel Academy of Sciences and Humanities.

The research for this book was supported by the Israel Science Foundation Grant no. 46/09, and my travel to Armenia in autumn 2010 in connection with the research was partly supported by the Jerusalem Armenian Studies Committee.

I am indebted to my friends Gohar Muradyan and Theo Maarten van Lint, who helped me with some knotty points of reading and decipherment. Ishayahu Landa, Oren Abelman, and Shira Golani were very supportive research assistants.

Michael E. Stone
Jerusalem, July 2011 ירושלים, תמוז תשע"א

ABBREVIATIONS

AAP	Michael E. Stone, Dickran Kouymjian, and Henning Lehmann, *Album of Armenian Paleography* (Aarhus: Aarhus University Press, 2002)
ALD	*Aramaic Levi Document*
ANF	Ante-Nicene Fathers
Apoc. Ab.	*Apocalypse of Abraham*
CBET	Contributions to Biblical Exegesis and Theology
CSCO	Corpus scriptorum christianorum orientalium
Eusebius	
Dem. ev.	*Demonstratio evangelica*
Hist. eccl.	*Historia ecclesiastica*
Praep. ev.	*Praeparatio evangelica*
fol., fols.	folio, folios
GCS	*Griechische christliche Schriftsteller*
HAB	Hṙč'ea Ačaṙyan, Հայոց անձնանունների բառարան *Dictionary of Armenian Proper Names.* 5 vols. (Beirut: Sevan Press, 1972)
IDB	G. A. Buttrick, ed., *The Interpreter's Dictionary of the Bible.* 4 vols. (Nashville: Abingdon, 1962)
Irenaeus	
Adv. haer.	*Adversus haereses*
JJS	*Journal of Jewish Studies*
John Chrysostom	
Hom. Gen.	*Homiliae in Genesim*
JSHRZ	Jüdische Schriften aus hellenistisch-römischer Zeit
JSP	*Journal for the Study of the Pseudepigrapha*
JSJ	*Journal for the Study of Judaism in the Persian, Hellenistic, and Roman Period*
JSJSup	Journal for the Study of Judaism in the Persian, Hellenistic, and Roman Period Supplements
Justin	
Dial.	*Dialogue with Trypho*
LAB	*Liber Antiquitatum Biblicarum*
MH	Մատենագիրք Հայոց *Medieval Armenian Literature* (cited by centuries and pages) (Antelias: Armenian Catholicosate Press)

MHB	Ṙ. S. Łazaryan and H. M. Avetisyan Միջին հայերենի բառարան *Mediaeval Armenian Dictionary.* 2 vols. (Erevan: Erevan State University Press, 1987–1992)
MX	Movsēs Xorenacʻi [Moses of Khoren], *History of the Armenians*
NBHL	G. Awetikʻean, X. Siwrmēlean, and M. Awkʻerean Նոր բառգիրք հայկազեան լեզուի *New Dictionary of the Armenian Language.* 2 vols. (Venice: St. Lazzaro, 1836–37)
OIP	Oriental Institute Publications
OLA	Orientalia lovaniensia analecta
OrChrAn	Orientalia christiana analecta
Ona	Onomastica Sacra
Origen	
Hom. in Gen.	*Homiliae in Genesim*
OTP	James H. Charlesworth, ed., *Old Testament Pseudepigrapha.* 2 vols. (New York: Doubleday, 1983)
Palaea	A. Vassiliev, *Anecdota graeco-byzantina* (Moscow: Imperial University Press, 1893)
PG	J.-P. Migne, *Patrologia cursus completus: Series graeca.* 162 vols. (Paris, 1857–86)
Philo	
Abr.	*De Abrahamo*
Cher.	*De cherubim*
Post.	*De posteritate Caini*
Rabbinic writings	
ARN	*Abot de Rabbi Nathan*
Babylonian Talmud	
Ned.	*Nedarim*
Qidd.	*Qiddušin*
BM	*Bet ha-Midrasch*
Gen. Rab.	*Genesis Rabbah*
Lev. Rab.	*Leviticus Rabbah*
PRE	*Pirqe de Rabbi Eliezer*
SBLEJL	Society of Biblical Literature Early Judaism and Its Literature
SBLMS	Society of Biblical Literature Monograph Series
SBLRBS	Society of Biblica Literature Resources for Biblical Study
SVTP	Studia in veteris testamenti pseudepigrapha
T. 12 Patr.	*Testaments of Twelve Patriarchs*
T. Ab.	*Testament of Abraham*
T. Job	*Testament of Job*
T. Levi	*Testament of Levi*
Theodoret of Cyrrhus	
Quaest.	*Ad quaestiones magorum*

ABBREVIATIONS

TSAJ	Texte und Studien zum antiken Judentum
TU	Texte und Untersuchungen
vol., vols.	volume, volumes
< >	signifies a change made to a text, either to the reading of another manuscript or to an emendation, as noted in the apparatus.
{ }	corrupt words in Armenian text whether or not they are translated
[ ]	physical lacuna in the manuscript
( )	words added by the translator either for stylistic or for semantic reasons
~	transposed
+	adds

List of Works Published Here by Date

Text No.	Name	Manuscript[1*]	Year
01	Lists	M2679	981
02	Story of Father Abraham	M8531	1400-1499
03	Biblical Paraphrases	M3854 M4231	1471 1400-1499
04	Memorial of the Forefathers	M1665 M6092 BLEgerton 708	1441 1600-1699
05	Genealogy of Abraham	Galata 154	1600-1699(?)
06	Poem on Abraham, Isaac, etc.	SBB-IIIE MS or quart 805	1600-1699(?)
07	History Concerning the Tree of Sabek	BLEgerton 708	1600-1635
08	Story of Holy father Abraham: Recension A	BnF Arm 0186 M0569	1618 1618
09	Story of Holy Father Abraham: Recension B	M3411	1600-1699
10	Abraham in an Elenchic Text	M10200	1624, 1634, 1666
11	The Story of Terah and of Father Abraham	M6340 BLHarl5459	1651 1698
11A	Concerning Abraham's Hospitality on the Way	Constantinople1730	1730
12	Sermon on the verse concerning the Sodomites	M5571	1657-1659
13	The Ten Trials of Abraham	M717	1700-1799
14	Memorial of the Great Patriarch Abraham	Synaxarium, Cple 1730.	1730
15	Sermon Concerning Hospitality	Paris Arm. Museum 62	1600-1799

1. Manuscripts are referred to using the system of sigla initiated by the Association Internationale des Études Arméniennes, see Bernard Coulie, *Répertoire de manuscrits arméniens* (Leiden: AIEA, 1994).

List of Manuscripts Published Here

Manuscript	Year	Text No.	Name
BLEgerton 708	1600-1635	07	History Concerning the Tree of Sabek
BnF0186 M0569	1618 1618	08	Story of Holy father Abraham: Recension A
Constantinople 1730	1730 (Misc.)	11A	Concerning Abraham's Hospitality on the Way
Constantinople 1730	1730 (Synax.)	14	Memorial of the Great Patriarch Abraham
Galata 154	1600-1699(?)	05	Genealogy of Abraham
M717	1700-1799	13	The Ten Trials of Abraham
M10200	1624, 1634, 1666	10	Abraham in an Elenchic Text
M1665 M6092 BLEgerton 708	1441 1600-1699 1600-1699?	04	Memorial of the Forefathers
M2679	981	01	Lists
M3411	1600-1699	09	Story of Holy Father Abraham: Recension B
M3854 M4231	1471 1400-1499	03	Biblical Paraphrases
M5571	1657-1659	12	Sermon on the verse concerning the Sodomites
M6340 BLHarl5459	1651 1698	11	The Story of Terah and of Father Abraham
M8531	1400-1499	02	Story of Father Abraham
SBB-IIIE MS or quart 805	1600-1699(?)	06	Poem on Abraham, Isaac, etc.
Paris Arm. Museum 62	1600-1799	15	Sermon Concerning Hospitality

List of Manuscripts Consulted in Appendix 1

M1425	1690	Ējmiacin	Miscellany
M4618	1569-1714		Miscellany
M6541	1830-1862		Miscellany
M10561	1600-1699		Miscellany

General Introduction

Character of the Armenian Abraham Traditions

The documents published here are chiefly narratives telling the story of Abraham, a subject in which the Armenians showed a deep interest. This interest was expressed not only in apocryphal narratives, the focus of the present study, but in poetry, art, and exegesis as well. To trace all this abundance is beyond the scope of the present volume, in which I seek only to make known to the broader public the chief ways in which the Armenians told the Abraham story as preserved in fifteen unpublished, late-medieval manuscripts in Armenian. This corpus is itself not exhaustive. After all, in its simple biblical form, Abraham's is a very dramatic story, moving from one exciting incident and episode to another: Abraham's emigration to the Land of Israel, the binding of Isaac, Abraham's battle against the four kings, the double narratives of Sarah in the palaces of pagan monarchs, the story of Lot, and the burning of Sodom and Gomorrah. Above all, in Christian thought, the visit of the three "men" and their annunciation of Isaac's birth to Abraham, as well as Abraham's offering of Isaac, came to play a pivotal role, foreshadowing the annunciation of Christ's birth and the crucifixion.

To these exciting events, enticing grist to the mill of any storyteller, were added clearly Christian theological dimensions, nearly all in expansions and reformulations of the biblical narrative. Indeed, Abraham's recognition of the true God was an old Jewish theme, and Christians emphasized Abraham's role as the father of all believers (cf. Rom 4:16) and the idea of the bosom of Abraham as the resting place of the righteous souls (Luke 16:23).[1] In Jewish and Christian stories, Abraham's discovery and recognition of God were a focus of fascination. There exist numerous versions of this event in varied sources, going back as far as *Jubilees*, and ancient traditions are mixed with newer ones in the stories retailed here.

The strange story of Abraham offering Isaac,[2] taken as paradigmatic but yet always puzzling, plays a major role. It is not just connected with a trial of the

---

1. This was a commonplace in Armenian writing. See, e.g., Zak'aria Catholicos, *MH* 9th century, 279; Maštoc', *MH* 9th century, 650, and many other sources.

2. See Shulman 1993 and Licht 1973, for two interesting perspectives. Obviously the scholarly and exegetical literature on this topic is enormous. The exegesis of the Aqedah material is analyzed by Kessler (2004), while its stark narrative in Genesis is finely presented by Auerbuch (1957, 3-23).

patriarch's faith, for Christians it prefigured God's offering of his Son, and so the central mystery of Christian faith and understanding of the world.[3]

When Abraham knelt down after offering the ram, Isaac's substitute, text no. 15.47 says: "[T]here was a voice from the heavens which said, '. . . in the same way, I too did not pity my beloved Son for your sake who, having come, will free all the children of Adam from Hell because of your goodness.'" So Abraham's willing sacrifice is not just a parade example of faith, drawn from the past, but it intimates and atemporally reflects God's sacrifice of his Son for the sake of Adam's offspring and, therefore, the central mystery and meaning of the world.[4] Such understandings transform the Abraham narrative from a single, punctual event to a multilayered, eternal foreshadowing of the redemptive dynamic of the cosmos.

This and other themes developed in this fashion were woven into an expanded biblical narrative, and that was moved from a past significance to playing a usually typological or paradigmatic role in the history of salvation, as viewed through a Christian prism. In the present work, a number of other incidents in the Abraham story will be discussed from this perspective. Some of these are readings of incidents in the biblical text, and others are apocryphal and have been added to the line of the narrative, either in Armenian circles or in preceding Syriac or Greek narrations.

Characteristically, this approach regards the biblical story as the presentation of an unified history of redemption from creation to crucifixion, resurrection and parousia. Narrative sequence governs the surface relation of the episodes of the story, but, in fact, the central redemptive event gives an atemporal unity that supersedes any narrative sequence. This led to certain specific Christian interpretations or exegeses of Old Testament events or texts, and to the reformulation of such events as prefiguring, indeed enfolding, the salvific life and death of Christ in which their meaning was found. Both of these tendencies appear in the texts published here.

Specific Exegetic and Narrative Traditions

Once we enter into this worldview, the modern contrast of "Old" and "New Testament Apocrypha" has no meaning,[5] yet, of course, the origin and content of the various narrative events and episodes can and, indeed, should be considered. The preceding remarks bear on how such events and episodes were understood by the Armenian Christian tradition.

---

3. See Kessler 2004, 108–14. The typological interpretation of the Aqedah is found often. See, e.g., Zakʻaria Catholicos, *MH* 9th century, 300.

4. Precisely this interpretation is opposed in *Aggadat Berešit* 31 (end).

5. See text no. 1 below and also Stone 1999, 30–31; Stone in press A.

It is worth observing, moreover, that the traditions and interpretations that formed the building blocks of these developed narratives were not exclusively Christian in origin. It has been remarked that it is misleading, at least for the first millennium C.E., to treat the various religious and literary traditions that derive from the Bible—Judaism, Christianity, Islam, and others—as if they lived and grew hermetically sealed off from one another, basically as independent traditions. Instead, the interrelations between them are complex and dynamic and involve not only diachronic transmission of shared "parabiblical" material but also mutual borrowing and influence over centuries. In light of these relations, an ongoing process of interpretation and reinterpretation took place.[6] For this reason as well, in this book I have not attempted exhaustively to trace exact genealogical lines of derivation for specific elements of tradition, though I have noted some references to striking parallels from Jewish, Christian, and, to some extent, Muslim sources. So often, the attempt to achieve genetic certainty is misleading, for the evidence at our disposal is, by the nature of things, partial, and the fit of the material is only probable and not compelling.

The narratives published here overlap one another at many points and on occasion are quite repetitive. Nonetheless, the different writings have diverse interests and highlight varied points of view. The manuscript copies that we have at our disposal are mostly of the late medieval period, but elements of the embroidered Abraham tradition already occur in the first substantial Armenian literary manuscript, of the year 981.[7] Samuel Kamrjajorecʻi, also of the tenth century, knows such embroidered Abraham traditions.[8] So the embroidery of traditions was already present by then.[9]

Of course, it would be difficult to trace in detail the sources, growth, and development of these Armenian biblical retellings without an extensive investigation of much of the Armenian literary tradition, for Abraham material in one form or another is very widespread.[10] We have already remarked on the difficulties attending the attempt to clarify the genetic origins of specific units of the narrative tradition. The issues of literary interrelationship of these whole Abraham texts are, for the most part, equally problematic. Where the literary

---

6. See, e.g., Reeves 1999; 2005. An interesting example is the material on Jewish and Christian "encounters" collected in Grypeou and Spurling 2009a. At another level, the movement of traditions between different Christian channels, often widely separated in time and place, is significant. Such is illustrated in Stone 2002. Firestone (1990, 3–21) outlines how Islam drew on both biblical and nonbiblical material in its construction of Abraham legends. Islamic sources subsume much material into the Islamic legend of Abraham, Sarah, and the Tyrant; see Firestone 1990, 30–38.

7. See Matʻevosyan 1995; 1997.
8. *MH* 10th century, 742–44.
9. See also Appendix 2, below.
10. I have carried out some analogous research into the very rich Adam tradition, and I hope that that research will be paradigmatic for those interested in Armenian biblical retellings. I will present it in *Traditions of Adam and Eve in Armenian Literature* (in preparation).

relationships are obvious, they have been discussed below. It is not these obvious instances that pose the most severe challenge. The most difficult matter is the failure (almost fated) of attempts to establish clear relations of literary dependence or derivation between many of the narrative texts. Some sort of relationship is evident: some elements are shared and some expressions or turns of speech are common, but in as many other points the texts differ in this or that way, and one is not obviously more pristine than the other, nor one clearly dependent on another. Yet the exact nature of these literary relationships remains obscure.

Such a pattern of both sharing and difference between text forms typifies what I have called "textual clusters." I invoked this term to explain the complex relationships among the Adam books and equally among the Esdras apocalypses.[11] Now I suggest that it is appropriate also for describing the relationship among these allied but different Armenian Abraham texts. Having said this, I readily admit that the *description* or *naming* of the phenomenon is not an *explanation* of it. The chief advantage of a description is that it helps us to perceive the phenomenon of textual clusters, by distinguishing it from other types of relationships between texts. It is clearly a type of textual transmission, but it does not yield to conventional stemmatic analysis,[12] and we must consider alternative paradigms of textual development.[13] I stress, the phenomenon exists, we have named it, but naming is not explaining. The etiology of textual clusters may lie in the way the documents were created and used. To resolve this issue is a challenge lying ahead as the study of allied corpora of medieval texts advances.

Our goals here, however, are limited and aim at a more modest level of discourse: (1) to publish a good selection of Armenian Abraham narrative apocrypha with English translations, annotations, and critical apparatus; (2) to indicate in expository notes not merely difficulties of translation or edition but also the biblical sources and the cross-references within the present corpus; (3) to note some parallels from Jewish, Christian, Islamic, and other sources even though we do not seek to provide an exhaustive motif history of these stories; (4) to give some examples, from time to time, of the use of the apocryphal themes of these stories in medieval Armenian literature, again without aspiring to be exhaustive.

---

11. Stone 2011, 151–71.

12. See Stone 2011, 157 n. 16, relating to Tromp's textual genetics of the primary Adam Book.

13. It may well be that, if the context of the use of the Abraham texts is clarified, that may contribute to resolving this issue. There may also be something to learn from the types of manuscripts preserving these texts, and equally about their *Vorlagen*. For that, a complete (or as complete as possible) inventory of all Armenian Abraham texts is required as well as their analysis.

Structure and Discussion of Selected Elements

Each document published in this volume is provided with an introduction dealing briefly with its particular character and manuscripts, as well as major points of interest in its narrative and other significant issues. The document is edited and the text is annotated, mainly with remarks either on issues of decipherment or on those of grammar and language. A full translation is given, the notes to which relate to the content, biblical parallels, similar views in the other texts in this volume, and so forth. When the manuscript situation makes it necessary, a critical apparatus is added between the text and the translation.

In the rest of this General Introduction, I will outline the main narrative units that combined and recombined to form an expanded Abraham tale, into which various traditions and literary sources are woven. The name "embroidered Abraham saga," designates a reservoir of traditions that, while maintaining a measure of stability, nonetheless combined differently in each document.[14] In the texts studied here, the range and selection of incidents, their combination and recombination, their inclusion and exclusion changed and changed again. This Abraham saga, which is a conceptual construct, does not exist in full in any given textual crystallization and indeed may well never have existed as a whole in any single document anywhere. Even the fullest existing texts do not contain all the episodes, nor do they coincide completely with one another.[15] Of course, it is precisely this state of affairs that led me to regard these narratives as a textual cluster rather than to analyze them as descendants of a single archetype (see above).[16] The overall repertoire of incidents and episodes forms the Armenian Abraham saga, but the reader should bear in mind that this saga is a conceptual construct that does not exist in any given textual crystallization.[17]

In table 1, I enumerate the chief narrative units or episodes of the Armenian Abraham saga. The list abides by the biblical order of events, introducing the nonbiblical incidents at appropriate points, usually at the junctures at which they occur in the actual texts. In the second column, I give the appropriate biblical reference, so a blank in the second column indicates an incident or episode that the Abraham saga introduced *de novo* into the biblical narrative line.

---

14. We have dealt with complex tradition transmission in Stone 2011, ch. 6.
15. It should be borne in mind that text no. 15 is another version of text no. 11.
16. We have dealt with complex tradition transmission in Stone 2011, 151–71.
17. At least of those we have published here or consulted.

TABLE 1: CHIEF NARRATIVE UNITS OF THE ARMENIAN ABRAHAM SAGA

1. Abraham's background	
2. Idols and the recognition of God	
3. Story of the Crows: recognition of God	
4. Both stories combined in some versions: recognition of God	
5. Abraham regards the luminaries: recognition of God	
6. Abraham burns the idolatrous temple	
7. His brother dies (for the fault of breeding of the mule)[1]	Gen 11:28
8. Terah dies in Haran	Gen 11:32
9. Abraham goes to Canaan	Gen 12:1–5
10. Abraham and Sarah go to Egypt and the incident with Pharaoh	Gen 12:10–20
11. Excursus: List of ten trials of Abraham	
12. Abraham increases in wealth: separation from Lot	Gen 13:1–12
13. Incident of four kings and Melchizedek	Gen 14
14. Melchizedek of Salem, stories about (not as an ascetic)	
15. Hagar and the birth of Ishmael	Gen 16
16. Circumcision of Abraham	Gen 17
17. The story of Mamrē	
18. Abraham's hospitality	Gen 18:1–5
19. Three men appeared	Gen 18:2
20. The meal	Gen 18:6–8
21. Annunciation to Abraham	Gen 18:9–15
22. Sodom and Gomorrah, destruction of, and Lot's hospitality	Gen 18:20–33; 19:1–29
23. Typology of Abraham and his sacrifice	
24. Abimelech of Gerar	Gen 20; 21:25–34
25. Isaac	Gen 21:1–13
26. Aqedah—binding of Isaac	Gen 22
27. Melchizedek story—Melchizedek as an ascetic	
28. Abraham, naming of	Gen 17:5
29. Sarah's death and burial	Gen 23
30. Rebekah	Gen 24

---

18. Achan's (Haran's) fault is not mentioned in the Bible.

31. Isaac marries Rebekah	Gen 24:67
32. Prophecy	
33. Descendants of Abraham	
34. Armenization of the genealogy	
35. Death of Abraham	Gen 25:8–10

This list of incidents reflects the major episodes of the narratives in the Armenian Abraham texts published here. It is instructive to compare the list of incidents with the biblical narrative. The Abraham saga adds major incidents or subjects to the biblical narrative. Particularly notable among these are the stories about the crows and the recognition of God, the Story of Mamrē, and the Story of Melchizedek the Ascetic.

TABLE 2: INCIDENTS ADDED TO THE BIBLICAL STORY

1. Abraham's background
2. Idols and the recognition of God
3. Story of the Crows: recognition of God
4. Both stories combined in some versions: Recognition of God
5. Abraham regards Luminaries: Recognition of God
6. Abraham burns idolatrous Temple
11. Excursus: List of ten trials of Abraham
14. Melchizedek of Salem, stories about (not as an ascetic)
17. The Story of Mamrē
23. Typology of Abraham and his sacrifice
27. Melchizedek Story—Melchizedek as an ascetic
30. Rebekah
31. Isaac marries Rebekah
32. Prophecy
33. Descendants of Abraham
34. Armenization of the genealogy

These items give a background to Abraham, in some texts extending back to the flood. They explain the idolatry against which Abraham reacted as emerging from the degeneration of the postdiluvian generations. Humans forgot God, and in some instances—for example, in text no. 15.1—the book of law is said to have been forgotten.[19] Notable are the various stories of Abraham's recognition

---

19. See texts nos. 11.1 and 15.1. On Jewish sources for the idea of God's being forgotten

of God. Several versions of this incident, also related in other traditions, are to be found in the Armenian texts. Abraham's role as the "father of all believers," which was noted above, and his recognition of the true God are major themes in both Jewish and Christian readings of this material. In Islamic tradition also, his discovery of God plays a major role.

MELCHIZEDEK AND THE STORY OF MELCHIZEDEK

The Story of Melchizedek as an ascetic (table 1, item 27) causes an inconvenience in the story line. It follows the Aqedah, itself sequential to the Story of Mamrē, the Annunciation to Abraham, and the Sodom and Lot incidents. This apocryphal Story of Melchizedek as an ascetic, which is most probably drawn from a Greek source,[20] occurs in two documents, texts nos. 6 and 11 + 15. In a number of other texts, however, the four kings and Melchizedek's welcome and blessing of Abraham, which we call the Expatiation on Melchizedek, precede the Story of Mamrē. Thus, in texts nos. 2, 7, and 12 there are variants on his greeting Abraham, based on (and in the case of text no. 12.15–16, very close to) Gen 14:18–20 including the tithe. It is notable that in no text do both these Melchizedek incidents occur.

In a third type of Melchizedek material, he is consulted as a counseling or oracular source of knowledge: see texts nos. 3 and 4. In these instances it is impossible to situate Melchizedek's entry into the story within the narrative sequence. The remaining texts do not include either the Story of Melchizedek or the four kings incident, mainly because of their limited narrative scope.

The Expatiation on Melchizedek (table 1, item no. 14) occurs in texts nos. 2, 7, and 12. This name designates expansions related to Gen 14 and not the Melchizedek Story found in texts nos. 6, 11, and 15 (table 1, item no. 27). The expatiation on the brief reference in Gen 14:18–20 is directly connected with Melchizedek's importance for Christians as a non-Levitical priest. This understanding is anchored in the Old Testament text ("a priest of the Most High God"; Gen 18:18) and occurs already in the Epistle to the Hebrews. Hebrews makes Jesus a member of a high-priestly line founded by Melchizedek (Heb 5:6, 10; 6:20; and 7:1–17) and argues for the primacy of the Melchizedek sacerdotal line over the Levitical, descended from Abraham.[21]

---

after Noah, see also Beer 1859, 105 and n. 50. In Eznik 3.15.2, the idea is present that, though idolatry was predominant, a measure of piety remained, as is witnessed by Melchizedek's title and taking the tithe (*MH* 5th century, 494). Text no. 11.1A has the idea of a second law, in force from Abraham on. On this idea, described as "unwritten law", see *2 Bar.* 57:2.

20. See Dochhorn 2004; and Piovanelli In press. Note the detailed introduction, German translation, and rich notes by Böttrich 2010. The combination of several versions of the story is found in the *Palaea*, certain of which are closer to the Armenian story here than others. Fully to analyze this is beyond the scope of this volume.

21. The rabbis make Abraham a priest, applying Ps 110:4 to him in *Gen. Rab.* 26:3; see

TABLE 3: MELCHIZEDEK INCIDENTS IN THE TEXTS

Text no.	4 Kings incident	Story of Melchizedek	Other Melchizedek
2	meets Abraham - brief		
4			Melchizedek as priest consulted by Rebekah
4			Predicts preeminence of Jacob
6		Melchizedek in forest	
7	bread & wine, type of Christ—brief		
11		Melchizedek in forest	
12	meets Abraham—close to Bible		

In Jewish sources of the Second Temple period, Melchizedek takes on a heavenly character and is identified in 11QMelchizedek as a savior figure.[22] In *2 Enoch* he is a type of divine man, born without a father and taken to heaven before the flood, to be brought down in Abraham's time (see *2 En.* 71–72). His connection with Noachic times is highlighted in the widespread view that he was Shem, son of Noah.[23] Thus, Hebrews is building on an anterior Jewish tradition connected with Gen 14 and bolstered by Ps 110:4.[24] For the Christian tradents of the Armenian Abraham texts, Hebrews' view is strengthened by the bread and wine that Melchizedek, the priest, is said to offer Abraham (see Gen 14:18), which offering was readily viewed as a sacrificial, eucharistic act, one of several found in the Armenian Abraham saga.[25] Thus, text no. 6.5 says of the meal Abraham prepared for the Three Men:

---

also on this issue Kessler 2004, 52–53. *Yalqut Shimʿoni Lek Lĕka* 14.74; 17.81 interprets the bread and wine offered to Abraham as priestly instructions.

22. See Steudel 2000.

23. Rabbinic sources are plentiful: see *b. Ned.* 32b, *PRE* 27. See also Ephrem, *Commentary on Genesis* 11 9 (Mathews and Amar 1994, 151) and Ginzberg 1909–38, 1:233 and 5:225 n. 102. On the descent of his priestly line from Noah, see ibid. The passage cited in *b. Ned.* 32b and also *Lev. Rab.* 25 speaks of why Melchizedek's priestly function was canceled. According to *PRE* 27, Abraham gives tithe to Melchizedek. Views on this varied and were determined by the opinion of Melchizedek that was espoused. See further Böttrich 2010, 32–33.

24. Hay 1973.

25. See also Böttrich (2010, 15, 37–38), who sees this as part of the *interpretatio christiana* of the story. Eucharistic connections are highlighted, sometimes indeed created,

Unleavened bread, wine and calf he slaughtered for the meal,
A type of unleavened (wafer) (and) chalice of the Mass.

Text no. 7.13–14, devoted to the Tree of Sabek, says of Melchizedek's offering to Abraham: "¹³Melchizedek took from the grapes of the tree and made wine. And having brought it he offered it to Abraham. And he broke unleavened bread beneath (it) when he came from cutting down the kings. ¹⁴Abraham, having taken it, he himself communicated and his 318 soldiers with him."

Similar reasons lay behind the adoption of the apocryphal Melchizedek story (item no. 27), which was known in Greek and incorporated into the Armenian Abraham story in two texts, nos. 6 and 11.[26] It serves to highlight the Christian perception of the events but shows no overt connections with the biblical text beyond association of Melchizedek, a priest, with Abraham. This story evokes a number of well-known incidents. Melchizedek discovers God in an event very much like those about Abraham in texts no. 11.5–6 and 15.4–5.[27] Melchizedek

---

elsewhere in the Abraham stories, such as in the repast of the Three Men with Abraham, in the household offering of Melchizedek, and in the highlighting of his foreshadowing sacerdotal function (text no. 15.48, 55). See also text no. 7.13–14; and *Palaea* 214. On Melchizedek in the *Palaea*, see Böttrich 2010, 8–9. The representation of Melchizedek's offering is placed over the altar in S. Maria Maggiore in Rome: the bread has crosses on it and an image of Christ is incorporated, which shows that the purpose of the image is eucharistic and not merely illustrative (fifth century). The motif is of course extremely popular in Christian literature; see Clement of Alexandria in *Stromata*, who states that Melchizedek offered wine and bread, the "consecrated food", as a type of the Eucharist (ὁ τὸν οἶνον καὶ ἄρτον τὴν ἡγιασμένην διδοὺς τροφὴν εἰς τύπον εὐχαριστίας; Stählin and Früchtel 1960, 15); cf. Eusebius of Caesara, *Dem. ev.* 5.3: "in exactly the same way our Lord and Saviour Himself first, and then all His priests among all nations, perform the spiritual sacrifice according to the customs of the Church, and with wine and bread darkly express the mysteries of His Body and saving Blood"; *Cave of Treasures* (Budge 1927, 148): "and Melchisedek made him [i.e., Abraham] to participate in the Holy Mysteries, [of] the bread of the Offering and the wine of redemption." Böttrich (2010, 30–35) discusses the use of Melchizedek material in *Cave of Treasures* and in *Conflict of Adam and Eve with Satan*. See also George Syncellus 112 (Adler and Tuffin 2002, 141).

26. Böttrich 2010; and Dochhorn 2004. See also the incisive remarks of William Adler in the introduction to his forthcoming translation of the Greek *Palaea Historica* (a work no earlier than the ninth century). The story has been taken into ch. 72 of the long version of *2 Enoch* in a different form, and there the connection with Abraham is not made (see the analysis by Böttrich 2010, 35–37). This leads us to speculate that it was an independent piece associated with Melchizedek (so also Böttrich 2010, 65–66) and connected to Abraham through Gen 14. It is also found in the *Palaea*, see n. 25 above. Much information on works associated with Melchizedek is to be found in Denis and Haelewyck 2000, 215–20. Böttrich (2010, 54–66) maintains that the story had a Jewish kernel and underwent a complex process of Christianization.

27. Below I discuss other aspects of the construction of the Melchizedek figure in conversation with that of Abraham. This connection is pointed out also in Böttrich 2010, 66.

lives as a "hairy ascetic" in a forest on Golgotha, in Jerusalem,[28] is found after eight years by Abraham with God's help, and becomes Abraham's household priest. His offering Abraham bread, indeed unleavened bread, and wine is stressed.[29]

In the Abraham saga, the Story of Melchizedek follows the story of Abraham's ordeal in the Binding of Isaac. In that ordeal, Abraham's willingness to sacrifice his son is regarded typologically as foreshadowing God's sacrifice of his only-begotten Son.[30] This is, of course, in tension with Melchizedek's father Melk'i's wish to sacrifice his son. Moreover, in the Story of Melchizedek the incident of the idolatrous sacrifices and the earth swallowing up both the idolatrous temple and all the people is reminiscent of the Korah incident in the book of Numbers (16:20–21, 31–33).[31] It also guarantees the purity of Jerusalem and Golgotha. This Melchizedek story, then, is adopted into the body of two of the texts, being itself created so as to form a typology of redemption: Melchizedek, like Abraham, recognizes God; Melchizedek's father sacrifices his other son to idols, and Melchizedek is saved (a reverse Aqedah); instead of redemption, the sacrifice of the son leads to a swallowing up of idolaters, while Melchizedek, saved from slaughter, offers the eucharistic sacrifice on behalf of the children of Adam. Christian themes of eremitic character, such as the hairy ascetic living isolated in the forest, are introduced, and Melchizedek, instead of being king of Salem (he is never that in the Story of Melchizedek!), becomes priest to Abraham's family. The forest is on the Mount of Olives (6.11) or in Jerusalem (Paris 72).[32] Redemption is on the mountain, identified with Golgotha.

---

28. See texts nos. 7.18 and 14.13 and notes there. Compare the discussion by Satran 1985, 345–69; N. Stone 2000, 63 note and 126 note; and Böttrich 2010, 57–59 with bibliography. On the figure of the forest-dwelling, wild ascetic, see N. Stone 2000, 63 note and 126 note.

29. Text no. 7.13. See above, p. 10.

30. See text no. 15.47, discussed above in connection with this theme. Further, see M1425 in Appendix 1, below. See most recently Orlov (2000; reprinted in Orlov 2007, 423–39), who discusses this legend.

31. The stress on the swallowing up of all those associated with evil is noteworthy. The result is the cleansing of Jerusalem from idolatry. Swallowing up by the earth is documented in Böttrich 2010, 95.

32. According to text no. 14.13, the Aqedah was on Golgotha, in the mountains of the Jebusites, which once more ties the place of sacrifice to Golgotha, so one has the sacrifice of Isaac, Melchizedek, and the crucifixion all on the one, central place. The texts lack clear geographical knowledge. In *Cave of Treasures* (Budge 1927, 151), which has a different combination of these events, we read:

> And Isaac was thirteen years old when his father took him and went up to the mountain of Yâbhôs (Jebus) to Melchisedek, the priest of God, the Most High. Now Mount Yâbhôs is the mountain of the Amôrâyê (Amorites), and in that place the Cross of Christ was set up, and on it grew the tree which held the ram that saved Isaac. And that same place is the centre of the earth, and the grave of Adam,

The chief problem that the Story of Melchizedek raises is its integration not with the Abraham narratives that include it but with the sequence of events that can be inferred from Genesis. In the three documents that have incorporated this story, texts nos. 6, 11, and 15, the other Melchizedek material relating to the four kings (Gen 14) is not found but is replaced by this Story of Melchizedek.[33] However, that produces anomalies in the biblical time line, and at least to that extent the Story of Melchizedek appears to be independent of Genesis. Its modifications contrast with Gen 14 and cause one to wonder about its origins. Moreover, as far as the Armenian Abraham saga is concerned, it is an import, most likely from Greek, and the primary questions of its origin and purpose must be answered from within the Greek tradition.

The Story of Mamrē

Item 17 in table 1 is the apocryphal story of Mam(b)rē.[34] Mamrē, Abraham's black slave, sets out to pasture the sheep. He is provided with three loaves of bread, and in three incidents *en route* he generously gives his loaves away to starving men.

---

and the altar of Melchisedek, and Golgotha, and Karkaftâ [i.e., skull], and Gefîftâ (Gabbatha). And there David saw the angel bearing the sword of fire. There, too, Abraham took up Isaac his son for a burnt offering, and he saw the Cross, and Christ, and the redemption of our father Adam. The tree (*i.e.*, thicket) was a symbol of the Cross of Christ our Lord, and the ram [caught] in its branches was the mystery of the manhood of the Word, the Only One.

See also *Cave of Treasures* (Budge 1927, 224): "In that very place where Melchisedek ministered as a priest, and where Abraham offered up his son Isaac as an offering, the wood of the Cross was set up, and that self-same place is the centre of the earth, and there the Four Quarters of the earth meet each other." See also the identification in a catena fragment attributed to Eusebius of Emesa (Petit, van Rompay, and Weitenberg 2011, 233; cf. Kessler 2004, 90). On the rabbinic "pre-history" of Jerusalem, see Gafni 1987, 10–15, and the response to changes of perception as Christian interest in holy places developed. The dominant tradition of the Greek Story of Melchizedek puts his dwelling on Mount Tabor: contrast text no. 11.47, which speaks of Jerusalem. This is documented throughout the introduction in Böttrich 2010, and it should be noted that the conflate version of Grigor of Tat'ew (in Appendix 1 below) has Mount Tabor. Certain sources, however, connect the events with Golgotha (and Adam's burial) and others with the Mount of Olives. See *Cave of Treasures*, where Noah and Melchizedek bury Adam's body on Golgotha (Budge 1927, 126–27). Compare also Böttrich 2010, 32–33. In the Athanasian recension of *Story of Melchizedek* 10.3 and in *Palaea* 1893, 210, Mount Tabor is identified with the Mount of Olives. In the Armenian texts published here, Mount Tabor is not given, and it should be observed that St. Gregory of Narek (tenth–eleventh centuries) also mentions the Mount of Olives; see below, n. 57. In the seventh-century Armenian description of Mount Tabor in pseudo-Ełišē's *Homily of the Transfiguration*, there is no mention of Melchizedek or a chapel dedicated to him or his cave; see Stone 2004.

33. The reverse situation, the presence of the Gen 14 material and the absence of the Story of Melchizedek, occurs in texts nos. 2, 7, and 12; cf. texts nos. 3 and 4. In 1QapGen 21–22 the story of the four kings is told at some length, but Melchizedek is not mentioned.

34. The introduction of a "b" following an "m" is observed elsewhere in Armenian

After this he reaches his goal and falls asleep, having stuck his oaken staff into the ground. When he awakes, the staff has become a great oak tree (cf. Gen 13:18; 14:13; and 18:1),[35] and he, a black slave, has turned white, together with his black sheep. He goes back to Abraham, who recognizes the miraculous nature of the event and returns with him and praises him. In another version, Abraham comes to him and likewise perceives that a miracle has taken place.

Here the origin of Abraham's famed hospitality is explained, which story is itself the lead-up to the story of the Annunciation to Abraham. Abraham observed the miracles that followed on Mamrē's hospitality and, taking this to heart, swore never to eat again without a guest at his table.[36] The narrative sequence—the Story of Mamrē followed by Abraham's oath, Satan's blocking of the way, and eventually the arrival of the Three Men—is found, *mutatis mutandis*, in texts nos. 2, 6, 8, 11, 12, and 15. Thus, this story complex is present in all the major narrative texts.

The Annunciation to Abraham or The Visit of the Three Men

The stress on the Annunciation to Abraham, that is, the visit of the Three Men (items 18–22 in table 1), is also characterized by Christian typology, and the story is thus integrated into the Christian history of redemption or proclamation of Christ. This is extremely explicit (see text no. 8.29). Some of the not very frequent images of Abraham in Armenian manuscript painting are of this Annunciation,[37] and it functions as does the Annunciation to the Virgin. It foreshadows redemption.[38] Similarly, the Binding of Isaac intimates the crucifixion,[39] and, according to text no. 14.13, Isaac was offered on Golgotha.[40] The ram, Isaac's surrogate, is given metacontextual significance, since it is identified as Abel's offering and was preserved alive in heaven from Abel's day until Sahak's birth. Then it was offered again by Abraham; so text no. 6.5.3–4:

---

transliterations; compare, for example, the Armenian name Smbat derived Shabbat. Compare Greek λαμβάνω.

35. Sextus Iulius Africanus F30 deals with this tree and also knows the tradition that it sprang from Abraham's servant's staff (Wallraff and Adler 2007, 66–67). See also below, text 2.10 and note there.

36. *Genesis Rabbah* 43:19 suggests that Abraham learned hospitality from Melchizedek; it is a common theme in rabbinic writing. See also *Gen. Rab.* 52:1

37. See M4818 (in Durnovo 1961, 145) of 1316 (depicting also cups, wine, and unleavened bread).

38. This is already clearly stated by Anania Širakac'i in *MH* 7th century, 702. On the artistic presentation of the Aqedah, see Kessler 2004, ch. 7.

39. See the statement of Anania Catholicos (tenth century) that Isaac showed the Lord's passion, see *MH* 10th century, 255, 297–98. See here text no. 3.18; Isaac was "a likeness and type of Christ" (texts nos. 4.24, and 11.46). See Kessler 2004, 66–67.

40. On the identification of Moriah and Golgotha, see Kessler 2004, 90–91

Unleavened bread, wine and calf he slaughtered for the meal,
A type of unleavened (wafer) (and) chalice of the Mass.[41]

In one form of the stories, the calf slaughtered by Abraham in the meal he prepared for the Three Men is resurrected, indicating the salvific meaning of these events. "The marrow of this ram is the sweet oil with which they anointed you," text no. 8.32 says, evoking the transformative oil of *2 En.* 22:8–9 and 56:2 and perhaps the marrow of Isa 25:6.[42] Of course, at another level it may refer to the myron, the oil of chrism, used for baptism and unction.[43]

Structurally the Annunciation story is well integrated into the narrative sequence.[44] In illustrations of the coming of the Three Men, Abraham is shown tenting under a tree, presumably the oak of Mamrē, see M4818, 1316 C.E.[45] The story is, of course, an etiology of the oaks of Mamrē in Genesis and is discussed in the following section.

THE STORY OF LOT AND THE DESTRUCTION OF SODOM

The stories of the incident of Lot and the destruction of Sodom follow the Annunciation story. The sequence is the same as in Genesis and is to be found in texts nos. 2, 8 (brief reference), 11, and 15. Lot is also mentioned in passing in a number of other texts. Not much is made of the Lot story beyond what is related in the biblical narrative, except that Lot is presented as hospitable after the pattern of Abraham.

OTHER NARRATIVE ELEMENTS

The additional items in the last part of table 1 above are of a technical nature. They account for Abraham's death and burial, his descendants, and an Armenized form of his genealogy.[46]

---

41. Cf. text no. 8.25.

42. Cf. *3 Bar.* 15:1–2; and see Kulik 2010, 366–68. See also Stone 2000b, 118, 124–27.

43. Compare the oil of joy or gladness in Isa 61:3, Ps 45:8. The marrow is associated with fatness and plenty; see Job 21:24; Ps 63:5; and Isa 25:6. The use of oil deriving from marrow for anointing is not mentioned by Dudley and Rowel in their book on Christian anointing (1993) or elsewhere. Abraham is anointed by God with oil of joy (*Yalqut Shimʿoni Lek Lĕka* 12.62).

44. It is missing from Grigor Magistros's poem, *Aṙ Manuchē*, which deals with the Annunciation to Abraham in line 125.

45. The tree is also shown bearing bunches of grapes.

46. In Stone In press A, I discusses the Armenization of biblical genealogies and other references, particularly in the context of Armenian apocryphal literature.

BIBLICAL AND NONBIBLICAL EPISODES IN THE ABRAHAM SAGA

The question can now be raised concerning which elements of the biblical narrative have been omitted from the apocryphal Armenian Abraham saga and which elements of the Abraham saga have no *point d'appui* in the biblical narrative.

First, let us consider those episodes and incidents that are present in the biblical narrative but do not occur in the Armenian apocryphal Abraham texts. In some instances the reasons for their omission seem virtually certain. These are cases where a number of omitted episodes or incidents share a feature or features of content that are absent completely from the apocryphal retelling of the Bible. It seems reasonable to assume that this shared feature provides the motive for omission of these episodes. The texts relating to the promise of the gift of the land to Abraham and his descendants are a good example. These are all omitted, as is the promise of the perdurance of his seed: Gen 12:7 (promise), Gen 15 (the covenant between the pieces and the prophecy of Abraham's descendants' future),[47] Gen 18:17–18 (promise to Abraham about his descendants).[48] These omissions, we suggest, are part of a Christian reading of the Abraham stories, for they all refer to the specific promises to or about the bodily descendants of Abraham, the "old Israel." In the writers' perspective, these divine undertakings were superseded by the revelation through Christ and the understanding of the Christians as the new Israel.[49] Abraham's promised bodily descendants are replaced by his role as father of all believers. In none of the apocryphal Abraham texts is any attempt made to handle the promises to Israel explicitly; they are simply omitted from the retelling—which is, of course, a way of handling them.[50]

In addition, Gen 25:12–18, dealing with the descendants of Ishmael, is not taken up. Moreover, the rather distasteful (to moderns) story of the daughters of Lot, which serves as an etiology of the Moabites and Ammonites and of attitudes to them (cf. Deut 23:3), is completely absent. Perhaps this seemed irrelevant to the Armenian tradents. If our primary observations here are to the point, they

---

47. The Armenian Abraham saga lacks future revelation to Abraham, for which the events of Gen 15 are a primary fruitful locus. Compare *Apoc. Ab.* ch. 9 and 4 Ezra 3:14–15. See Stone 1990, 71, where further sources are cited.

48. The subjects are found throughout early Armenian literature, which makes the incidents' omission from the Abraham saga the more striking. The increase of Abraham's seed is mentioned in texts nos. 11.28, 15.29, and 15.43. It should be remembered that texts 11 and 15 are closely related.

49. This omission is not found in such authors as Stepʻanos Siwnecʻi, *Fragments of Commentary on Genesis* in *MH* 8th century, 2.109.

50. Ephrem in *Commentary on Genesis* 12 does deal explicitly with these promises (see Mathews and Amar 1994, 152–53) as does Eusebius, *Hist. eccl.* 1.4.11 (differently from Ephrem).

confirm the conclusion that the Abraham stories were of interest for their role in the history of salvation and not just because they are found in Scripture.[51]

What is more surprising is that the incidents of the four kings and Melchizedek's meeting with Abraham are given only in brief compass and not expansively (texts 2.8, 6.11-12, 7.13, and 12.15–16). The chronological problems involved in relating the two Melchizedek incidents, the one connected with Gen 14 and the other being the apocryphal story, are dealt with in text no. 6.11–12 (see the note there and also the discussion above, p. 12).[52] However, the typological potential of the four kings story is not fully realized, perhaps precisely because of the enhancement of Melchizedek's role elsewhere by the inclusion of the ascetic Story of Melchizedek within the Abraham cycle, even though the two Melchizedek incidents do not occur in any single text.[53]

Thus, the general outline of the Armenian Abraham saga shows a profoundly Christian, and occasionally distinctive,[54] selection and editing of material drawn for the main part from the biblical Abraham texts and certain apocryphal sources. A Christian perspective is expressed not only by the (to us) anachronistic use of "Christ" for "God" (e.g., text no. 8.6), but by the introduction of the Melchizedek material and by many typological exegeses.[55] Certain biblical passages, particularly those relating to Abraham's descendants, are omitted completely. All these elements result in a story line that is quite exciting and which is read naturally as part of a revelation by God that is deemed unitary and seamless.

Date of the Abraham Saga

Because virtually all the manuscripts we have seen are late, the Abraham saga cannot be dated from them except to a date *ante quem* of the fifteenth century (M8531). The material in M2679 of 981 C.E. does not bear distinctive signs of the embroidered Abraham saga, though it does have extrabiblical traditions. How-

---

51. There are Armenian texts that are basically scholarly and learned. One such is in Galata 154, text no. 5 in this book. Probably the list of the Ten Trials of Abraham also belongs to this category, though it came to be included within narrative texts. See text no. 13 and its reuse in text no. 5. Numerous other copies exist, see the introduction to text no. 5. On Armenian learned literature related to the Bible, see Stone 1996b, 627–28.

52. In the section on "Melchizedek and the Story of Melchizedek," this incident is discussed in detail.

53. Compare the synthetic treatment by Gregory of Tat'ew with discussion of M6524 in Appendix 1, below.

54. The "covenant between the pieces" (Gen 15), which was used for Christian exegesis, is omitted, though the four hundred years' bondage, prophesied there, is found in our texts. See, e.g., Zak'aria Catholicos in *MH* 9th century, 178. See texts nos. 5.8 and 8.28 below.

55. These are pointed out in the notes to the individual texts.

ever, the tenth-century author Samuel Karmrǰajorec'i refers to the Mamrē story and so knows this element of the tradition in the tenth century.[56]

The Story of Melchizedek is known to St. Gregory of Narek (945?–1003), and, since its source is non-Armenian and most likely Greek, St. Gregory's familiarity with it only means that it was known in Armenia by the tenth century but indicates nothing about the date of its incorporation into the Abraham saga.[57] He knows about Melchizedek's living at Golgotha on the peak of the Mount of Olives. Of course the Armenian Abraham tales cannot be older than the fifth century, at which time the Armenians began to write their own language. Moreover, the date of the constitutive traditions is not necessarily the date of any particular literary formulation of that tradition.

Moreover, there exists a *Commentary on Genesis* attributed to the fifth-century author Ełišē available in an edition prepared by Levon Khachikyan from extracts embedded in the *Commentary on Genesis* of Vardan Arewelc'i (1200?–1271).[58] The editor attributes the text to the fifth-century Ełišē, and it contains a number of distinctive traditions, such as that on the birds in Terah's time, considered in the next section. Somewhat similarly, it knows the metaphor of the dry wood that bore fruit for Sarah (see text no. 12.47), which occurs in a number of places (see note on text no. 12.46 for its possible sources). Neither of these cases is distinctive enough for us to date all of the Abraham saga back to the fifth century.

Nonetheless, Ełišē's *Commentary on Genesis* has certainly served as a literary source for text no. 12 here. It shares traditions and formulations with that text in §§12.36, 12.38, 12.41, and 12.47 and is cited verbatim in §§12.43–44a, 12.44b–46, and 12.52 (somewhat more distant from Ełišē's text). It has a less literal, but still clear, connection with text no. 2.7, 2.14, and 2.16 and possible connections also occur in text no. 4.5, 4.24. Thus, Ełišē's *Commentary on Genesis* has served as a source for a number of texts relating to Abraham, though we cannot tell

---

56. *MH* 10th century, 704 and 736.

57. Grigor Narekac'i 1985, 622 (93.5):, Ո՛չ ապա Մելքիսեդեկ յարինակ ճշմարտիդ ահատրութեան ի Ձիթաստանեաց լերինն, ուր յետոյ ոտք մարմնացելոյդ աստուծոյ գետեղեալ կացին, ի վերնոց անտի հրեշտակաց ի պտղոց տեղւոյն իղեգաւ. ուստի շիրմի սկզբնահաւրն պաշտպան եպիսկոպոսական արքայապատիւ ճոխութեամբ ի քեն հանդերձեալ նստաւ. . . ." "Was not Melchizedek anointed as a type of your true fearsomeness on the Mount of Olives where afterwards the feet of God incarnate stood, by the celestial angels in the place of fruits (i.e., olives), where by the power put on You from the grave of forefather, protector through episcopal royal power, he sat . . ." (my translation). Observe the differing tradition preserved by Vardan Aygkec'i, cited below in the note on text no. 7.2–7, which reflects yet another combination of Melchizedek material.

58. See Khachikyan and Papazian 2004; the original edition was Xač'ikyan 1992. The text is also reprinted in *MH* 5th century. Note the methodological and conceptual remarks of Zekiyan 1997, esp. 106–8.

whether it was by the intermediary of Vardan Arewelcʻi or directly, since all our knowledge of the text comes from Vardan. Perhaps other, unpublished Armenian commentaries on Genesis might also contain source material utilized by the Abraham texts. The determination, however, must await the publication of those commentaries.[59] In any case, the issue becomes one of the "chicken or the egg": Do the apocryphal narratives draw upon the commentaries, or do the commentaries incorporate material drawn from the apocryphal narratives? In the case of text no. 12, the answer is clear, because of sections of word-for-word citation.[60]

Sources of the Abraham Saga: The Ravens

In a fine study, S. P. Brock compares the story of the ravens or crows (see item 3 in the table above) as it occurs in *Jub.* 11–12 with various forms of this story found in Syriac sources.[61] He lists eight points in which the Syriac sources differ significantly from *Jubilees*.

1. In *Jubilees*, the ravens are sent by Mastema, and in Syriac sources, by God.
2. Abraham is fourteen years old according to *Jubilees* and fifteen according to Syriac sources.
3. In *Jubilees*, Abraham is acting with his family; in Syriac sources his father sends him alone.
4. Abraham easily chases off the birds in *Jubilees*. In the Syriac sources, exhausted by his efforts, he converses with God, who identifies himself.
5. *Jubilees* introduces the invention of the seed plough as a result of the ravens incident. Syriac does not have the seed plough but introduces the ravens incident as a lead-up to Abraham's calling.
6. Abraham, fourteen years later, tries to divert his father from idolatry (*Jubilees*), and the Syriac sources put this event right after the ravens. In *Jubilees*, he tries to convert his brothers. Syriac mentions Nahor, but not in detail.
7. In the burning of the idolatrous temple, Syriac explicitly mentions it as of Qainan, the mighty god.
8. *Jubilees* then mentions Terah's departure to Canaan, with no causal connection between it and the temple burning. The Syriac traditions record that the Chaldeans threatened Terah, who consequently fled.[62]

---

59. No published ancient commentaries are mentioned in Petrosyan and Ter-Stepanyan 2002.

60. The attribution to Ełišē is commonly accepted, but perhaps it should be reexamined.

61. Brock 1978. See Michael the Syrian 2.6 (ed. Chabot 1899, 26–27), Gregor bar Hebraeus, *Chronography* (trans. E. A. W. Budge; repr., Piscataway, N.J.: Gorgias Press, 2003), 10.

62. Brock 1978, 140–41.

When the Armenian versions of this episode and its ensuing results are compared with this list, the following may be observed.

1. God raises up the crows (not Mastema or Satan) (2.3, 12.4, 14.2, 15.3); crows appear (4.2, 8.5).
2. Abraham was fifteen years old (2.3, 4.4, 12.5).[63]
3. His father sent him alone (2.3, 8.5, 12.5); Abraham went on his own (15.3); Abraham considers the birds and concludes that God exists (15.4).
4. Abraham, exhausted, sat down to rest (2.3, 12.5); he observed the luminaries, he was an astronomer, he received enlightenment (2.3, 12.5-6, 14.3, 15.4).
   He has conversation with God who reveals himself (2.4-5, 8.6-7; cf. 12.6).
   Abraham prays and the ravens disappear (4.3, 12.7, 15.5-6).
   The birds do not eat Abraham's fields (15.6).
   Terah departs for Canaan and stops in Haran (2.5, 12.9).
   Abraham at age sixty moves to Haran (14.5).
5. The invention of the seed plough is not mentioned (2, 4, 8, 15).
6. Abraham burns Terah's idolatrous temple (2.6, 4.6, 12.10, 14.6,[64] 15.7).
7. The temple's deity is not specified (all texts).
8. Terah dies, no date mentioned (2.7, 4.7, 12.12, 14.7).
   Abraham departed Haran at age seventy-five (4.8, 14.7);[65] at age seventy-two (8.7).[66]

Text nos. 2 and 15 are full stories, though text no. 15 concludes this episode after the burning of the temple, when Abraham's family is angered at him and he flees and ends up in Egypt; text no. 4 is brief, while text no. 6 is brief and poetic:

1. Concerning the flocks of crows in the fields,
   Who mentioned God on high and the ravens fled.
2. Then there came to his mind the clear thought,
   (That) it is the Creator, God, who does miracles.

---

63. Abraham was fourteen years old: note George Syncellus 111 (Adler and Tuffin 2002, 138), also on Abraham as an astronomer.
64. Although John Malalas 57.1 (Jeffreys et al. 1986, 28) mentions Abraham's conflict with Terah over idolatry, he does not mention the burning of the temple. That is found in George Syncellus 112 (Adler and Tuffin 2002, 138). He dates the burning of the idols to Abraham's sixty-first year; cf. Symeon Metaphrastes 33; George Monachus 1.93.16-94.16.
65. Compare also George Syncellus 112 (Adler and Tuffin 2002, 140).
66. For a discussion of the age of seventy-five (the reading of the Masoretic Text and the LXX of Gen 12:4), compare George Syncellus 106–7 (Adler and Tuffin 2002, 130–31). This subject does not appear in the earlier chonography of John Malalas.

He burnt the house of idols secretly in the night,
And the inventor of the mule perished with it.

Since in none of these instances does the Armenian agree with *Jubilees* against the Syriac traditions, the close connection of Armenian and Syriac becomes evident, or at least the dependence of Armenian on a form of the ravens tradition later than that in *Jubilees*.

Observe further that in the *Commentary on Genesis* by Ełišē on Gen 11:32, we read: "A good secret was announced to Terah by God, and he went to Mesopotamia and dwelt in Haran in the land of the Chaldees, because he often visited the magi. The Lord punished them with birds, which ate their fields. And they established a guard to drive them out."[67] This text knows a tradition of an attack of birds connected not with Abraham but with Terah. In the fragment of surviving text, no discovery of God is mentioned and no relationship with Abraham. What is clear is that, as far as this text goes, it knows a tradition different from that in the Syriac and Armenian sources, and different again from that in *Jubilees*.

Sources of the Abraham Saga: Early Armenian Commentaries on Genesis

In the course of this General Introduction and the introductions in the chapters below, we have referred quite often to the *Commentary on Genesis* attributed to Ełišē *vardapet*.[68] It will not be discussed in detail in this section, for its intersections with the documents cited here are chiefly in the treatment of some detailed aspects of the narrative and it does not show easily identifiable points of direct contact with the texts of the Abraham Saga.

More like our texts, however, is the *Commentary on Genesis* attributed to Step'anos Siwnec'i, an author of the late seventh and early eighth century.[69] This work, extant in fragments, was recently published.[70] It presents what is more or less a running narrative sequence of Abraham stories, in this respect resembling the literary texts published in the present work.

---

67. Khachikyan and Papazian 2004, 113.

68. We have consulted three editions, but mainly Khachikyan and Papazian 2004; cf. Xač'ikyan (Khachikyan) 1992. Xač'ikyan's text is reprinted with an introduction in *MH* 5th century, 765–929. The text is attributed to Ełišē, but we regard this as uncertain. Its antiquity, however, is clear.

69. For the text of Step'anos Siwnec'i, see "Fragments of the Commentary on Genesis" in *MH* 8th century, 1:105–29. Introductory information is to be found in ibid., 95-104. In general, see also Thomson 1995, 138–39.

70. See *MH* 8th century, 95–105; the extracts were preserved in a number of manuscripts in the Matenadaran, the oldest of which is dated to the eleventh–twelfth centuries. In all these cases, the fragments of Step'anos Siwnec'i's commentary have been preserved as citations in other works.

In some sections, it follows the biblical narrative quite closely, but in the passages given below it seems to be familiar with material resembling the embroidered Abraham saga, though the resemblances are not specific enough to make it possible to posit a direct relationship. Note, in particular, its very simple form of the story of Mamrē, which exhibits the main points of the embroidered form of it given in the texts published here but lacks numerous distinctive details. Step'anos Siwnec'i's *Commentary on Genesis* is one of the oldest known witnesses to Mamrē story. The paucity of shared, explicit details prevents my saying that it was a direct source of the material in the Abraham saga, but the story must have developed in an anterior extrabiblical source of some kind.[71]

Different is the list of the Ten Trials of Abraham, which may well be a list or school text imported into Step'anos Siwnec'i's *Commentary on Genesis*. That in itself is an important piece of information, throwing light on Armenian biblical studies and scholasticism at a relatively early date.[72] The list's order and, to greater or lesser measure, its language are remarkably fixed down to the seventeenth century, which strengthens the idea of its independent origin.

What Step'anos Siwnec'i's *Commentary on Genesis* does show is that the Abraham saga has early roots in Armenian tradition, but the narrative texts we introduce to the public for the first time here are considerably more detailed and complex than the material adduced in the seventh–eighth century by Step'anos Siwnec'i. We translate the following extracts from the edition in *MH* 8th century, having supplied the subject headings and some annotations.[73]

STORY OF MAMRĒ[74]

> (p. 109) 68 And it came to pass after this, God appeared to Abram while he was sitting by the oak-tree of Mamrē. 69 They say that Mamrē was Abraham's shepherd. 70 And having seen Abram's good life, his strong faith and his merciful conduct, he learnt his virtue from him and acted mercifully.[75] 71 And, one day, Mamrē gave mercy to poor people and through hope in that, mercifully he planted his oaken staff in the earth. It struck root, greened and became a great

---

71. See Stone 1999, esp. 24; and Stone 1996b, 627–28.

72. See n. 90 below, where the four versions of this list extant in the documents below are discussed. Many more copies exist, in different types of manuscripts.

73. Page numbers are indicated in the translation. The section numbers of *MH* are indicated.

74. See above pp. 21–22.

75. Mamrē's merciful character is discussed in text no. 11.12. Above, p. 21, the story of the three loaves of bread is discussed. It is not found in Step'anos Siwnec'i, nor is the whitening of a black Mamrē and his sheep. Likewise, the story of the Annunciation to Abraham in Step'anos Siwnec'i lacks many specific details found in the Abraham saga.

tree[76] by which Abram, going off alone, prayed and contemplated the divine things[77] and looked at the coming of guests on the road to him.

Abraham's Hospitality and the Three Men

72 And he promised in his mind that he would not eat bread without a guest and he passed many days in hunger and did not see a guest, for Satan had obstructed the guests' path.[78] 73 And while Abram was sitting by the oak of Mamrē, lifting up his eyes he saw and behold, 3 (men) were coming above it.[79] 74 Abram arose, ran to greet and bowed down to them upon his face. 75 And, having brought them, he sat them down by the oak of Mamrē, for he recognized the might of their being in the(ir) coming, that they went above the earth and did not tread on (it). 76 And Abram hastened to Sarah and said, "Hasten and knead three measures of flour; make three loaves with finest flour." 77 And having taken the milk and butter, which is butter (*another word*) and the unleavened bread that she had baked, he brought (it) and put it before them. 78 And Abram ran to the herd, that is the flock, took a calf to slaughter and, having brought it, had it roasted and set (it) before them. 79 Abram recognized that he is God;[80] for that reason he did not order his servants to attend (them), but he himself and Sarah served the Lord's face.[81] 80 The Lord (p. 110) said to him, "Where is your wife, Sarah?" 81 Abraham said, "Behold, she is in the tent." 82 And the Lord said, "In this time I will come to you, on the very same day, and Sarah will have a son in her bosom." 83 When Sarah heard, she laughed in her mind, 84 and the Lord said, "Why did Sarah laugh?" 85 Then Sarah was afraid (and) said, "I did not laugh, but I was afraid, Lord." 86 The Lord said, "No, you laughed." 87. And see that Sarah served but she conceived. On account of (her) modesty she slighted the promise of good news, (and) it was allotted to her children to remain in servitude for 400 years.[82]

---

76. The complex incident of the oak tree, the shade, and so on, as found in the Abraham saga is not found here: compare text no. 2.9–10, 11.16, 11.18–19, 12.19–20, and 15.17.

77. See texts nos. 2.11–12, 11.16–20. The oak tree as a place of prayer is highlighted in text no. 12.23. Compare the similar phraseology but different context in text no. 12.8. In 12.36 it says of the oak of Mamrē that "Mamrē's field became a royal seat and the oak tree more than paradise of Eden."

78. Satan's obstruction of travelers is a widespread theme: see texts nos. 2.12, 11.24–25, 12.24, and 15.25. The number of days, forty, is absent from Stepʻanos Siwnecʻi.

79. Compare the similar description in text no. 12.27.

80. Contrast texts nos. 2.13 and 12.28–29, where Abraham is of two minds whether the traveler is God. 11A.28 says that Abraham did not know that he was the Lord, compare 12.40, 15.29. This is a prominent theme throughout text no. 12.

81. That is, in the Lord's presence. Abraham and Sarah served the Three Men themselves; see the developed discussion of this in texts nos. 2.15, 12.28, 12.37–38, and 12.42.

82. Not all the Abraham saga texts connect this servitude with Sarah's laughter. The length of the servitude is 460 years in 11.29 and 15.30. See further the discussion of this

88–96 *Story of Lot and the destruction of Sodom.*

97–110 *Abraham receives the commandment of circumcision and discussion of its significance.*

THE BINDING OF ISAAC

111 And Abraham being 100 years, and Sarah 90, Isaac was born, which means, "laughter." 112 And when Isaac was 15 years old,[83] and some say 27, He asked Abraham to sacrifice Isaac. 113 And Abraham gladly was willing to slaughter Isaac, because he knew that He can raise up even from the dead. 114 Because the calf, which the Lord ate with the angels on the day of the good news, (when) he blessed (him) with seed, after its being eaten he saw it gamboling with (its) mother.[84] 115 And Abraham was made firmer in his faith because, in Isaac's sacrifice, he took the ram from the tree of Sabek and, having been delivered, Isaac lived. 116 And the tree[85] indicates the Virgin Mary and the Cross, and the ram—Jesus.[86] 118 And when Isaac was 37 years old, Sarah died. 119 And Sarah was Abraham's sister from (his) father, daughter of Terah. 119 And Abraham's mother's name was Malkʻatʻu and Sarah's mother's (name was) Zmrut.[87]

TEN TRIALS OF ABRAHAM

120 And Abraham encountered 10 trials from God.[88]
First, the going forth from (his) land and family (people), and this is a great trial, to leave his native land and homeland.
Second, the dragging of Sarah to the house of Pharaoh.
Third, contention and strife between his and Lot's shepherds.

---

figure in note 13 on 11A.29. It is missing from text no. 12. The same idea occurs in Stepʻanos Siwnecʻi, *Fragments of Commentary on Genesis* in *MH* 8th century, 2.108, §49. He too knows four hundred years. Th. M. van Lint contributed to the translation of this sentence.

83. See 4.22 note, on fifteen as the ideal age of a youth. The origin of the number twenty-seven is unknown to me.

84. The resurrection of the calf occurs in texts no. 8.29 and 15.29 in connection with the meal of the Three Men. Its implications for the Binding of Isaac are not taken up in the Abraham saga texts. It is an old tradition, see note 95 on text no. 8.29.

85. The tree's name, Sabek, is mentioned here and in texts nos. 4.22, 6.6.1, 7 passim, 8.31, 11.45, 14.14, and 14.45. See also the introduction to text no. 4 and note on text no. 4.22.

86. Observe the clear typology here laid forth.

87. The names are not found in the Abraham saga texts.

88. On the Ten Trials, see below, texts nos. 5.2, 6.6–7, 6.13, and 14.12. Except for the poetic treatment in text no. 6, the other texts are identical but with some variation in order. The broad circulation of this list evidences its independent origin.

Fourth, not taking of the booty of Sodom.
Fifth, it was said to him that his seed would increase like the stars of heaven, and he did not doubt.
Sixth, that he delivered Hagar into Sarah's power.
Seventh, that he made Ishmael and his mother apart from him.
Eighth, that Abimelech took Sarah.
Ninth, the He said to him to be circumcised in the time of (his) old age.
Tenth, indeed a great and fearful trial from God, is that, that God asked his son as a sacrifice.
121 And it is known that there was a famine twice, and Abraham was in foreign lands; and Sarah was taken from him twice and Abraham said (that she was) his sister; and she remained untempted by sin, for they gave her back to Abraham and they gladly blamed Abraham (saying), "Why did you say that she (is) your sister." Pharaoh gave Hagar. 122 Abimelech the Philistine king of the Gerarites (gave) 1,000 staters of silver. 123 And the reason that Sarah remained untested (is that) her/his buttocks swelled.[89] 124 And an angel of the Lord God appeared to the two kings and said, "That woman is wife of that man. Give her to her lord and do not sin against the servants of the living God, as David says, 125 (Ps 105:15) . . . "

Affinities of Armenian

Brock's study of the relationship of Syriac with *Jubilees* in one complex incident and our application of the criteria he isolated to the comparison of Armenian, Syriac, and *Jubilees* shows that the Armenian resembles the Syriac sources rather than *Jubilees*. This is, of course, not surprising, for *Jubilees* did not exist, apparently, in Armenian, and *Jubilees*—like traditions in Armenian—may have come through an intermediary source, most likely Syriac or Greek. Below I mention certain of the Abraham traditions in the Greek chronographies. The incident of the ravens does not appear in the Greek *Palaea*, while parallels to various narrative Abraham traditions are to be found in Greek chronographers and are recorded in annotations to the text.

I am conscious of the limited nature of the treatment above and I indicated that to investigate fully the genealogy of the traditions taken into the Armenian Abraham saga would extend beyond the limits set for this research. Indeed, further studies of individual episodes and incidents by experts in the Greek and Syriac traditions at least, will be required, like Brock's of the Ravens story.

Editorial Procedures

When Armenian has numerals, in English numerals are also used.

I use capital letters for *nomina sacra*, personal and proper names. Certain manuscripts use a minuscule letter following the end of sentence punctuation

---

89. See also Khachikyan and Papazian 2004, 115. Contrast text no. 4.11 and note there.

mark ":". In addition, in some manuscripts, a majuscule letter follows a major break marked by a single dot. Although these instances contradict modern Armenian usage, we have preserved them in our transcriptions. In the translations we give the usual English forms of biblical names, unless the Armenian is itself exceptional.

The sigla for Armenian manuscripts follow the system of AIEA.[90]

In the translation, we have introduced elided possessives in instances where the words have a suffixed demonstrative, without marking them all specifically.

In the texts, aorist participles are used (and often translated) as finite verbs (cf. Meillet 1913, 115). In such instances as required, "and" is added in brackets. We do not seek absolute consistency in this usage, but to produce a readable English text.

For convenience, I use an author-date documentation system. Full details of all the works to which I refer are recorded in the bibliography at the end of the book.

---

90. See http://aiea.fltr.ucl.ac.be/aiea_fr/home_french.htm and also Coulie 1994.

TEXTS AND TRANSLATIONS

1. Lists and Chronology (M2769)

M2679 is the oldest Armenian manuscript on paper and was copied in the year 981 C.E. A facsimile edition of it was published by the late Artašes Matʻevosyan, and the second volume of his work contains a full transcription of the manuscript.[1] The manuscript is written in a mixed *erkatʻagir-bolorgir* script,[2] and it is the oldest Armenian manuscript in this script and also the earliest dated manuscript that contains literary texts.[3]

The manuscript includes, together with other material, retellings of biblical stories, and among them are two short texts on Abraham. These are not narratives, as are most of the documents published below, but belong to the school literature of chronology and lists, also reflected in a much later list published here from M717 (below, no. 13), which is also included in another, late scholastic text, Galata 154 (text no. 5, below).

The first text occurs on fols. 36v–37r of the manuscript.[4] It deals with the number of years from Reu to Abraham[5] and continues in a semi-narrative form with the year spans from Abraham to Moses. This text is drawn from a chronology written by Pʻilon Tirakacʻi (seventh century) and may be found among the edition of his works in the collection *Armenian Literature* (*MH*).[6]

The second text that we present here is extracted from a longer "Chronology of the Hebrews, Elamites, Byzantines, Egyptians, Hellenes, Ethiopians, Syrians, Greeks" that runs from fol. 156r to fol. 165v, concluding with a number of calendar tables. The origin of this text is unknown. The extract relating to Abraham extends from fol. 156v, line 20, to fol. 157r, line 11.[7] Such lists played a considerable role in Armenian learned literature. Other lists, some preserving traditions allied with the pseudepigrapha, have been preserved, and a number have been published. The tenth-century example given here shows how old this genre is.[8] Text no. 5 below, Galata 154, is a typical example of such scholastic texts.

---

1. Matʻevosyan, 1995; 1997.
2. Stone 1998; 2002; see also *AAP* plates 10, 11. Most early Armenian manuscripts are Gospels or, sometimes, Service Books.
3. See Stone 1999.
4. Matʻevosyan 1997, 2:92
5. We have compared this with the descendants of Shem in MX 1.5 (Thomson 2006, 71–72). That section of MX has many genealogical lists.
6. *MH* 7th century, 912 §140.
7. See Matʻevosyan 1997, 2:224. On fols. 201v–202 are correlations of legendary history with that of Abraham and Isaac drawn from a chronography.
8. I have published other chronological and substantial lists elsewhere. See, e.g., Stone

In transcribing these texts, we have changed the line division and paragraphing of the original to enhance legibility. The other editorial procedures follow those outlined in the last section of the General Introduction above.

For ease of reference, we present three tables here. The first two are of the biblical chronology as presented in texts 1 and 2, while the third gives the names of the wives of the patriarchs drawn from M2679. Both types of material have been published elsewhere as well.[9]

Table 1: Text 1 fols. 36v–37

Item or Event	Genealogy (M2769)	MT	LXX	*Jubilees*[10]
Peleg begot Reu	130	30	130	1579
Reu begot Serug	132	32	132	1687 (108)
Serug begot Nahor	130	30	130	1744 (57)
Nahor begot Terah	109	29	79	1806 (62)
Terah begot Abraham	70	70	70	1876 (70)
God's command to Abraham	75	75	75	1953 (77)
Abraham begot Isaac	75+25=100	100	100	~1987 (111)
Isaac begot Jacob	60	60	60	2046 (59)
Jacob begot Levi	87	—	—	2127 (80)
Levi begot Kohath	46	—	—	
Kohath begot Amram	60	—	—	
Amram begot Aaron	70	—	—	2327[11]
Aaron's age at the Egypt Exodus	83			

1982a, 174–75; 1996a, 82–83, 88–89, 98–100, 135–40; 158–66; and others. The types of transmission of Armenian apocryphal traditions are discussed in Stone 1996b.

9. On the wives of the patriarchs, see Lipscomb 1978, Stone 1996a. I am indebted to O. Ableman, who prepared the tables below.

10. Total years from creation, based on VanderKam 1989. The patriarch's age is indicated in brackets.

11. This is based on the date given for Moses.

Table 2: Text 2 (M2679 156v-157r)

Item/Event	Genealogy (M2769)	MT	LXX	Jubilees	ALD
Rahab begot Serug	132	32	132	1687	
Rahab's lifetime	132+207= 339	32+207= 239	132+207=339		
Serug begot Nahor	130	30	130	1744	
Serug's lifetime	130+200= 320	30+200= 230	130+200= 320		
Nahor begot Terah	80	29	79	1806	
Nahor's lifetime	80+122= 202	29+119= 148	79+129= 208		
Terah begot Abraham	70	70	70	1876	
Terah's lifetime	70+35= 105	205	205		
Abraham begot Isaac	100	100	100	~1987	
Abraham's lifetime	100+75= 175	175	175	(175)	
Isaac begot Jacob	60	60	60	2046	
Isaac's lifetime	60+120= 180	180	180		
Jacob begot Levi	83	—	—	2127	
Jacob's lifetime	83+62= 145				
Levi begot Kohath	45	—	—		34
Levi's lifetime	45+80= 125	—	—		137
Kohath begot Amram	64	—	—		
Kohath's lifetime	—	—	—		
Amram begot Moses	75	—	—	2330	
Amram's lifetime	75+62= 137	—	—		

Table 3: List of Wives' Names in M2679

Patriarch	Wife M2679	Wives of the Forefathers
Rahab (Reu)	Ura	Soria
Serug	Milchah	Melk'ea (Milchah)
Nahor	Edna	Yesk'a
Terah	Arna	Yedna
Abraham	Sarah	Sarah
Isaac	Rebecca	Rebecca
Jacob	Leah	Rachel and Leah
Levi	Kaxat'am	Milka III (Milchah) (ALD)
Kohath	—	
Amram	Jochebed	Jochebed (ALD)

It will readily be observed that in tables 1 and 2 the life spans in M2769 resemble those of the Septuagint (and the Armenian Bible), while in table 3 the names are basically the same as those in the Septuagint, though there are differences is spelling and in the names of the wives of Nahor and Terah. Lipscomb 1968 disused these names in much detail. Some comparisons with Movsēs Xorenac'i may be found in the annotations, but they do not indicate any special relationship.

TEXT 1

M2679, fol. 36v–37r

Պարտ եւ պատշաճ է այսուհետեւ ընթանալ զհետ ամացն թուոց. զդաւիթ քահանայ յիշեսջիք ի ՔՍ.
Փաղեգ եղեալ ամաց ՃԼ ծնաւ զՌագաւ՝
Ռագաւ եղեալ ամաց ՃԼԲ ծնաւ զՍերուք՝
Սերուք եղեալ ամաց ՃԼ ծնաւ զՆաքովր.
Նաքովր եղեալ ամաց ՃԹ[12] ծնաւ զԹարայ.
Թարայ եղեալ ամաց Հ ծնաւ զԱբրահամ.
Աբրահամ էր ամաց ՀԵ ի ժամանակի իբրեւ հրաման ետ Աստուած ելանել նմա ի տանէ հարց իւրոց եւ ել յերկիրն քանանացւոց:
Արդ առնին ի բաժանմանցն երկրի մինչեւ ի գալ / fol. 37r / Աբրահամու յերկիրն Քանանացւոց ազգք Ե ամք ՌՃՁ եւ յԱդամայ ազգք Ի ամք ՎՅՁՂ:
Բ[նակէ]աց Աբրահամ յերկրին քանանացւոց ամս ԻԵ եւ ապա ծնաւ զԻսահակ՝ Իսահակ եղեալ ամաց Կ ծնաւ զՅակովբ՝ Յակոբ եղեալ ամաց ՁԷ ծնաւ զՂեւի՝ Ղեւի եղեալ ամաց ԽԹ ծնաւ զԿահաթ՝ Կահաթ եղեալ ամաց Կ ծնաւ զԱմրամ՝ Ամրամ եղեալ ամաց Հ ծնաւ զԱհարովն՝ եւ յամին ութսներորդի երրորդի կենացն Ահարովնի ելին որդիքն Իսրայելի յերկրէն Եգիպտոսացւոց ի ձեռն Մովսէսի առաջնորդին իւրեանց՝

It is a duty and fitting henceforth to follow after the numbers of the years.[13]
Peleg having lived 130 years begot Reu,[14]
Reu having lived 132 years begot Serug,[15]
Serug having lived 130 years begot Nahor,[16]
Nahor having lived 109 years begot Terah.[17]

---

12. ՀԹ in P'ilon Tirakac'i §140: see *MH* 7th century, 912.
13. Here, a short colophon by the scribe is added: "Remember David *k'ahanay* to Christ".
14. In the Masoretic Text the numbers are less by 100. See Gen 11:18. In Xorenac'i 1.5 it is 133 years; see Thomson 2006, 71.
15. Gen 11:20, MX 1.5.
16. Gen 11:22, MX 1.5.
17. Gen 11:24, but it gives twenty-nine years. MX 1.5 has seventy-nine years. See table above.

Terah, having lived 70 years, begot Abraham.[18]
Abraham was 75 years old at the time when God commanded (him) to go out of his fathers' house and he went forth to the land of the Canaanites.[19]
Now there were made, from the divisions of the earth[20] until Abraham came to the land of the Canaanites, 5 generations 616 years, and from Adam—20 generations, 3,384 years.
Abraham lived in the land of the Canaanites for 25 years and then he begot Isaac.[21] Isaac having lived for 60 years, begot Jacob.[22]
Jacob having lived for 87 years begot Levi.
Levi, having lived for 46 years begot Kohath.
Kohath having lived for 60 years, begot Amram.
Amram having lived for 70 years begot Aaron.
And in the eighty-third year of Aaron's life, the children of Israel went out of Egypt through the hand of Moses, their leader.[23]

Text 2

M2679 156v–157r

Ռագաւ ամաց ՃԼԲ ծնաւ qՍերուք յՈւրալ՝ եւ եկեաց առ նովաւ ամս՝ ՄԷ՝ միշտեւ ի Հէ ամս Նաքովրա: Ի Ռագաւա ՃԻԷ ամին Վ ամ լցաւ դարս Գ ի չրիեղեղէն qՓաղէկ ազգբ Ե ամք ՇԻԵ:

Ս[երուք ամաց ՃԼ ծնաւ qՆաքովր ի Մեթքեա՝ եւ եկեաց] առ նովաւ ամս Մ՝ միշտեւ ի ՕԱ ամս Աբրահա]մու:

Նաք[ովր ամաց] Չ ծնաւ qԹարա՝ յեղնաէ՝ եւ եկեաց [առ նո]վաւ ամս ՃԻԲ, միշտեւ ի ՕԲ ամս Աբրահամու:

Թարա Հ ամաւ ծնաւ qԱբրահամ, յԱռնաէ, եւ եկեաց առ նովաւ ամս ԼԵ, մինչեւ ի ԼԵ ամս Աբրահամու. եւ մեռաւ Թարա ի Խառան:

ՅԱդամայ մինչեւ յաւետիքն Աբրահամու Վ[ՃՁԴ] ամք. սա էր նախնի նախապետ ազգին հրէից՝ առ սովաւ ասորւց, եւ ասիացւց, թագաւորեաց Նինոս եւ Շամիրամ կին իւր, [աստա]նաւր լինի սկիզբն ձառայութեան յեզիպտոս՝ ՆԼ ամին, ի Ճ ամին ծնաւ qԻսահակ, ի Սառայէ, եւ եկեաց առ նովաւ ամք ՀԵ, մինչեւ ի ԺԵ ամս Յակոբ:

Իսահակ ամաց Կ ծնաւ qՅակոբ՝ ի Ռեբեկա, եւ եկաց առ նովաւ ամս ՃԻ մինչեւ ի ԼԵ ամս Դեւեայ:

Յակոբ ամաց ՁԳ ծնաւ qԴեւեա ի Լիայէ. եւ եկեաց առ նովաւ ամս ԿԲ

---

18. Gen 11:26, MX 1.5.
19. Gen 12:4. This date is common to all texts.
20. That is, from the Tower of Babel.
21. Gen 21:5.
22. Gen 25:26.
23. Exod 7:7.

մինչեւ ի ՋԹ ամս Կախաթու, ի մահուանէն Յակովբայ գնահն[24] Մովսէսի են ամք ՄԼԴ.

Ղեւի ամաց ԽԵ ծնաւ զԿախաթ ի Կախաթամա, եւ եկեաց առ նովաւ ամք Ձ մինչեւ ի ԼԱ ամս Ամրամա:

Կախաթ ամաց ԿԴ. ծնաւ զԱմրան Յոբոբեդա. ամք ՃԼԵ.

Ամրան ամաց ՀԵ ծնաւ զՄովսէս, Յոբոբեդնաէ դստերէ հաւր եղբաւր իւրոյ, եւ [եկեա]ց առ նովաւ ամս ԿԲ. մինչեւ ԿԲ ամս Մովսէսի, ի սորա. Ձ ամին յետքն յեգիպտոսէ: Յաւետեաց Աբրահամու մինչեւ ցելսն ամք ՆԼ. եւ Խ. ամ յանապատին:

Յա[դամա] գվախճանէն Մովսէսի ամք ՎՊԿԲ:

Reu at 132 years[25] begot Serug from Ura, and he lived during his lifetime for 207 years,[26] until the 75th year of Nahor. In Reu's 127th year, 3000 years were completed, 3 eras (millennia) from the flood, 5 generations from Peleg, 525 years.

Serug at 130 years begot Nahor from Milchah (Mełk'ea), and he lived during his lifetime for 200 years[27] until the 51st year of Abraham.

Nahor at 80 years begot Terah from Edna, and he lived during his lifetime for 122 years,[28] until the 52nd year of Abraham.

Terah in his 70th year begot Abraham from Aṙna, and he lived during his lifetime for 35 years, until the 35th year of Abraham. And Terah died in Haran.[29]

From Adam up to the Annunciation to Abraham was 3,184 years. He was the first forefather of the people of the Jews. During his (i.e., Abraham's) lifetime, Ninos and Šamiram his wife ruled over the Syrians and the Asians.[30] Now the beginning of the enslavement in Egypt was for the 430 years.[31] In the 100th year he begot Isaac from Sarah,[32] and he lived during his lifetime for 75 years, up to the 15th year of Jacob.[33]

---

24. գմահն would be expected here. This is a common graphic variant.
25. The figures agree basically with those of the above list.
26. Gen 11:28-29.
27. Gen 11:22-23.
28. Gen 11:24-25. In the Masoretic Text the figures are twenty-nine years and 119 years. Nahor lived eighty years before the birth of Terah; see MX 1.5 and Text 1 here, which has seventy.
29. Gen 11:32.
30. Semiramis; see MX 1.5 (Thomson 2006, 73–74); cf. 1.6. Her exploits are described in MX 1.15–16 (Thomson 2006, 94–98). Here Xorenac'i's combination of biblical chronology with other chronological systems is to be noted. This is, of course, typical of the chronographic tradition.
31. That is, after the descent into Egypt; see Exod 12:41; cf. Gal 3:17.
32. Gen 21:5.
33. Gen 25:7.

Isaac at 60 years begot Jacob from Rebekah[34] and he lived during his lifetime for 120 years,[35] up to the 35th year of Levi.
Jacob at 83 years begot Levi from Leah, and he lived during his lifetime for 62 years,[36] up to the 19th year of Kohath. From the death of Jacob to the death of Moses is 233 years.
Levi at 45 years begot Kohath[37] from Kaxat'am, and he lived during his lifetime for 80 years until the 62nd year of Moses up to the 31st year of Amran.[38]
Kohath at 64 years begot Amran from Jochebed: 135 years.[39]
Amran at 75 years begot Moses from Jochebed, the sister of his father's brother,[40] and he lived during his lifetime for 62 years up to the 62nd year of Moses.[41] From him it was 80 years to the exodus from Egypt.[42]
From the Annunciation to Abraham up to the exodus was 430 years and there were 40 years in the desert.[43]
From Adam to Moses' death was 3,862 years.

---

34. Gen 25:26.
35. Gen 35:28.
36. Gen 47:28. Based on the figures in the Masoretic Text, Jacob should have been eighty-five at Levi's birth.
37. *ALD* 11:4 has Levi as thirty years old and marrying Milchah III. See Greenfield, Stone, and Eshel 2004, 181–82 and genealogical table there. *T. Levi* 11:4 puts Levi at thirty-five but has a different wife. Levi's wife's name here is unique.
38. That is, Amram. This form of the name appears here and in the next sentences. From this section we may infer that Levi lived 125 years. According to Exod 6:16 he lived 137 years.
39. According to Exod 6:18, 133 years was the length of Kohath's life. The form of Jochabed is here in the ablative in –ոյ from which the final –յ is missing. Note the ablative form Յոքորեդնաէ, in the next line, which looks more familiar than that in -ոյ.
40. Exod 2:1.
41. That is, Amran (Amram) lived 137 years; cf. Exod 6:20.
42. Exod 7:7.
43. Exod 16:35. The period is usually reckoned to be that in servitude in Egypt. Michael the Syrian (Chabot 1899, 34) reckons this period from Abraham's departure for Canaan, when he was seventy-five years old. According to Michael the Syrian (1871, 25), the 430 years were counted from Abraham's seventy-seventh year, when he left his father's house. This may be another instance of the common Armenian variation of "5" and "7".

2. Story of Father Abraham

M8531 is a Miscellany of the fifteenth century.[1] The work from it that we are publishing is entitled Պատմութիւն հայր Աբրահամու *Story of Father Abraham*, and it is found on fols. 82v–90v. H. Anasyan first drew attention to the existence of *Story of Father Abraham* in his entry on Abraham in his *Bibliology of the Armenians*.[2]

The manuscript is written in formal minuscule script (*bolorgir*), and the place and exact date of copying remain unknown. Immediately preceding *Story of Father Abraham* are works on Noah's Ark, the Tower of Babel, and the Ark (i.e., of the covenant).[3] It is followed by other, more theological writings, including Vardan Aygkec'i's *Confession of Faith*. The orthography is unremarkable, and there is extensive use of ideographs and the single stroke abbreviation for ա. On the whole, the punctuation of the manuscript has been preserved, but occasionally a single dot (*kēt*) has been introduced to avoid confusion. Capitalization follows the manuscript, except that all proper nouns are also capitalized. I have introduced section divisions, and the rest of the editorial practice accords with that outlined in the General Introduction above.

This text contains a very full form of many of the Abraham incidents, including the following:

- Birth of Abraham in Babylon 1
- Crows (including Abraham as an astronomer 3) 2-4
- God's speech to Abraham before he leaves Ur 5
- Terah's idolatry; Haran's death and its reason 6
- Abraham goes to Canaan: Egypt, Pharaoh, and Sarah 7
- Separation of Lot from Abraham 7
- The four kings; mention of Melchizedek 8
- Story of Mamrē in full 9-11
- Abraham's hospitality introduced and his oath 11
- Abraham's hospitality; Satan's intervention; the three travelers 12
- The story of the Annunciation to Abraham 13-16

---

1. See Ēganyan, Zeyt'unyan and Ant'abyan 1970, col. 766.
2. Anasyan 1959, 138, no. 2. He also mentions a possible second copy in V290, fol. 93v. According to Čemčian 1996, 771–72, manuscript V290 is a different work. However, the notorious confusion of numbers in the Venice collection may be to blame for this lack of clarity.
3. Folios 13r ff. contain a work on Adam and Eve, titled in the catalogue, *Story Concerning Adam and Eve*.

- Sodom and Gomorrah and the flight of Lot 17-21
- Colophon 22

Folios 53v–55r of manuscript M4618 contain another copy of the *Story of Father Abraham* (text no. 2) in a form very close to that in M8351, on which manuscript the text published above is based. The very tiny script of M4618 renders it illegible in photographs. M4618 is a Miscellany containing several apocryphal texts, as listed in the catalogue.[4] These include texts concerning Adam and Eve, Noah's Ark, Cycle of Four Works, Hezekiah and Isaiah. It is to be hoped that these will be edited in the future.

On a visit to the Matenadaran in Erevan in autumn of 2010, I made sample collations of M4718 *in situ*.[5] These are given in Appendix 1 below, and they show that the two manuscripts are very similar.

Պատմութիւն Հայր Աբրահամու:

1. Եւ յետ աշտարակին լեզուացն բաժանելոյ. մոլորեցան մարդիկք եւ անկան ի կռապաշտութիւն. եւ եհան Աբրահամ. որ նա ծանեօ զճշմարիտ Աստուած եւ հայր եղեւ հաւատոյ. անուն հաւրն Թարա. կռապաշտ էր յառաջն. / fol. 83r / եւ իւր ծնընդեան տեղիքն Բաբիլոն. երկիրն Բաբելացոց:
2. բարիքն շատ բնակիչքն ուտե<ին>[6] եւ ըմպէին եւ բուծին զմարմինն: եւ ոչ դաղարէին ի մեղաց. եւ ի պոռնկութենէ. բարկացաւ Աստուած. սով եւ սղութիւն ետ նոցա:
3. ճաեկ յարուց որ ուտէին զվաստակս նոցա. եւ Աբրահամ ժե ամաց էր. առաքեաց հայրն պահել զարտորայս. եւ նա գնացեալ շատ ջանաց. եւ ոչ կարաց հալածել. ներացաւ ստաւ նաեցօ ի վեր եւ եսեւ գշրշագայութիւն երկնից. գաստեղս զարեզական եւ զլուսին. եւ ինքն ճա[րտ]ար[7] աստղազէտ էր. ծագեաց լոյս ի սիրտն Աբրահամու. եւ ի միտս իւր եկեալ ծանեաւ զմոլորութիւն.
4. եկաց ի վերայ ծնկաց. զբազուկս տարածեաց յաղօթս. եւ ասաց. անծանօթ եւ արարիչ ամենայնի. / fol. 83v / եւ ստեղծիչ. այս թռչոցս դու տուր հրաման. զի հեռասցին. եւ նոյնժամայն ի չիք դարձան. ուրախացաւ Աբրահամ. զի եզիտ զճշմարիտն Աստուած. եւ եկեալ պատմեաց հօրն. եւ ասաց թէ շատ աղաչեցի զկպաշտելիս ձեր. եւ ոչ եղեւ լսելի. եւ ապա ծանեա զճշմարիտն Աստուած. եւ նորա հրամանօքն հալածեցան թռչունքն.

---

4. See Ēganyan, Zeytʻunyan, and Antʻabyan 1965, cols. 1247–48.
5. Thanks are expressed to the Director, Dr. Hrach Tamrazian and Dr. Georg Ter-Vardanian, Keeper of Manuscripts, for making this possible.
6. The form in the text is singular, but a plural is required.
7. Two letters erased.

5. Եւ ի լուսանալ առաւօտուն. առանձնացեալ Աբրահամ եկաց յաղօթս. եւ երեւեցաւ Աստուած եւ ասէ. ել յերկրէ քումէ եւ յազգէ. եւ եկ երկիր զոր ցուցից[8] քեզ. վասն այտորիկ երեւեցա քեզ. զի ճշմարիտ եւ հաստատ ճանաչել տամ զիս քեզ: մի բնակիր ընդ անհաւատս: Եւ առ Թարա զորդիս իւր. գնաց երկիրն Քանանացոց. բնակեցո ի Խառան.
/ fol. 84r /
6. Եւ շինեաց Թարայ տուն կռոց ի Խառան. եւ բարկացաւ Աբրահամ. կամեցո այրել հրով. եղբայր Աբրահամու հայր Ղովտա կամեցաւ շիջուցանել զհուրն: եւ անկեալ ի տաճարն այրեցաւ եւ մեռաւ առաջի հաւրն. զի յետ ջրհեղեղին այլ չէր մեռեր[9] որդի առաջի հաւրն: իմացաւ զծնունդն ջորոյ. հակառակ Աստուծոյ արարչութեան. զի Աստուծոյ կամքն այն է. որ ամէն ազգ իւր ազգէն ծնանի. վասն այն ոչ ունի ծնունդ. զի չէ արարած Աստուծոյ այլ մարդիք իմացան ի հնարից Սատանայի:
7. մեռաւ Թարա ի Խառան: Եւ ասէ Աստուած ցԱբրահամ. ել յերկրէ քումէ. եւ եկ{ն}[10] ի Սամարիա: Եւ եղեւ սով. եւ էջ Աբրահամ յԵգիպտոս. եւ առին զՍառա ետուն փարօնի. եւ[11] / fol. 84v / եւ պատժեաց Աստուած զփարաւոն. եւ դարձոյց զկինն առ Աբրահամ. եւ եղեւ բազմանալն խաշանց եւ անասնոց Աբրահամու եւ Ղովտա. եւ ասէ Աբրահամ ցՂովտ. չէ պարտ խռովութիւն ի միջի մերում. քանց կռուով միատեղ կեցած. սիրով բաժանած լաւ եմք. եւ բաժանեցաւ Ղովտ յԱբրահամէ. եւ եկն բնակեցո ի Սողոմ. եւ առ իւր կին. եւ Աբրահամ բնակեցաւ ի Քեբրոն:
8. եկին չորս թագաւորք յարեւելից առին զՍողոմ. եւ զ[ ].[12] եւ Աբրահամ ՅԺԸ ընդոճինաւք կոտորեաց եւ դարձուց զգերին. Մելքիսեդեկ թագաւոր [Սա]ղիմա. ել ընդ առաջ Աբրահամու. աւծ զնա թագաւոր. եւ եղեւ Աբրահամ Ճ ամաց եւ Սառա Ղ ամալ էր.
9. զի Մամր/ fol. 85r /էն սեւ ծառա եւ հովիւ էր Աբրահամու. եւ ոչխարքն սեւ էին վասն ջերմութեան աշխարհին. եւ եղեւ սով. եւ յետ Աբրահամ Մամրէի հաց մի. եւ ասաց յարաւտ[13] տանել զոչխարն. եւ տեսեալ Մամրէ աղքատ մի նուաղեալ ի սովու. եւ անկեալ ի վերայ ճանապարհին. եւ ասէ աղքատն ցՄամրէ. քո Աստուծոյ սիրուն համար. թէ ունիս ինձ մի պատառ հաց տուր. ոչ կարեմ գնալ. եւ նա վասն Աստուծոյ սիրուն. հանեալ զհացն ետ աղքատին. եւ աղքատն

---

8. gl° over q p.m.
9. Non-classical form.
10. Corrupt for եկ.
11. Erased line, of which the first three letters, սատ are legible. There is a dittography of u at the beginning of fol. 84v.
12. Erasure of five letters follows.
13. Corrupt for յարաւատ.

2. STORY OF FATHER ABRAHAM

եկեր զ .. [ ][14] եւ գնաց. եւ ինքն մաաց սովա[ծ] ի տալթյն. ցցեց [կ]ադնի ցուպն հովակման շուք արար. եւ ինքն նստեալ ննջեաց.

10. զարթեաւ եւ տեսեալ արմատացեալ. զկադնին. բարձրացեալ եղեւ ծառ մեծ. եւ շուք էր / fol. 85v / արարեալ ի վերայ իւրն եւ ոչխարին. զոհացաւ Աստուծոյ. եւ սպիտակեալ էր ինքն. եւ ոչխարն. եւ երեկոյին յորժամ դարձաւ ի տունն. եւ գնաց Աբրահամ ընդ առաջ նորա. եւ հարցանէր թէ ով ես դու. եւ նա ասաց ես եմ Մամրէ հովիւն քո. եհարց թէ վասն յէր ես սպիտակացեալ. դու եւ ոչխարքդ.

11. եւ նա ասաց թէ քո Աստուածն արար. զԱ. հացն որ ինձ պաշար տուիր ես նորա սիր[ու]ն[15] աղքատին տուի. զայս ամենայն բար[ու]թիւնս արար Աստուած. եւ զարմացաւ Աբրահամ զոհացաւ զԱստուծոյ. եւ ուխտ եդ անձին իւրոյ. առանց աղքատի այլ հաց մի կերիցէ. մինչեւ ի յԱբրահամ թոյս մորվաք մեռանէին. իսկ հայրն հաատոյ Աբրահամ ծաղկեցաւ ալեւաք. / fol. 86r / եւ առաւօտուն առաջնորդեալ Մամրէ տարեալ էցոյց Աբրահամու զկադնին. եւ նա տեսեալ աւրհնեաց զԱստուած. եւ աւրն Գ անգամ ադաւթէր.

12. եւ նստէր ընդ հովանեաւ ծառոյն. մաւտաւոր ճանապարհի էր անցօրաց, զով որ տեսանէր կերակրէր վասն Աստուծոյ սիրուն. Սատանայ կապեաց զճանապարհին. Խ աւր. հիւր ոչ եկն. ալյազզիքն զայն բարի սովորութիւն յԱբրահամէ ունէին. որ զեւլիա շինեն ի վերայ ճանապարհին. եւ հաց տան աղքատաց. հիւր ոչ եկն Աբրահամու. եւ հասեալ աւաք հինգ շաբաթի. հասարակ աւրն. կայր աղաւթս առ կաղնեաւն. Մամրէի. եւ երեւեցաւ Աստուած Բ ընդ իւր ունելով ի կերպարան. / fol. 86v / առանց. անփոփոխ բնութիւն է Աստուած. այլ վասն մարդասիրութեան խոնարհի. փոխի ի տեսութիւն մարդոյ:

13. յառաջն տարակուսեցաւ ի միտս իւր. եւ ասաց թէ Աստուած է ընդէր մարդակերպ երեւի. եւ թէ մարդ է մարմաւոր. որպէս իջանէ յերկնից. իմաստուն էր Աբրահամ ի միտս ասաց. թէ ընդյեր ես տարակուսեր. յառաջ գնա մեծարէ. մարդասէրն աստուածասէր է: ընթացալ ընդ յառաջ. երկիր եպագ ի վերայ երեսաց. զի Տէրն կամեցաւ փորձել զհաւատն. եւ զկատարեալ սէրն Աբրահամու յառաջն ասաց մեք ճանապարհորդեմք. կու գնամք ի մեր ճանապարհին. ապա տարաւ իշ/ fol. 87r /ոյց զՏէրն ի խորանին. եւ լուաց չրով զոտս նոցա:

14. Եւ Սառայի ասաց. փութա. արա երիս նկանակ բաղարճ. եւ Աբրահամ առեալ որթ կաթնակեր զենեալ. եւ եւտ ի ծառայ եվել. եւ Սառա հասոյց բաղարճն. եւ էած Աբրահամ սեղան. նախ. կաթն եւ կարաք կերան. եւ ապա զորթն մատաղ. ծեր էր Աբրահամ. մոռացալ զիւր ծերութիւն. եւ անձամբ սպասաւորէին ինքն եւ Սառա. զի վարձքն իւրեանքն առցեն. Ոչ թէ առ աշատք. այլ ճշմարիտ կերան զկերակուրն անմարմինք գոլով. եւ մաքրեաց հուրն աստուածային.

---

14. Erasure in the manuscript.
15. We restore սիրուն, a dative of սէր.

15. Եւ Աբրահամ կանչեաց կայր. դեռ տարակուսի էր. / fol. 87v / թէ մարդկան է թէ Աստուած. եւ ասէ Տէրն. ուր է Սառա կին քո. եւ Սառա կայր յետեւ խորանին. եւ ունգն դներ բանից նոցա. յորժամ ասաց զանուն կնոջն. ապա Ճշմարիտ գիտաց Աբրահամ թէ Տէրն է. պատասխանի ետ Աբրահամ. եւ ասէ ի խորանին է. քեզ որդի լինի. յայտնի արար զինքն։ եւ պարզեաց զի Տէրն է. եւ լուաւ Սառա ծիծաղեցաւ ասելով. թէ մինչեւ ցայժմ չեղեւ որդի. ի ծերութեան ժամանակիս լինի։
16. Եւ ասէ Տէրն զԱբրահամ. զի է զի ծիծաղեցաւ Սառայ. մատ ի յիս ծեռն ու տղան մի է. երբ կամենամ չոր ծառեն որպէս դալարէ պտուղ բերեմ. յառաջ եկաց յերկ/ fol. 88r /իւղէն ասաց թէ ոչ ծիծաղեցա. թէ թերեհաւատութեամբ էր ծիծաղին. դատապարտեալ լինէր իբրեւ Զաքարիա. շատ աղքատաց կ[ար]աւտեր¹⁶ ցցեր Աբրահամ. եւ ինքն կարօտեր զաւակի. մեծ փառք է Աստուծոյ հուր զայն Բ հրեշտակաւք։ Եւ ապա աւրհնեաց զտունն եւ զեղղանն. եւ ելեալ երթայր այր ի տանէն. եւ երթայր Աբրահամ յուղարկել զնոսա։
17. Եւ ասէ Տէրն գԱբրահամ աղաղակ Սողոմացոց եւ Գոմորացոց ել առաջի իմ. եւ ասէ Աբրահամ մի կորուսեր արդարն ընդ ամբարշտին. եւ ելաց առաջի Աստուծոյ Աբրահամ. երկիր եպագ եւ ասէ Տէր. ես հող, եւ մոխիր եմ. գիտող եւ մոխիրս հետ քեզ խօսելոյ արժան արիր. թէ Օ արդար / fol. 88v / գտան ի մէջ նոցա կու կորուսանի այլոց մեղացն. եւ ասէ Տէրն ոչ կորուսից. թէ պակաս լինի Ե. ասէ Տէրն թող լինի. Խե. եւ եկն ի ԽՁ ի Ժ արդար. Դ. էր Ղովտ եւ կինն եւ ադչիկն. այլ արդար ոչ գտաւ. եւ զինչ է չարիք նոցա. արուագէտ էին. որձն հետ որձի. հետ անասնոց. անողորմ էին դիմաց աղքատին. դուռն փակէին դէմ աղքատաց. եւ ապա հաց ուտէին. աւտար հուրն հանդիպէր փոխանակ պատուելոյն եւ կերակրելոյն. բռնէին հետն չարիք գործէին։
18. Եւ ասէ Տէրն. Բ հրեշտակացն թէ գնացէք ի Սողոմ. եւ զԱբրահամու եղբաւր որդին գՂովտ իւր տանդվա հանեցէք. Աբրահամ/ fol. 89r / ու սիրուն համար. եւ Աբրահամ երկիր եպագ Աստուծոյ. եւ գնաց Աստուած մեկնեցօ ի տեղոջէն. եւ եկին Բ հրեշտակն ի Սողոմ. եւ Ղովտ նստեր աո դրանն. եւ նա իւր բարի վարպետեն Աբրահամէ էր ուսեալ զհուրընկալութիւն. եւ երկիր եպագ. զոր տեսեալ Ղովտ զգեղեցկութիւն պատկերի նոցա. ասաց ի միտս թէ սոցա նման գեղեցիկ մարդ ի քաղաքս չէ մտեր. քաղաքացիքս սոցա գլուխն մեծ չար կու բերեն.
19. կամէր Ղովտ գաղտ պահել. եւ ծածուկ ճանիւ դնել. զի մի իմասցին չարագործքն. ի քուն մտեալ էր. պատեցին զտունն Ղովտա. ծածկել ջանաց Ղովտ այլ տեսեալ էին մեծ քաղաքին. յառաջն պատեցին զտունն. / fol. 89v / զի մի գաղտ դռնով փախիցէ. ասացին Ղովդա

---

16. The word, as it appears in the text, is unknown: կաւտէր. Perhaps it is corrupt for կ[ար]աւտէր.

թէ ուր են արքն որ մտին ի տուն քո. տուր մեզ. եւ ել Ղովտ առ նոսա յետ նա փականել զդուռն. դարձեալ սկսաւ աղաչել զնոսա Ղովտ թէ. Ի դուստր ունիմ հարսնացու. ձեզ տամ զնոսա. սովրեալ էին յարուագիտութիւն. որ ի կին մարդ ոչ նաէին ամէնեւին:
20. Իբրեւ գիտացին հրեշտակքն զՂովտա վիշտն. բացին գդուռն. զՂովտ ի տուն առին. եւ փչեցին յերեսս նոցա կուրացան. եւ ասին հրեշտակքն գՂովտ. անմիտ դու գիտես մեք մեղաւոր մարդ եմք. մեք հրեշտակք ամենակալին եմք եւ ասին գՂովտ. էր ո աստ ընդանի. հան. եւ ել Ղովտ. եւ ասաց փեսա/ fol. 90r /ային որ առնելցոյ էին գդուստերսն եւ ոչ հաւատացին. այլ ծաղր արարեալ. եւ ասին հրեշտակք գՂովտ. զամենայն գիշերս աշխատ եղար. եւ չգիտեր գոք արժանի:
21. Կալան գձեռնանէ նոցա եւ հանին արտաքոյ քաղաքին. դարձաւ կինն Ղովտա յետս. եւ եղեւ արձան աղի: Սոդոմացի էր կինն. պատուիրեցին հրեշտակքն յետս չդառնալ. մնաց Ղովտ. եւ Բ դստերքն. գնացին փութով. հուր եւ ծծումբ<ք> առ հասարակ թափեցո. մէկ ժամ այրեցաւ մարդ անասուն այգի: եւ ապա սեւ ջուր թանձր իբրեւ զկուպրն ի վեր երեկ յանդնդոց. որպէս մեռած մարդ ոչ շարժի. այսպէս մեռած ծով անուանի. եւ յորդանան անցանէ ոչ ի գետի / fol. 90v / չրէն ի ծովս խառնի եւ ոչ ծովէն ի գետն:

Colophon: Տէր Աստուած Յիսուս Քրիստոսի ողորմեա անարժան գծող տէր Մարգարէիս. կարդացողացն եւ լսողացն. առ հասարակ ողորմեցի եւ նմա փարք յաւիտեանս ամէն:

Story of Father Abraham

1. And after the Tower (and) the separation of tongues, men erred and fell into idolatry. And he brought forth Abraham, who recognized the true God and became father of faith.[17] (His) father's name was Terah. He was an idolater[18] at first and the place of his birth (was) Babylon,[19] the land of the Babylonians.
2. The inhabitants ate and drank and nourished (their) body very well. And they did not cease sinning and fornication. God became angry and gave (caused) them famine and exiguity.

---

17. Rom 4:11. See further Maštoc' of Erivart in *MH* 9th century, 650.

18. Cf. Josh 24:2; Didymus the Blind, *On Genesis* [209]: "It is not by chance that God orders Abraham to leave his land and his relatives but because he sees in him . . . his faith in God. But it was not fitting that the one who had faith in God should remain among perverse people—the father of Abraham was in fact an idolater—because the company of the wicked often does harm to zealous people, especially to those whose zeal is new." Cf. Procopius of Gaza, *Commentary on Genesis*, col. 320; John Malalas, *Chronography*, 55, 57 (Jeffreys et al. 1986, 27, 28); Ishodad of Merv (Vosté and van den Eynde 1950–55, 155); George Syncellus, 106–7 (Adler and Tuffin 2002, 132–33), and implied by Symeon Metaphrastes 32.27–29 (Wahlgren 2006, 37). Terah was widely reputed as an idolater in rabbinic sources; see also Beer 1859, 9 and notes there.

19. Also in texts nos. 4.1, 8.2, and 13.3; cf. 6.8, where Ur is called Babyon.

3. He raised up ravens that ate (the fruit of) their toil.[20] And Abraham was 15 years old.[21] (His) father sent (him) to guard the fields. And he, having gone, strove greatly and was unable to chase (them) away. He was distressed, he sat down, he looked up and saw the circuit of the heavens, the stars, the sun and the moon. And he was a ski[lf]ul astronomer.[22] Light shone in Abraham's heart[23] and, coming to his mind (senses) he recognized (his) error.

---

20. This incident is not biblical. A variant form of it is found in *Jub.* 11:11–21, though it is not connected there with a discovery of God. It also occurs in texts nos. 2.3, 4.2–3, 6.1.3, 8.5–6, and 9.6 and has become an integral part of the story of Abraham's discovery of God. See the General Introduction, under "Sources of the Abraham Saga: The Ravens," where Brock's study of this tradition is discussed. Compare also Michael the Syrian (Chabot 1899, 26) and the Armenian version (Michael the Syrian 1871, 22). Observe that the Armenian version of Michael the Syrian in the 1871 edition has considerable expansions, including to the Abraham material. The expansions were discussed by Haase 1915.

21. No biblical basis for this age is to be found, but it is widespread; see also texts nos. 4.4, 12.5, 14.4, and 15.1 in the same context as here. Compare the General Introduction (p. 23). It is also found in Syriac sources, while *Jubilees* has 14: see the General Introduction (p. 42). The two angels who entered Sodom were youths, said to resemble fifteen-year-olds: see texts nos. 11.34 and 15.35; Isaac was fifteen at the time of the Aqedah (4.22; Michael the Syrian [Chabot, 1899, 34–35] has an alternative view of seventeen or thirty); and Joseph was fifteen when he shepherded with his brothers: see text no. 5.7. Thus, fifteen seems to have been the ideal age when a youth came to be considered an adult. Michael the Syrian has fifteen for the incident of the ravens (Chabot 1899, 26); the Armenian version has seventeen (p. 22), though this might result from a common graphic error.

22. Astronomical contemplation is related to the discovery of God in texts nos. 3.11, 12.5, 14.3, and 15.4. See already *Jub.* 12:16–18; the implications of *Apoc. Ab.* 7:7–9; Pseudo-Eupolemus *apud* Eusebius *Praep. ev.* 9.17.4, 8 and 9.18.2; Michael the Syrian 1871, 22; Artapanus *apud* Eusebius *Praep. ev.* 9.18.1; and apparently *Orphica* A.26–29 (*OTP* 2:799); Synagogal Prayer 2:14; and *LAB* 26:7. See further Josephus, *Ant.* 1.167–68. Philo in *De Abrahamo* talks of Abraham's education as an astrologer (69–70) but opposes astrology energetically (71, 77–79, etc.), as do the rabbis (see Ginzberg 1909–1938, 5:227; cf. *Gen. Rab.* 44:5. Compare also the view of astrology in Adler 2008, 50. The vigor of the opposition to Abraham's association with astrology or astronomy evinced by both Philo and the rabbis witnesses to the currency of such traditions. Bowley (1994, esp. 227–33) discusses Jewish Hellenistic views of Abraham as an astrologer. Note George Syncellus 111 (Adler and Tuffin 2002, 138) on Abraham as an astronomer. The same idea is found in Anania Širakac'i (seventh century) in *MH* 7th century, 725; Tiran *vardapet* in *MH* 10th century, 966. See also *Aggadat Berešit* 37 (in a different context); Fabricius 1713, 350–78; *Palaea* 201–2. Abraham as an infant discovered God through the luminaries according to the late *Ma'aseh Abraham* (*BM* 1.26). Perhaps also his heavenly vision of the arrangements of the stars in *LAB* 18:5 reflects this same tradition, since only astronomical revelation is mentioned. See the discussion of this theme in Kister 1994, 23; and Lowin 2006, 89–91. Lowin (2006, 90–96) has a schematic analysis of the astronomical argument used by Abraham for his belief in God. This is also current in Islamic sources from the Qur'an (6:76–80) on; see ibid., 98–105.

23. In most texts it is "light of grace (շնորհաց)"; in Michael the Syrian 1871, it is "light of mercy" (ողորմութեանն), which seems to indicate the independence of its text at this point.

2. STORY OF FATHER ABRAHAM

4. He remained on his knees, stretched out his arms in prayer.[24] And he said, "Unknown One and Maker of all and Creator. Give a command to these birds to be distant." And, at that very time they turned into nothing. Abraham rejoiced, for he had found the true God. And having come, he related (this) to his father and he said, "I beseeched your reverenced ones (i.e., gods) greatly, and it was not heard, and then I recognized the true God, and at his commands the birds were chased away."[25]

5. And when it dawned, Abraham went off alone (and) prayed. And God appeared and said, "Go forth from your land and family, and come to the land that I will show you. For this reason I appeared to you, that I may cause you to recognize me truly and firmly. Do not dwell with the faithless." And Terah took his sons; he went to the land of the Canaanites.[26] He dwelt in Haran.[27]

6. And Terah built a house of idols in Haran and Abraham became angry. He wished to burn (it) with fire.[28] Abraham's brother, the father of Lot wished to extinguish the fire and having fallen into the temple he was burnt up and died before his father.[29] For, after the flood, no other son died before his father. He learned the breeding[30] of the mule, (which was) against God's creation, for

---

24. Observe this kneeling *orans* position. Compare texts nos. 8.24, 12.6, and 14.3. It occurs at major prayer junctures in the various stories.

25. An address to Terah after Abraham's recognition of God, it found already in *Jub.* 12:2–5 and in a number of the texts below: nos. 8.3, and 12.7.

26. This must be corrupt for "Babylonians." Note that here, as in 5.1, 12.9, 13.5, and other places, the command of Gen 12:1 is doubled and used of the departure from Ur (Babylon) as well as the later departure from Haran. This stresses the divine purposiveness of the events and is based on Gen 11:31, which says that Terah set out for Canaan but stopped in Haran. The double departure is to be observed also in the *Palaea* 203. It occurs in Jacob of Edessa, and its background lies in the integration of Acts 7:3–4 with Genesis; see Adler 2008, 56.

27. Gen 11:31. Note the omission of the names of Abraham's brothers, Haran and Nahor. The text here reports a command to Abraham, but that Terah went to Haran. This command and the two moves, from Ur to Haran and from Haran to Canaan, are handled differently in the various texts. Here, in §7, a second command is given to Abraham, but oddly, he is told to go to the land of Samaria. There are different views of Terah's death; see texts nos. 2:7, 12.12, and 14.7; and compare Adler 2008, 58.

28. Note the words attributed to Abraham in one recension of *Apoc. Ab.* 7:2: "because fire burns your gods." In *Jub.* 12:12, Abraham burned the idolatrous temple; so also Michael the Syrian (Chabot 1899, 26) and Armenian version (Michael the Syrian 1871, 23). A similar story is to be found at the beginning of *T. Job*, with the actual burning of the idolatrous temple described in ch. 5.

29. Gen 11:28. The Bible puts (H)aran's (without the Ḥ, as also in the Armenian Bible) death in Ur, while our text and other Armenian sources put it in Haran; see texts nos. 4.6, 11.7, 12.10, and 14.6. It is always connected with Abraham's burning of the idolatrous temple. See further *Palaea* 202; Michael the Syrian (Chabot 1899, 27) and Michael the Syrian 1871, 23.

30. Literally, "birth," that is, that the mule was born from the crossing of a horse and a donkey. The tradition that the reason for Aṙan's untimely death is the miscegenation of the

it was God's will that every sort should bear its own sort. For that reason it (i.e., the mule) does not have offspring, for it is not created by God, but men have learned (its breeding) through the wiles of Satan.

7. Terah died in Haran. And God said to Abraham, "Go forth from your land and come to Samaria."[31] And there was a famine and Abraham went down to Egypt.[32] And they took Sarah, gave her to Pharaoh's house,[33] and God punished Pharaoh and he returned the woman to Abraham.[34] And Abraham's and Lot's sheep and beasts multiplied and Abraham said to Lot,[35] "Disorder should not be between us. We were better to be separated lovingly than to live contentiously in one place." And Lot was separated from Abraham and he came (and) dwelt in Sodom and he took a wife for himself. And Abraham dwelt in Hebron.[36]

8. Four kings came from the east. They took Sodom and [ ]. And Abraham with 318 domestically born men[37] cut (them) down and returned the booty.[38] Melchizedek king of [Sa]łim went forth to meet Abraham.[39] He anointed him king.[40] And Abraham was 100 years old and Sarah was 90. She was barren.

9. For[41] Mamrē was Abraham's black servant and shepherd[42] and the sheep

---

horse and donkey is to be found in several Armenian Abraham writings; see texts nos. 4.1, 6.2.4, and 12.10. It is not biblical. *Jubilees* 12:12–14 relates that Abraham burned the idolatrous temple and Haran died in the attempt to extinguish it, but the issue of the birth of the mule is not present. It is to be found in Ełišē, *Commentary on Genesis* 74.45 in *MH* 5th century, 818.

31. Gen 12:1. This is anachronistic as far as the name is concerned, but Shechem, Abraham's first stop (Gen 12:6) is indeed in the area later called Samaria.

32. Gen 12:10. At this point, preceding the descent to Egypt, the biblical text introduces a promise of the land. This is omitted by all the Armenian Abraham texts; see the General Introduction, p. 15, above.

33. Gen 12:15.

34. This incident is related in greater detail in texts nos. 4.8–12, 8.7–15 (which gives a very detailed version), 9.7–10, 12.14, 14.8–9, and 15.8–11. It derives from Gen 12:17–20. Pharaoh's punishment is made very explicit in 1QapGen (1Q20) 20:16–17. In *Palaea* 204 the hero of this incident in not Pharaoh but Ephron the Hittite. The picture of Pharaoh is emphatically negative in Philo, *Abr.* 94–95.

35. Lot occurs in Gen 13:1–12, where the separation of Abraham from Lot is also related. See also text no. 12.14–15.

36. Gen 13:12 and 13:18.

37. Gen 14:14. See the General Introduction, p. 92, n. 27, on the typological application of this number.

38. Literally, "captive." This incident is related in Gen 14:1–17, 21–24.

39. Gen 14:18-20.

40. It is not made explicit who anointed whom. Observe also that the offering of bread and wine is not mentioned in this text as it is in text no. 12.6 and in a different context in the Story of Sabek, texts nos. 7.13 and 15.55.

41. The word "for, since" does not fit smoothly into context here. The Story of Mamrē occurs here and in texts nos. 8.17–24, 12.18–21, and 15.13–21.

42. In *Gen. Rab.* 41:13, there is a discussion of what the name Mamrē designates. In

were black because of the heat of the land. And there was a famine. And Abraham gave Mamrē one (loaf of) bread and he said to take out the sheep in the morning. And Mamrē saw a poor man who had fainted from hunger and fallen on the road. And the poor man said to Mamrē, "For the love of your God, if you have (it), give me a piece of bread. I cannot walk (go)." And he, for the sake of the love of God, having taken out the bread, gave it to the poor man. And the poor man ate the [ ][43] and went, and he himself remained hungry in the heat. He drove in his oak staff (and) he made a shady shelter.[44] And he, having sat down, fell asleep.

10. He awoke (and) saw that the oak had struck root. Grown high it became a great tree and it was shading him and the sheep. He praised God. And he had become white and the sheep (as well). And in the evening, when he returned to the house, Abraham went to meet him and asked, "Who are you?" And he said, "I am Mamrē your shepherd." He asked, "On account of what have your face and the sheep become white?"[45]

11. And he said, "Your God did it. The 1 (loaf of) bread, which you gave me as provisions, through love of him, I gave to the poor man. All these benefits God did." And Abraham was amazed, he praised God and resolved[46] not to eat bread again without a poor man. Up to Abraham people would die with a dark beard, but Abraham, father of faith, flowered with grey hair.[47] And in

---

the view of R. Nehemiah it was a man and is connected with the King Mamrē in Gen 14:24. Mamrē is celebrated as giving Abraham pious advice in connection with his circumcision.

43. Erasure in the manuscript.

44. Ishodad of Merv (ca. 850 C.E.) says, "Ce chêne appartint à un homme qui avait nom Mamrē, le frère d'Aner et d' Ešcol" (Vosté and van den Eynde 1950–1955, 172). The formulation here is an etiology of the name "oaks of Mamrē" based on the biblical text. The connection of the three names derives from Gen 14:24, where these three accompanied Abraham in the four kings incident. However, Ishodad does not know the Story of Mamrē as it is found in the Armenian Abraham books.

45. At the basis of this story stands an apparent confusion of Mamrē of the "oaks of Mamrē" (Gen 13:18; 14:13; 14:24) and Eliezer, Abraham's servant or slave (Gen 15:2). Note the valuation of white and black, which is not mentioned in Genesis. This reflects partly the role of Ethiopian and African slaves in medieval Islamicate regions; see Brunschvig 2011. See further the perceptions of the descendants of Ham and Canaan as black and servants, e.g., in Gregor bar Hebraeus, *Scholia* to Gen 9:22 (Sprengling and Graham, 1931, 40–41). Other variants of the story occur in the Abraham texts, but the basic elements are stable. See texts nos. 2.9–12, 6.3.1–4, and 8.17–24.

46. Literally, "made an agreement with himself".

47. This reflects the socially high estimation of grey hair. Contrast the rabbinic tradition that with the birth of Isaac, Abraham's hair, formerly grey, turned black in a process of rejuvenation. This occurs in tenth-century Armenian sources; see *MH* 10th century, 967. See also texts nos. 4.28, 6.3.3–4, 12.22, and 14.15–16 concerning Abraham's grey hair. *Aggadat Berešit* 34 and 40 remark that from Adam to Abraham, the Bible does not mention old age. The verb "flowering" is used in all these contexts and, in some of them, is also applied to Abraham's good deeds. In *Kitāb al-ma'ārif*, Ibn Qutayba (d. 889 C.E.) says that Abraham was

the morning Mamrē led (and) brought Abraham (and) showed him the oak tree. And he, having seen (it), blessed God and he prayed three times daily.[48]

12. And he sat under the shade of the tree. The path of the passersby (was) close. Whomever he saw, he fed for the sake of the love of God.[49] Satan ensorcelled the road, for 40 days no guest came.[50] Foreigners have this good custom from Abraham that they build the cell[51] on the road and they give bread to the poor. No guest came to Abraham. And when the day equivalent to Maundy Thursday arrived,[52] he prayed by the oak tree of Mamrē.[53] And God appeared, having 2 (beings) with him in the form of men.[54] God is an unchanging nature (being), but for the sake of the love of humans he humbled himself, he changed into the appearance of a man.[55]

13. First, he (Abraham) doubted in his mind and said, "If he is God, why does he appear in human form, and if he is bodily man, how does he descend from the heavens?" Abraham was wise; he said to himself, "Why are you doubting, go forward (and) pay your respects. He who loves God loves man." He ran to meet (them), bowed down upon (his) face. For God wished to test Abraham's faith and perfect love. He spoke first, "We are traveling; we are

---

the first with grey hair; see Lowin 2006, 206. Abraham's grey hair is mentioned in *Yalqut Shim'oni Lek Lěka* 15.77 as a wonder.

48. Three daily prayers is, of course, the Jewish custom and is first mentioned in the book of Dan 6:10. Armenian custom in ecclesiastical usage differs, though the daily prayers are often centralized in three services.

49. See text no. 3.11 note.

50. In Islamic sources fifteen days are mentioned, and Firestone (1990, 55) suggests that this derives from a Jewish explanation that God prevented guests from coming because Abraham was recuperating from his circumcision. *Genesis Rabbah* 48:1 *Tanḥuma Vayera'* 1; *PRE* 28; and *Aggadat Berešit* 19 speak of God visiting Abraham as he was recuperating from circumcision.

51. This is a rare word. See MHB, s.v. զկիխա: "monastic cell, chapel."

52. Thus, this document puts the epiphany to Abraham into the events of Holy Week and Easter.

53. This was the site of a popular festival down to the time of Constantine. It was also called "Terebinth": see Thomsen 1907, 110–11; Wilkinson 1977, 173–74. The narrative has established the place and origin of the oak of Mamrē in the previous part of the tale.

54. Zak'aria Catholicos (ninth century) identifies the three men as the Word, Michael, and Gabriel (*MH* 9th century, 263), while Sahak Mrut identifies them less precisely, as God (*MH* 9th century, 403). On their identity, see further Grypeou and Spurling 2009a, 184–86. That a divine company visited Abraham is found in *Gen. Rab.* 48:1. The idea of a demon blocking the road occurs in *Palaea* 214. A discussion of the identity of the three men is to be found in Philo, *Abr.* 107–18.

55. This theological concern, as a sort of aside, is continued in the next section. Unclarity may be observed in *b. B. Meṣi'a* 86b and *Gen. Rab.* 48:1, which say that Abraham saw God or the Shekhina and subsequently identify the three men as Michael, Gabriel, and Raphael (*Gen. Rab.* 48:2) or as angels. These names are also found in *Gen. Rab.* 48:8. The exegetical issue in Gen 18:2–3 is set forth very clearly by Grypeou and Spurling 2009a, 182, with Christian identifications given on 190–93

going on our way." Then he brought the Lord and seated[56] (him) into the tent and washed their feet with water.[57]

14. And he said to Sarah, "Hasten. Make three cakes of unleavened bread."[58] And Abraham, having taken a milk-fed calf, having slaughtered (it), gave it to servants to cook.[59] And Sarah offered the unleavened bread and Abraham brought a table (or: meal, feast): first, they ate milk and butter and then the slaughtered calf. Abraham was old; he forgot his age and he and Sarah were themselves serving, so that they might receive their reward.[60] They did not just seem to eat, but truly they ate, though they were bodiless. And the divine fire purged (i.e., the food).[61]

15. And Abraham remained standing. He still was doubtful whether he was human or God. And the Lord said, "Where is Sarah your wife?" And Sarah was standing behind the tent and attended to their words. When he said the woman's name, then truly Abraham knew that he is the Lord. Abraham answered and said, "She is in the tent." "You will have a son," he revealed to him. And it was clear that he was the Lord. And Sarah heard, she laughed saying, "Up to now there was no son, will there be (one) in this time of (my) old age?"[62]

---

56. Literally: "made descend."

57. Genesis 18:1-16 relates this incident, though there Abraham does not bring them into his tent but entertains them in the shade of a tree (18:4). Compare Abraham washing Michael's feet in *T. Ab.* A3:7–12 and B3:6–10, where the washing of the feet is accompanied by miracles. That the chief of the three angels was Michael is the view of R. Ḥiyya in *Gen. Rab.* 48:3. That sequence is built on the one here, including the slaughter of animals from the flock as an expression of hospitality. The matter is not mentioned in *Jubilees*. In *T. Ab.* A 6:6 and B 6:13 Abraham, later in his life, recognizes the feet of one of the three men that he washed. See §16 below, for interpretations of the three men.

58. Gen 18:6.

59. Gen 18:7.

60. In the biblical text, Sarah's serving is not mentioned nor the motive that Abraham and Sarah wished to win their reward. Stress on the virtue of Abraham's personal service occurs in *b. B. Meṣiʻa* 86b. This point is made by Ełišē, *Commentary on Genesis* (Khachikyan and Papazian 2004, 131), comments on Gen 18:9 and Stepʻanos Siwnecʻi §79 (above, p. 23, n. 82).

61. A similar theological concern is expressed in §§12–13. On angelic eating, see *T. Ab.* A 4:9–10, where the food the angel Michael ingests is consumed by a specially appointed "all-consuming" spirit. See E. P. Sanders's comment in *OTP* 1:884 note e; and Grypeou and Spurling 2009a, 188–89. Compare text no. 12.40. See also Philo, *Abr.* 118, who argues that the angels neither ate nor drank but gave the appearance thereof: so also *Gen. Rab.* 48:5; 48:8. See on the issue of the angels or God eating, Justin, *Dial.* 57: the patristic evidence is discussed further in Grypeou and Spurling 2009a, 194–95. Another approach to this issue is the Islamic one, where the angels reveal their true nature as an explanation of why they are refraining from food: see Al-Tabari's treatment and others', cited in Firestone 1990, 54–55. See also Grypeou and Spurling 2009b,

62. Gen 18:9–12. This theme is taken up in the Qurʾan 11:67–69 and 51:24–29; see Firestone 1990, 52, 57–58.

16. And the Lord said to Abraham, "Why is it that Sarah laughed (saying)? 'Whether an old man or a young man approaches me, (even) when I wish, can I bring forth fruit from a dry tree as from a green tree?'"[63] She came forward from fear; she said, "I did not laugh."[64] If laughing were through little faith, she was guilty like Zechariah.[65] Abraham de[sir]ed (and) filled[66] many poor, and he himself desired seed. It is a great honor that God came with two angels, as a guest.[67] And then he blessed the house and the table and, going forth the man went from the house and Abraham went to accompany them on their way.[68]

17. And the Lord said to Abraham,[69] "The cry of the Sodomites and the Ghomoreans has ascended before me." And Abraham said, "Do not destroy the righteous with the wicked." And Abraham wept before God, he bowed down and said, "Lord, I am dust and ashes. Make me, this dust and ashes, worthy to speak with you. If 50 righteous are found among them, will it (i.e, the city) be destroyed (because) of the sins of the others?" And the Lord said, " I will not destroy (it)." "And if 5 lack?" The Lord said, "Let there be 45." And he came to 46,[70] 20, 10 righteous.[71] There were 4—Lot and his wife, and the daughters.[72] No other righteous person was found. And what was their evil? They were homosexuals, man with man, and with beasts; they were merciless toward the poor; they shut the door against the poor and then ate bread;

---

63. Compare this same image in al-Tabari, in the citation by Firestone 1990, 109: "Sarah said to Gabriel: 'What is a sign of this?' He took a dry twig in his hand and bent it between his fingers. It quivered and turned green." This same theme is concretized in the Mamrē story of the planting of his staff and its turning green. It is hard to derive this recurrent theme from the one similar biblical verse in Ezek 17:24: "I dry up the green tree and make the dry tree flourish." More remotely, it evokes the incident of Aaron's staff in Num 17:5–10. See text no. 12.46 and note there. It occurs in Ełišē, *Commentary on Genesis* (Khachikyan and Papazian 2004, 131) and is applied from that source to Sarah in text no. 12.46 (see note there).

64. Gen 18:13–15.

65. Luke 1:18–20. See text no. 12.47.

66. That is, with food.

67. This is the common Christian interpretation of the three men: see also Justin, *Dial.* 56 (ANF 1:355). See also Eznik, 22.19 (*MH* 5th century, 457), Agathangelos, *Teaching,* 28.4 (*MH* 5th century, 1,446). A different tradition lies behind the statement in *T.Ab.* B 2:10: "I heard about you when you went apart forty stadia and took a calf and slaughtered it, entertaining angels as guests in your house" (*OTP* 1:896). This interpretation must be built on exegeses like Philo's in *Abr.* 113. In §143 Philo says that the chief of the three men was God.

68. Gen 18:16. The blessing of the table and the house is not in the biblical story, nor is the preceding sentence. It occurs also in texts nos. 11.30, 11A.29–30, 11A.42, 12.51, and 15.29.

69. Gen 18:20–23.

70. One would expect "30" here.

71. From this point on the story departs from the biblical text. The numbers of righteous given at this point in the narrative by the various Abraham texts vary from one another.

72. The form is singular but must designate Lot's two daughters, as is clear from context.

2. STORY OF FATHER ABRAHAM   49

a foreign guest encountered instead of honor and nurture, (that) they seized (him) from behind,[73] they did evil.

18. And the Lord said to the two angels, "Go to Sodom and bring forth Lot, Abraham's nephew, with his household, for the love of Abraham." And Abraham bowed down to God.[74] And God went, departed from that place.[75] And the 2 angels came to Sodom, and Lot was sitting by the gate[76] and he had learned hospitality from his good teacher Abraham.[77] And he bowed down,[78] to those the beauty of whose countenance Lot had seen. He said to himself, "A man as beautiful as them has not entered the city. These citizens (dwellers in this city) will bring great evil on their heads."

19. Lot wanted to keep (it)[79] secret, and secretly to set (them) on the way, so that evildoers should not learn of it. When he fell asleep, they surrounded Lot's house. Lot tried to hide, but they had been seen in the city. First, they surrounded the house, so that he should not secretly flee by the door. They said to Lot, "Where are the men who entered your house? Give (them) to us." And Lot went out to them, closing the door behind him. Again Lot began to beseech them, "I have two marriageable daughters. I give them to you."[80] They were so used to lying with men that they completely ignored women.[81]

20. When the angels apprehended Lot's difficulty, they opened the door; they took Lot into the house. And they blew in their faces; they became blind.[82] And the angels said to Lot, "Foolish one, do you consider that we are sinful men? We are angels of the Omnipotent." And they said to Lot, "Bring forth whoever is your family here."[83] And Lot went forth and he said to his sons-in-law, who were going to take his daughters (i.e., in marriage) and they did not believe, but mocked.[84] And the angels said to Lot, "All this night you labored and you did not know who was worthy (i.e., of being saved)."[85]

21. They took them by the hand and brought them out of the city.[86] Lot's wife turned back and became a pillar of salt.[87] The woman was from Sodom; the

---

73. The Armenian is not quite clear.
74. Down to this point, this section is not found in the Bible.
75. Gen 18:33.
76. Gen 19:1a.
77. Lot learned hospitality from Abraham (*Tanḥuma Vayera'*, 15).
78. Gen 19:1b. The text is expanded from this point.
79. That is, their coming.
80. From "They said . . ." to the end of this section, see Gen 19:4–8.
81. This sentence is not in the biblical text.
82. Gen 19:11. According to *Palaea* 217, the angel consumed them with a fire-bolt.
83. Gen 19:12. The word ṭp at the beginning of the phrase is difficult. It could be an auxiliary to be construed with hutʻ.
84. Gen 19:14.
85. This sentence is not in the biblical text.
86. Gen 19:16.
87. Gen 19:26. The prohibition to look back and its punishment come later in the section

angels commanded not to turn around. Lot and his 2 daughters remained. They went quickly. Fire and sulphur poured down equally.[88] Men, beasts, vineyards were burnt all at once.[89] And then black water, thick as sulphur came up from hell. Just as a dead man does not move, thus it is named the Dead Sea. And the Jordan passes through. Nothing of the river water is mixed with the sea and nothing of the sea with the river.[90]

22. Colophon: Lord God Jesus Christ. Have mercy on the unworthy scribe, me Rev. Margarē. Let him have mercy upon the readers and the listeners together. Glory to Him forever. Amen.

---

here. There are two traditions, one that she turned into stone, the other that she turned into salt. Both are to be found in *Palaea* 217. Ephrem, *Commentary on Genesis* 16.7 (Mathews and Amar 1994, 162) has only the pillar of salt.

88. Gen 19:24.
89. Gen 19:25.
90. This passage is not biblical. It exhibits popular geographical concepts.

3. Biblical Paraphrases on Abraham

An introduction to the document as a whole is to be found in the full edition of *Biblical Paraphrases*.[1] Two manuscripts have been edited. Ms A is M3854 of the year 1471 and Ms B is M4231 of the fifteenth century. This work differs in genre from the narrative documents that we publish elsewhere in the present volume, but, despite that, its apocryphal traditions often bear the same character. It contains a sort of summary of biblical verses in sequence, integrating among them apocryphal sections and apocryphal traditions. This character is different from, say, text no. 2 above, which, though it follows the biblical story line in broad terms and though it uses biblical words and phrases, is still far from being a series of excerpts from the biblical text.

This document was first published in 1982.[2] Here we quote that edition exactly. That edition adopted the practice of giving only the nonbiblical parts of the text in full and listing sequentially the biblical verses that are excerpted or paraphrased between the apocryphal segments. We have chosen to include the sections dealing with Abraham. As in the 1982 edition, the text and translation alternate by segments. We note any changes to the published text.

TEXT AND TRANSLATION

10. Gen 11:10, 22, 24, 26, 29, 30.

11. **Ms A** եւ յայնմ ժամանակին մարդիք գաստուած ոչ ճանաչէին՝ զի կռապաշտք էին, ումանք գաւդն եւ այլք զջուրն. եւ հայէր աբրահամ յաստեղսն եւ կարծէր թէ նոքայ են աստուած. մինչ եկն լուսինն. եւ ասաց թէ այս է որ մեծ է. մինչ եկն արեգակն. ասէ այս է աստուած որ քան զայլն մեծ է եւ լուսատու. մինչ տեսաւ որ ամէնքն զային եւ զնացին. որպէս ծառայք թուեցաւ նմայ. եւ այս ասէ ոչ են աստուած. այլ ծառայք են:

And at that time men did not know God, for they were worshippers of idols—some of the air and others of the water.[3] And Abraham looked at the stars and thought that they are God. When[4] the moon came, he said, "This it is which is great." When[5] the sun came, he said, "This is God, which is

---

1. See Stone 1982a, 93–95.
2. Stone 1982a, 92–95. These excerpts are published by permission of the Israel Academy of Sciences and Humanities, which holds the copyright.
3. This detail does not occur in the other Abraham documents.
4. Or: until ... and.
5. Or: until ... and.

greater than the other and more light-giving." When he saw that all these came and went, they seemed to him like servants, and he said this, "They are not God but servants."

Յայնժամ ի վեր կալաւ զձեռն եւ ասէ՝ աստուած որ ի ծածուկդ ես եւ ոչ երեւիս եւ այս ամենայն քո ծառայք են՝ գոյց ինձ քեզ: Եւ առ ժամայն երեւեցաւ նմա աստուած եւ ասէ՝ Ետու զայակիս քում զերկիրս զայս:

Then he held his hands on high[6] and said, "O God! who are hidden and not seen, and all these are your servants, show me yourself." And God appeared immediately unto him and said, "I have given this land to your seed."[7]

Եւ շինեաց Աբրահամ սեղան ո<ւ>ր երեւեցաւ նմա տէր: Ահա կռապաշտ եւ տխմար՝ բայց տեղեկեցաւ աստուծոյ. եգիտ զաստուած եւ եղեւ նման աստուծոյ: Եւ հայր ամենայն հաւատելոց. որ ամենայն արժանաւոր ի գոգն նորա հանգչին:

And Abraham built an altar where the Lord had appeared to him. Behold! He was an idol worshipper and unlearned, but he recognized God. He found God and he became like God and father of all believers, in whose bosom all the worthy rest.[8]

ի ջրհեղեղէն մինչ ի յաբրահամ թձխբ. տարի է:

From the Flood up to Abraham is 942 years.[9]

Եւ բնակեցաւ աբրահամ ուր էր խորանն առաջին, եւ էր նա հիւրասէր՝ եւ առանց հիւրի հաց ոչ ուտէր: Եւ սատանայ արգելեաց զճանապարհն՝ եւ քառասուն աւր հիւր ոչ եկ<ն> նմա, եւ նա հաց ոչ եկեր. եւ կայր առ դրան խորանին.

And Abraham dwelt where the first tent was and he was hospitable and did not eat food (or: bread) without a guest.[10] And Satan obstructed the way and

---

6. The kneeling, found in other texts at similar junctures, is missing from *Biblical Paraphrases*.
7. Note the promise of the land, given later in the biblical narrative (Gen 12:7) and also omitted from all the other Abraham apocrypha, as discussed in the General Introduction, p. 17. The command of Gen 12:1 is not mentioned here.
8. For the "bosom of Abraham," see Luke 16:22; for "father of all believers," see Rom 4:16.
9. On the chronology in this text, see Stone 1982a, 83. Elsewhere this document gives this period as 944. In the *Acts of Pilate*, this period is 1,137 years. In Stone 1996a, 99, a text is given with a total 930 years. The whole issue of these chronological summaries in Armenian remains unstudied, but it should be remarked that often, as in some of the texts mentioned in this note, the grand totals are out of synchronization with the totals that are gained by adding up the specified year spans between specific events.
10. This story is found repeatedly in the literature, sometimes as a brief allusion and sometimes in considerable detail. See texts nos. 2.12 (a very short version), 11.22–27, 12.22–24, and 15.23–25.

for forty days no guest came to him, and he ate no food (or: bread). And he was by the entrance of the tent.

Ms B

Եւ յայնմ ժամանակին. մարդիք զաստուած ոչ ճանաչէին. զի կռայպաշտք էին։ Եւ աբրահամ ասաց թէ աստուած արեգակն է. եւ լուսին։ Եւ տեսանէր զի երթային եւ գնային։ Եւ ասէ թէ սոքայ ծառայք են աստուծոյ. եւ յայնժամ զձեռն ի վեր կալաւ եւ ասէ. աստուած որ ի ծածուկ ես եւ ոչ երեւիս։ Եւ այս ամենայն քո ծառայք են. զքեզ ցոյց ինձ։

And at that time, men did not know God, for they were idol-worshippers. And Abraham said, "The sun is God, and the moon." And he saw that they came and went,[11] and he said, "They are servants of God." And then he held his hands on high and said, "God, who are hidden and not seen, and all these are your servants, show yourself to me."

Եւ առ ժամայն երեւեցաւ նմա աստուած եւ ասէ. տաց<ի> զալակի քում զերկիրս զայս. եւ շինեաց աբրահամ սեղան ուր երեւեցաւ նմա տէրն։ Եւ յորժամ ծանեաւ իմաստութեամբ զաստուած եղեւ հայր հաւատոյ ամենայն քրիստոնէից։ որք արժանաւորք են ի գոգն նորա հանգչին։

And immediately God appeared to him and said, "I will give this land to your seed."[12] And Abraham built an altar where the Lord appeared to him. And when he recognized God by means of wisdom, he became a father of faith for all the Christians. Those who are worthy rest in his bosom.[13]

ի ջրհեղեղն մինչեւ ի յաբրահամ ՋԽԲ տարի է.

From the Flood to Abraham is 942 years.

Եւ բնակեցաւ աբրահամ ... (*like A*)

And Abraham dwelt ... (*like A*)

12. Gen 18:2, 3, 4, 7a, 8, 9, 10 + 14, 18, 20, 21, 23, 24, 26.

13. Ամենայն մարդոյ պարտ է զսուրբն եւ զարդարն սիրել եւ ընդունել՝ զի ձեզ բարի եւ շահ լինի զմեղաւորն եւ զչարագործն ատել եւ ոչ ընդունել եւ ընկերանալ. այլ խափանել զչարն. զի չարն ոչ պակասի ուր պիղծն լինի։

It is the duty of every man to love and accept the holy and righteous. For you it is good and advantageous to hate the sinner and the evildoer and not

---

11. That is, rose and set.
12. Gen 12:7; see note 7 above.
13. See p. 212, n. 42.

to accept or befriend him, but to oppose the evil. For the evil does not lack where abomination[14] is.

14. ի սոդոմ եւ ի գոմոր դովտ էր արդար. Աստուած եհան զնա ի քաղաքէն՝ եւ ապա զհուրն յերկնից առաքեաց ի նոսա. եւ անշիջելի դեռեւս յայրեցման է:

In Sodom and Gomorrah, Lot was righteous. God brought him forth from the city and then he sent fire from heaven upon them, and it is still unextinguished in (its) burning.

15. Gen 16:3, 4a, 15
որ են իսմայելացիք՝ քուրդ ազգդ անդ իցեն:

who are the Ishmaelites, the Kurdish people are there.[15]

16. Gen 17:16, 18:11
A 110v ուստի լինի այդ. եւ ասէ դիւրին է աստուծոյ ի քարանցդ յայդմանէ յարուցանել որդիս աբրահամու. եւ հաւատային.

"Whence shall this be?" And he said, "It is easy for God to raise up this son for Abraham from these stones."[16] And they believed (cf. Gen 18:14).

Gen 21:2, 3, 5, 4, Gen 17:27.
B զի աստուած հրամայեաց թլփատել. որ էր նշան եւ մատանեհար աստուծոյ՝ թէ մտի ունիցիս զիս. որպէս ի ջրհեղեղն՝ աղեղն յամպս նոյի.

For God commanded him to circumcise,[17] which was a sign and seal of God, that they might bear me in mind, as in the case of the flood the rainbow (was) for Noah.

18. *Typological exegesis:* Abraham is the type of God the Father, Isaac is Christ, the wood is the wood of the Cross, Abraham's sacrifice is God's sending of his Son.[18]

---

14. The late N. Bogharian suggested reading, "the abominable one".

15. The identification of biblical ethnonyms with medieval peoples and tribes is quite common. It is worthy of a separate study. See text no. 5.4 below.

16. Matt 3:9. Note that elsewhere Sarah compares herself to a dry stick that cannot bring forth green leaves; see text no. 2.16, etc. The metaphor is transferred into a miracle in the Story of Mamrē; see texts nos. 2:10, 11.16, 12.20, and 15.17, where it provides an etiology of the "oak of Mamrē."

17. Abraham's circumcision is mentioned in a number of the texts; see nos. 4.13, 5.2.6, 5.3, 13.8, and 14.12.

18. Above (General Introduction pp. 1–2) we have discussed the typology of the sacrifice of Isaac, which is specifically mentioned only rarely in the narrative texts.

4. The Memorial of the Forefathers Abraham, Isaac, and Jacob

The title of this text, "On that day is the memorial of the Patriarchs Abraham, Isaac, and Jacob," signals its hagiographical character, referring to the appropriateness of the story of Abraham for "the same day," that is, for some specific date. Such titles are common in the Synaxarium, itself called in Armenian *Yaysmawurkʻ,* which means "On that day . . . ."[1] Hagiographical collections of various sorts formed a significant context for the preservation (and perhaps to some extent for the creation) of apocryphal narratives, among other types of material. Indeed, text no. 14 below is the Abraham story drawn from the 1730 edition of the Armenian Synaxarium.

Here I publish three copies of *The Memorial of the Forefathers*. The first, which serves as the text, is drawn from M1665 fols. 173v–182v, a Miscellany written in 1445. It is in the *bolorgir* script, and it was copied in the village of Tayšoł in the Vaspurakan region of Greater Armenia by Stepʻannos *erēcʻ* for the priest Karapet.[2] In addition to the document published here, the manuscript contains a number of other hagiographical and associated works.

Another copy of the same text is found in M6092 fols. 338r–344r. That manuscript is another Miscellany, copied in the seventeenth century.[3] It contains many narratives (titled պատմութիւն) including among the titles listed in the catalogue: Stories of Joachim and Anna, of Abraham, Isaac and Jacob, and of the prophet Elijah. It is written in a clear *notrgir* script, of rather large size. The manuscript seems to have been copied from a faulty exemplar in which much text was displaced. Thus, for example, the text at the top of p. 338v does not follow upon that at the end of 338r, but apparently commences in the middle of the incident of the birds. I note a number of further points of the influence of displacement in this corrupt exemplar in the apparatus and notes.[4]

---

1. See Mécérian 1953; and, further, Thomson 1995, 257–63.
2. Ēganyan, Zeytʻunyan, and Antʻabyan 1965, 1:604.
3. Ēganyan, Zeytʻunyan, and Antʻabyan 1970, 2:248–49.
4. Note that words իւր ի կնութիւն ". . . himself as wife" conclude an incomplete sentence in §18 at the beginning of the folio and are repeated in §19 in the second line re Abimelech. Other examples are noted below. Because some of these *non sequiturs* occur in the middle of pages of the manuscript, manuscript M6902 itself cannot be the manuscript in which the pages have been misplaced. This must have taken place in an earlier exemplar probably in the course of resewing and rebinding.

The third copy of this document is found in BLEgerton 708, fols. 158v–161r. Frederick Conybeare, in the catalogue of the British Museum, sets it in the eighteenth century, but it might be somewhat earlier.[5] It is written in *notrgir*, informal minuscule script. The manuscript contains a series of hagiographic works and Պատմութիւն "Stories," including texts devoted to the Ark of the Covenant, Daniel, and Nebuchadnezzar, and others. The title *Lives of the 12 Patriarchs* of the text published here (MS E) is not related to the twelve sons of Jacob, but to twelve forefathers of Israel, starting from Abraham.[6]

All three copies of the writing, therefore, are drawn from manuscripts that contain tales additional to that about Abraham. In order to provide an example of the character of this additional material, in the Appendix to the present document I provide a transcription and translation of the stories from Isaac down to Joseph as found in M1665. It is in such contexts that stories about Abraham often occur.

In the text, I have kept the punctuation of the oldest manuscript (M1665) with a very few minor adjustments for clarity. The orthography of that manuscript is regular and fairly standard in character. This situation contrasts with the much less formal character of M6092, while Egerton 708 holds the middle ground between the other two. The language of M6092 is a late form of Ancient Armenian with a number of orthographic peculiarities, while the Armenian language and orthography of the Egerton 708 are a fairly standard form of later Ancient Armenian. Its script is clear and offers few difficulties of decipherment.

The manuscripts are designated as:

M   M1665
Y   M6092
E   Egerton 708

The Character of the Document

The sequence of the text and a good deal of its wording follow the biblical order rather closely. Major incidents of the biblical Abraham stories are omitted, such as the Annunciation to Abraham, the affair of Sodom and Lot, the war of Abraham with the four kings, the meeting with Melchizedek, the naming of Beersheba, the Covenant between the Pieces and others.[7] *Memorial of the Forefathers* stresses quite strongly the two incidents of Sarah in kings' palaces.

The document introduces apocryphal episodes such as the crows and Abraham's faith (§§2–3); the death of Achan because of the miscegenation of the mule

---

5. For a description of the manuscript, see Conybeare 1913, 218–25. Conybeare does not mention any basis for dating, but it seems likely to have been paleographical and, today, on paleographical grounds, I think a date up to a century earlier might be entertained.

6. There exist quite numerous copies of such collections of "Stories of..." (պատմութիւն) that very often start with the *Cycle of Four Works*. They require separate investigation.

7. See above the General Introduction, under "Biblical and Nonbiblical Episodes" on this.

(§§1, 6); Terah as the builder of idols and of an idolatrous temple (§6); Abraham's burning the idolatrous temple (§6); and the death of Achan in extinguishing the fire (§6). Moreover, apocryphal exegeses of biblical events and apocryphal details are also included. Among them we may observe the following:

- The wives of Abraham and Nahor were Achan's daughters, Sarah = Isca and Nahor's wife is Milcah (Melk'a, §5).
- Hagar was given to Sarah as a maidservant by Pharaoh (§12).
- Ishmael means "seeing of God" (§12): derived exegetically from Gen 16:3–14.[8]
- The source of "the tree of Sabek" (§22) is a misunderstanding of a transliteration in the LXX of Gen 22:13. Traditions about the tree of Sabek are much more developed in other Armenian narratives; see especially text no. 7 *History Concerning the Tree of Sabek*.[9]
- Sarah died in Abraham's 137th or 138th year (§28).
- Shechem is identified as Hebron in this context as is found elsewhere; see text no. 14.16 below.

A number of cases seem to allude toEłišē's *Commentary on Genesis*.[10]

REMARKS ON THE TEXT, COLLATIONS, AND APPARATUS

1. M1665 exhibits the following noteworthy orthographic and grammatical peculiarities, among others, and a number of such readings as these have been included in the apparatus.

• էր instead of էր (imperf. 3 ps)	§§1, 2, 6, 13, 25
• ն for ո	§§2, 24
• ուէ / վէ	§12
• շ for ջ	§§13, 19
• irregular use of *nota accusativi*	§2
• nom/acc for dative	§21
• superfluous initial յ-	§§3, 16
• omission of initial յ- with loc.	§5

2. In general, in the presentation of the variants, a number of regularly occurring orthographic variants were not noted unless they affect the meaning of the text. They include:

---

8. In OnaV 231 Ishmael is said to be "God's listening". See Stone 1981, 180–81.

9. It is notable that inEłišē, *Commentary on Genesis* 96.22 in *MH* 5th century, 835, a literal explanation of the word "Sabek" as bush is given.

10. See the General Introduction, under "Date of the Abraham Saga."

- ա / այ
- աւ / o
- ու + V / ւ + V
- spelling variants of proper names.

3. In the critical apparatus, the text of M1665 is the lemma and variant readings of M6029 and Egerton 708 are recorded in the apparatus. Only a couple of instances were found in which the text of M1665 seemed inferior to the other two manuscripts. Such instances are clearly marked in the apparatus. Variants are translated in the apparatus only when they substantially affect the meaning of the text. A few notes on the origins of variants have been added.

Ի սմին աւուր յիշատակ նախահարցն.
Աբրահամու. Իսահակայ եւ Յակոբայ.

1. Աբրահամ որդի Թարայի. եւ էին Քաղդեացիք. ազգաւ Ասորիք. եւ բնակէին ի Բաբելոն։ Եւ ունէր Թարայ Գ որդիս, զԱռան. եւ զԱբրահամ եւ զՆաքովր. եւ Առան մեռաւ առաջի հօրն իւրոյ Թարայի. վասն զի արար զնունդ չորոյն:

2. Եւ մաց Առանայ որդի Ղովտ. եւ Բ դուստր քոյր Ղովտայ. Մելքա. եւ Եսքա։ Եւ եղեւ բազմանալ ճայից. եւ ունէին զբերս երկրին Քաղդեացոց. շատ աղաչեցին զկուռսն. եւ ջեռեւ հնար փրկութեան:

3. Ապա՝ Աբրահամ ձեռն Աստուծոյ ձգեաց. եւ ասաց անտես արարիչ. դու հայեաց ի տարապանս մեր. եւ սաստեա տարմից հալուցս։ Եւ ընդ ասելն ի չիք դարձան. եւ այլ ոչ երեւեցան / fol. 174r / յարտորայսն Աբրահամու:

4. Եւ այն եղեւ սկիզբն եւ պատճառ աստուածպաշտութեան Աբրահամու. եւ ոչ երկմտեաց ի հաւատոցն. եւ էր Աբրահամ յայնժամ ԺԷ ամաց:

5. Եւ առին Աբրահամ եւ Նաքովր իւրեանց կանայս զդստերսն Առանայ.[11] զեքսա որ է Սարա[12] Աբրահամ էառ. եւ զՄելքա Նաքովր։ Եւ էառ Թարա զորդիսն իւր՝ եւ ել ի Քաղդեացոց՝ եւ եկեալ բնակեցաւ ի Խառան:

6. Եւ անդ շինեաց տուն կռոցն Թարայ եւ կանգնեաց կուրս զի պաշտեցեն։ Եւ Աբրահամ վառեաց հուր զի այրեցի մեհեանն. եւ Առան ջանաց շիջուցանել զայն. եւ անկաւ ի հուրն՝ եւ այրեցաւ. եւ զի հնարեալ էր զնունդ չորոյն. վասն այսորիկ սատակեց զնա Տէր:

7. Եւ Թարա ևս անդ մեռաւ ի Խառան։ Եւ յետ / fol. 174v / այնորիկ երեւեցաւ Աստուած Աբրահամու եւ ասաց ել յերկրէ քումէ եւ յազգէ. եւ եկ յերկիր զոր ցուցից քեզ։ Եւ առ Աբրահամ զՍարա կին իւր. եւ զՂովտ եղբօր որդին իւր. եւ ել գնաց յերկիրն Քանանու:

---

11. Spelling variant ո/ու here in E and elsewhere; see next note.
12. The spelling of Sarah varies; see the confusion in §23.

4. THE MEMORIAL OF THE FOREFATHERS

8. Եւ էր Աբրահամ ՀԵ ամաց. յորժամ ել ի Խառանու եւ գնաց ի Քանան. եւ բնակեցաւ անդ: Եւ եղեւ սով յերկիրն Քանանու. եւ էջ Աբրահամ յեգիպտոս. եւ ասաց Սարայի. ահա կին գեղեցիկ ես դու երեսօք. գուցէ թէ գիտասցեն Եգիպտացիք. թէ կին իմ ես դու. զիս սպանցեն եւ զքեզ առցեն:

9. այլ ասա թէ քոյր եմ ես նմա. թերեւս զի եւ ես ապրեցայց վասն քո: Եւ իբրեւ մտին յեգիպտոս՝ տեսին Եգիպտացիքն զգեղեցկութիւն Սարայի. եւ գովեցին զնա առաջի փարաւոնի. եւ կոչեաց փարաւոն զԱբրահամ՝ եւ եհարց զնա վասն Սարայի:

10. Եւ Աբրահամ ասաց թէ քոյր իմ է Սարայ: Եւ առ փարաւոն / fol. 175v / զԱառա ի տուն իւր. եւ ոչ գիտաց զնա. զի պատժեաց Տէր զփարաւոն հարուածովք յերանսն: Եւ երեւեցաւ Տէր փարաւոնի եւ ասաց. մի մերձենար յօտարայ իմ. եւ մարգարէից իմոց մի մեղանչէք:

11. Կոչեաց փարաւոն զԱբրահամ եւ ասաց. զի՞նչ գործեցեր ընդ մեզ՝ զկին քո քոյր ասելով: Արդ աւասիկ¹³ կին քո. առաջի քո առ եւ գնա ի բաց. եւ պատուէր ետ փարաւոն վասն Աբրահամու՝ յուղարկել զնա եւ զկին նորա խաղաղութեամբ:

12. Եւ բազմացան Աբրահամու յեգիպտոս անդեայք՝ եւ ոչխարք, էշք, եւ ուղտք: Ետ եւ փարաւոն զՀագար աղախին Սարայի. եւ ել Աբրահամ յեգիպտոսէ. եւ գնաց մինչեւ ցԲեթէլ. Սառա կինն Աբրահամու ոչ ծնանէր. զի ամուլ էր. վասն որոյ ասաց Աբրահամու թէ որդիհետու արգել զիս Տէր ի ծնանելոյ. մուտ առ աղջիկդ իմ. զի արարից ինձ որդի ի դմանէ. եւ ծնաւ Հագար որդի Աբրահամու. / fol. 175v / եւ կոչեաց զանուն նորա Իսմայէլ. որ է տեսումն Աստուծոյ. եւ է Աբրահամ ՁՁ ամաց ի ծնանելն Իսմայէլի:

13. Եւ իբրեւ եղեւ Աբրահամ ՂԹ ամաց. երեւեցաւ նմա Տէր Աստուած եւ ասաց. թէ թլփատեա դու զանփլփատութիւնն անձին քո. եւ զզաւակաց քոց. մանուկ ութօրեայ թլփատայի ձեր ամենայն արու յամենայն ազգս ձեր. ընդոծինն եւ արծաթագինն. եւ այն եդիցի ձեզ նշան աստուածպաշտութեանն: զի ես եմ Տէր Աստուած ձեր:

14. Իբրեւ թլփատեցաւ Աբրահամ. էր ՂԹ ամաց. եւ Իսմայէլ ԺԳ ամաց թլփատեցաւ. եւ Իսահակ Ը օրեայ թլփատեցաւ: Եւ յետ այրմանն Սոդոմայ. չուեաց Աբրահամ անտի յերկիրն {քան}¹⁴ հարաւոյ. եւ բնակեցաւ ի Գերարա: Եւ անդ եւս ասաց Աբրահամ վասն Սարայի թէ քոյր իմ է:

---

13. In M6092 there is displacement here, and the text on fol. 340r does not follow the preceding. It takes up in the middle of the story of Abraham in Egypt.

14. These three letters are apparently the beginning of an error, reading քանանու "of Canaan," the end of which was overwritten by հարաւոյ.

15. Եւ առ Աբիմելէք[15] արքայ փղշտացի զՍառա իւր ի կնութիւնն:[16] Եւ երեւեցաւ Աստուած Աբիմելէք ի տեսլեան գիշերոյ. եւ ասաց նմա ահա / fol. 176r / մեռանիս վասն կնոջն զոր առեր. զի կին առնակին է դա:

16. Եւ Աբիմելէք ոչ մերձեցաւ ի նա. եւ ասաց Աստուծոյ. Տէր զազգ մի անզէտ եւ արդար կորուսանիցե՞ս: Նա ասաց թէ քոյր իմ է. եւ սա ասաց թէ եղբայր իմ է. եւ ես սրբութեամբ սրտի. եւ արդարութեամբ ձեռաց արարի զայս: Եւ ասէ ցնա Աստուած. եւ ես գիտացի զի սրբութեամբ արարեր զայդ. բայց արդ տուր զկինդ յայր իւր. զի այր մարգարէ է: ‹Եւ նա արասցէ աղաւթս վասն քո եւ կեցցես:›

17. ապա թէ ոչ տացես գիտասջիր ‹զի› մեռանիս դու. եւ ամենայն որ ինչ քոյ է: Եւ ի վաղիւն կոչեաց Աբիմելէք զամենայն ծառայս իւր եւ զաղախնեայս. եւ զնախարարս՝ եւ խօսեցաւ զամենայն բանս զայսոսիկ. յականջս նոցա:

18. Եւ ասաց Աբրահամու առաջի նոցա. զի՞նչ[17] գործեցեր դու զայդ ընդ մեզ. միթէ մեղաք մեք ինչ քեզ. զի ածեր ի վերայ մեր մեղս մեծամեծս. գործ զոր ոչ ոք գործէ՛ գործեցեր ընդ մեզ / fol 176v / զինչ տեսեալ ի մեզ արարեր զբանդ զայդ: Ասէ Աբրահամ զուգէ ասացի. թէ լինի ոչ զուգէ աստուածապաշտութիւն ի տեղոջս յայսմիկ. եւ զիս սպանցեն վասն կնոջ իմոյ.

19. Այլ արդարեւ քոյր իմ է ի հօրէ. եւ ոչ ի[18] մօրէ: եւ եղեւ ինձ կին: Եւ եղեւ յորժամ եհան զիս Աստուած ի տանէ հօր իմոյ. ասացի ցդա զայդ արդարութիւն արասցես ընդ իս: յամենայն տեղիս ուր երթիցուք, ասա վասն իմ թէ եղբայր իմ է:

20. Եւ ետ Աբիմելէք Աբրահամու Ռ սատեր արծաթոյ. այլ եւ արջառս. եւ ոչխարս. եւ Սառա կին իւր. եւ ասաց նմա. ահաւասիկ երկիրդ իմ առաջի քո է. ուր եւ հաճի սիրտ քո բնակեսջիր անդ համարձակ. եւ ասէ ցՍառայ ահա ետու Ռ սատեր արծաթոյ եղբօր քո Աբրահամու. այն եղիցի ի պատիւ երեսաց քոց:

21. Եւ զի փակեաց Տէր զամենայն արգանդ ծնընդեանն ի տանն Աբիմելէքեայ. / fol, 177r / վասն Սառայի կնոջն Աբրահամու: Եւ եկաց Աբրահամ յաղօթս առ Տէր Աստուած եւ բժշկեաց զնոսա: Եւ յետ այնորիկ ապա յղացաւ Սառա՛ եւ ծնաւ որդի Աբրահամու զԻսահակ որ թարգմանի ծաղր եւ խնդութիւնն:

22. Եւ յարբունս հասեալ Իսահակայ եղեւ. ԺԷ ամաց. եւ Աստուած խնդրեաց յԱբրահամու զԻսահակ պատարագ. եւ Աբրահամ

---

15. In M6092, this verse is clearly incomplete, and the surviving text must reflect a lacuna. Only էք *ek'* is found in the first line of the folio. Since it is in the middle of the line, again this indicates that the displacement of folios must have taken place in an ancestor of this manuscript. In all these instances, the displacement reflects the situation that obtained in the ancestor.

16. Again, displacement occurs here in M6092, reflecting its exemplar.

17. Displacement occurs again here in M6092, reflecting its exemplar.

18. The reading իմ E is corrupt for ի, which is found in the other manuscripts.

մատուցաներ յօժար կամօք: Եւ Տէր ետ ի ծառոյս Սաբեկայ գլոյն փոխանակ Իսահակայ. եւ գնեաց յԱբրահամու գրահակ իւր ծառայ:
23. Եւ ասաց Աստուած Աբրահամու թէ ոչ եւս կոչեսջիս Աբրամ. այլ Աբրահամ եղիցի անուն քո: Նոյնպէս կնոջ քո Սարայի ոչ եւս կոչեցի Սարա. այլ Սառա. որ եղիցի Սառա:[19] Եւ ի ՃԼԷ ամի կենացն Աբրահամու. մեռաւ Սառա: Եւ Աբրահամ գնեաց զայրն ի Քեբրոն. որ է Սիկիմ: / fol. 177v / յորդոցն Եմովրայ ի ՊԾ սատեր արծաթոյ. եւ անդ եդ զՍառա. եւ այն եղեւ գերեզմանատուն նոցա:
24. Եւ յետ Գ ամաց մահւանն Սառայի ի Խ ամին Իսահակայ բերաւ Հռաբեկկին նորա ի Խառանայ. դուստր Բաղուելի որդոյ Նաքովրայ. եղբօրն Աբրահամու: Եւ Ի տարի ոչ մերձեցաւ ի նա Իսահակ. վասն ողջախոհութեան իւրոյ: զի նման եւ օրինակ էր Քրիստոսի:
25. Իսկ Ռաբեկ ներեղեցաւ. եւ գնաց զանգտեցաւ Մելքիսեդեկ քահանային: Եւ նա ասաց նմա թէ համբերեա դու. եւ մի կարճամտեր. զի աւա տեսանեմ յարգանդի քում. Բ նահապետութիւնս ազգաց: Եւ յետ հարսանեացն Իսահակայ էառ Աբրահամ այլ կին զՔետուրայ. յորմէ ծնաւ Զ որդիս. յորոց մին զմեւս եղբայրն եսպան: Եւ այլքն եղին յարեւելս:
26. Եւ այսպէս եղեն ծնունդք Աբրահամու. յերից կանանց. Նախ ի Հազարա եգիպտացոյ Իսմայէլ: ուստի ազգն Իսմայելացւոց: Եւ ի Սառայէ լինի Իսահակ, ուստի ազգն Հրէից: Եւ ի Քետուրայ եղեն ազգն Պարսից եւ Պարթեւաց: Յորոց քաջն Արշակ նախնին ազգաց Պալհաւկեան. եւ Արշակունեաց:
27. Արդ կեցեալ Աբրահամ յետ ծնանելոյն գրահակ ամս ՀԵ: Եւ Աբրահամ լեալ ՃՀԵ ամաց եւ մեռաւ եւ յաւելաւ առ հարսն իւր. լի աւուրք. ալեւորեալ:
28. Եւ արդ գիտելի է. զի մինչ ի յԱբրահամ այլ ոք ի նախահարցն. որ յառաջ քան զնա յԱդամ հետէ. ոչ են ծերացեալ. թէպէտ եւ շատ ամօք ապրէին. թուխ մուրուշ մեռանէին: Իսկ Աբրահամ որ հաւատաց յԱստուած. եւ ծաղկեցաւ հոգով ի հաւատս. եւ ի գործս բարիս նոյնպէս մարմնով ալեւորեալ ծաղկեցաւ ծերութեամբն եւ թաղեցին զնա Իսահակ եւ Իսմայէլ որդիք նորա առ Սառայի. ի կրկնումն այրին. յազարակին Եփրոնի. զոր ստացաւ Աբրահամ գնող արծաթոյ:

The document continues with the stories of Isaac, Jacob, etc.

---

19. See Gen 17:15, which has Սարա and Սառա. The form Սառայ does not occur here.

Variant Readings

Title in Y: Պատմութիւն նահապետացն Աբրահամու Իսահակայ եւ Յակորայ եւ այլոցն "History of the Patriarchs Abraham Isaac and Jacob and of the others" Y

Title in E: վարք ժէ նահապետաց "Lives of the 12 Patriarchs" E | ամին աևւր] omit E | յիշատակ] յիշատակն E

1. որդի] + եր Y + էր E | էրն] է ինքն Y | Գ որդիս] որդի Y | առան] զառան Y | աբրաամ E | hopն] hopն Y : note orthography | իւրոյ] om Y | զի] զի նայ Y | զծնունդ] ծնունդ Y զծնունդն E
2. առան] առ նայ Y : graphic corruption | քոյր դովտայ] omit E | մեշբա] մեշբեա Y | էաբա] եաբեա Y | Ճայից] ամենեցին Y Ճայիցն E | ուտէին] ուտել E | զբեր E | երկրին] յերկրին Y | չեղեւ] ոչ եղեւ Y E
3. աստուծոյ] աստուած Y յաստուած E | արարիչ] + աստուած E | տարմից] տարերից E | ասեին] ասելոյն աբրահամ Y ասելն աբրահամու զայս E "Abraham said" (+ this E) | դարձան] + հաւքն E | յարտորայան] արտորայան Y
4. եւ այն -- աբրահամու] omit Y : perhaps due to exemplar | եղեւ2°] omit E | ոչ] այլ ոչ E | աբրաամ յայնժամ] ̃ E | ժէ] ԺԷ Y : 17 instead of 15
5. եւ առին աբրահամ "and Abraham ... took"] omit Y : perhaps due to exemplar | իւրեանց կանայս] omit Y | իւր] omit E | առանայ "of Aŕan"] նաթանայ "of Nathan" Y : corrupt արանայ E | զմելքա] զմելքիթեայ Y | էառ2°] առեալ Y
6. եւ անդ] անդեն Y | տուն կռոցն] կռոց տունա Y | կուռս] կռոցս Y | hուր] omit Y | այրեցից] այրեցէ Y E | մեհեանն] զմեհեանն Y | շանաց շիջուցանել զայն] շիջուցանել կամեցաւ E | զի3°] omit Y | զայն] զնայ Y | այստրիկ] այնորիկ Y
7. եւ թարայ] թարայ Y | եւս] եւ Y | անդ] follows խառան E | յերկրէ] ի յերկրէ Y | քումէ] քումմէ E | յազգէ] ազգէ Y + քումմէ E | յերկիր] յերկիրն Y E | զտարա] զտառայ E | կին] կինն Y | զդովտ] դովտ Y | եղբօր] եղպոր Y : note orthography | յերկիրն] երկիրն E
8. խառանու (8) – աւասիկ (11)] omit due to faulty exemplar Y | երկիրն E | սարայի] սառայի E | եգիպտացիք] յեգիպտացիքն E
9. մտին յեգիպտոս] omit E | եգիպտացիքն] յեգիպտացիքն E | սառայի] սառայի E
10. զտառա] զտառայ E | զիտաց] զիտացին E
11. եւ ասաց] ասաց E | ասելով] + մեզ E | եւս] Y resumes here | աւասիկ] ահաւասիկ E | ի բաց] ուր եւ կամիս "wherever you wish" E | պատուէր] պատվէր Y | վասն] om Y | յուղարկել] ուղարկել Y | զկին] զկնի Y : corrupt
12. անդեայք] անդէայք եւ Y | զհագար] զհաքար E | աղախինն E |

4. THE MEMORIAL OF THE FOREFATHERS

սառայի] սարայի E | եզիպտոսէ E | աբրահամ յեզիպտոսէ] յեքիպտոսէ աբրահամ Y | սառա] եւ սառայ Y սարայ E | կինն] կին E | զի] քանզի Y | որոյ] որ Y այս E | ասաց] + սառայ Y | թէ որովհետեւ] իւրով հետեւ Y | թէ] զի E | մուտ] մօտ Y | աղջիկդ] աղչիկդ Y | դմանէ] եմանէ Y | ծնաւ] ծնար Y | հագար] ագար E | իսմայէլ] իսմէլ Y | որ է] որ Y | է] էր E

13. իբրեւ] om Y E | Ղ.Թ] իբրեւ Ղ.Թ E | երեւեցաւ] եւ երեւեցաւ Y | եմա տէր ասաուած] ասաուած աբրահամու Y | եմա] omit E | ասաց] ասէ Y | դու] զդու Y | զանքթլիատութիւնն] զանքթլիատութիւն Y E | զզաւակաց] զաւակաց Y E | թլիատայի] թլիատեցի E : perhaps to be preferred | յամենայն ազգու] ամենայն յազգու Y | ընդօծինն] ընդօծին E | արձաքագինն] արձաքագին Y | ասաուածպաշտութեանն] ասաուածպաշտութեան Y

14. եւ իսահակ — թլիատեցաւ] omit : homoeoarchton Y | աբրահամ անտի] անտի (անդի E) աբրահամ Y E | յերկիրն] յերկրին E | սառայի սարայի E | քոյր] զքոյր Y | fin] + իւր ի կնութիւն Y : corruption

15. եւ առ] om Y | աբիմելէք] էք Y : corruption | աբրայ] omit E | փողշտացի] փողշտացոց Y | կնութիւնն] կնութիւն Y E | կնօշ] կնշ քո Y | առնակին] omit Y

16. անգէտ եւ արդար] ~ E | արդար] + մի Y | թէ1°] omit Y | թէ2°] omit Y | ասէ նա] ասա Y : corrupt by haplography | սրբութեամբ] արդարութեամբ Y | ձեռաց] omit E | արդ] omit Y | զկինդ] զիկինդ Y | յայր] այր Y | է] omit Y : haplography | եւ նայ (omit E) արասցէ աղաւթս (յաղաւթս Y) վասն քո զի կեցցես "and he will pray for you so that you live"] Y E omit M

17. զի] Y E omit M | մեռանիս] մեռանես Y | որ ինչ] ~ Y E | քոյ] քո M Y | զադախնեաու] զադախնայն Y

18. աբրահամու] աբրամու E | զինչ] զոր Y | զայդ] զայտ Y | մեզ մեղա] մեղա Y : haplography | զործ զոր] զործա զորա Y | զործեցեր] + դու Y E | տեսեալ] տեսար Y | մեզ] մեզ եւ Y | աբրահամ] աբրամ E | զուցէ1°] զի Y E | յայսմիկ] այսմիկ Y E | զիս] the text of Y continues on fol 343r with §24 ողջախոհութեամբ | կնօշ] կնօշու E

19. այլ] արդ E | ի] իմ E : see footnote 224

20. աբրահամու] աբրամու E | արշարա եւ ոչիարա] ~ E | սառա] զսարայ E | է] omit E | գսառա] գսարայ E | արձաթոյ] omit E | աբրահամու] աբրամու E | ի] omit E

21. փակեցաց տէր] ~ E | արգանդ] following սարայի deleted E | աբրահամու] աբրամու E | ծնընդեանն] ծնընդեան E | սառայի] սարայի E | աբրահամու2°] աբրամու E | աբրահամ] աբրամ E | տէր] omit E | ապա] եւ ապայ E | սառա] սարայ E | որդի աբրահամու] աբրամու որդի E | խնդութիւնն E

22. եւ1° — ամաց] omit E | յաբրահամու1°] աբրամու E | աբրահամ] աբրամ E | տէր ետո] ետ տէր E | իսահակայ] իսահակ E | յաբրահամու2°] աբրամու E

23. աբրահամու] աբրամու E | նոյնպէս] + եւ E | ոչ եւս կոչեցի2°] այլ E | սարա] սարրայ E | ՃԼԷ] ՃԼՀ E | յորդւոցն] որդոցն E | զսառա] զսարա E
24. մահւանն] մահւան E | կին] կինն E | ի տարի] ի ի տարի E | քրիստոսի] not visible in photo E
25. ետղեցաւ] ետղացաւ (-o Y) Y E | զանզւեցաւ] զանզատ եսաւ Y զանկուեցաւ E | քահանային] քահանայն E | եմա] omit Y | եւ մի] դու եւ մի Y | կարճամտեր] կարճմտեցեր Y կարճմտէր E | նահապետութիւնս] նահանգայպետութիւնս Y | իսահակայ] omit Y | զբետուրայ] բետուրայ Y | յորժէ] յորոց E | մին] մինն E | զմեւս] զմիւսն Y E | եղբայրն] omit E | եսպան] + զեղպայրն իւր Y սպանեաց զեղբայրն E | այլքն] յայլքն Y | արեւելյ E
26. եղեն1°] եղեւ Y եղէն E | ծնունդք] ծնունդն Y ծնունդքն E | հաբարայ E | եզիպտացոյ] եբեպտացոց Y | լինի] omit Y | իսմայելացոց E | իսահակ] իսահակայ Y | եղէն2° E | ուստի3°] omit Y | բաչն] բաչն Y
27. զիսահակ] իսահակայ Y | Հէ] Հէ Y | ՃՀԵ] ՃԿԵ Y ՃՀ եւ Ե E | ամաց եւ] ամաց Y | յաւելաւ] աւելաւ Y | առ] ընդ E | հարսն] հարս Y | աւուրբբ E : preferable | ալեւորեալ] + եւ ծերացեալ and aged Y E
28. մինչ] մինչեւ Y | յաբրահամ] աբրահամ Y | յաղամ հետէ] յաղամայ հետէ Y E | են] omit Y | ապրին] ապրեալ այլ Y | մուրուք] մորսվք Y մորոք E | մեռանէին] էին մեռացեալ Y | նոյնպէս] + եւ E | մարմուս E | իսահակ եւ իսմայել] ~ E | յաստուած] աստուած Y | բարիս -- արձարոյ] omit Y

ON THIS DAY IS THE MEMORIAL OF THE FOREFATHERS, ABRAHAM, ISAAC, AND JACOB

1. Abraham (was) son of Terah, and they were Chaldeans, Syrians by race, and they were dwelling in Babylon. And Terah had 3 sons, Achan and Abraham[20] and Nahor.[21] And Achan died before his father Terah[22] because he made the begetting of the mule.[23]
2. And Lot, Achan's son, remained and two daughters, sister(s) of Lot, Melk'a and Ēsk'a. And it came to pass that the ravens multiplied and they were eating the yield of the land of the Chaldeans.[24] They besought the idols greatly, and no salvation was feasible.

---

20. The spelling of Abraham varies throughout. We give either Abraham or Abram, depending on the Armenian.

21. Gen 11:26–27.

22. Gen 11:28.

23. A different story, related to the Nimrod incident, is to be found in *Gen. Rab.* 38:28 and many other Jewish and Christian sources. It is not found in the texts in the present corpus.

24. Here and in texts nos. 11.3, 12.5, and 15.3, the ravens eat the produce of the fields or the seed; in 8.4 they eat fruit of the vineyards. The ravens are also mentioned in texts nos. 2.3, 6.1, 9.6, 13.2, and 14.2. In Michael the Syrian 1871, 22, it is produce of the fields that they eat.

3. Then, Abraham stretched forth (his) hand to God and said, "Unseen Creator. Regard our sufferings and destroy the flocks of birds." And as he said (this) they turned into nothing and disappeared from Abraham's field.[25]
4. And that was the beginning and the cause of Abraham's worship of God, and he did not doubt the faith. And then Abraham was 15 years old.[26]
5. And[27] Abraham and Nahor took the daughters of Achan to themselves as wives. Abraham took Ēskʻa,[28] who is Sarai, and Nahor, Mēlkʻa.[29] And Terah took his sons and went forth from the Chaldeans, and he came (and) dwelt in Haran.[30]
6. And there, Terah built a house of idols and set up idols that they might worship (them). And Abraham kindled a fire so that the pagan temple would be burnt. And Achan tried to extinguish that and fell into the fire and was burnt up. And because he devised the birth of the mule, because of this the Lord killed him.[31]
7. And Terah also died there in Haran. And after that God appeared to Abraham and said, "Go forth from your land and family, and come to the land which I will show you."[32] And Abraham took Sarai his wife, and Lot his brother's son and went forth, proceeded to the land of Canaan.[33]
8. And Abraham was 75 years old when he went forth from Haran[34] and went to Canaan, and he dwelt there. And there was a famine in the land of Canaan, and Abraham went down to Egypt.[35] And he said to Sarah, "Behold you are a beautiful woman in your countenance. Perhaps, if the Egyptians will learn that you are my wife, they will kill me and take you.[36]
9. But say, 'I am a sister to him.' Perhaps I will be saved for your sake."[37] And when they entered Egypt, the Egyptians saw Sarah's beauty and praised her before Pharaoh.[38] And Pharaoh summoned Abraham and asked him about Sarah.
10. And Abraham said, "Sarah is my sister." And Pharaoh took Sarah to his

---

25. See text no. 2.4, note for this incident.
26. Compare text no. 14.1.
27. Gen 11:29.
28. See Ełišē, *Commentary on Genesis* 74.47 in *MH* 5th century, 819.
29. The identifications are exegetical, but see Gen 11:29.
30. Gen 11:31.
31. See notes on text no. 2.6 about this incident. In this text Achan's death is related twice, once here and once in §1 as part of a genealogical preface.
32. Gen 12:1.
33. Gen 12:5.
34. Gen 12:4. According to the *Book of the Bee* (Budge 1886, 42), at this age he moved to Haran.
35. Gen 12:10.
36. Gen 12:11-12. In *Palaea* 204, Sarah suggests this ruse to Abraham, thus minimizing his culpability. For this issue, see text no. 4.19 note below.
37. Gen 12:13.
38. The paean of praise to Sarah's beauty in 1QapGen (1Q20) col. 20 is particularly notable.

house,[39] and he did not know her,[40] for the Lord inflicted upon Pharaoh an affliction in his groin.[41] And the Lord appeared to Pharaoh and said, "Do not draw near (sg.) to this anointed one of mine and do not sin (pl.) against my prophets."[42]

11. Pharaoh summoned Abraham and said: "What did you do to us by saying that your wife is (your) sister? Behold, your wife (is) before you, take her and go away." And Pharaoh gave a command concerning Abraham, to despatch him and his wife peacefully.[43]

12. And Abraham's flocks multiplied in Egypt, and sheep, donkeys, and camels. Pharaoh also gave Hagar as a handmaiden for Sarah.[44] And Abraham went forth from Egypt and he went as far as Bethel.[45] Sarah, Abraham's wife, did not bear child, for she was barren,[46] on account of which she said to Abraham, "Because the Lord has prevented me from bearing child, go in to my maid so that I may make myself a son by her."[47] Hagar bore a son to Abraham and he called his name Ishmael,[48] which is "seeing of God."[49] And Abraham was 86 years old when Ishmael was born.[50]

---

39. Gen 12:14-15.
40. Gen 12:15. Theodoret of Cyrrhus remarks that "some commentators have claimed that Pharaoh had relations with Sarah" (*Quaest.* 63); however, the majority of Christian exegetes stress that Sarah remained untouched; see John Chrysostom, *Hom. Gen.* 32.21; 32.7.
41. 1QapGen 20.16–17 also apparently says that Pharaoh had a genital affliction that prevented him from having intercourse with Sarah. This must have been inferred from the less-explicit biblical phrasing in Gen 12:17, with which compare *Jub.* 13:13. *PRE* 26 says that Abimelech became impotent in the parallel story. Pharaoh is stressedly wicked in Philo, *Abr.* 94–95. Philo also omits Abraham's statement about Sarah being his sister.
42. 1 Chr 16:22.
43. Gen 12:18-20.
44. This is inferred from Gen 16:1, which says that Hagar was an Egyptian. Hagar as Pharaoh's gift to Sarah is mentioned in *Cave of Treasures* (Budge 1927, 148). It is found already in 1QapGen (1Q20) 20.32. The increase of flocks here is not explicit in the Bible but can be inferred from Gen 12:16 and 13:2. The idea is found in 1QapGen (1Q20) 20.32; Ephrem, *Commentary on Genesis* 13 (Mathews and Amar 1994, 155). See Firestone 1990, 40–44, on Islamic versions. See also Beer 1859, 25 and notes.
45. Literally: "Bedēl." See Gen 13:3. In Gen 13:1 the place is "the Negeb." Bethel is not in the Negeb, and for Bethel, see Gen 12:8.
46. Gen 16:1; cf. 11:30.
47. Gen 16:2.
48. Gen 16:15.
49. Or: "vision of God." This onomastic gloss is incorrect for "Ishmael" and is known elsewhere as the meaning of "Israel." See Stone 1981, Ona V 231. In that text, Ishmael is "God's listening" [lur Asstucoy]. The etymology found here may be derived from later in this chapter, where Hagar calls the deity as he appears to her "El-Roi," which in meaning resembles this etymology. See Gen 16:13-14. See also Firestone 1990, 39, on an Islamic etymology of Ishmael as "God heeds."
50. Gen 16:16. This is the date also in George Syncellus 113 (Adler and Tuffin 2002, 141).

13. And when Abraham was 99 years old, the Lord God appeared to him and said,[51] "Circumcise your own[52] uncircumcision and that of your seed. At eight days all your male babies[53] shall be circumcised for all your generations, house-born and purchased with silver.[54] And that will be a sign for you of worship of God. For I am the Lord your God.
14. When Abraham was circumcised he was 99 years old. And Ishmael was circumcised at 13 years[55] and Isaac was circumcised at 8 days.[56] And after the burning of Sodom,[57] Abraham proceeded thence to the land {than}[58] of the south, and he dwelt in[59] Gerar.[60] And there also Abraham said of Sarah, "She is my sister."
15. And Abimelech the Philistine king took Sarah[61] to himself in marriage. And God appeared to Abimelech in a night vision and he said to him, "Behold, you (will) die because of this woman whom you took, for this woman is a married woman."[62]
16. And Abimelech did not draw near to her,[63] and he said to God, "Lord, will you destroy an unknowing and righteous people? He said, 'She is my sister,' and she said, 'He is my brother,' and in purity of heart and righteousness of hands I did this."[64] And God said to him "Indeed, I know that you did this in purity,[65] but now give the woman to her husband, for (her) husband is a prophet, and he will pray on your behalf and you will live.[66]
17. If you do not give (her back), know that you (will) die and everything that

---

51. Gen 17:1.
52. "Body" is also a possible meaning of ւմածն in these texts.
53. Literally: a baby of all your males.
54. Gen 17:10–13.
55. Gen 17:24–25.
56. Gen 21:4.
57. Both the Annunciation to Abraham and the full narrative of the Sodom incident are omitted from this text and just referred to glancingly here.
58. See the General Introduction above, under "Biblical and Nonbiblical Episodes." The word translated "than" might be a torso of "Canaan," started by error and then left in the text.
59. The text is very elliptic here.
60. Gen 20:1.
61. Gen 20:2.
62. Gen 20:3.
63. Gen 20:4. Abimelech is pictured much more positively than Pharaoh in the previous incident. Pharaoh's feast is described in much greater detail in text no. 8.8-14. Elements from the Pharaoh incident are transferred to Abimelech in *Gen. Rab.* 52.18
64. Gen 20:4b–5.
65. Gen 20:6.
66. Gen 20:7. Manuscript M omits the last clause. Abraham's prophetic role is highlighted in other texts in this corpus in the same context as here and also in connection with the Binding of Isaac; see texts nos. 4.10 above, 11.45, 11A.45, and 15.46. See, in a slightly different context, Kessler 2004, 94.

is yours."⁶⁷ And on the morrow Abimelech summoned all his servants and maid-servants and nobles and he spoke all these word in their ears.⁶⁸

18. And he said to Abraham before them, "Why did you do this to us? Did we commit any sin against you, that you brought a very great sin upon us? You have done to us a deed that no one does. What did you see in us that you did this thing?"⁶⁹ Abraham said, "'Perhaps,' I said, 'there will perhaps not be worship of God (piety) in this place, and they will kill me on account of my wife.'"⁷⁰

19. But, indeed, she is my sister from (my) father and not from (my) mother⁷¹ and she became a wife for me.⁷² And it came to pass, that when God brought me out of my father's house, I said to her, 'Do me this favor.⁷³ In all places where we go, say about me, "He is my brother'."⁷⁴

20. And Abimelech gave Abraham 1,000 staters of silver, and also oxen and sheep, and Sarah his wife, and he said to him, "Behold this land of mine is before you. Where your heart pleases, dwell there freely."⁷⁵ And he said to Sarah, "Behold, I have given 1,000 staters of silver to your brother Abraham. Let that be for the honor of your face."⁷⁶

21. And since the Lord had closed every child-bearing womb in Abimelech's house because of Sarah, Abraham's wife, Abraham also prayed to the Lord God and He healed them.⁷⁷ And after that, then Sarah conceived and bore a son to Abraham,⁷⁸ Isaac, which is translated, "laughter and joy".⁷⁹

22. And Isaac, having reached puberty, was 15 years old.⁸⁰ And God asked Isaac

---

67. Gen 20:7b.
68. Gen 20:8. This phrase means, "in their hearing."
69. Gen 20:9-10.
70. Gen 20:11.
71. See the same idea and a narrative explanation in *Cave of Treasures* (Budge 1927, 148).
72. Gen 20:12. Ancient exegetes discuss the issue that Abraham's deception here raises; see Harl 1986, 186. Abraham's words to Isaac on the occasion of the Aqedah are called prophecy, which implies ambiguity and deception; see texts nos. 11.45, 11A.45, and 15.46. It is made explicit in 11A.45, "Abraham said, 'God will prepare the sacrificial offering,' for in that way Abraham deceived Isaac, but (in fact) he prophesied through God." Ephrem, *Commentary on Genesis* 20.2 (Mathews and Amar 1994, 168) refers to this speech as prophecy.
73. Literally: "righteousness".
74. Gen 20:13.
75. Gen 20:14–15. Here, as expected, the text draws on the Armenian Bible and the LXX, in contrast to the Masoretic Text.
76. Gen 20:16.
77. Gen 20:17–18. Note the difference of the affliction in the two incidents.
78. Gen 21:2.
79. The whole Annunciation story, the visit of the three men and Abraham's famous hospitality are passed over here, with no comment. Ona 5.226 gives "Isahak, laughter": see Wutz 1914–15, 585, 745, 759, 812–13, 899, etc.
80. See the discussion of the age of fifteen in the notes to text no. 2.3. Isaac was fifteen

4. THE MEMORIAL OF THE FOREFATHERS   69

as a sacrifice from Abraham,[81] and Abraham offered him with a willing desire. And the Lord set[82] the ram in the tree of Sabek[83] instead of Isaac.[84] And he purchased Isaac his servant from Abraham.

23. And God said to Abraham, "No more will you be called Abram, but Abraham will be your name.[85] Likewise your wife Sarai will no longer be called Sarai, but Sarra, which will be Sarah.[86] And in the 137th year of Abraham's life, Sarah died.[87] And Abraham bought the cave in Hebron, which is Shechem,[88] from the sons of Emovr[89] for 400 staters of silver. And there he placed Sarah, and that was their mausoleum.[90]

24. And 3 years after Sarah's death, in Isaac's 40th year, Rabek (Rebekah) his wife was brought from Haran, daughter of Bathuel son of Nahor, Abraham's brother.[91] And for 20 years Isaac did not draw near to her on account of his modesty (chastity), for he was a likeness and a type of Christ.[92]

---

at the time of the Aqedah, according to Step'anos Siwnec'i, *Commentary on Genesis* §112 and Tiran *vardapet MH* 10th century, 968.

81. From this point on in BLEgerton 708, "Abram" is found, not "Abraham"; cf. Gen 22:2.

82. Manuscript E has ետ ("gave"), which is probably a corruption of եդ ("set").

83. Deriving from Hebrew סבך in Gen 22:13. This word, transliterated, is taken as a proper name in some texts. The LXX has ἐν φυτῷ σαβέκ, and Sabek is found also in various hexaplaric witnesses. It is both a translation and a transliteration. The Armenian Bible has քօառոյն Սարեկայ ("the tree of Sabek"). Compare text 7, which is a development of the Sabek tradition. The thicket is mentioned by this name in texts nos. 6.9.1, 8:24, 8:31, and 11A:45. See also *Palaea* 221. The root *sbk* is used in the exegesis in *Gen. Rab.* 56:13.

84. Gen 22:13.
85. Gen 17:5.
86. Gen 17:15. The different English spellings reflect an Armenian variation.
87. Cf. Gen 23:1.
88. This is, of course, a geographical anomaly. It arises, conceivably, from a confusion with Joseph's burial in Shechem: compare Gen 33:18–19; 50:13–14; Josh 24:32 (Sh. Golani).
89. That is, "sons of Hamor" or else "the Amorites," but there is some confusion, for Abraham bought the field from Ephron the Hittite; see Gen 23:8–18 and 49:30. Note that according to Gen 33:18–19 Jacob bought a field for burial near Shechem, which may have led to the confusion (Sh. Golani).
90. This is a paraphrase of Gen 23 or perhaps more specifically of Gen 23:19–20. Note that *T. Ab.* A 20:11 sets Abraham's burial at the oaks of Mamrē.
91. Gen 25:20.
92. Isaac's sacrifice prefigured Christ's. This idea is found also in Ełišē, *Commentary on Genesis* 95.21 (*MH* 5th century, 834). It is common in patristic literature; see, e.g., Origen, *Hom. in Gen* 8.6–9 (see Petit 1991–96, frg. 1252); Ephrem the Syrian, *Commentary on Genesis* 20.3 (Mathews and Amar 1994, 169); John Chrysostom, *Hom. Gen* 47.14; Cyril of Alexandria, *Glaphyra* (*PG* 69:140A). In Genesis there is no hint at Isaac's twenty years' continence, and the idea reflects Christian ascetic values. The number 20 comes from a comparison of Gen 25:20 with 25:26. But since Gen 25:12 says, "Isaac prayed to the Lord for his wife, because she was barren," one is led to assume that the plain sense of the Bible is that they had fruitless intercourse during the twenty years. The three days of Abraham's travel after which is the

25. But Rebekah was afflicted and she went and complained to Melchizedek the priest.[93] And he said to her, "Be patient and be not impatient. For, behold, I see two patriarchs of nations in your womb."[94] And after Isaac's marriage, Abraham took another wife Keturah, from whom he begot 6 sons. One of these killed his brother and the others went forth to the east.[95]
26. And thus were the descendants of Abraham from three wives. First, from Hagar the Egyptian, Ishmael, whence the nation of the Ishmaelites. And from Sarah, Isaac, whence the nation of the Jews. And from Keturah were the people(s) of the Persians and the Parthians (Part'ews), of whom was valorous Aršak, ancestor of the Palhavikean family and the Arsacids.[96]
27. Now, Abraham lived 75 years after Isaac's birth. And Abraham, having become 175 years old,[97] died and was gathered to his fathers, full of days, grey-haired.
28. And now it is known that up to Abraham, no other of the forefathers who were before him from Adam on had grown old. Although they lived for many years, they died with black beards. But Abraham, who believed in God and flowered spiritually in faith and, likewise in bodily good deeds, having gone grey, flowered in old age.[98] And Isaac and Ishmael his sons buried him by

---

offering of Isaac are compared to the three days of Christ on the cross by Tiran *vardapet* (*MH* 10th century, 967).

93. Rebekah does not converse with Melchizedek in the other versions of the story given here. This is an interpretation of Gen 25:22, which reads, "She went to inquire of the Lord," which implies consulting an oracular source. Rebekah's consulting with Melchizedek occurs in Ephrem, *Commentary on Genesis* 11 (Mathews and Amar 1994, 151) and in Michael the Syrian (Chabot 1891, 35; Michael the Syrian 1871, 25); *Cave of Treasures* (Budge 1927, 154); compare van Rompay 1997, 114–16. It is found also in Ełišē, *Commentary on Genesis* 97.42 (*MH* 5th century, 839); cf. Eusebius of Emesa (Petit, van Rompay and Weitenberg 2011, 139, 239, on Gen 25:22, 26).

94. See Gen 25:23.

95. Gen 25:1–4. The incident of the killing is unclear but occurs elsewhere, e.g., text no. 5.4.

96. Here, the genealogy is Armenized. On this process, see Stone 2009a, 629–46. The same connection of Abraham with the Arsacids is given in Movsēs Xorenac'i 2.2 and 2.68. Thus we read in Movsēs Xorenac'i 2.68: Յադամայ բանակերորդ առաջներորդ նահապետ մեզ զԱբրահամ աստուածայինքն ցուցանեն պատմութիւնք, եւ ի նմանէ եղեալ ազգդ Պարթեւաց: "The divine histories show us that the twenty-first patriarch from Adam was Abraham, and from him the race of the Part'ews (Parthians) issued." In Ełišē, *Commentary on Genesis* on 17:6 it says, "He says that you will be a father of kings, of David, Solomon, the Arsacids and the Ishmaelites, and then . . . the heavenly king" (Khachikyan and Papazian 2004, 129). That Aršak the Brave was a descendant of Abraham is found in the variant to §221 in the seventh-century Chronicle of P'ilon Tirakac'i (*MH* 7th century, 92).

97. Gen 25:7.

98. This is an exegesis of Gen 25:8. The term "good old age" is first used of Abraham in the Bible; see Gen 15:15, which point is picked up by the exegete here. Perhaps this term is considered to indicate grey hair as well.

4. THE MEMORIAL OF THE FOREFATHERS

Sarah, in the double cave in the field of Ephron, which Abraham had got for its price in silver.[99]

Appendix
Continuation of M1665 down to Jacob

29. Իսահակ / 178v / երթայր եւ զաւրանայր. զի <S>էրն[100] էր ընդ նմա: Եւ եղեւ սով ի ժամանակին յայնմիկ. եւ գնաց Իսահակ յերկիրն Գերգերացւոց. առ Աբիմելէք արքայ. եւ նա եւս զկինն քոյրն անւանեաց: Եւ յաւուր միում ետես Աբիմելէք ի պատուհանէն զԻսահակ որ խաղայ ընդ Հռաբեկայ կնոջ իւրոյ. եւ մեղադրեաց սիրով թէ ընդէր զկինդ քո քոյր ասացեր քեզ:
30. Եւ նա ասաց զի կին գեղեցկապատկեր է: ասացի մի գուցէյափրշտական յինէն. եւ զիս սպանանէն: Եւ Աբիմելէք ասէ ցնա. մի երկնչիր աևա երկիրդ իմ ամենայն առաջի քո. Ուր եւ հաճոյ թուի յայս քո. բնակեաց անդ. վասն հօր քո Աբրահամու. զի եղբայր մեր էր նա. բարի կամօք եւ սիրով:
31. Եւ բնակեաց Իսահակ յերկիր փոքրտացւոց. ուր ցանեաց զարին արար մինն Ճ, եւ ապա եղեն նմա Բ որդի ի մհոջէ անկողնոյ. ի միոյ / fol. 79r / արգանդէ. ի Կ ամի կենացն Իսահակայ եղեն նմա Բ որդիք. որպէս ասաց քահանայ Աստուծոյ Մելքիսեդեկ. թէ էրեցն կրսերոյն ծառայեսցէ. երեւեցաւ այն ի ծնունդն զի Յակոբ ունէր զամոլաշին Եսաւայ:
32. Եւ եղեւ Եսաւ այր զազանաբարոյ. վայրազամիտ՝ եւ որսական. թաւ մազով: Եւ Յակոբ էր լե<ր>կամարմին.[101] հեզ եւ հանդարտ:
33. Եւ յաւուր միում գնաց Յեսաւ[102] ի յորս երեցց եւ ոչ ինչ կալաւ. դարձաւ ի տուն քաղցեալ եւ ետես զՅակոբ զի ուտէր ոսպաթան. եւ ասաց տուր եւ ինձ զի կերայց: Եւ նա ասաց տուր զանդրանկութիւն քո ինձ եւ ապա տաց քեզ գոսպնութանս.
34. Եւ նա վասն միոյ կերակրոյ ետ նմա զանդրանկութիւն: Եւ դարձեալ էառ Յակոբ զաւրհնութիւն զանդրանկութեան: Եւ եղեւ զի Իսահակ տկարացաւ. եւ պակասեաց լոյս աչացն եւ կայր անկեալ ի տան:
35. Եւ յաւուր միում ասաց Եսաւայ՝ գնալ յորս էրեցց. եւ բերել նմա միս վայրի. զի կերայց աստ եւ աւրհնեցից զքեզ. / fol. 179 v / Եւ նա գնաց. եւ Ռաբեկ լուաւ զայն. եւ կամէր զաւրհնութիւն Իսահակայ Եսաւայ.[103] Յակոբայ: Իբրեւ գնաց յեսաւ աստ մայրն ցՅակոբ. որդեակ երբ բեր ի խաշանց մերոց Բ ուլ. եւ զեն. զի արարից հօր քո խորտիկս զի կերիցէ եւ աւրհնեսցէ զքեզ:

---

99. Gen 25:9–10. See the variant tradition on §23 above.
100. Corrected from corrupt form ձեռն.
101. So correcting the corrupt form, լեկամարմին.
102. Written over Յակոբ.
103. Two illegible letters.

36. Ասէ Յակոբ հայր իմ յեղբօրէ իմմէ խնդրեաց զմիսն որսոյ. զի զնա աւրհնեցէ. եւ ի մեր մատուցանելին զուցէ զիտասցէ հայրն իմ. եւ փոխանակ աւրհնութեան անիծանէ մեզ։ Ասէ մայրն յիմ վերայ անէծքն այն. զոր հայր քո ասէ քեզ.
37. Եւ զնացեալ Յակոբ էած Բ ուլս. եւ եզեն. եւ առեալ Հռաբեկ զմիսն արար խորտիկս անուշահամ. որպէս եւ ախորժէր Իսահակ. եւ զմորթին խուզեալ՝ մկրատով. արար պատան պարանոցին Յակոբայ. եւ բազպան եւ ահոյց զպատմուճան Եսաւայ. զոր թողեալ էր ի տունն[104] Յակոբայ.
38. Եւ եդ ի ձեռն զխորտիկն որ առեալ տարաւ առ Իսահակ եւ ասաց յարիցէ հայր իմ. եւ կերիցէ միս որսային / fol. 180r / զոր եւ խնդրեաց։ Ասէ Իսահակ զիարդ եկիր փութով որդեակ։ Եւ նա ասաց Աստուած հայր քո աշողեաց ինձ վաղվաղակի ունել եւ դառնալ։
39. Ասէ Իսահակ ի մօտ եկ առ իս որդեակ զի համբուրեցից զքեզ. եւ զնաց Յակոբ մերձ հօր իւրոյ. զոր[105] կալաւ զղաստակ ձեռացն. եւ եւտես մազուտ. եւ էառ զհոտ պատմուճանին Եսաւայ։ {եւ առեալ եկեր զմիսն. եւ սկսաւ աւրհնել զնա եւ զնաց յակոբ մերձ հօր իւրոյ. զոր կալաւ զղաստակ ձեռացն. եւ եւտես մազուտ՝ եւ էառ զհոտ պատմուճանին Եսաւայ.} զի մշկահոտ էր՝ եւ համբուրեալ զնա ասաց. ճայնդ՝ ճայն Յակոբայ. եւ ձեռքդ ձեռք Եսաւայ. եւ առեալ եկեր զմիսն՝ եւ սկսաւ աւրհնել զնա յերկնէ եւ յերկրէ. ի ցօղէ եւ ի ցամաքէ. ի հրեշտակաց սրբոց. յԱստուծոյ եւ մարդկանէ.
40. Եւ ասաց յաղթօղ եւ զօրաւոր լիցիս ի վերայ թշնամեաց քոց։ Եւ ապա եկն յեսաւ յորսոյն. եւ ոչ զիտեր զինչ եղեալն էր։ Եւ առեալ մայրն հասոյց զայն եւս խորտակին։ Եւ ետ ի ձեռն Եսաւայ. զոր առեալ տարաւ առ հայրն. եւ ասաց. արի հայր եւ կեր / fol. 180v / միս յորսոյ իմմէ եւ աւրհնեա զիս։ Ասէ Իսահակ որդեակ բերիր եւ կերայ։
41. Ասէ Եսաւ ես աւասիկ դերեւս եկի. Ասէ Իսահակ եղբայր քո եկն եւ խաբեաց զիս. եւ էառ զաւրհնութիւն անդրանկութեան։ Ասէ Եսաւ այս երիցս որ նա էառ զանդրանկութիւն իմ։ Արդ աւրհնեա եւ զիս հայր։ Ասէ Իսահակ զիարդ աւրհնեցից զքեզ որդեակ իմ. զի նա էառ զաւրհնութիւնն անդրանկութեան։ Ասէ Եսաւ են եւ քո աւրհնութիւնք զանազան. հայր իմ աւրհնեա եւ զիս։
42. Ասէ Իսահակ զնա տէր արարի եւ զքեզ ծառայ. այլ ոչ զոյ անդրադարձութիւն։ Յայնժամ սկսաւ Եսաւ զոռալ եւ լալ դառնապէս։ Եւ Իսահակ աւրհնեաց զնա՝ եւ մխիթարեաց՝ այլ ոչ լիապէս։ Եւ յայնմ օրէ ոխ[ացա]լ յեսաւ ընդ Յակոբայ՝ եւ ընդ ակամբ հ[այ]էր ի նա։ Եւ փախեաւ Յակոբ յեսաւայ. եւ զնաց ի Խառան առ քեռին իւր

---

104. A locative would be expected.
105. զ- is anomalous as often in late texts, where its role as *nota accusativi* has undergone change. See also the introduction to text no. 12. On uses of the *nota accusativi*, see p. 180, n. 7 and p. 182, n. 14 below.

Լաբան. եւ իառ[106] գդւստերս նորա զԼիայ եւ գՀռաքէլ վասն ԺԴ ամ[ա]g հովութեան. եւ եղեն նմա որդիք ԺԲան. Զ ի Լիայէ. Ռուբէն՝ Շաևոն. Ղեւի. Յուդայ՝ / fol. 181r / Իսաքար. Զբողոն. եւ Դինա քոյր նոցա. եւ Զելփայէ. յաղախնոյն Լիայ. Դան. եւ Նեփ[թ]աղիմ եւ Բ ի Բալլայէ յաղախնոյն Հռաքէլ[ի] Յովսէփ. եւ Բենիամին:

43. Եւ էին ամենեքեան ոք անւանիք. գորեղք եւ գեղեցկատեսիլք։ Չէ ամաց էր Յակոբ. եւ ծնաւ Լիա նմա որդի զՌուբէն. եւ յՁՉ ամին ծնաւ Շմաւոն. եւ յ[ՁԷ] ծնաւ Ղեւի. եւ յՁԸ ամին ծնաւ Յուդա։ Եւ յետ որդւոցն ծնելոյ. այլ եւս եկաց չիւ Յակոբ Լաբանու քեռոյն իւրոյ. եւ ան[եր]- ոյն. ամս Է. եւ էառ վարձ զիայտ խայրիք յանասնոցն յամենայնէ։ Եւ հրեշտակ Աստուծոյն հօրն իւրոյ ասաց Յակոբայ. առնուլ փայտ դալ[ար] ընկուզի. ուշի. եւ ոսփի. կեղեւել զայն նկարէն. եւ դնել յաւազանս ջրարբացն:

44. Եւ ջոկեալ զատոյց Լաբան կամօքն. եւ բանին Յակոբայ զամենայն գորշ եւ զկապոյտ. եւ զխայտ խայրի. եւ սպիտակ ի խաշանց իւրոց. [.] յ[....] իսն իւր եւ ասաց հեռանալ ի վայրաց [.]տին. Գ աւուրց ճանապարհաւ. եւ տանել յայ[ն տե]ղի.[107] եւ զամենայն համադրման. եւ զմիազոյն / fol. 181v / թողեալ ի ծեռն Յակոբայ. արածել ի սովորական տեղիսն. զայն այնպէս արարին. զի բան էր ի մէջ Լաբանու եւ Յակոբայ. որ ամէն կէտջ վասն է ամ հովիւ կացեալ էր Յակոբ Լաբանու. եւ ԴԺան ամացն առեալ էր վարձ գԲ քորսն:

45. Եւ է ամ այլ արածէր զնորա խաշինսն՝ եւ առևոյր վարձմ՝ գսպիտակն եւ գգորշսն՝ զմիով տարոյ ծնունդսն: Եւ ի դնել զնկարէն կեղեւալ փայտոս ի յաւազանսն՝ եւ ամենայն խաշինքն եւ անասունքն ի ջուր խմեն տեսանէին զկեղեւեալ փայտոսն նկարէն ի ջուրսն. եւ կծկէին: Եւ ի գալ տարոյն ամենայն խաշինքն եւ անասունքն խայտագորշ ծնան. անսղալ. որ ոչ կրիպեցան. այլ ամենեքեան երկւորիք էին: Եւ այն ամենայն Յակոբայ եղեն ի վարձ վաստակոց իւրոց:

46. Եւ ի լինելն Յակոբայ ի տանն Լաբանայ ԻԱ տարի. եւ եղեն նմա Դ կանայս. եւ ԺԱ որդիս եւ դուստր մի ի Խառան. եւ բազում ոչխարք եւ անասունք՝ եւ ուղտք եւ էշք. Եւ ասաց ընդ աներ քեռին իւր Յակոբ. առնուլ զկալ/ fol. 182v /նայն եւ զորդիսն եւ զամենայն ինչսն. եւ գնալ դառնալ առ ծնողսն իւր: Եւ նա ասաց թէ ոչ երթ ի բարի:

47. Եւ չուեալ Յակոբայ գնաց ընդ Եփրատ. եւ դիմեաց երթալ յերկիրն Քանանու. եւ հասեալ ի հունն Յորդանանու. յետ Լ աւուր ելանելոյ նորա ի Ճանապարհի: Եւ անցոյց զամենայն տունն եւ զիաշինսն յայնկոյս գետոյն. եւ ինքն մնաց միայն եւ գոհանայր զԱստուծոյ.[108] թէ ի գնալն իմ յԱսորիս. ցուպ ի ծեղին միայն անցի ընդ Յորդանան: Եւ

---

106. Note ի for է in իառ.
107. There is a lacuna, and this seems a reasonable restoration in view both of sense and space.
108. More usual would be գոհանալ Աստուծոյ. In addition, in the next line, the –u on դառնելու is unusual.

ի դառնելս իմ ի քանան. յերկուս բանակս եղէ. կանամբք եւ որդովք. եւ բազում բոզակօբ: Եւ մինչ նա կայր միայն եւ աղօթէր. եւ նսեմացաւ երեկն. ահա այր մի կալաւ գՅակոբ եւ գօտեկռիւ մարտեաւ ընդ նմա. յերեկորեայ մինչեւ ցառաւօտն ի յեյս արեւուն:

48. Եւ Յակոբ զահի հարեալ ջանայր սպանանել զնա՝ զի մի սպանցէ զինքն: Եւ յորժամ լուսացաւ. ասէ ցնա տէր. թող զիս զի ահա լուսացաւ: Եւ Յակոբ ասէ ցնա ոչ թողից / fol. 182v / գբեզ մինչեւ ասիցես զանուն քո: Ե[ւ] նա ասէ ցնա զի հարցանես զանուանէ իմ. անուն իմ սքանչելի է: Բայց դու Յակոբ ոչ կոչեսցիս. այլ Իսրայէլ եղիցիս անուն քո. զի ժուժկալեցեր ընդ Աստուծոյ. թող զիս. եւ Յակոբ ոչ թողոյր զնա ի բաց. մինչեւ կալաւ զամողաջէն Յակոբայ: որրեաց գծալելիսն ի ներբոյ ծնկանն. եւ կաղացոյց զնա. եւ ապա անէրեւույթ եղեւ ի Յակոբայ. եւ Յակոբ ի միտս իւր եկեալ տայր փառս Աստուծոյ:

TRANSLATION

29. Isaac became increasingly mighty for the <L>ord was with him. And there was famine in that time, and Isaac went to the land of the Gergerites, to king Abimelech. And he too called his wife (his) sister. And one day Abimelech saw from the window, Isaac who was sporting with Rebekah his wife, and he accused him in a friendly fashion, "Why did you say that your wife is your sister?"

30. And he said, "Because she is a woman of beautiful appearance, I said, 'Perhaps they will seize (her) from me and kill me.'" And Abimelech said to him, "Fear not. Behold all my land (is) before you. Where it seems pleasing to your eyes, dwell there, for the sake of your father Abraham, for he was our brother with good will and love."[109]

31. And Isaac dwelt in the land of the Philistines, where he spread. One (i.e., ewe) made 100 lambs. And then he had 2 sons from one intercourse, from one womb. In the 60th year of Isaac's life he had two sons, as Melchizedek, priest of God had said, that the older will serve the younger.[110] This was seen in the birth, for Jacob was grasping Esau's heel.

32. And Esau was an animal-like man, wild minded and a hunter, with thick hair.[111] And Jacob was smooth skinned, mild and peaceable.

33. And one day Esau went hunting deer and caught nothing. He returned home hungry and saw Jacob who was eating lentil soup. And he said, "Give me (some) too so that I may eat." And he said, "Give your birthright to me and then I will give you this lentil soup."

34. And he, for the sake of one food, gave him the birthright. And again, Jacob

---

109. Paraphrase of Gen 26:1–11.
110. Compare text no. 4.25 above.
111. Compare text no. 5.5 and see Gen 25:25 and 25:27.

received the blessing of the birthright. And it came to pass that Isaac grew weaker and the light of his eyes diminished and he remained lying in his house.[112]

35. And one day he said to Esau to go hunting deer and to bring him venison,[113] "So that I may eat," he said, "and bless you."[114] And he went. And Rebekah heard that and wished Jacob to have Isaac's blessing of Esau [for]. When Esau had gone, his mother said to Jacob, "Son, go and bring two kids from our flock and slaughter (them), so that I may make the stew for your father, so that he may eat and bless you."

36. Jacob said, "My father asked my brother for venison,[115] so that he might bless him. And when we offer him (i.e., the goat's flesh), perhaps my father will realize (what we have done) and instead of the blessing he will curse us." His mother said, "Let that curse (be) upon me, which your father says to you."

37. And Jacob went (and) brought two kids and he slaughtered (them). And Rebekah took the meat and prepared a sweet-tasting stew, just as Isaac liked. And shaving the skin with shears, she made a wrapping for Jacob's neck, and armbands, and she dressed (him) in Esau's cloak, which he had left in Jacob's house.

38. And she put the stew into (his) hands, and he took (it) and brought it to Isaac and said, "Let my father arise and eat this venison, which he requested." Isaac said, "How did you come (so) quickly, my son?" And he said, "The God of your father made me successful in catching (it) quickly and returning."

39. [116] Isaac said, "Approach me, son, so that I may kiss you." And Jacob went close to his father, who grasped his wrist and saw that (it was) hairy. And he received the smell of Esau's cloak, for it was leather[117] scented, and he embraced (or: kissed) him and said, "The voice is Jacob's voice and your hands are Esau's hands." And taking, he ate the meat and he began to bless him by heaven and earth, by the sea and the dry land, by the holy angels, by God and man.

40. And he said, "You will be victorious and mighty over your enemies." Then Esau came from the hunt and he did not know what had happened. And his mother took and cooked that stew too. And she put it in Esau's hand. He took it and brought it to (his) father and said, "Arise, father, and eat my venison and bless me." Isaac said, "My son, you brought and I ate."

41. Esau said, "Behold, did I come in vain?" Isaac said, "Your brother came and deceived me and he took the blessing of the birthright." Esau said, "This is

---

112. Paraphrase of Gen 26:27–34 and 27:1.
113. Literally: "meat of the field, plain".
114. The following is paraphrased from Gen 27.
115. Literally: "meat of the hunt".
116. There is major dittography in this section. The duplicate text is omitted from the translation.
117. Reading մաշկահոտ. Alternatively, translate մշկահոտ as "musk scented."

three times[118] that he has taken my birthright. Now, bless me too father." Isaac said, "How will I bless you, my son, for he took the blessing of birthright." Esau said, "You have further various blessings, my father. Bless me too."

42. Isaac said, "I made him master and you, servant. There is no returning it again." Then Esau began to become angry and to weep bitterly. And Isaac blessed him and he comforted (him), but not fully. And from that day on Esau held a grudge against Jacob and he lo[ok]ed askance at him. And Jacob fled from Esau and went to Haran,[119] to his uncle Laban, and he took his daughters, Leah and Rachel, (in exchange) for 14 years' shepherding and he had twelve sons, six from Leah: Reuben, Simeon, Levi, Judah, Issachar, Zebulun, and Dinah their sister, and from Zilpah, Leah's maidservant: Dan and Naphtali, and two from Bilhah, Rachel's maidservant: [*text lost which must have read like:* "Gad and Asher, and two from Rachel,"][120] Joseph and Benjamin.

43. And they were all famous, mighty and handsome. Jacob was 95 years old and Leah bore him a son, Reuben; and in his 96th year Simeon was born; and in [his 97th year] Levi was born; and in his 98th year Judah was born. And after begetting the children, Jacob remained further under the roof of Laban his uncle and his father-in-law for 7 years and took as his wages the spotted get of all the beasts. And an angel of the God of his father said to Jacob to take fre[sh] sticks of the walnut, of the willow and of the plane tree, to peel them (to make them) multicolored and to put them in the watering pools.

44. And Laban separated (and) set apart at his desire and at Jacob's word all the grey and blue and spotted get and the white of his flocks, his [......] and he said to lead (them) 3 days travel from the field (plain) of [ ] and to bring them to tha[t pla]ce, and for all those of one aspect and one color to be left in Jacob's hands to pasture in the customary places. They did this in that way, for it was bespoken between Laban and Jacob that for each wife Jacob would serve Laban as a shepherd for 7 years, and for 14 years he had taken the two sisters as wages.

45. And for a further 7 years he pastured his (i.e., Laban's) sheep and took as wages one year's white and grey get.[121] And by placing the multicolored, peeled sticks in the pools, and when all the sheep and the beasts drank water they saw the peeled, multicolored sticks in the water and they contracted.[122] And in the coming year all the sheep and beasts were born with grey spots, with no miscarriages. They did not wander away, but all were twins. And all that was Jacob's as wages for his labors.

---

118. See Gen 27:36, but there it is "twice".
119. This is paraphrase of Gen 28–31.
120. Probably lost by homoioarchton in the Armenian.
121. This seems somewhat confused; see Gen 30:35–36.
122. The word must mean "mated".

4. THE MEMORIAL OF THE FOREFATHERS

46. And when Jacob had been in Laban's house for 21 years, he had 4 wives and 11 sons and one daughter in Haran, and numerous sheep and beasts and camels and donkeys. And Jacob said to his father-in-law uncle that he would take his wives and sons and all his possessions and would go back to his parents. And he said, "Go well for good."
47. And Jacob set out and went across the Euphrates. And he set his face to go to the land of Canaan.[123] And he arrived at the ford of the Jordan, after he had been 30 days on the road. And he brought all (his) household and sheep across to the other side of the river. And he himself remained alone and praised God,[124] "When I went to Syria, I crossed the Jordan with only the staff in my hand,[125] and when I return to Canaan, I have become two camps, with wives and sons and much wealth." And while he was alone and praying, the evening darkened. Behold a man seized Jacob and wrestled with him, from evening until morning, to the rising of the sun.
48. And Jacob, smitten with fear, tried to kill him, lest he kill him. And when it became light, the Lord said to him, "Leave me, for behold it has become light." And Jacob said to him, "I will not leave you until you say your name." A[nd] he said to him, "Why to you ask about my name? My name is wondrous. But you will not be called Jacob, but Israel will be your name, for you resisted God. Leave me." And Jacob did not leave him go until he seized Jacob's heel. He twisted the joint below the knee and lamed him. And then he disappeared from Jacob. And Jacob, coming to his senses, gave glory to God. *The text continues the story of Jacob. A different scribe has written 184v–185r. The story continues down to the death of Joseph, on fol. 189v.*

---

123. Paraphrase of Gen 32.
124. The case ending of "God" is anomalous.
125. Gen 32:10.

5. Genealogy of Abraham

The manuscript Galata 154, now in the Library of the Armenian Patriarchate of Istanbul, is a Miscellany. It is undated but written in *notrgir* script by a number of scribes and may reasonably be assigned to the seventeenth century.[1] On p. 298 is a later colophon of the year 1741.

This text, occurring on pp. 300–305, contains not so much a narrative retelling of biblical events as a school tradition that in the fashion of list texts, enumerates a series of numbers and measurements relating to events and persons in the Old Testament.[2] We have edited a body of text basically referring to material parallel to Genesis and Exodus. Biblical sources of most traditions could be located and have been noted. The ten trials of Abraham (§2 here) also occur in a number of other Armenian manuscripts, such as the eighteenth-century M717 published separately below (text no. 13).

This text forms part of the treatment of Abraham in an extended context. In the Galata manuscript, after the material dependent on Genesis and Exodus that we have edited, the text continues on p. 305 with the some incidents from the period of the divided monarchy, the exile, and events of the time of the monarchy. Some botanical details follow, relating to the oil of anointment and its ingredients.[3]

/p. 300 / Ազգաբանութիւն Աբրահամու

1. Թարա ծնաւ զնաքովր, զԱռան եւ զԱբրահամ։ Ի ՃԺ ամին ճանաչեաց Աբրահամ զԱստուած, ի Կ ամին ասաց Աստուած ել յերկրէ եւ յազգէ քումմէ։ որ եւ բնակեցան ի Խառան։ Եւ ՀԵ ամին ել ի Խառանայ ի Պաղեստին. ուր եւ Ժ փորձանաց հանդիպեցաւ։
2. (Ա.) Նախ, ելանել յերկրէն եւ յազգէն։
   Բ. քարշին Սարայի, ի փարաւոնէ։
   Գ. բաժանին Ղովտայ։
   Դ. ոչ ինչ առնուլ յաւարէն Սողոմայ։
   Ե. քարշին Սարայի յԱբիմելէքէ,

---

1. See Kiwleserean 1961, cols. 975–90.
2. On the list texts, see Stone 2006, 132–33.
3. Thanks are expressed to H. B. Mesrob II, Patriarch of Istanbul, who some years ago encouraged me to photograph and publish this text. I am glad finally to be able to carry out his wishes.

5. GENEALOGY OF ABRAHAM

Զ ի ծերութեան թլփատին:
Է. տալ գՀաքար ի ձեռն Սառայի:
Ը. ի բաց հանել Հաքարայ որդովքն:
Թ. աւետեացն Աստուծոյ ոչ երկմտելն:
Ժ. որդին պատարագելն:

3. Ի ՁՁ ամին ծնաւ գԻսմայէլ: ՂԹ ամին թլփատեցաւ: Ճ ամին ծնաւ գԻսահակ. եւ Սառայ Ղ ամաց: Եւ մեռաւ Սառայ ՃԻԷ ամաց: Եւ խառ կին Աբրահամ գՔետուր յորմէ ծնաւ որդիս Զ. գԵմրան. եւ գՅեկդան. եւ գՁմադան. եւ գՄադիան. եւ գՅեզբոկ: եւ գՍովէ:

4. Մինն գմինն սպան, եւ այլքն լցին գերկիր. որոց մի են Թուրք որ եւ Պալհաւունիք կոչին յադագս Պահլ քաղաքին, եւ Արշակունիք վասն Արշակայ քաջին. եւ մեռաւ Աբրահամ ՃՀԵ ամաց:

5. Իսահակ խառ կին գՌեբեկայ, թոռն Նաքովրայ եղբօրն Աբրահամու, եւ ծնաւ գՅակոբ. եւ գԵսաւ: Եւ Եսաւ էր վայրագ. գազանամիտ անասնաբարոյ մարդատեաց յորվանամոյ. անձնասէր եւ ոչ աստուածասէր. վասն որոյ ասաց Աստուած. գՅակոբ սիրեցի եւ գԵսաւ ատեցի:

6. Յակոբ փախեալ յԵսաւայ գնաց ի Խառան. եւ խառ գԲ. դստերսն Լաբանայ քեռյն իւրոյ. զԼիա, եւ գՀռաքէլ: եւ ծնաւ որդիս ԺԲ. Ռուբէն, Շմաւոն, Ղեւի, Յուդայ: Իսաքար. Զաբողոն, Եւ Դի<ն>այ⁴ քոյր նոցա. ի Լիայ կնոջէն: Դան եւ Նեփթաղիմ. ի Զելփայէ աղախնոյ նորին: Գաթ. եւ Ասեր. ի Բալլայէ աղախնոյն Հռաքելայ: Յովսէփ եւ Բենիամին ի Հռաքելայ: Իսահակ / p. 302 / մեռանի ՃՁ ամաց: Եւ Յակոբ ի գնալն Խառան. անդ՝ ուր ննջեաց եւ ետես. սանդուխ կանգնեալ յերկրէ յերկինս եւ Տէր ի նմա. եւ կանգնեաց⁵ անդ՝ սեղան. եւ անուանեաց տուն Աստուծոյ: եւ ասի չիրող տեպեան:

7. Եւ այն որ չիրող ասի երդման. այն է գոր Աբիմելէք արքայ փղշտացւոց եկն առ Աբրահամ. եւ երդուան զի մի չար ինչ արասցեն միմեանց: Եւ նախանձեալ եղբարքն յով<ս>եփայ, վաճառեցին գնա ԺԵ ամաց⁶ եւ ԺԳ ամ եկաց ի տան դահճապետին. եւ Բ ամ ի բանտին: Եւ թագաւորեաց Լ ամաց, եւ ապրեցաւ այլ եւս Զ ամ. եւ մեռաւ ՃԺ ամաց.

8. Եւ Յակոբ էջ յԵզիպտոս ՀՄ հոգով. Յովսէփի եւ կին. եւ Բ որդիքն որդով լինին ողիք Հէ. Այտ Ն ամ գերութիւնն Իսրայէլի. յետ աւետեացն Աստուծոյ. ԻԵ. ամին ծնաւ Աբրահամ գԻսահակ. Եւ Իսահակ Կ ամին ծնաւ գՅակոբ: Եւ ՃԼ ամին. էջ յԵզիպտոս, որ լինի ՆԼ ամ:

9. Այս են Ժ հարուածքն Եզիպտացոց: Առաջին. գջուրն յարիւն փոխել: Բ. գորտն: Գ. մունն: Դ. շանաճանճն: Ե. խաշնամահն: Զ. կեղ եւ

---

4. ն is omitted by the manuscript.
5. q is written over կ in the ms. See Stone and Hillel 2012, Index of Variants, s.v.
6. ամաց is in margin.
7. From this point on, the text more or less follows the biblical course of events. However, list-type material is introduced and little narrative is to be found. This tendency also occurs in §§1–8, but henceforth it is more marked.

խաւարտն: Է. Կարկուտն. եւ հուրն: Ը: մարախն: Թ. Խաւարն շօշափելի:
Ժ. Անդրանկաց մահ:
10. Ի պատառելն գծովս Մովսէսի, ասաց. այսպէս. յառաջ / p. 303 / ձգեալ զգաւազանն ասէ: Այիայ այսպէս Աստուած իմ. առաջի իմ: յաշ կողմս Շարայիս. դու հաներ զմեզ Աստուած: Ձախ կողմս Ադոնիա Տէրդ տերացն. ընդ մեզ: Ընկղմեցաւ փարաւոն Ո կառօք:
11. Ի պաշտել որթոյն, կոտորեաց Մովսէս ԳՌ. Աւրէնք տուան յետ Ծ աւուր անցանելոյն ընդ ծովս: Եւ է այս Ժ բան օրինացն:
    Ես եմ Տէր Աստուած քո:
    Մի արասցես քեզ կուռս:
    Մի կոչեսցես զանուն իմ ի վերայ սնոտեաց:
    Պահեա զշաբաթս իմ սրբութեամբ:
    Պատուեա զհայր քո եւ զմայր:
    Այս է Ե յանձնառական:
    Մի շնար:
    Մի գողանար:
    Մի սպանաներ:
    Մի սուտ վկայեր:
    Մի ցանկար ինչից եղբօրն:
    Այս հրաժար{ը}ական:
12. Թէ որ չափ էր տապանակ ուխտին: Երկայն. Բ կանգուն եւ կէս: Լայնն կանգուն եւ կէս: Բարձր կանգուն եւ կէս:
    Եւ կայր ի մէջն տապանակ օրինացն. սափորն ոսկի լի մանանայիւ. Գաւազանն Ահարոնի որ ծաղկեցաւ. Բուրվառն պղնձի որ եղեւ ոսկի ի ձեռն Ահարոնի:
    Խորանն վկայութեան յետ ելիցն. Ե ամսոյ սկսան. եւ է ամիսն կատարեցաւ. խորհուրդ է աւուր արարչութեանն. եւ կանգնեցաւ սկիզբն երկրորդի ամին:
13. Եւ էր չափ խորանին Ժ փեղք. երկայնութիւն / p. 304 / փեղքին ԻԸ կանգուն, եւ լայն Դ կանգուն: ի կարմրոյ ի կապուտոյ: ի բեհեզոյ: ի ծիրանոյ:
    Ադաշանքն Մովսէսի առ Աստուած այս էր: Գրթած ես եւ ողորմած. Երկայնամիտ: Բազմադորդում: Եւ ճշմարիտ: Այսպէս գթած առ որդիս: Ողորմած առ դարձեալս: երկայնամիտ. առ անդարձս. Բազմադորդմաց առ բա<գ>մապարտսն:[8] Ճշմարիտ ի հատատուցումս բարեաց:
14. Սօնք հնդն այս են: տարեմուտն եւ ամսամուտն: բաղարձակերացն

---

8. The manuscript has բամապարտսն.

Եւ եղիցն: Տոչութեան օրինացն: քաւութեան որ զղջոյն: Եւ տաղաւարահարացն: վասն ...⁹ ի նորս: Ե նաւակատիս կատարեմք¹⁰:
15. Եւ թէ քանի էր պատարագն. ի հնումն. ասեմք թէ Դ.
Նախ, զոհն որ զոհութեան էր: Բ պատարգն ֆրկութեան: Գ վասն մեղացն: Դ ողջակէզն Աստուծոյ որ է կամաւոր:
16. Այս է Է. ազգն:
Ամովրհացին: Քետացին: Փերեզացին: Քանանացին: Գերգեսացին. Խեւացին: Երուսացին:

GENEALOGY OF ABRAHAM

1. Terah begot Nahor, Achan and Abraham. In his 18th year, Abraham recognized God.[11] In his 60th year,[12] God said, "Go forth from your land and family, who lived in Haran." In his 75th year[13] he went forth from Haran to Palestine, where he encountered 10 trials.
2.1 First, going forth from (his) land and (his) family[14]
2.2. The dragging away of Sarah by Pharaoh[15]
2.3. The separation from Lot
2.4. Taking nothing from the booty of Sodom
2.5. The dragging away of Sarah by Abimelech
2.6. Being circumcised in old age
2.7. Giving Hagar into Sarah's hand[16]
2.8. Expulsion of Hagar with her children
2.9. Not doubting God's Annunciation (i.e., that Sarah would give birth)
2.10. The offering of his son

---

9. This is an abbreviation, most likely reading վասն որոյ, "on account of which, this". The middle letter of the abbreviation is unclear.

10. The last two words are reversed in the text and corrected to the order we give here.

11. According to *Tanḥuma Vayera'* 22 he was three years old.

12. Michael the Syrian (Chabot 1899, 27) also has the age of sixty.

13. Gen 12:4. The sentence may be construed to mean that Abraham went forth in his sixtieth year. The dates are odd, for God's command was given in Abraham's sixtieth year (which has no biblical basis), but his execution of the command is set in his seventy-fifth year. It seems that two events are combined, his going forth from Ur to Haran, traditionally put in his sixtieth year (see text no. 14.5) and in his seventy-fifth year he went forth from Haran to Canaan. Michael the Syrian put this after fourteen years in Haran (see Chabot 1899, 27; Michael the Syrian 1871, 24).

14. See the General Introduction above, under "Ten Trials of Abraham," p. 21, n. 72, on such lists.

15. The famine that drove Abraham to Egypt is described as a "trial" (փորձութիւն) by Ełišē, *Commentary on Genesis* 76.5; and see *MH* 5th century, 819.

16. That is, power.

3. In (his) 86th year he begot Ishmael.[17] (In) (his) 99th year he was circumcised.[18] In (his) 100th year Isaac was born and Sarah was 90 years old.[19] And Sarah died at 127 years.[20] And Abraham took Ketur(a) as wife, from whom he begot 6 sons, (Z)Emran, and Yektan, {Z}Medan, and Midian, and Yezbok (i.e., Ishbak), and Sovē (i.e., Shuah).[21]
4. They killed one another, and the others filled the earth. One of them are the Turks who are also called Palhavounis on account of the city of Pahl[22] and Aršakunis on account of valorous Aršak.[23] And Abraham died when he was 175 years old.[24]
5. Isaac took Rebekah as wife, the grandchild of Nahor, Abraham's brother and he begot Jacob and Esau. And Esau was fierce (savage), with a bestial mind and animalian habits, misanthropic, crazy for food,[25] self-loving and not God-loving. Because of that God said, "I loved Jacob and I hated Esau."[26]
6. Jacob, having fled from Esau, went to Haran. And he took the 2 daughters of Laban his uncle,[27] Leah and Rachel. And he begot 12 sons: Reuben, Simeon, Levi, Judah, Issachar, Zebulun, and Di(n)a their sister, from his wife Leah; Dan and Naphtali from Zilpah her handmaid; Gad and Asher from Bilhah, Rachel's handmaid; Joseph and Benjamin from Rachel. Isaac died at 180 years.[28] And when Jacob went to Haran, there, where he fell asleep {and} he saw a ladder standing from earth to heaven and the Lord on it.[29] And he set up an altar there and he called it "House of God." And it is called "Well of Vision."[30]

---

17. Gen 16:16.
18. Gen 17:24.
19. Gen 17:17 and 21:5.
20. Gen 23:1.
21. See Gen 25:1–4. The genealogy is not Armenized here, as it is in the next section. Note that the biblical forms are "Zimran" and "Medan." In Armenian, the initial z- has become confused, Zimran being treated as zEmran and Medan as ZZmedan, that is, the *nota accusativi* is lost from Zimran and doubled on Medan.
22. See Thomson 2006, 129, for a discussion of Pahl. See the analogous tradition in text no. 4.26, which seems somewhat clearer.
23. On Aršak, founder of the Aršakuni dynasty, see Movsēs Xorenacʻi 2.2, cf. 2:1, where he is said to be a descendant of Esau. The Palhavunis are presumably to be viewed as the Parthians; see text no. 4.26 note.
24. See Gen 25:7.
25. Presumably because of the "mess of pottage" or stew; see Gen 25:29–34. The source of this list of epithets is not clear. Compare text no. 4.32 on Esau.
26. Mal 1:2–3, quoted in Rom 9:13; cf. 4 Ezra 3:16.
27. The word means specifically, his mother's brother.
28. Gen 35:28.
29. Gen 28:12. The biblical text refers to "angels of God," but compare Gen 28:13.
30. Gen 28:17–19. "Well of vision" seems to be confused with another well, Beer-lahai-roi, mentioned in Gen 16:14 in connection with the Hagar story; see Gen 24:62 and 25:11. See the etymology of Ishmael given in text no. 4.12.

5. GENEALOGY OF ABRAHAM

7. And that (is the well) that was called "Well of Oath," that (well concerning) which Abimelech king of the Philistines came to Abraham, and they swore that they would do no evil to one another.[31] And Joseph's brothers, being envious, sold him at the age of 15 years.[32] And for 13 years he lived in the house of the chief executioner and for 2 years in the prison.[33] And he reigned at 30 years[34] and he lived another 80 years and he died at 110 years.[35]
8. And Jacob went down to Egypt with 71 souls.[36] Joseph and (his) wife and (his) two sons, which makes 75 souls. Those 400 years (were) the captivity of Israel.[37] 25 years after God's pronouncement, Abraham begot Isaac. And Isaac at 60 begot Jacob[38] and in the 130th year he went down into Egypt, which is 430 years.[39]
9. These are the 10 plagues of the Egyptians.[40] First, the water changes to blood, 2 the frogs, 3 the worms (midges), 4 the dog-ticks, 5 the murrain, 6 the ulcers and gloominess, 7 the hail and fire, 8 the locusts, 9 the terrible darkness, 10 the death of firstborn.
10. When Moses split the sea it (Scripture) said thus, "First, he stretched out his staff and said, 'Ayiay, thus my God (is) before me. On the right side (is) Šarayiay. You brought us forth, O God. (On the) left side (is) Adonia, O Lord of the lords (you are) with us.'"[41] Pharaoh was drowned with 600 chariots.[42]
11. In the worshiping of the calf, Moses cut down 3,000.[43] The Law was given 50 days after the crossing of the sea.[44] And these are the 10 words of the Law:

---

31. An etymology of Beer-sheba; Gen 21:31.
32. *Jubilees* 39:2 and 46:3 have 17; cf. Gen 37:2.
33. *Jubilees* 46:3 speaks of three years in prison. Genesis 41:1 mentions that Joseph spent two years in prison, but he was already a prisoner before the point in time referred to by that verse.
34. See *Jub.* 40:11.
35. Also *Jub.* 46:3. The figures are as follows: 15 + 13 + 2 = 30; 30 + 80 = 110. In Gen 50:22, Joseph is said to live 110 years. The second "30" must be Joseph's age when he became viceroy. Genesis 37:2 says that Joseph was sold at seventeen years. The thirteen years in Egypt are inferred from Gen 41:46, where Joseph is said to enter Pharaoh's service at the age of thirty.
36. Genesis 46:26–27 and Exod 1:5 have seventy, not seventy-one. The calculation yielding seventy-five is not biblical.
37. Compare Gen 15:13. Exodus 12:41 puts the exodus after 430 years. The same difference of 400 and 430 years is discussed by Tiran *vardapet MH* 10th century, 966.
38. Gen 25:26.
39. See Gen 47:9.
40. This is a widely known list and there exist a number of further copies, e.g., M0605 fols. 25v (seventeenth century), M2188 fols. 244–46 (fifteenth century), and M6897 (1317). See above p. 21.
41. This is an invocation in magical style of three angels of the presence. These seem to be variants on divine and angelic names. For Adonia, see Stone 1982b, 140. "You brought forth" is related to the popular Armenian etymology of *Astuac* ("God"); see *NBHL*, s.v.
42. Exod 14:7.
43. Exod 32:28.
44. The figure is not biblical, however, and it is the number of days of the seven weeks

I am the Lord your God.[45]
Do not make idols for yourself.
Do not call my name upon vanities.
Observe[46] my Sabbaths with holiness.
Honor your father and mother.
These are 5 positive (commandments).
Do not commit adultery.
Do not steal.
Do not kill.
Do not bear false witness.
Do not covet your brother's goods.

12. Of what measure was the Ark of the Covenant? 2 and a half cubits long, a cubit and a half wide and a cubit and a half high.[47]
And there was inside: the table of the Law,[48] a golden urn full of manna,[49] Aaron's staff which flowered,[50] the bronze censer which became golden in Aaron's hand.[51]
The Tent of Witness after the exodus: they began in the 5th month and the plan was completed on the 7th month, on the 7th day of its fashioning, and it was set up at the beginning of the second year.[52]

13. And the measure of the 10 curtains of the tent was—length of the curtain was 28 cubits and 4 cubits wide of red, of blue of purple (crimson) linen.[53]
This was the prayer of Moses to God:[54] You are pitying and merciful, long-suffering, greatly merciful and true. Thus: pitying toward (his) children, merciful to those who repent, long-suffering to the impenitent, greatly merciful to the most guilty, true for the recompense of good.

14. These are feasts of the Old (Testament): New Year and New Moon, Eating of Unleavened Bread and Exodus, Giving of the Law, of Atonement which (is) of confession of sins, and of Tabernacles. On account of this in the New, we perform 5 festivals.[55]

---

between Passover and Pentecost, which is between the exodus and the giving of the Torah. The fiftieth day is that after the seven weeks.

45. See Exod 20 and Deut 5.
46. This is the verb found in Deut 5:12.
47. Exod 25:10.
48. Exod 25:21.
49. Exod 16:32-34.
50. See Num 17:25 and compare this statement with Heb 9:4.
51. The incident with the censer referred to here is not biblical.
52. See Exod 40:2. The origin of the preceding dates is unclear.
53. See Exod 26:2 and 36:9, which also give 28 x 4. For the colors, see Exod 26:31 and 36.
54. Exod 34:6.
55. See Stone 1988, 5–12, where the typology of the Christian festivals is to be found.

15. And how many offerings do we say are in the Old (i.e., Testament)? We say 4. First, the offering which is of praise; 2 the offering of redemption; 3 on account of sins; 4 the holocaust to God, which is a free-will offering.
16. These are the 7 peoples: the Amorite, the Hittite, the Perezite, the Canaanite, the Gergeshite, the Hivite, the Jebusite.[56]

---

56. Compare the lists in Exod 23:23; Deut 7:1 and many other places.

6. Poem on Abraham, Isaac, Melchizedek, Lot

This poem is found in Berlin Staatsbibliothek SBB IIIE MS or quart 805, fols. 279r–280r.[1] The manuscript has 317 folios in various hands and is apparently from the seventeenth century. It is written in *bolorgir* script on paper. This poem is a section of a much longer verse retelling of biblical stories. This passage on Abraham is immediately preceded by a poetic section dealing with the period from Adam to Noah and is followed by a similar poem on Jacob, Joseph, and the patriarchs. It is desirable, of course, that the whole poetic composition, of which the Abraham poem is a section, be published. The same manuscript also preserves other works including the *History of Alexander* as well as demonological texts. It also contains a number of illustrations, none of which relates to the biblical stories.

Stanza 24 of the poem mentions Yovasap' as the author, without giving any further details. The only poet of this name mentioned in Bardakjian's *Reference Guide* is Yovasap' Sebastac'i (ca. 1510–after 1564). In his discussion of Yovasap''s works, Bardakjian does not mention a rhymed biblical retelling.[2] Our purpose here, however, is not to resolve literary problems nor to study Yovasap''s poetry in its own right, but to make available this retelling of the Abraham traditions, which is closely related to the narrative texts also presented in this volume. Whether this poem is by Yovasap' Sebastac'i or not, the language indicates that it is from the sixteenth century or later.

It is significant to note that whole lines of this poem are incomprehensible without knowledge of the narrative traditions. This is an indication of the wide circulation of the "embroidered" Abraham traditions, which was such that apocryphal incidents can be referred to incidentally.[3] In addition, Yovasap' departs from the biblical details to make homiletic or typological points. Instances of this are pointed out in the notes to the translation below.

The poem is in a monorhyme in *-in,* and we present it in numbered stanzas of four lines each.

---

1. See Assfalg and Molitor 1962, no. 23, 93–100
2. Bardakjian 2000, 35–38. On Yovasap', see also Ačaṙyan, *HAB*, 3:535. This poem is not mentioned by Abełian 1955.
3. I am grateful to Th. M. van Lint, who made a number of suggestions relating to the interpretation of this work.

Ոտանաւոր Աբրահամու Սահակայ
Մելքիսեթեկի Ղովտա

1. Հայր Աբրահամ ասեմ որդի Թարային.
   Որ ի նմայ է աստուածպաշտութիւն.
   Վասն երամից ճայիցն որ յարտորանին.
   Յիշել զվերինն Աստուած ճայքն հալածին։
2. Ապայ եկեալ ի միտ. եւ խորհուրդ յայտնին.
   Ըստեղծող Աստուած նայ է որ հրաշագործին.
   Կոզց տունն այրեցեալ զադտ ի գիշերին.
   Եւ հնարող ջորոյն կորեալ ընդ դմին։
3. Ի Մամրէ երեւեալ հատի ոչխարին.
   / fol. 279v / Տէրն եւ Բ սրբք կերպիւ մարդկային.
   Մազոբ սպիտակացեալ ծաղկի նմանին.
   Որ մինչեւ յԱբրահամ. սպիտակ տեսել չին։
4. Զոր հաստատեցաւ հաւատ ճշմարիտին.
   Հիւրոք նստեր ի ճաշի ժամս եղանին.
   Մինչեւ տէր զթացաւ ի գործս նորին.
   Բ սրբքհիւք եկեալ ի ճաշին։
5. Եւ խոստացաւ նմայ զանտրանիկ որդին.
   Զոր եկեալ մարմնացո ի յորդոց նորին.
   Բազարչ գինի եւ որթ զենեալ ի ճաշին.
   Յորինակ բազարչոյ. Բաժակ խորհրդին։
6. Եօթն փորձքն որ անց ընդ հօր հաւատին.
   Եւ զպանտըխտանալն յոտար երկրին.
   Չի Հաքար աղախին փարոնին.
   Եւ քոյր ասել զկնոջն գրեալ կայ գրին։
7. Ծնեալ զորդին Սահակ ամուլ Սառային.
   Փորձեաց Տէր զԱբրահամ խնդրել զպատանին.
   Իսկ նայ բառնայր զփայտ իւր ողջակիզին.
   Հանեալ ի Գողգոթայ յօրինակ խաչին։
8. Կապեաց զորդին Սահակ եդ ի սեղանին.
   Էառ սուսեր կամէր զենուլ զիւր որդին.
   Հրեշտակ երեւեցո ցյայր Աբրահամին.
   Ասաց մի մխեր զսուրտ ի պատանին։
9. Եցոյց զԱաբէկ ծառն որ ի տեղին.
   Եւ խոյ մի կախեալ կայր յԲ եղջերին.
   Գնաց եղեաց վերա կափարիճ վիմին.
   Էառ զխոյն Աբէլի զենեաց ի տեղին։
10. Գոհացո զՏէր Աստուած զղած մարդկային.
    Որ յամէն ժամ որսայ զմարդիք ի բարին.
    Այն է երկրպագու փառաց վերին.
    Որ հաւատով ի նայ դիմէն ի սրտին։

11. Եցոյց զՄելքիսեդեկ որ կայր յանտառին.
    Ասէ առածել իմ կրաս ի կարգին.
    Գնայ ի ձիթենեաց լեառն ի խիտ մայրին.
    Չայնեաց զանուն նորա Տէառնէ հրամանին:
12. Չի քահանայ լինի աստուածային.
    Եւ է ամ որ անտես է նայ մարդկային.
    Վասըն սասելոյ յահէ արարչին.
    Եւ վասն ընկղման ծնդացն եւ երկրին:
13. Գնաց հայրն Աբրահամ որպէս հրամային.
    Արար այնպէս ըստ Տէառն պատուիրանին.
    Նայ գոհացաւ հոգով զԱստուած կենտանին.
    Որպէս լլան կարգիւ զիրաշս արարչին:
14. Դարձեալ գնաց առ նայ հայր Աբրահամին.
    Յորժամ որ կոտորեաց զգողող Գումրին.
    ԳՁ ոգով եւ ԺՀ-ին.
    Յորինակ սուրբ հարանց որ ի Նիկիին:
15. Որպէս նայ հալածեաց զգողող Գումրին.
    Սուրբ հարքն զհերձուածողսն ի Տէառնէ սիրին.
    Նոքա կերակրեցան բաղարջ ի գինին.
    Սուրբ հարքն զկենաց հացն ճշմարտեցին:
16. Զոր անմահ թագաւորն յօրինիչ նորին.
    Արժանէ զմեզ մարմնոյ արենին. / fol. 280r /
    Քրիստոնեաց ոգնող յուսըն ահեղին.
    Ողորմեցի փրկէ զմեզ ի գեհենին:
17. Կամիմ զՂովտ յիշել ի յայսմ կարգին.
    Չի էր եղբօր որդի հայր Աբրահամին.
    Ասէ Տէր զայրացայ ի գործ Սոդումին.
    Անասելի չարք որ ի նմա գործին:
18. Աբրահամ աղաչեաց զՏէրն ամենին.
    Մի բարկանար դու Տէր հանուրց քաղաքին.
    Իցէ բազում արդարք ի նորա միջին.
    Չի մի ի մեղաւն եղծեալ կործանին:
19. Ասէ Տէր եթէ ոչ կայ ի նա բարի<ն>.[4]
    Բայց միայն գտայ զՂովտ արդար ի միջին.
    Ես առաքեցից հրեշտակ պատգամին.
    Եւ զնայ ազատեմ ի պատուհասին:
20. Երկու հրեշտակ առին հրաման յԱրարչին.
    Մտան Սոդոմ քաղաք կերպիւ մարդկային.
    Տունն Ղովտայ մտին ի կերպ օտարին.
    Եւ Ղովտ պահեաց զնոսա չարէ Սոդումին:

---

4. We assume that a final ն is lost here because of the monorhyme in -ին that is universal in the poem, except for this line and stanza 23.1.

21. Ասէ հրեշտակն ցասումն հասու Սոդոմին։
    Արի ել ի քաղաքէս զի մի կործանին։
    Եհան զՂովտ ընդանեաւքն ի յայն քաղաքին։
    Յայնժամ մեք եւ մրրիկ զՍոդոմ պատեցին։
22. Հուր եւ ծծում իջեալ ի վրայ քաղաքին։
    Եւ պատառեալ անտունք եւ ջուր բխեցին։
    Երայր որպէս կաթաց եւ ծուխ մրրկին։
    Գոչիւն եւ շառաչիւն սաստիկ ահագին։
23. Իսկ կինն արդար Ղովտայ ի յետս նայի։
    Ի Սոդոմ քաղաքին միտքն էր ի շարին։
    Արձան աղի դարձաւ քարացաւ մարմին։
    Նրբայ զարհուրացեալ թողեալ զնացին։
24. Զոր աղաչեմք զհայր Աստուած եւ զՀզին։
    Փրկել զմեզ մաղթեմք ի մեղաց պատժին։
    Յովասափ անարժան գործով Սոդոմին։
    Եւ մեղաւք զավրացեալ ի մէջ մարդկային։

Poem on Abraham, Sahak, Melchizedek, Lot

1. Father Abraham, I say, (was) son of Terah,
   In whom is service of God (piety),
   Concerning the flocks of crows in the fields,[5]
   Who mentioned God on high and the ravens fled.
2. Then there came to (his) mind the clear thought,
   (That) it is the Creator, God, who does miracles.
   He burnt the house of idols secretly in the night,
   And the inventor of the mule perished with it.[6]
3. By Mamrē the flock of sheep was revealed,
   The Lord and two seraphs in human form,[7]
   With whitened hair like a flower,[8]
   Which was not seen as white until Abraham.[9]

---

5. This is a plural արտորայ + նի plural suffix; no locative ending was added because the monorhyme needs to be preserved (Th. M. van Lint: oral communication). On the incident of the crows, see text no. 2.3 note.

6. On this legend, see text no. 2.6. It is an explanation of the death of (H)Achan, Abraham's brother.

7. Here the poet appears to identify the three old men who accosted Mamrē with the three men of the Annunciation to Abraham; cf. text no. 6.4.4. This connection is not made in the other texts.

8. Mamrē and his sheep turning white (text no. 2.9–10 and note) are conflated with Abraham's being the first with white hair (text no. 4.28). This latter incident uses the same term for flowering as text no. 4.28.

9. Abraham was the first to have grey hair; see text no. 2.11 and note.

4. He who established the true faith,
   Sat with guests when mealtime came around,[10]
   Until the Lord pitied his work,[11]
   (And) came with two seraphs to the meal.[12]
5. And He promised him a firstborn son,
   He who came incarnated to his (i.e., Abraham's) sons.
   Unleavened bread, wine, and calf he (Abraham) slaughtered for the meal,
   As type of unleavened (wafer) (and) chalice of the Mass.[13]
6. Seven[14] trials which passed over the father of faith,
   And the sojourning in a foreign land;
   Hagar the maidservant of Pharaoh;
   And calling his wife, sister, is written in the book.
7. Having begotten his son Isaac from barren Sarah,
   The Lord tested Abraham, asking for the youth,
   Then he (Abraham) took up the wood of his sacrifice,
   Brought (it) forth to Golgotha, a type of the Cross.[15]
8. He bound his son Sahak, he placed (him) on the altar,
   He took the blade, he wished to slaughter his son,
   An angel appeared to Father Abraham,
   He said, "Lay not the sword upon the youth."[16]

---

10. Note the stress in text no. 2.14 on Abraham and Sarah's standing by the table and serving the three visitors; cf. Gen 18:8, "and he stood by them under the tree while they ate."

11. Or: "creation." Satan's stopping guests arriving is assumed but not mentioned (text no. 2.12).

12. On the identity of the three "men," see text no. 2.12 note.

13. In fact, in the biblical text, wine is not mentioned.

14. Ten is the usual number of the trials; see the General Introduction above, p. 21; texts nos. 5.1–2 and 14.11–12. However, the next three lines of this stanza list another three trials, thus making ten. Two of these, the sojourning and Hagar are in the list in text no. 5.2; cf. text no. 14. "Calling his wife sister" is not included in those lists, though the Abimelech incident is.

15. The sacrifice of Isaac took place, in this view, on Golgotha, which doubly emphasizes that Isaac's sacrifice was a type of Christ's. On Golgotha in such contexts, see the General Introduction, p. 29 and n. 34, text no. 14 and especially text no. 7 and its sections 3 and 14. *Palaea* 229 also implies this. Earlier, in *Jub.* 18:13, it is said to be Mount Zion. Melchizedek is on the Mount of Olives; see text no. 6.11.3 below and text no. 7.6; see also the General Introduction above, p. 12, n. 32. The carrying of the wood is a type of Christ's carrying the cross; see Kessler 2004, 112. Isaac as a type of Christ is naturally a very common motif in patristic literature; see, e.g., Origen, *Hom. in Gen.* 8.6–9 (see Petit 1991–96, frg. 1252); Ephrem the Syrian, *Commentary on Genesis* 20.3 (Mathews and Amar 1994, 169); John Chrysostom, *Hom. Gen.* 47.14; Cyril of Alexandria, *Glaphyra* (*PG* 69:140A).

16. Cf. Gen 22:12.

6. POEM ON ABRAHAM, ISAAC, MELCHIZEDEK, LOT   91

9. He showed him the tree of Sabek,[17] which is in that place,
   And a ram was hung by its two horns.[18]
   He went forth upon the flat rock,[19]
   He took Abel's ram,[20] slaughtered it in the place.
10. He praised the Lord God, merciful to men,
    Who at every time hunts[21] men for the good,
    That is the worship of the supernal glory,
    Which by faith he encounters in his heart.
11. He pointed out Melchizedek who was in the forest,
    He said, "I wandered; you bore in (your) turn,"[22]
    He came to the Mount of Olives to the bushy wood,
    He called his name at the Lord's command.
12. So that he might become a godly priest,
    And for seven years[23] for which he was unseen by men,
    On account of terror, through fear of the Creator,
    And on account of the swallowing up of (his) parents and land.[24]
13. Father Abraham went according to the commandment,
    He did this according to the Lord's command,
    Behold, he praised the living Lord with his spirit,
    Just as the wonders of the Creator were heard in order.[25]
14. Again, Father Abraham went to him,[26]

---

17. See text no. 7, below.
18. Gen 22:15. According to rabbinic sources, the ram was special, one of ten things created on the evening of the sixth day of creation; see *ARN* B.37; *Tanḥuma Vayera'* 23. Its horn will be blown before God to mark the redemption (ibid.). See also *Gen. Rab.* 66:13. The same idea is found in *Tĕ'ĕzāza Sanbat* (Leslau 1951, 28).
19. This feature is not in Gen 22.
20. In Islamic sources, as here, Abraham's ram is the same animal that was sacrificed by Abel; so Ibn 'Abbas cited by Firestone 1990, 129–30. In our texts, Abel's ram is not only identified with that offered by Abraham, but in other texts also with the heifer that Abraham slaughtered for the three men; see on this beast, texts nos. 8.32, 11.27, 11A.28, and 15.28–29. The point appears to be the perfect nature of the sacrificial victim—Abel's, Abraham's, and God's sacrifice of his Son. The Qur'an also knows that this is a choice calf; see 51:24–30 and later Islamic sources cited by Firestone 1990, 55–57. A similar identification is made in *PRE* 30, where Abraham's donkey in the Aqedah is identified with Moses' donkey (Exod 4:20) and the Messiah's donkey (Zech 9:9).
21. That is, in a trial or test. This may be a deliberate reversal of the image of Satan as hunter or fisherman of souls.
22. This line is obscure. Th. M. van Lint suggests, "I offered/gave; you suffer(ed) in your turn".
23. The *Palaea* 210 has forty years for this period.
24. This is, of course, a reference to the Story of Melchizedek; see the General Introduction, 8–12; see texts nos. 7, 11.46–54, and 11A.46–54.
25. Or: "in the poem"; see §17.1 below for this meaning of "order."
26. Here the difficulty of sequence is dealt with. Melchizedek is connected with

      When he cut down abominable Gomorrah,
      With three hundred and eighteen souls,
      In the pattern of the holy fathers in Nicaea.[27]

15. Just as he pursued the abominable Gomorrah,
      The holy fathers loved those who had fallen away from God,[28]
      They were fed unleavened bread in wine,
      The holy fathers averred the bread of life.[29]

16. Which the immortal King, their Creator,
      Made us worthy of body, of blood,
      Carer for Christians on the fearful day,
      He will have mercy, he saves us from Gehenna.[30]

---------------------------------[31]

17. I wish to remember (mention) Lot in the poem,[32]
      For he was Father Abraham's brother's son,
      The Lord said, "I am wroth at the action of Sodom,
      The unspeakable evils that in it were done."[33]

18. Abraham beseeched the Lord of all,
      "Be not angry, Lord, with the whole city,
      There are many righteous in it,
      Let them not be destroyed together."[34]

19. The Lord said, "There is no good person in it,
      But I only found Lot righteous in it.
      I will send an angel (with) a message,
      And I free him from punishment."[35]

---

the incident of the four kings, which is much before the revelation of Melchizedek in the apocryphal story, where it follows the Binding of Isaac.

27. Athanasius (*Ad Afros epistola synodica* 2) says that there were 318 bishops present at the Council of Nicaea. In *Barn.* 9, the letters IH = Jesus are interpreted as 318. In early Armenian literature, 318 bishops are mentioned, but they are not related to Abraham's servants. The connection with Nicaea is found in the pseudo-Athanasian Greek text; see Böttrich (2010, 7, 14–15), who traces this tradition back to the fourth century C.E. (p. 66 and note on p. 105, where he adduces numerous sources).

28. I am indebted to Th. M. van Lint for this proposed translation. The typology is somewhat forced.

29. The bread and wine that Melchizedek fed Abraham, the type of the Eucharist, were life saving as were the dogmatic asseverations of the Nicene Creed and council.

30. The verb tenses here are somewhat confused. The "fearful day" is the day of judgment.

31. A new section, a poem about Lot, starts here with an enlarged initial. §16 formed an appropriate final subscription of the Abraham poem.

32. Literally: "order."

33. Gen 18:20.

34. Gen 18:23–32; "together" means "the righteous and the wicked together."

35. This divine address is an addition to the biblical narrative. Text no. 2.17 says that there were four righteous, "Lot and his wife, and the daughters."

20. Two angels received a command from the Creator,
    They entered the city of Sodom in human form.[36]
    They entered Lot's house in the form of strangers,
    And Lot preserved them from Sodom's evil.[37]
21. The angel said that wrath had come upon Sodom,
    "Arise, go forth from this city," lest they perish.[38]
    He brought forth Lot with his household from that city.
    Then fog and storm surrounded Sodom.[39]
22. Fire and sulphur descended upon the city,[40]
    And the deeps were split and water flowed forth.
    The storm of smoke boiled[41] as it dripped down,
    Cry and rumbling, terrible and fearsome.
23. But the wife of righteous Lot looked back,
    Her mind was toward Sodom for evil.
    She turned into a pillar of salt, her body petrified.[42]
    They, astounded, left her, went.
24. We beseech God the Father and the Spirit,
    To save us, we beg, from the punishment of sins.
    Yovasapʻ unworthy, with works of Sodom,
    And grown strong in sins among men.

---

36. This is implied by Genesis.
37. Gen 19:3–9. Alternatively, translate "from evil Sodom."
38. Gen 19:12; 19:15.
39. This detail is not found in the Bible.
40. Gen 19:24. The splitting of the deep is not mentioned.
41. Gen 19:28
42. Gen 19:26.

7. The Tree of Sabek and Melchizedek

For a general description of the manuscript BLEgerton 708 and its various habits, scribal and orthographic, see the introduction to text no. 4 above, which is drawn from the same manuscript. The present text is found on fols. 80r–81v quite independently of text no. 4. It differs from it, in that its contents are further from the biblical text than those of text no. 4 and include many extrabiblical elements.

This document presents a combination of various traditions. It opens with an apocryphal genealogy of Melchizedek: viz., Arpachshad, Salim, Melkʻi, and Sēdēk. Sēdēk is then invoked, together with Shem, to explain the burial sites of Adam and Eve, Adam's head on Golgotha, and Eve's remains in the grotto in Bethlehem.[1] Odd onomastic traditions are found in these sections, one of Palestine as "Place of Arena"; Golgotha is called "heart of earth."[2]

Then elements related to the Melchizedek story are invoked: God ordained Sēdēk as a priest on the Mount of Olives and renamed him Melchizedek. He planted a cypress on Golgotha to honor Adam's grave.[3] That tree became called "Tree of Sēdēk." This tree is identified with the Tree of Sabek[4] (see text no. 6.14) as the place where Abraham offered Isaac.[5]

---

1. See Stone 2000a. The *Book of the Bee* (Budge 1886, 33–34) strongly asserts that Melchizedek had parents but that they are not mentioned in Genesis. On Melchizedek's genealogy, see Böttrich 2010, 86 note 1,2 a. The main point he makes is the tension between the genealogy and Heb 7:3, which we too have noted above. See further Böttrich (2010, 63), who discerns in the very existence of a genealogy an argument for the ultimately Jewish origin of the material.

2. It is not clear that "How far, Shem?" is indeed an onomastic explanation of the name "Jerusalem"; see §4 below.

3. *Adam Fragment 2*, §8 preserves the tradition of a tree from Eden planted on Adam's grave (Stone 1982a, 11). This is part of the Rood Tree legend, discussed below in a note on §10. See further Stone 2000a.

4. See text 5, Introduction, and text no. 4.22, and note there on the origin of this name, and text no. 6.9.1. See text no. 4.22.

5. Oxford, Bodleian Arm f 11 (1651–1656), fols. 93r–94, contains an incomplete copy of the Story of Melchizedek; see Conybeare 1913, cols. 115–16. We made some manual copies of the *incipit* and *explicit* some decades ago, which read: . . . 93r լայր դառնապէս. աւէ հայրն իմ ըևդ մօրն իմոյ ըևդէր լաս. զի վիճակ արկցուբ ի վերայ Բ որդոց մերոց ում ելցէ վիճակն զևա զեևգուբ. երբ որ վիճակն արկ նորա եկաւ հայրն մի. այսպէս թուբր թէ վիճակն ինչ անկանէր ի մեռանել վասն կոցև. դարձեալ երեբ անգամ վիճակ արկին. վիճակն անկանէր եղրօրև իմ մեռանել վասն կոցև ... *explicit*: fol. 93v զի այս եղեւ առաջի բահանայ եւ առաջի պատարագող հացիւ եւ զինով. զի մելքիսեդեկ

7. TREE OF SABEK AND MELCHIZEDEK

A vine went forth and eventually joined with the cypress,[6] and the wine that Melchizedek offered Abraham came from grapes from this wondrous tree-vine. The wine and bread that Melchizedek offered Abraham were the Eucharist. In §16 there is a tradition about Joseph's tree, and the text concludes with further traditions about the tree.

It is notable that the basic Melchizedek material of this text is developed from the Genesis narrative, with the addition of some apocryphal embroidery and the strong tradition of the Rood Tree from the Garden together with a Christian typology. The legend of Melchizedek is discussed above in the General Introduction.[7]

Պատմութիւն վասն ծառոյն Սաբեկայ:

1. Յետ ջրհեղեղին. Սէմ Նոյեա որդին. ծնաւ զԱրփաքսաթ: Եւ Արփաքսաթ ծնաւ զՍաղիմ: Սաղիմ ծնաւ զՍադայ: Սադայ ծնաւ զՄելքին: Մելքին ծնաւ զՍեդեկ:

2. Եւ իբրեւ եղեւ Սեդեկ ամաց երեսնից. առ Սէմ ընդ իւր զՍեդեկ. եւ երկուսն բերին զնշխարսն Ադամայ: եւ Յեւայի. յերկիրն Պաղեստին. որ թարքմանի տեղի ասպարիսի:

3. Եւ ի այրն Բեդղէեմի եդին զնշխարսն Յեւայի: եւ ի լեառն Սիոփա զնշխարսն Ադամայ. եւ զգլուխն ի Գողգոթայ որ է բարձրագոյն. եւ կոչի սիրտ երկրի:

4. Եւ ասէ Սեդեկ մինչեւ ուր Սէմ[8] վասն տանելոյն զլխոյն Ադամայ ի Սիոնէ ի Գողգոթայ. Եւ կոչեցո անուն տեղւոյն Յերուսաղէմ:

5. Եւ հրամանաւ Սէմայ մնաց Սեդեկ անդ միայնացեալ: Քանզի ոչ որ գոյր այնմ վայրի. ոչ մարդ եւ ոչ անասուն եւ ոչ սողուն: Այլ հրեշտակք պահէին զնա: Եւ / fol. 80v / կացեալ անդ երիս ամիս:

6. Եւ եկեալ առ Սեդեկ Աստուած Բանն եւ կոչեալ եհան զնա ի սուրբ լեառն ձիթենեաց: Եւ եղեալ զաշն աստուածային ի վերայ զլխոյն նորայ.

7. Եւ ետ նմա զաւծումն քահանայութեան եւ զպատիւ թագաւորութեան. եւ կոչեաց զնա մականուամբ հօրն Մելքիսեդէկ. աւրինակ իւր զոր ասէ Դաւիթ: Դու ես քահանա յաւիտեան ըստ կարգի Մելքիսեդէկի:

8. Ուստի եւ ի բազմանալ ազգի մարդկան եկեալ որդիքն Սէմայ ի վիճակ ժառանգութեան իւրեանց աշխարհին Պաղեստին. եւ արարին շէնս եւ քաղաքս ամուրս. եւ գեօղս եւ յագարակս:

եղեւ առաջին քահանայն որ օրինակ էր քրիստոսի. Զի ադամայ մինչեւ աբրահամ քահանայ հրեշտակ էր. այլ մարմնաւոր քահանայ ոչ կայր ադամայ եւ աբէլի եւ եւայի երիցութիւն եւ այլոցն ամենեցուն հրեշտակք արարին:

   6. See §12 and note there.
   7. See the General Introduction, 8–12.
   8. This is apparently a wordplay rather than an etymology: Armenian (*minč'ew*) **ur Sēm** being seen as "(until) Jerusalem" and not just "(until) where Sēm?".

9. Տնկեցին այգիս. ճիթենիս. եւ թզենիս հանդերձ ամենայն պտղաբերաւք:
10. Ընդ որս եւ ինքն Մեղիսեդեկ ի Գողգոթայ ի վերայ գազաթանն Ադամ տնկեաց ուղէշ մի կիպարեայ ի պատիւ գերեզմանին Ադամայ: Զոր եհատ ինքնին ձեռօքն իւրովք ի մայրիցն Լիբանանու եւ բերեալ տնկեաց ի Գողգոթայ:
11. Եւ եղեւ ծառ մեծ եւ գեղեցիկք[9] հովանի առնելով զլխոյն Ադամայ եւ ամենեքին քայլին առ նայ եւ հանգչէին ընդ / fol. 81r / հովանեաւ նորա. եւ կոչեցին զայն ծառ Սեդեկի՝[10] քանզի Սեդեկ տնկեաց զնա:
12. Այլ եւ ի խնամոցն Աստուծոյ էր ուր մի խադողոյ ընդ ծառոյն կիպարեայ եւ պատուաստեալ միաւորեցաւ ի նմայ. եւ աճեալ ընդ ծառոյն ծածկեաց զծառն. Եւ տայր պտուղ բազում եւ ողկոյզս մեծամեծս եւ գեղեցկատեսիլս եւ քաղցրահամս. եւ եղեն երկուսն մի ծառ պատուաստելով որթոյն ընդ կիպարոյն:
13. Եւ եղեւ զի եհատ Մեղքիսեդեկ ի ծառոյն խադողոյ եւ շինեաց գինի՝ եւ տարեալ մատոյց Աբրահամու. եւ հատ[11] բաղարջ կոտորեալ ի ներս յորժամ զայր ի կոտորածէ թազաւորացն:
14. զոր առեալ Աբրահամու հաղորդեցաւ ինքն. եւ ԳՃԺԸ զաւրականքն իւր ընդ նմա: Եւ եղեւ ըստ աւետեացն Աբրահամու ի Սառայէ որդի Իսահակ եւ Աբրահամու լցեալ հաւատով. առեալ զԻսահակ որդին իւր եւ տարեալ ի նոյն տեղին Գողգոթայ եհան ի սեղան Տեառն յոշակէզու:
15. Զոր եւ ի սոյն ծառոյ կախեցաւ խոյն յեղջերացն փոխանակ Իսահակայ. որ գուշակեաց Քրիստոս ի խաչին, ի / fol. 81v / նոյն տեղի Գողգոթային: այլ եւ գինին եւ հաց բաղարջին զոր տարաւ Մեղքիսեդեկ Աբրահամին աւրինակ մարմնոյ եւ արեանն Քրիստոսի:
16. Եւ ծառն կացեալ մաացեալ եհաս մինչեւ ի Յովսեփի. եւ եղեւ տեղին ծառովն Յովսեփիայ՝ զոր քահանայապետքն առ ատելութեան Յովսեփիա հատին զծառն զի իբրեւ զդէտ էր բուրաստանի նորա:
17. Եւ հրեայքն ձեռացուցին զայն խաչ ի նոյն տեղին որ վերստին պտղաբերեաց. եւ եբեր պտուղ անմահութեան զՔրիստոս որդին Աստուծոյ ի փրկութիւն աշխարհի:
18. Եւ դարձեալ ասեն թէ ի դրախտէն Ադամայ բերաւ ի հրեշտակաց ճիւղն այն տնկեցաւ ի մայրսն Լիբանանու, եւ անտի բերաւ ձեռամբն Մեղքիսեդեկի ի սուրբ լեառն Սիովփի. ի սուրբ Գողգոթայ որ եղեւ փրկութիւն ի նմանէ բոլոր տանս Ադամայ եւ ծննդոց նորա. որ է աւրհնեալ յաւիտեանս ամէն:

---

9. This is formally a plural. However, the final ք is produced by phonetic corruption of the final palatal; see Stone and Hillel 2012, Index of Variants, s.v.

10. Unclear variant in the manuscript.

11. Probably corrupt for hաց.

7. TREE OF SABEK AND MELCHIZEDEK

Story Concerning the Tree of Sabek

1. After the Flood, Shem, son of Noah, begot Arpachshad.[12] And Arpachshad begot Saɫim, Saɫim begot Saɫa.[13] Saɫa begot Melkʻi. Melkʻi begot Sēdēk.[14]
2. And when Sēdēk was thirty years old,[15] Shem[16] took Sēdēk with him and those two brought the remains of Adam and Eve[17] to the land of Palestine, which is translated, "place of arena."[18]

---

12. Gen 11:10. It is noteworthy that in this Melchizedek story that he has a genealogy, in light of Heb 7:3, where he is said to be "without father, without mother, without genealogy." See above in the introduction to this text.

13. Gen 11:12 deals with Shelah, which name is Saɫa in the Armenian Bible. Saɫim is a duplicate variant of Saɫa, influenced, doubtless by "Shalem." From this point on the genealogy is not biblical. An analogous, but not identical, genealogy is found in the pseudo-Athanasian recension of *Story of Melchizedek* 1.1 (Böttrich 2010, 85–86).

14. The figure of Melkʻi is not biblical. In the Bible, in addition to Melchizedek there is Adoni-Zedek in Josh 10:1 (see van der Toorn, Becking, and van der Horst 1995, 1750–58). A Melchi is mentioned in the genealogy of Luke 3:24 and 3:28, but he is different from this figure. This genealogy, however, has several points in common with that put forward by John Malalas in his *Chronicle* (sixth century C.E.). Melchizedek, according to Malalas, is the second name of Sedek, son of Melchi, founder of Salem on Mount Sion. Melchi was a descendant of Sidos, son of the emperor of Libya. The incident of Abraham and the story of Melchizedek's ascetic life are not given. See Jeffreys 1986, 28, §§57–58.

15. The age of thirty was considered auspicious; see Stone, 1996a, 18, 204, and the literature is extensive. For example, Joseph became viceroy of Egypt at thirty; see text no. 5.7. Similarly, Christ was baptized at the age of thirty; see Stone 2006a, 204; Adam was created at the age of thirty, according to Aṙakʻel Siwnecʻi, *Adamgirkʻ* 1.22.35 (Stone 2007, 212), and other sources.

16. The occurrence of Shem here is notable. By the genealogy given here, Sēdēk is the fifth generation from Shem; compare *Book of the Bee* (Budge 1886, 34); cf. *Cave of Treasures* (Budge 1927, 126–27): "And Shem took the body of Adam and Melchizedek, . . . And when they arrived at Gâghûltâ (Golgotha), which is the centre of the earth, the Angel of the Lord showed Shem the place [for the body of Adam]. And when Shem had deposited the body of our father Adam upon that the four quarters [of the earth] separated themselves from each other, and the earth opened itself in the form of a cross, and Shem and Melchizedek deposited the body of Adam there (i.e., in the cavity). And as soon as they had laid it therein, the four quarters [of the earth] drew quickly together, and enclosed the body of our father Adam, and the door of the created world was shut fast. And that place was called 'Ḵarkaphtâ' (*i.e.* 'Skull'), because the head of all the children of men was deposited there. And it was called 'Gâghûltâ,' because it was round [like the head], and 'Reṣîphtâ' (i.e., a trodden-down thing), because the head of the accursed serpent, that is to say, Satan, was crushed there, and 'Gefîftâ' (Gabbatha), because all the nations were to be gathered together to it." The points of similarity with our text are quite striking. On the onomastic etymology of Golgotha, see Wutz 1914–15, 649, 711, 881, 1027.

17. See *PRE* 20; Stone 1996a, 116–17; Stone 2006, 141–45.

18. In OnaV 152 we find մոխրով արկեալ ("Cast with ashes") as also in Wutz 1914–15, 438). This makes no obvious sense. "Place of arena" may be connected with Latin *palaestra* < Greek παλαίστρα.

3. And in the cave of Bethlehem they placed Eve's remains and on Mount Zion, Adam's remains,[19] and (his) head in Golgotha, which is the highest and is called "heart of earth".[20]
4. And Sēdēk said, "Unto where, Shem?" on account of bringing Adam's head from Zion to Golgotha.[21] And the name of the place was called Jerusalem.
5. And at Shem's command, Sēdēk remained there alone, for there was no-one in that place, not man, nor beast, not crawling thing. But the angels guarded him, who remained there for three months.[22]
6. And God the Word came to Sēdēk and having summoned (him) he brought him forth to the holy Mount of Olives. And having placed his divine right hand upon his head
7. he also gave him the anointing of priesthood and the honor of kingship.[23] And he called him by his father's name, Melchizedek. His example, which David said, (is), "You are a priest forever according to the order of Melchizedek" (Psalm 110:4).
8. Thence also when the race of men multiplied, the sons of Shem came to the portion of their inheritance, the land of Palestine[24] and they made buildings and stout cities and villages and fields.
9. They planted vines, olive trees, and fig trees as well as all fruit-bearing trees.
10. Along with these, Melchizedek himself also planted a branch of a cypress in Golgotha, at Adam's peak, to honor Adam's grave. He cut this himself with his hands from the forests of Lebanon and, having brought (it), planted (it) in Golgotha.[25]

---

19. See Stone 2000a, 241–45.

20. Note the location of Golgotha on the Mount of Olives, which is part of the procedure of this text, which tends to identify a number of holy places or sites of biblical events with one another. On Golgotha and Jerusalem, see texts nos. 6.7.4, 7.18, and 14.13 and notes there. In some versions of the story found in the *Palaea*, the event took place on Mount Taburion, surely Mount Tabor, which is there related to the Mount of Olives (p. 206). A fragment cited from Xosrow, Rhetor of the Armenians (otherwise unidentified) by Vardan Aygkec'i (1170?–1235) states, "Melchizedek distributed unleavened bread and uncorrupted wine upon the tomb of Adam, which shows the uncorrupt coming of our God from heaven" (K'ēosēyan and Hayrapetean 1988, 405). Rather than being a reference to the ascetic Melchizedek, this appears to be an interpretation of Gen 14.

21. Usually, the oldest witness to this idea is said to be Origen on Matt 27:33. See Golgotha, *IDB* 2:439; and see the preceding note.

22. This incident has no parallel in the texts examined here; it may, of course, occur in other sources.

23. This ceremony of consecration of a priest has three elements: laying on of hands, anointing, and royal honor. In §7 there is also a renaming. The role of Ps 110:4 is well known in Melchizedek traditions.

24. Contrast Gen 10:31–32; see *Sons of Noah* §1 in Stone 1981, 224–25. Is there some reminiscence of the tradition that the Sethites lived on mountains? See Stone 1996a, 205.

25. On the role of cypress and cedar trees, see Stone (In press A). The connection of the tree and Adam's grave figures quite often elsewhere; see, e.g., *Adam Fragment 2* (Stone

7. TREE OF SABEK AND MELCHIZEDEK 99

11. And it became a great and beautiful tree, making shelter for Adam's head. And all came to it and rested under its shade.[26] And they called that "The Tree of Sēdēk," because Sēdēk planted it.
12. But through God's care there went forth a branch of a vine joined with the cypress tree, it was united in it. And having grown with (the) tree, it hid the tree. And it gave much fruit and bunches of grapes, very great and beautiful-looking and sweet tasting. And the two became one tree of joined vine with the cypress.[27]
13. And it came to pass that Melchizedek took from the grapes of the tree and made wine. And having brought it he offered it to Abraham.[28] And he broke unleavened bread[29] beneath (it) when he (i.e., Abraham) came from cutting down the kings.[30]
14. Abraham, having taken it, he himself communicated[31] and his 318 soldiers with him. And, according to the good news (Annunciation)[32] Abraham had a son from Sarah, Isaac. And Abraham, filled with faith, took Isaac his son and brought him to the same place of Golgotha. He offered (him) as a sacrifice on the Lord's altar.[33]
15. Also from this same tree the ram was hung by the horns in place of Isaac,

---

1982a, 10–11). Cypress is one of the three woods of the Rood Tree. Most typically, the cedar is associated with the forests of Lebanon; however, in general this text shows little knowledge of the actual geography of the Holy Land.

26. Here features of the World Tree may be observed. The fruitful garden described in §9 is also an evocation of Eden. On both of these topics, see Stordalen 2000.

27. Compare the vine and the cedar in Ps 80:8–10; the cypress and vine do not occur together in the Hebrew Bible. See Stone, In press A, 8–9, but we noted above that here the cypress has assumed some of the cedar's qualities. Note Stordalen's remark (2000, 173).

28. See Gen 14:18. Vardan Aygkec'i (in K'eosēyan and Hayrapetyan 1988. 405) quotes a fragment from a certain Xosrov Rhetor of the Armenians whose identity unclear:

Մելքիսեդեկ հաց բաղարջ եւ անապական գինին բաշխեր ի վերա գերեզմանին Ադամայ, որ ցուցանէ զանապական գալուստն Աստուծոյ մերոյ յերկնից:

Melchizedek distributed unleavened bread an uncorrupted wine upon the tomb of Adam, which shows the uncorrupt coming of our God from heaven.

29. There is a strange orthography of this word; see n. 11, above. The element "unleavened" is added to the biblical "bread," because of the typology of the Eucharist. On the issue of leaven, Melchizedek's bread, and the Eucharistic wafers, see Böttrich 2010, 45–46.

30. This incident, described in Gen 14, is scarcely raised in the Armenian Abraham texts published here.

31. That is, received communion. This makes the eucharistic nature of Melchizedek's wine and bread offering to Abraham explicit; see the General Introduction, 9.

32. See Gen 18:10. This Annunciation by the three angels described in Genesis is seen as a precursor of the annunciation of Christ's birth; see Luke 1:26–38. Isaac is identified elsewhere as a type of Christ; see texts nos. 4.24 and 11.46, and the General Introduction, 1–2, 11.

33. Note the concentration and overlaying of sacred places and sacred acts, typical of this document; see p. 99, n. 21 above.

which foretold Christ on the Cross, in the same place of Golgotha.[34] But also the wine and unleavened bread, which Abraham brought to Melchizedek is a type of the body and blood of Christ.

16. And the tree remained and stayed until Joseph. And the place was near Joseph's tree, which tree the high priests in the hatred of Joseph cut down, for it was like a guard of his garden.[35]
17. And the Jews formed that cross in the same place, which again bore fruit and bore fruit of immortality, Christ son of God, for the redemption of the world.[36]
18. And again they say that from Adam's garden that branch was brought by angels, (and) it was planted in the forests of Lebanon. And then it was brought by the hands of Melchizedek to the holy Mount Zion, to holy Golgotha from which salvation came about for all the house of Adam and his descendants.[37] Which is blessed forever. Amen.

---

34. Isaac was a type of Christ; see above, text no. 4.24. Zak'aria Catholicos (ninth century) says that the cross was erected on the site of the Tree of Sabek and the ram (see *MH* ninth century, 196 and 227, 230).

35. This does not refer to an incident in a canonical Gospel.

36. The typology of the tree is extended here.

37. Here Golgotha, already identified with the Mount of Olives and the Tree of Sabek, is also identified with Mount Zion. The narrative is part of the Rood Tree legends, also known in other forms in Armenian, and in many other languages. See Stone 1982a, 11–12 (*Adam Fragment 2* 9–11; *Words of Adam to Seth* 6.13). See in general, Napier 1894; Quinn 1962; and Murdoch 2000, 142–51. An associated legend of three trees—pine, cedar, and cypress—found by the Nile, which flowed from paradise, may be observed in *Palaea* 218 and other sources.

8. Story of the Holy Father Abraham and of Isaac, His son, and of Mamrē, His Servant

Recension A

This document is a narrative not very different in overall character from text no. 4. We have two manuscript copies of it at our disposal. The first copy is Bibliothèque nationale de France BnF186 dated 1618, fols. 187v–192v.[1] The manuscript is a Miscellany and in addition to *Story of the Holy Father Abraham*, it contains a mixture of astronomical, apotropaic, homiletic, and other texts, including embroideries on biblical stories. *Story of the Holy Father Abraham* is followed by *The Wisdom of Ahikar* and preceded by philosophical admonitions.[2] The manuscript is in *notrgir* script.

Erevan Matenadaran M0569 is also a Miscellany.[3] It was written in Lwow, Poland in 1618 and contains a variety of works, chiefly of ecclesiastical interest. *Story of the Holy Father Abraham* is the only work of its genre in the manuscript, and it occurs on fols. 254v–267v. It is followed by a chronological text starting from Abraham. The manuscript is written in *notrgir* script. It is quite remarkable that the two manuscripts were written in the same year.

The variants between the two manuscripts are not very significant, and there are no groups of readings that lead us to an absolute preference of one manuscript over the other on textual grounds. The decision to use BnF186 as the text is fairly arbitrary. This manuscript is written in a less "normative" form of medieval Armenian than M0569 particularly as regards orthography.[4] Since M0569 also has a number of non-normative forms, we have assumed that these are more original to this document and that M0569 is somewhat "classicizing."[5]

I have, therefore, prepared a diplomatic edition of the text of BnF186 and I have included occasional readings from M0569 in the text. Such instances are

---

1. Kévorkian and Ter-Stépanian 1998, 725.
2. For the Armenian text of Ahikar, see Martirosyan 1969–72.
3. Ēganyan et al. 2004, cols. 1303–6.
4. I express my thanks to Dr. G. Muradyan of Erevan, who verified my collation of BnF186.
5. This is not a necessary conclusion from this situation. The differences that would be engendered by using M0569 would have minor impact on the narrative, though they would affect aspects of style and orthography.

clearly marked and noted. Consequently, in the *apparatus criticus* the lemma is usually the reading of BnF186, while the variant following the square bracket is drawn from M0569. Any other situation is marked distinctly. The apparatus follows upon the text and is itself followed by the translation.

Another recension of this work is preserved in M3411. This manuscript is only partially at my disposal, and I give it following the present document, as text no. 9. M10561, which contains excerpts of text no. 8 including Պատմութիւն հօրն Աբրահամու: Աբրահամու հօրն Թարայ էր *Story of the Father Abraham. Abraham's Father was Terah* is described in the Appendix below. This text starts on fol. 133v and continues to the text corresponding to the end of section 6 of text no. 8. Then, on fol. 134v we find Պատմութիւն Սահակայ որդոյ Աբրահամու զոր խոստացեալ էր Աստուծոյ մատաղ առնել *Story of Sahak, son of Abraham, whom he promised to make an offering to God*, which corresponds text no. 8.31–32.

ORTHOGRAPHIC VARIANTS

The chief consistent orthographic variants between the manuscripts are included in the following lists. Such orthographic variants are not noted in the apparatus except in cases in which they are in some other way unusual.

այ / ա
աւ / օ
եա / ե
էր / էր
է / ի
թ / դ especially in երթամ / երդամ
ոյ / ու
չ / շ

CONTENTS OF STORY OF HOLY FATHER ABRAHAM

The main topics of this work are the following:

- Abraham breaks the idols (1–3)
- The crows and Abraham's prayer and recognition of God (4–6)
- Abraham in Egypt (7–14, in much greater detail than Gen 12.[6]
- Abraham returns to Jerusalem; the birth of Ishmael; Ishmael is three years old (15–16)
- The Story of Mamrē (17–24)

---

6. O. Ableman has pointed out that this whole section seems to be influenced or inspired by the story of Joseph and his brothers in Gen 42–44.

8. STORY OF ABRAHAM, ISAAC, AND MAMRĒ

- Abraham's hospitality and the blocking of the road (25)
- The three visitors and their meal (25)
- The Annunciation to Abraham and Sarah's laughter (25–27)
- Prophecy of enslavement in Egypt (28)
- The resurrection of the calf and the proof of divinity (29)
- Sin and punishment of Sodom, not including the story of Lot (29–30)
- Sacrifice of Isaac (31–32)
- Chronology of the patriarchs (33)

Պատմութիւն սուրբ հօրն Աբրահամայ եւ Սահակայ որդոյ նորա, եւ Մամբրէի ծառայի իւրոյ

1. Աբրահամու հաւրն անուն Թարայ էր. Աբրահամ յորժամ տղայ էր. նայ հայր նորա կուռք շինէր. յաւուր միում բարձել էր Աբրահամ. զկուռքն⁷ պարկով ի վերայ իշոյ. եւ կու տանէր ի ծախ եւ էշն ընկաւ ի շախխին⁸ մէջն եւ կուռքն ամեն չարդեցան⁹ եւ շուդախ¹⁰ եղեն.
2. Աբրահամա խիստ. բարկացաւ եւ վախեց ի հաւրէն. եւ ասաց կռօցն եւ վայ ու եղուկ ի ձեր վերայ ինչ չաստուած էք դուք: որ չի¹¹ պահեցէք գձէզ ի այնմ շադախէ որպէս պատասխանի տվից հաւրս կամ որպիսի աւգնականութիւն գտից ի ձէնջ. Բարկացաւ յուժ¹² եւ զամէնն. չար<դ>եաց¹³ եւ ի շողախին¹⁴ ընկղղմեց եւ ասաց յայտ որ էք յարժանի. որ ի շախիդ¹⁵ մէջն պարկիք եւ գնաց ի տուն իշովս սրտնեդ եւ դառնացեալ յոյժ. Եւ տեսեալ հաւրն Դար/ fol. 188r /այի¹⁶ գորդին իւր սրտնեդ. եւ դառնացեալ յոյժ ասաց Աւրամ ինչ սրտնեդես:
3. Պատասպանի ետ հաւրն եւ ասէ գնացի ի Ա շադախի մս հանդ<իպ>եցայ¹⁷ ի Ճանբանն եւ էշն իմ ոչ կարաց. անցանել ընկաւ էշն շադախին մէջն եւ մեր չաստուածքն կոտորեցան. եւ ես. սիրտնեդ եղայ եւ բարկացայ յոյժ եւ ասացի ցնոսա թէ ձեր գօրութիւնն այս է

---

7. ո written above the ը; cf. above and apparatus.
8. Corrupt for շադախին.
9. For չարդեցան. There are many unusual spellings in BnF186; see the introductory remarks above.
10. Read as շադախ.
11. For չի and the variation չ / շ is frequent.
12. For յոյժ and often ոյ / ու.
13. Emending չարեաց and so M0569.
14. For շադախն.
15. So both manuscripts, for շադախիդ.
16. For Թարայի.
17. BnF186 reads հանդեցայ, corruptly; see M0569.

քարեր առի ի ձեռս եւ զամէնն չարդեցի. եւ դարտակ¹⁸ եկի ի տունն. եւ ասէ հայր այս մեր աստուածցն գործութիւն ինչ է. որ զԱ էշն չի պահեց. որ ի շախէն անցել էր. ու ինքն ջեր կոտրել երբ որ ինքն զինքն չի կարաց պահել. ապայ մեզի ինչ պիտի աւգնէ:

4. Ասաց հայրն որդի դու ոչ կացիր էգի¹⁹ կայր իւրեանց. ասաց հայրն Աբրահամու որդի գնայ. գէգին պահէ. որ ճայեկներն չուտեն.

5. Գնաց Աբրահամ ի էգին. եւ էտես որ խիստ. վրան²⁰ թափել էր. Ճայեկներն եւ կուտէին. գխաղողն. ձայն էած Աբրահամ. եւ ասաց. Ճայեկներ իմ հայրն աստուած կու շինէ. եթէ նա է ստեղծել. գձեզ նազայ. զաւրութեամբ հրամանք կանեմ ձեզ. որ այլ չուտէք. զմեր խաղողն.

6. Ապա թէ այլ աստուած կայ. որ զմեզ ստեղծել է եւ գձեզ. որ գերկինք եւ գերկիր ստեղծել է. նայ է Ճշմարիտ Աստուած երկնի եւ երկրի. նարա զաւրութենէ. թչիք եւ երթայք. ասել բանին վերացան ճայեկներն. նայ Աբրահամ հիացաւ եւ ի վեր համբարձ չայս իւր եւ ասաց. Ով²¹ թազաւոր երկնի եւ երկրի. դու ես Ճշմարիտ Աստուած մինչեւ գխաղողն կթեցին այլ ոչ Ա ճայեկ եմ²² չի նստաւ եւ ոչ անցաւ ի յայն էգոյն վրայ մինչեւ մեծ զարմանալեաւք կու զարմանային եւ կու հիանային այլ էգեպանին.²³ ի այն տեղն հաւատաց Աբրահամ Ճշմարիտ հոտով. զՔրիստոս. / fol. 188v /

7. Եւ երեւեցաւ Աստուած Աբրահամու եւ ասաց. Աբրահամ.²⁴ Ել ի երկրէ քումէ թող գհայր քո եւ զմայր եւ եկ գնի իմ որ տեղ որ ես ցուցանեմ քեզ եւ էգոյց նմա Տէր որ տեղ որ երդայլու էր. ՀԲ տարու էր Աբրահամ եւ գնաց ի Մսր. յետ Սարային. կնկանն հետ. ոչ մալ ոչ գանձ ոչ ոսկի եւ ոչ արծաթ. ի²⁵ հետ չի բարձան բայց ԱԱ հայալ ունէին ու²⁶ Ա էշ մի ունէր. Աբրահամ իդիր գկինն. Սարան ի վերայ իշոյն. եւ ինքն հետեւակ. եւ գնացին հասան ի Մսր.

8. Եւ խիստ պատկերաւք էր. Սարայ ունց որ ի քաղաքն. մտան. նայ տեսան. քաղաքացիքն. որ գնաց Աբրահամ. եւ իշեւանեցաւ. ի քարվասարան. եւ պատուիրեաց Աբրահամ Սարայի. վեր Աստուած վարի քեզ թէ հարցանեն քեզ ինձ համար. թէ այս. մարդ քեզի. նայ դու ասես թէ իմ. յեղբարս է. Եւ համբաւեցին. թազաւորն. վասն Աբրահամու. յղղաց թազաւոր ի զարվարարան եւ գտան զԱբրահամ.

---

18. Variant form of դատարկ; see M0569.
19. Reading as այգի; cf. M0569.
20. M0569 reads վերա, and so we translate.
21. Recension B, which is incomplete, starts here.
22. Corrupt for մ, the indefinite article in this text; cf. M0569.
23. I.e., այգեպանին.
24. A title, as if of a new text, occurs here.
25. Perhaps read արծաթի հետ; cf. Recension B. Alternatively, ի հետ occurs as a variant of հետ, but in that case, the absence of a genitive ending would be odd.
26. So M0569.

8. STORY OF ABRAHAM, ISAAC, AND MAMRĒ

եւ զՄարան. եւ տեսան որ խիստ. պատկերաւքն էր Սարան. հարցան
առ Աբրահամ. թէ ինչ մարդ ես. կամ որ յաշխարհէ ես. պատասխանի
ետ թէ ի Պաղտատոյ եմ. հարցին ցնայ թէ որպէս եկել ես կամ ոյ
կերթաս. ասաց թէ խարիպ մարդ եկել եմ. որ ի քաղաքս. բնակրեմ.
աս<ա>ցին. եկ փարաւոն թագաւոր կոչէ զքեզ. էթող Աբրահամ.
զՄարան. եւ գնաց առ փարօնն եւ երկիր էպագ թագաւորին. տեսաւ
փարաւոն գշարժուածքն որ բատուշահի²⁷ վար կու շարժէր. եւ
գարմացաւ յոյժ. հարցաւ թէ որ աշխարհէ ես. կամ որ յազգէ.

9. Պատասխանի ետ Աբրահամ եւ ասէ. Թարային որդի եմ. ասաց
փարօնն բարի եկիր. ինչու համար ես եկել. ար/ fol. 189r /ուեստ ինչ է.
ասաց թէ շինական եմ. լուծք վարել գիտես. ասաց ոչ ոչխարպան եմ.

10. Եւ ասաց փարաւօն. այն կինն ինչ է քեզ. ասաց թէ իմ գոյր է. եւ ասէ
փարաւօն տուր ինձ որ կին անեմ. պատասխանի ետ Աբրահամ եւ
ասէ. թագաւոր քո հրամանք է. փարաւօնն ողեաց պարօնայք եւ
թագուհիք. եւ փառաւք առին. զՍարան.²⁸ եւ տարան առ թագաւորն.
գիպարսանիքն պատրաստեցին. կերան եւ արբին. ի նոր իրիկունն.
եւ սեղնին գլուխն. ստել էր փարաւօն. եւ մեկ ալ գլուխն Սարայ.
եւ զԱբրահամ. տարան. ի այլ տուն. եւ ժողովքն ամէնն գնացին. եւ
պահապանքն. եւ դրնապանքն. գդրներն. փակեցին. եւ մաց միայն.
փարօնն. եւ Սարայ. որպէս օրէնն է. եւ ճրագն ի վառման կայր:

11. Եւ Աստուծոյ հրամանաւն ընկաւ թըմբութիւն ի վերայ փարասնի եւ
գուն տարաւ. բայց Սարան ոստած կայր. ի սեղնի գլուխն. եւ տեսո
փարաւօն. ի էրազին գիրէշտակն. եւ գարհուրեցաւ հրեղեն թուրն ի
ձեռն. եւ խօսեցօ հրեշտակն առ փարօնն եւ ասէ. չի լինայ թէ ի յայդ
կինն մերձենաս. եւ Աբրահամու կինն է այն. ի քէն վախեց եւ ասաց.
իմ գոյր է. Աստուծոյ հայր է. Աստուած ի նարայ յազգեն պիտի ծնանի.
թէ անկարծ մա. որ դու նացայ. իրք մա շար անես գիտացիր որ այս.
թրովա զքեզ պիտի սպանանեմ. եւ զքաղաքդ ցամենայն ի սպր պիտի
անցնեմ.

12. Նայ փարաւոն. ի ահեն զարդեւ. էտես որ բոլորն մարդ ոչ քո. ճայն ետ.
պահապանացն. եւ եկին պահապանքն եւ հրամայեաց. զԱբրահամ
կոչել եկին եւ տարան առ թագաւորն. եւ Աբրահամ ահիւ լեալ եւ
թօդայր թէ ի սպանումա կու տանէն. երէկ Աբրահամ / fol 189v / առ
թագաւորն եւ ասաս²⁹ փարօնն առ Աբրահամ. թէ որպիսի կամ ինչ
մարդ ես. դու էր սուտ զուրուցեցեր ինձ կուզէիր որ զիս. սպանել
տայիր. քո Աստուծոյոյն.³⁰ Սարա քո կինն է: եւ դու նարայ այրն ես. ու
ինձիկ սուտ զուրուցեցեր թէ իմ գոյրս է. եւ Աբրահամ ասաց. թագաւոր
այդպես է. վախեցայ եւ այդպես ասացի. իմ կինն է:

---

27. Reading as an alternative spelling of փատիշահի.
28. Recension B is longer here, but the photographs available come to an end at this point.
29. Corrupt for ասաց as in M05697
30. Sic! M0569 has Աստուծոյ, which is correct.

13. Պատասխանի ետ փարաւօն. զթշ էր զԱստուածն տեսայ ի երազու։ Եւ Աբրամ ասաց թէ թագաւոր ան իմ Աստուածն չէ. զայն որ տեսար. նայ իմ Աստուծոյոյն[31] ծառայն է եւ սպասաւոր. եւ ասաց փարօնն. եթի այն սպասաւորն է որ հանց լոյս է. եւ զարհուրեցի. ապայ նարայ ստեղծաւղն ինչ է։
14. [Պատասխանի] ետ Աբրահամըն եւ ասէ թէ թագաւոր ճար ու հընար.[32] չիքայ որ մարդկային բնութիւնն կարենայ զիմ Աստուածն տեսնուլ. եւ թ դաաւ հրեշտակաց ոչ կարեն տեսանել. Եւ հրամաեաց փարօնն եւ ասէ պահապանացն. տարէք զԱբրահամ եւ գկինն ի այլ դարպասն իմ. եւ հանգուցէք զնուսայ. բարութեամբ. եւ պահեցէք զնուսայ մինչեւ առաւաւտն. եւ այն գիշերն. լուսացօ եւ կոչեաց թագաւորն զԱբրահամ եւ զՍարան ի ճաշք. եւ պատուեաց զնուսա եւ պարգեւ մեծամեծ շնորհեաց նոցա. եւ ըզհազար. ախչիկն. բեշգաշ երետ Սարայի. եւ մեծաւ պատուով պատուեաց. զնուսա. հրամանք անաւ պարոնաց եւ նշան երետ թէ չի լինայ որ մարդ դոցայ. յույժ անէ յոր տեղ որ ուզենայ երթալու. թող բարով երթան.
15. Եւ էլ Աբրահամ ի Մարայ եւ գնաց ի Երուսաղէմայ[33] բյլորն. Աբրահամու քաղաք կայ. գինքն ի հօն թաղած. է ոչխարն եւ ծառայն շատացան եւ ժամանակ մա անցօ. եւ յիշատակ չունին.
16. Եւ ասաց Սարայ Աբրահամու ես ծերացայ եւ դու ծեր ես. Եւ / fol. 190r / յիշատակ չունենք. արի առ զհազար. եւ տղայ արայ որ տղայ լինայ մեզ եւ յիշատակ. հրամանք առաւ եւ երետ Սարայ Աբրահամու գհազար որ Իսմայէլ տղայ եղօ. եւ Գ տարու եղաւ այն տղան. որ է անուն Իսմայէլ։

Վասն Մամրէի որ էր ծառայ Աբրահամու եւ արածէր զխաշինս ի լերինն։

17. Մամրէ յանուն ծառայ մա ունէր Աբրահամ սեւ Արաբ. ոչխար կու արծէր. ասաց պարոն մատիկա. խոտ հատաւ. եւ ոչխարքն կու թախցի.[34] կու երդում ի հեռուն. ինձի Գ աւուր հաց տուր. Գ օրն ապա թէ զամ եւ հաց առնում. եւ խաղ Գ աւուր հաց ու գնաց.
18. եւ կերդար ճանբով տեսանէր հեռագոյն որ Ա մարդ մա. հայեւոր կու գայր. կանկնեցաւ Մամրէ երեկ ի մօտն. ասաց բարեւ քեզ որդի. ասաց. բարի եկիր հայր. ասաց. որդի Գ օր է անաւթի կու գամ. եւ խիստ. քաղցել եմ եթէ իսկի հաց ունիս. տուր ինձ հացեդ որ ուտեմ ու գքեզ օրհնեմ. եւ Մամրէն երետ զԱ օուրն հացն եւ այն հայեւորն ի այն պահն. կերաւ. ու ասաց որդի. խիստ եմ քաղցել. եւ Մամրէն ասաց.

---
31. See the preceding section for this form.
32. These two words are synonyms.
33. The form is unclear.
34. Reading as if it were թախծի (G. Muradyan).

8. STORY OF ABRAHAM, ISAAC, AND MAMRĒ

հայր գնա իմ պարոնին մօտն. իմ պարոն խիստ ողորմած մարդ է. նա քեզ շատ հաց տայ. հասայ մօտիկս է. եւ ասաց պատուելի հայր. ինձ Գ աւուր հաց է տված եւ հեռու կու երդամ Գ օր. ապայ պիտի դառնամ ի տուն հաց առնուլ. Պատտասխանի ետ ծերն եւ ասէ. ես ծեր եմ եւ հեռու տեղաց եմ եկել եւ խիստ աւզնել եմ. եւ Մամրէն այլվի էրետ զԱ օուրն հացն զան ալ կերաւ:

19. Դարձեալ ասաց. որդի. Գ աւուր ճանապարի ալ ունիմ / fol. 190v / եւ անշէն է եւ մարդ. չի քայ {ինձ ողորմութիւն} որ ողորմութիւն անէ արա ինձ ողորմութիւն. եւ տուր ինձ հաց. որ կարենամ ի տեղ հասանել. եւ ասաց Մամրէ ի միտս իւր. Գ օուր հաց է տված ինձիկ. լաւ է թէ ես Գ օր անօթի կենամ. եւ այս ծերս թող կուշտ լինայ. որ չի քաղցենայ ի ճանապարին.

20. Եւ ասաց առ հայլորն. հայր իմ եւ պատուելի ծեր ինձ Գ աւուր հաց է տված. որ երդամ. ղօչխարն. արձեմ. թող ես Գ աւր անաւթի կենամ. դու ի քո ճանապարիրն. բարով գնայ որ չի քաղցենաս. իթող գնաց <Մամրէ>.[35] քիչ մի տեղ. եւ ծերն ձայն էրետ. ասաց արեկ որդի որ զքեզ աւրհնեմ. եւ Մամրէն երեկ. եւ աւլորն այն ձեռքն ի վերայ զլխոյն իդիր եւ ասաց. օրհնած կենաս. որդի. որ զիս կշդացուցեր. ղայս ասաց. եւ ծերն. չէրեւցաւ ալ.

21. Տեսաւ Մամրէն. որ ձեռքն սպիտակ եղօ. աշեց ի անձն վրայ. տեսաւ որ բոլոր յանձն ճերմակ դարձաւ հիացաւ յոյժ թէ այս ինչ բան է. ես սեւ էի. հիմի ճերմակ եմ եղել. ասաց ի իւր մտին թէ իմ պարոնին. Աստուածն որ զայս. սքանչելիքն արար. Մամրէն ի ձեռքն. չոր փայտ. ցաւազան ունէր. ասաց ի հօս տնկեմ. որ նշան կենայ. որ ասեմ իմ պարոնին թէ ի այս տեղս տեսայ. իթող ղօչխարքն եւ ասաց երդամ. իմ պարոնին ասեմ թէ զքո զԱստուածն տեսայ.

22. Ի դարեն ի վար կու գայր. Մամրէն նայ Աբրահամ. նստել էր աթոռովս վրանին դուռն. նայեցօ եւ էտես. յԱբրահամ. մեկ մս կու գայ. Վազել են. ասաց թէ անձրն Մամրէի է. եւ հալաւն. բայց էրեսն ճերմակ է ձայն էրետ Աբրահ/ fol. 191r /ամ ասաց Սարայ<ի>.[36] մեկ մս կու գայ հալաւն Մամրէի է և անձ չէ. ելաւ Սարայ տեսաւ ասաց ճշմարիտ. հալաւն Մամրէի է անձն չէ.

23. Երեկ Մամրէ եւ Աբրահամու ուոն ընկաւ եւ ասաց. զքո Աստուածն տեսայ. ասաց Աբրահամ. որդեակ. դու ով ես. ասաց ես եմ Մամրէն. ասաց Աբրահամ. որդի Մամրէն սեւ էր. դուն ճրմակ ես. ասաց. աղքատի միջ հանդիպեցայ. եւ հաց տվի նմա եւ նայ օրհնեաց զիս եւ սպիտակացոյց զիս. ասաց որդի գտեղն. ցոյց ինձ թէ ուր հանդիպեցօ քեզ. Նայ ասաց. զցաւազանս որ էր ի ձեռս իմ. տրն<կ>ել եմ ի այն տեղ նշանով:

24. Աբրահամ գնաց. յետ Մամրէի. գտան զցաւազանն նշանով. ծառ

---
35. Corrected from մարրէ, and this is also the reading of M0569.
36. So M0569.

բուսեալ. եւ էհարց Աբրահամ գՄամրէ. թէ ծառ կայր երբէք այս տեղն. նայ ասաց ոչ. ճանաչեաց Մամրէ ծառի վերայ զնշանն եւ ասաց. այս է հայր իմ Աբրահամ. իմ զաւազան որ էծառս կանանչել: Երեկ Աբրահամ. եւ ի ծնկացն ընկաւ եւ աղօթեաց առ Աստուած եւ ասէ. Ո արարիչն արարածոց. Աստուած մարդասէր. փառք քո արարչութեանդ. որ անչափ փառաւորէ ողորմութիւնդ քո. որ զանհնարին. հնարաւոր կանես զանձառելին ճառակաւոր. զեւ սպիտակ արարեր. եւ գշոր փայտն. դալար. կանանչ.[37] ծառ եղօ տերեւով. Սաբէկայ ծառն այն է:

25. Եւ ընդ Աստուծոյ ուխտ եղիր Աբրահամ եւ ասէ: թէ արարիչ Աստուած. դու միշնորդ կացիր ինձ. երփ գ<ող>որմութիւնն[38] այնչափ պատուական է նայ ես առանց աղբատի հացչուտեմ. նայ խորայմանկն Սատանայ ոսխին մէր. գճանապարհքն. կալա<ւ>աւոր արար Խ օր հաց ոչ էկեր Աբրահամ յետ Խ ուր. քաղցեաւ Աբրահամ / fol/ 191v / եւ էտես հեռատասանէ[39] Գ մարդ որ գային. առ Աբրահամ. եկին առ նայ եւ Աբրահամ երկիր էպագ նոցա. եւ աս<աց>[40] եկեայք տերք իմ. ընդ սենեակզ իմով. եւ լուացից գոտս ձեր. եւ կերիչքր հաց ընդ սեղանս իմ. քանզի ընդ էրեկա է: եւ նոքայ ասեն գնայ. որպէս կամիս եղի<գի>[41] ըստ հրամանի քո. եկին ի վրանն էբեր ջուր եւ լուաց գոտս նոցա. եւ հրամայեաց Սարայի բաղարձ էփէլ. եւ առեալ Աբրահամու գհորդն եւ էզէն եփեց գհորդն. եւ էբեր առաջի նոցա. բայց ոսկր հորդոյ ոչ կոտորեաց. եւ էբեր գբաղարճն եւ կաթակ. կերաւ Քրիստոս. բերանն էառ ճշմարիտ. եւ ծամեց. բայց կուլ ոչ եւս. գէրայ ի Դ տարերացն ի տարերքն. կերաւ Քրիստոսն եւ ասաց. Աբրահամ. այլ տարի այս աւր գամ. Սառայի գաւակ լինայ. Սահակ անուն նորա:

26. Ձայ լուաւ Սառան եւ ծիծաղեցաւ եւ ասաց թէ ես <Ղ>[42] տարու եմ եւ Աբրահամ. ճ տարու. քանի որ տղայքն էաք: գաւակ. չեղօ հիմի պիտի լինայ. որ ծերացեալ ենք.

27. Ասաց Քրիստոս Աբրահամ. ահայ Սարայ կին քո չի հաւատաց. եւ ծիծաղեցաւ. եւ ասաց Աբրահամ. թէ չէ Տէր ծիպյտեցօ.

28. Դարձեալ ասաց Քրիստոս. ծնանի քեզի գաւակ. ապա ԴՃ եւ Խ տարի. ի ծառայութիւն կենայ ի մռայ որ Էգիպտոս. Եւ այն խոսիցն վերայ ի ծառայութիւն կացան.

29. գիշերեց. եւ կովերն եկան եւ մին կովա. կու բորչեր հարցաւ Քրիստոս թէ Աբրահամ. այն կովա ինչ կու բորչէ. նայ ասաց Աբրահամ թէ այն կովին հորդն էր որ մորդեցի. հրամայեց Տէրն մէր Յիսուս Քրիստոս.

---

37. Some letters are obliterated; the text is restored and is equivalent to M0569.
38. Corrupt: corrected according to M0569; see *apparatus*.
39. So M0569. In BnF186 we read հոէասատանէ, "from Judea", which is corrupt by graphic error.
40. So M0569; BnF186 is corrupt.
41. So M0569; BnF186 is corrupt.
42. So we emend Ը "8" of manuscript BnF186, in accordance with M0569. The two numerals are similar in form.

8. STORY OF ABRAHAM, ISAAC, AND MAMRĒ   109

Աբրահամու եւ ասէ. ժողովէ զիորդոյն ուկրն. եւ արկ ի կաշին մէջ եւ բեր. եւ արար Աբրահամ զոր եւ փրկիչն հրամայեաց. եւ Քրիստոս խաչ էհան. եւ յարոյց զիորդն. եւ ապայ զիտաց Աբր/ fol. 192r /ահամ թէ Քրիստոս է. եւ ելեալ. Յիսուս հրեշտակօրէն. եւ երդայր նայեաց Քրիստոս ի Սոդոմայեացոց երեսն[43] եւ ձայն ետ Աբրահամու եւ ասէ. շատացաւ մեղքն Սոդոմաեցոցն. եւ բազմացո յուժ առաջի իմ կամիմք հրով զնոսա այրել եւ ջնջեցից ի վերայ երկրի ի մեծամեծաց մինչեւ ցփոքու. եւ Ղուվոն Աբրահամու. գրոչն որդի էր եւ էր ի Սոդում. եւ Աբրահամու խեղճ թվաց. ասաց քաւ լիցի Տէր միթէ զարդարն ի հետ մեղաւորին կորսնեա. եւ Քրիստոսն ասաց ոչ:

30. Ասաց Աբրահամ առ Տէր. [Ո՛][44] Տէր իմ եւ Աստուած իմ եթէ մեղօր ծառայոյ քո. էջիա շնորհս առաջի քո. եթէ լինիցի անդ. Ծ արդար կորսբնեա. վասն Ծից. ասաց ոչ եւ եթէ լիցի Խ կորսնեա ասաց ոչ. եւ թէ լինայ Լ կորսնեա ասաց ոչ. եւ եթէ լիցի Ի. ասաց թէ ոչ եւ եթէ լիցի Ժ ասաց թէ ոչ. եթէ լիցի Ե ասաց ոչ. եւ դադարեցաւ Աբրահամ. այլ չի տեսաւ զՔրիստոս. դարձո Աբրահամ իր վրանն եւ պատմեց Սարային:

Վասն Սահակայ որդոյ Աբրահամու:

31. Երբ եղաւ Սահակ Լ տարու խոստացեալ էր Աբրահամ զՍահակ Աստուծոյ մատաղ անել զորդին. ասաց որդի Սահակ գնայ բեր Ա էշ մա. որ երդանք Աստուծոյ մատաղ անենք. գնաց. Սահակ եւ էբեր {էր}[45] բարձաւ փայտ եւ իդիր զգուռն ի վերայ. եւ կրակ իատ զՍահակ. եւ Բ ծառայ եւ գնաց ի Սաբեկայ ծառն. ունց որ ի դարին. տակն գնացին. իատ Աբրահամ. զփայտն ի վայր եւ զսուրն եւ ասացին ծառային. դուք սստէք ի հոտ. ես ու Սահակ երդանք ի ծառին տակն մատաղ անենք Աստուծոյ եւ զանք եւ ասաց Սահակ հայր ահայ փայտ սուր եւ կրակ եւ ուր է ոչիւսար. ասաց Աբրահամ. որդեակ Աստուած տեսնու իրեն գոչիարն եւ ասաց Աբրահամ. որդեակ, զքեզ խոստացել եմ որ Աստուծոյ մատաղ անեմ պարկէ. ի վայր նայ Սահակն. նստաւ ի վայր եւ ասաց հայր. մարդոյս մինս եւ մարմինն զնքուշ է առ ջուվան. ձեռվի կապէ. եւ գոտս. երբ մորդես նայ ձեռքս եւ ոռքս չի շարժի որ աղեկ կարենաս մորթել.

32. Եւ Սահակն Լ տարու էր. կապեց Աբրահամ. գձեռվին եւ գոտն պարկեցոյց երկանօք ի ծառին տակն. իատ գղանակն ի ձեռքն. եւ էբեր շնեցն ի վերայ. ունց որ ի մինն հասոյց նայ ձայն երեկ երկնից եւ ասաց. Աբրահամ Աբրահամ. Բ տարպայ. թէ ահեղ կանչեր նայ. կու մորդեր ասաց Աբրահամ ի վեր աշեց տեսաւ Աբրահամ

---

43. The word երեսն "face" occurs in the upper margin of BnF186 at this point and in the text of M0569. This appears to be the correct reading.
44. Illegible; omitted by M0569. We have made the restoration.
45. Corruption of էշ "donkey"; not found in M0569.

զհրեշկտակն. ասաց հրեշտակն. մի մորդել զորդիդ հաճեցօ Աստուած ի քո պատարագն. Սահակի համար. առ զխոյն որ <կ>ախվել է ծառի վար եւ մորթէ եւ պատարագ արայ Աստուծոյ. էառ զխոյն եւ մորթեց փոխանակ. Սահակին. մատաղ առօ. այս խոյիս. ըղեղն է եւղ անուշ. որ աւծեցին զքեզ. եւ այս խոյս. Հաբելին խոյն էր որ ընկալաւ Տէր ի պատարագն Աբելի. եւ Կայենի ոչ ընկալաւ. եւ զայս խոյս. ողջամբ ընկալաւ երկինք. եւ կայր պահեալ. մինչեւ ի ծնունդն. Սահակայ. զոր Աբրահամ. խոստացել էր Աստուծոյ. որպէս գրեալ է:

33. Աբրահամու մինչեւ Իսահակ. Ճ տարի:
Իսահակայ մինչեւ Յակոբ Կ:
Յակոբայ մինչեւ Յովսէփ. ՂԳ:
Ի Յովսեփայ եգիպտոս տանել ՃԺ :
յԵգիպտոս որ կեցան ՃԽԴ տարի.
Լըման ամէն Աբրահամայ մինչեւ ի Մովսէս. որ ելան Եգիպտոսէ ԵՃ
եւ ԿԷ տարի է.

Variant Readings

1. կուրք] կուռք | շինէր] կու շինէր | բարձեալ] արձկել | զկուրքն] զկուռքն | իշոյ] իշոյն | տաներ] տանէր | շախին] շախախին | ամէն] ամեն | շուղախ] շարղախ
2. ու վայ] Ո ու վայ | ինչ] ինչպէս | յայտմս] յայտմ | տվից] տաց | չար<դ>եաց] չարդեաց | շողախն] շաղախին | պարկիք] պառկիք | դարայի] թարայի | յոյժ] om
3. ի1°] om | հանդ<իպ>եցայ] հանդեցայ BnF186 | էշն] իշն | դարտակ] դատարկ | հայր] հայրն | շախէն] շաղախէն | կոտրել] կոտորել
4. էզի] այզի : and elsewhere
5. ի1°] om | էտեւ] ետեւ : and numerous instances throughout | վրան] վերա BnF286 | թափել] թափելն | եր] om | նացա] նոցա : and often
6. ապա] illegible | զաւրութենէ] զօրութեամբ | նարա] նորա : and often | ոյ] ո | նմ] մս : preferable | վրայ] վերա | ճայեակներն] ճաեկներն | նմ] մս | այզիոյ] էզոյն | վրայ] վերայ | էզեպանին] այզէպանն | այն] յայն
7. աստուած] քրիստոս | ի1°] omit | նմա] նմայ | մսր] մըսր | յետ] հետ | իդիր] եդիր
8. ու M0569] ո BnF186 : graphic | ունց] հանց | քաղաքացիքն] քաղաքացիք | վարի] վար | քեզ1°] զքեզ | քեզի] քեզ ինչ է | ասես] ասա | թագաւորի] թագաւորին | զարվարարան] քարավանսարան | սարան] սարայ | յաշխարհէ] աշխարհէ | խարիպ] ղարիպ | աս<ա>ցին] ացին BnF186 | վար] վերա
9. արուէստ] արուվեստ | ոչխարպան] ոչխարապան
10. զոյր] քոյր | ասէ] ասաց | ըղեաց] յըղեաց | սարայ] ասրան | այլ] յայլ | դրնապանքն] դռնապանքն | զդրներն] զդռներն

8. STORY OF ABRAHAM, ISAAC, AND MAMRÊ   111

11. փառասոնի] փարաւնի | զուն] քուն | էրագին] յերագին | փառօնն] փարաւնն | յայտ] յայդ | գոյր] քոյր | նոցայ] նորա | մ̃ս2°] մի
12. զարդեւ] զարդեաւ + եւ | ոչ քո] չկայր | թողայր] դողայր | ասաս] ասաց BnF186 : preferable | զուրուցուցեր] զրուցուցեր | աստուծոյոյ] աստուծոյն | գոյրս] քոյրս | նարայ] նորա | ու] om | ինձիկ] ինձ էր | զուրուցուցեր] զրուցուցեր | գոյրս] քոյրս
13. փառաւն] փարաւն | զքո էր] թէ զքո | զաստուածն] աստուածն | աբրամ] աբրահամ | ան] այն | նայ] + իմ | եփ] երփ | ապայ] ապա | նարայ] նորա
14. կարենայ] կարէ | տեսնուլ] տեսանել | զնուսայ] + մինչեւ which is erased | զատրան] զատրայն | բէշքաշ] բիշգաշ | անաւ] առաւ | երդայլու] երթալու : and throughout
16. չունենք] չունիևք | տողայ2°] om | մեզ եւ] մեզ | տողան] տողայն | անունն] անուն | իսմաել] իսմայել | զխաշինս] խաշինս |
17. արաք] արապ | արծեր] արածեր | խոտ] խոտն | թախցի] թախսրի | օրն] աօրն
18. կերդար] ի երթայն | ճանքով] ճանապարհին | մ̃] մի | հայեւոր] հայեւոր որ | իսկի հաց] հաց | հացէր] om | ուր] օր | ի այն] ի յայն | մօտն] տունն | իմ պարոն] om : homoeoarchton | հասայ մօտիկս] ի մօտ | օր] օրն | հայր] հայրն | զան աւ] զայն այլ
19. ալ] այլ | ունիմ] + երթայլու | չի քայ] չկայ + ողորմութիւն BnF186 : secondary | որ] որ + ինձ | առա] արայ դու | կարենամ M0569] կարէնայի BnF186
20. հայէորն] հայէվորն | ծեյր] ծէր | արծեմ] արածեմ | իթող] եթող | ասաց] եւ ասաց | ալէորն] ալեւորն | իդիր] եդիր | ալ] այլ
21. աշէց ի] հայեցաւ | անձն վրայ] անձին վերա | յանձն] անձն | եդել] եմ եդել | ի իւր] իւր | մամրէն ի] մամրէի | հոս] hos | այս տեղիս] յայս տեղս | իթող] եթող | քո] զքո | զաստուածն] աստուածն
22. վար] վայր | մեկ] մէկ | են] էն | ասաց սարայ<ի>] ∼ | սարայ<ի> M0569] սարայ BnF186 | մեկ] մէկ | բայց] եւ | տեսաւ] + եւ
23. աստուածն] զաստուածն | մամրէն] մամրէ | սեւ էիր] ով էր | դուն] դու հիմի | ճրմակ] ճերմակ | զոհեաց] աւհնեաց | տն<կ>ել] տնել BnF186 + եմ | ի այն | ի յայն | տեղ] տեղն
24. յետ] հետ | զզաւազանն] զզաւազան | բուսեալ] + էր | երբէք] երբէք | այս] ի յայս | այս է] follows աբրահամ | զաւազան] զաւազանս | ծառ] ծառս | կանաչել] կանաչ | զևէլ] զևէնն
25. ղ<ող>որմութիւնն] ողորմութիւնդ | նայ] նա | խորայմանկն | խորհամանկն | կալա<և>աւոր] կալաաւոր BnF186 | հեռեստանէ M0569] հրէաստանէ BnF186 | աս<աց> M0569] աս BnF186 | եկեայք] եկայք | եղի<ցի> M0569] եղի BnF186 | զբաղարճն] զբաղարչն | աբրահամ] աբրահամու
26. սարան] սարայն | <Ո> M0569] Ը BnF186
27. սարայ] սառայ | չէ] omit BnF186

28. մրայ] մրսրր | կացան] կացին
29. գիշերեց] գիշերուց օր եկ | բռշեր] բարշէ | բռշէ] բարշէ | մորդեցի] մորբեցի | որկզն] որկրն | մէշ] մէշ | քրիստոս] քրիստոսն | սողոմայեցոց] սողոմայեցոց + երեսն M0569 and in margin BnF186 | յուժ] յոյժ | գրոշն] քրոշն | զարային] սարայի
30. [Ո՛]] om | կորսրնեա] կորուսանեա | իր] ի | սարայի] սարային
31. Աբրահամու 1°] + զոր խոստացեալ էր աստուծոյ մատաղ անել "whom he promised to make a sacrifice to God" | եւ 1°] om | ունց] անց | տեսնու] կու տեսնու | զնքուշ] ենքուշ | առշուվան] առշեւան | ճերվի կապէ] կապէ զճեվիս | ճերքս] ճեռն | գուտս] ուտս | կառենաս] կարենաս
32. սահակն] սահակ | զճերվին] զճերն | իատ] եւատ | ճերքն] ճեռն | ունց] հանց | ահեդ] ա.հեդ | մորդեր] մորբթր | աշեց] հաեց | պատարագն] պատարագս | սահակի] սահակին | <կ>ախվել M0569] ճախվել BnF186 | սահակին] սահակայ | գրեալ է] + կայ

Story of the Holy Father Abraham and of Isaac, His Son, and of Mamrē, His Servant

1. Abraham's father's name was Terah. When Abraham was a boy, behold, his father made idols.[46] One day Abraham loaded the idols in a bag upon a donkey and it was swinging to the left and the donkey fell in the mire and all the idols were broken and became <muddy>.[47]

2. Abraham became very angry and was afraid of his father and said to the idols, "Woe, alas upon you. What false gods you are, who did not keep yourselves from this mire! What sort of answer shall I give my father and[48] what sort of help shall I find from you?" He became very angry and bro<k>e them all and submerged them in the mi<r>e and said, "(It is) clear that you[49] are worthy of this, who lie in this mi<r>e." And he went home with the donkey,

---

46. The tradition of Terah as a builder of idols is found in a number of places; see also 8.5, 11.2, 15.2; cf. *Gen. Rab.* 38:28. For different versions of the story of Abraham and idols, see Beer 1859, 9–11; cf. *Tanḥuma Lek Lĕka* 2.2. See also *Apoc. Ab.* 1–3. None of the material Beer adduces contains a story exactly like that here, though the point of the narratives is similar. On Abraham's family business being the manufacture of idols, see *Gen. Rab.* 38:13, *Yerahmeel* 4.5 (Yassif 2001, 131) drawn from *Seder Eliyahu Rabbah* (see Yassif 2001, 475). The recognition story there is different from that in the Armenian Abraham texts.

47. This form of the story occurs only here in the published texts. It is a variant on the idols' inability to chase off the ravens and the idols' inability to prevent the burning of their temple. The same theme is greatly developed in the narrative of *Apoc. Ab.* 5–6. The idea that Terah was an idol builder or an enthusiastic idol worshiper is to be found frequently, e.g., in *Apoc. Ab.* 5–6; and here in texts nos. 2.1, 2.6, 4.6, 12.3, 15.2, etc. See also, in a different historical context, *Ma'aseh Abraham* (*BM* 1.30). The story of the breaking of the idols occurs also in ibid., 32.

48. Literally: "or."

49. Literally: "you who."

8. STORY OF ABRAHAM, ISAAC, AND MAMRĒ

afflicted of heart and very bitter. And (his) father Terah, having seen his son afflicted of heart, said, "Avram. Why are you afflicted of heart?"

3. He answered (his) father and said, "I went. I en<co>untered mire on the way and my donkey could not pass. The donkey fell in the mire and our gods were broken. And I was afflicted of heart and became very angry. And I said to them, 'Is this your power?' I took stones in (my) hands and I broke (them) all, and I came home empty." And he said, "Father, the power of these gods of ours, what is it, that it did not preserve a donkey so that it passed through the mire and it (i.e., the god) was not broken up? When[50] it was unable to preserve itself then how will it avail us?"[51]

4. (His) father said, "Son, you be well." They had a vineyard. (His) father said to Abraham, "Son, go guard the vineyard, so that the ravens will not eat (i.e., its produce)."[52]

5. Abraham went to the vineyard and he saw that the ravens had strongly attacked and were eating the grapes. Abraham cried and he said, "Ravens, my father builds a god. If he has created you, by their power I command you that you no longer eat our grapes.

6. "But if there is another God who created us and you, who created the heavens and the earth, he is the true God of heaven and earth. By his power, fly and go!" At the saying of this speech, the ravens rose up. Indeed, Abraham was amazed and raised up his eyes on high and said, "O king of heaven and earth. You are a true God." Until they harvested the grapes, not one more raven perched in or passed over that vineyard, so that they wondered and were amazed by a great wonder[53] at the other Gardener. In that place Abraham came to believe in Christ with true faith.[54]

7. And God appeared to Abraham and he said, "Abraham! Go forth from your land. Leave (your) father and mother and come after me to the place which I will show you."[55] And the Lord showed him the place to which he was to go. Abraham was 72 years old and he went to Egypt with Sarah, with (his) wife.[56] They took with them no belongings, no treasure, no gold, and no

---

50. That is, "if".

51. This incident is not biblical. Observe that Terah does not contradict Abraham's assertions. Another form of the incident where the idols fall off a donkey and are broken is to be found in *Apoc. Ab.* 2–3. One wonders whether the river Gur mentioned in *Apoc. Ab.* 2:9 might not be an inner-Greek graphic error for the Babylonian river Sud (*Bar* 1:4). Note that a Dead Sea Scrolls text refers to a river Sur or Sor (4Q389a frg. 3.7), graphically similar to Sud in Aramaic script and even in Greek.

52. The incident of the ravens is told rather briefly. See also the General Introduction, pp. 18–20 and notes on text no. 4.2.

53. That is, "greatly."

54. This incident is not biblical; see text no. 2.3. Its end is abbreviated in Recension B text no. 9.6.

55. Gen 12:1.

56. In 5.1 Abraham's leaving Haran is put in his seventy-fifth year, in accordance with

silver, but each had one garment and he had one donkey. Abraham put (his) wife Sarah upon the donkey and he, himself, on foot.[57] And they went and reached Egypt.

8. And Sarah was very beautiful,[58] so that when they entered the city, behold, the citizens saw that Abraham went and took up lodgings in a caravanserai. And Abraham commanded Sarah, "God above controls you. If they ask you about me, 'Is this your husband?' Behold, you say, 'He is my brother.'"[59] And they reported to the king concerning Abraham. The king sent to the caravanserai and they found Abraham and Sarah, and they saw that Sarah was very beautiful.[60] They asked Abraham, "What man are you? From which land are you?" He answered, "I am from Baghdad."[61] They asked him, "How did you come and where are you going?" He said, "I am a foreigner. I came so that I might dwell in this city." They said, "Come, King Pharaoh is summoning you." Abraham left Sarah and went to Pharaoh and prostrated himself to the king. Pharaoh saw the gesture that he made[62] below the king,[63] and he wondered greatly. He asked, "From which land are you? Of which people?"

9. Abraham answered and said, "I am the son of Terah." Pharaoh said, "Welcome. For which reason have you come? What is your profession (craft)?" He said, "I am a country man." (He said,) "Do you know how to plough?" He said, "No, I am a shepherd."[64]

10. And Pharaoh said, "What is that woman to you?" He said, "She is my sister." Pharaoh said, "Give (her) to me so that I may make her (my) wife." Abraham answered and said, "King, it is your command." Pharaoh dispatched the

---

Gen 12:4. The origin of the date here is unclear, and in Recension B (text no. 9) it is seventy-five. Michael the Syrian (Chabot 1899, 31) put it in his eighty-first year. The promise that Abraham receives on reaching Canaan is missing from the story here, as from all the other Armenian Abraham retellings; see the General Introduction, p. 15.

57. Abraham's poverty and Sarah's riding a donkey do not occur in the most versions of this incident; cf. text no. 4.9, but see text no. 8.7. In text no. 4.12, however, the multiplication of Abraham's flocks is discussed, and that is made even more remarkable by stressing his absolute poverty when he went initially to Egypt. Sarah riding a donkey led by Abraham is reminiscent of the descent into Egypt (Matt 2:13-14), not as described in the Gospel text, but as painted by artists in medieval manuscripts. See Der Nersessian 1973, 72 and fig. 392 and Mathews and Wieck 1994, catalogue nos. 13, 78, 80, 87, and fig. 76. So also *Proto. Jas.* 17:2.

58. Literally: "by/with appearance".

59. Gen 12:11–13.

60. Gen 12:15. All the details that follow are apocryphal expansions. In Recension B the preceding narrative is much more detailed.

61. Recension B has "Babylon".

62. Literally: "moved, gestured".

63. This phrase remains obscure. In Gen 42:6 Joseph's brothers also prostrate themselves before an Egyptian ruler (i.e., Joseph). That story may well have influenced the narrative here.

64. This is close to the answers Joseph's brothers give to Pharaoh in Gen 47:2–4.

lords and royal women.⁶⁵ They took Sarah with pomp and brought her to the king. They prepared the wedding, ate and drank until the next evening. And at the head of the table Pharaoh was seated, and at the other head, Sarah. And they took Abraham to another house and all the assembly went away, and the guards and the door-keepers closed the doors. And Pharaoh and Sarah remained alone as is customary. And the torch was in the sconce.

11. And at God's command, deep slumber fell upon Pharaoh and he slept, but Sarah remained seated at the head of the table. And Pharaoh saw the angel in a dream and he was terrified (at) the fiery sabre in (his) hand. And the angel spoke to Pharaoh and said, "It shall not be that you have intercourse with this woman, and she is Abraham's wife. He feared you and said, 'She is my sister.' He is a father of God; God is going to be born of his family. If you do any unexpected evil to them, know that I will kill you with this sabre and all this city of yours will be put to the sword."

12. Behold, Pharaoh awoke from fear. He saw that there was no one there. He called to the guards and the guards came and he commanded to summon Abraham. They came and brought (him) to the king, and Abraham was fearful and trembling, lest they were taking him to execution. Abraham came to the king and Pharaoh said to Abraham, "What sort of or which man are you? Why did you tell me a lie? Did you wish to cause me to be killed by your God? Sarah is your wife and you are her husband and you told me a lie, 'She is my sister.'" And Abraham said, "King, it is thus: I feared and said thus, 'She is my wife.'"⁶⁶

13. Pharaoh answered, "Was it your God (that) I saw in my dream?" And Abraham said, "King, that is not my God. The one whom you saw is the servant of my God and (his) attendant." And Pharaoh said, "When⁶⁷ that is the attendant who is thus light and terrible, then what is his Creator?"

14. Abraham [answer]ed and said, "The king is clever and talented. There is no human body that can see my God and the 9 classes of angels⁶⁸ cannot see (him)." And Pharaoh commanded and said to the guards, "Bring Abraham and (his) wife to my other palace and make them rest with goodness and guard them till morning." And that night became light and the king summoned Abraham and Sarah for a meal. And he honored them and bestowed upon them very great gifts. And he gave Hagar as a gift, as maidservant to Sarah. He honored them with great honor. He commanded the lords and he gave a sign lest any man of them act with force; and wherever he wishes to go, let them go gladly.⁶⁹

---

65. Or: "queens," The text of Recension B differs and the available data from Recension B conclude here.
66. Perhaps a confusion for "my sister," or translate "feared (the result if) I said."
67. That is, "if".
68. Stone 2006, 429–30, 433–34.
69. Gen 12:20.

15. And Abraham went forth from Egypt and he went to Jerusalem.[70] All the city is Abraham's. He himself was buried there.[71] (His) sheep and servants multiplied[72] and some time passed and they had no memorial.[73]
16. And Sarah said to Abraham, "I have grown old and you are old, and we have no memorial. Come, take Hagar and make a child, so that we may have a child and a memorial."[74] The command was accepted and Sarah gave Hagar to Abraham, so that there was a child, Ishmael, (from her). And that child, whose name was Ishmael, was three years old.[75]

Concerning Mamrē, Who Was Abraham's Servant and Pastured Sheep on the Mountain.

17. Abraham had a servant Ma\<m\>rē who was a black Arab.[76] He pastured sheep. He said, "Master, the grass close by is cropped and the sheep are sad. I am going far off. Give me bread for 3 days. (On) the third day, then I shall come and take bread." And he took 3 days' bread and went.
18. And he was going on the way (and) he saw from afar that a grey-headed man was coming. Mamrē stopped. He came close (and) he said, "Greetings to you, son." He said, "Welcome, father." He said, "Son, for three days I am coming famished and I am very hungry. If you have any bread at all, give me (some) of your bread so that I can eat and bless you." And Mamrē gave (him) one day's bread and that grey-haired man ate (it) at that moment (i.e., all at once). And he said, "Son, I am very hungry." And Mamrē said, "Father, go to my master nearby. My master is a very merciful man. He (will) give you a lot of bread. Go there, he is close by." And he said, "Venerable father, he gave me three days' bread, and I am going far, for three days (i.e., journey), then I will return home to take bread." The old man answered and said: "I am old

---

70. Contrast Gen 13:3. This is another example of the tendency to identify holy places with one another; seethe comment on text no. 7.3.
71. In Gen 25:9 and most of the apocryphal Abraham texts, he is buried near Hebron in the Cave of Machpelah, in the field of Ephron the Hittite. The tradition reflected here, rather uniquely, connects Abraham's burial with Jerusalem.
72. Gen 13:2.
73. That is, "offspring."
74. Gen 16:2.
75. The biblical source of this age is not evident.
76. See Gen 14:13, where he is said to be an Amorite. The form of the meeting with the old men related here differs from that in text no. 2.9–11, where Mamrē has only one encounter with an old man, and one gift of bread. The story is not found in text no. 4, and in text no. 7 it is mentioned in passing, mainly in relationship to grey hair (7.3.1). Here the incident of Mamrē's sleep and the etiology of the oak tree are barely mentioned, though they figure prominently in text no. 2.9–10. The tradition occurs in a less developed form below in §§23–24.

and I have come from distant places and I am very tired." And again Mamrē gave one day's bread. That also[77] he ate.

19. Again he said, "Son, I have a further 3-days' road and it is uninhabited[78] and there is no man to have mercy on me. Have mercy on me and give me bread so that I might be able to reach the place." And Mamrē said to himself,[79] "He (i.e., Abraham) gave me three days' bread. It is better if I remain hungry for 3 days and let this old man be satisfied, so that he will not be hungry on the way."

20. And he said to the grey-haired man, "My father and honorable elder. 3 days' bread has been given to me to go and pasture the sheep. Let me remain hungry for three days, you go well on your way, so that you do not hunger." <Mamrē> left, went a little place (i.e., way) and the old man spoke up. He said, "Come, son, so that I may bless you." And Mamrē came and that grey-headed man placed his hands upon (his) head and said, "You will be blessed, (my) son, since you satiated me." The old man, having said this, disappeared.

21. Mamrē saw how his hand became white. He looked at (his) body,[80] he saw that all his body had turned white; he wondered greatly what was this matter. "I was black and I have become white," he said to himself.[81] "Is it my master's God who did this wonder?" Mamrē held in his hand a dry wooden staff. He said, "Here I am planting it so that a sign may be (remain), so that I say to my master, 'I saw (him) in this place.'" He left the sheep and he said, "Let me go and say to my master, 'I saw your God.'"

22. Mamrē came down from the heights. Behold, Abraham was seated on the chair at the doorway of the tent. Abraham looked and saw someone come running; he said, "The body is Mamrē's and the clothing, but the face is white." Abraham gave[82] voice (and) said to Sarah, "Someone is coming. The clothing is Mamrē's and the body is not." Sarah went out, saw, she said, "True, the garments are Mamrē's and the body is not."

23. Mamrē came and fell at Abraham's foot and said, "I saw your God." Abraham said, "Son, who are you?" He said, "I am Mamrē." Abraham said, "Son, Mamrē was black: you are white." "I met a poor man and I gave him bread and he blessed me and he made me white." He said, "Son, show me the place where he met you." He said, "The staff which was in my hand I have planted in that place as a sign[83]."

---

77. Here we read as if the text was զայն այլ.
78. Or: "unbuilt."
79. Literally, "in his mind" and so elsewhere.
80. Note this meaning of the word մահն and that of բնութիւն in this text, which also means "body."
81. Literally: "in his mind.. The higher estimation of white is discussed in text no. 2.11 note.
82. Apparently a word has been omitted. "Sarah" is in an odd case.
83. Instrumental case.

24. Abraham followed Mamrē. They found the staff as a sign, having grown into a tree. And Abraham asked Mamrē, "Was there ever a tree in this place?" He said, "No." Mamrē recognized the sign upon the tree[84] and said, "This is, Father Abraham, my staff, which is this greened tree." Abraham came and fell on his knees[85] and prayed to God and said, "O Creator of creatures (creations), God lover of humans, glory to your creation which glorifies your mercy beyond measure, who make the impossible possible, the ineffable effable. You made black white and dry wood fresh (green). It became a green, leafy tree." That is Sabek's tree.

25. And Abraham made a covenant with God and he says, "You Creator, God, be a mediator for me. If[86] mercy is so honorable, behold I (will) not eat bread without a poor man."[87] Behold, the cunning Satan our adversary blocked the ways. For 40 days Abraham ate no bread (i.e., food). After 40 days Abraham became hungry and he saw from afar three men who were coming to Abraham. They came to him and Abraham bowed down to them and he said, "Come my lords, into my room and let me wash your feet and eat bread at my table, for it is towards evening." And they said to him, "As you wish, let it be according to your command."[88] They came to the tent; he brought water and he washed their feet and he commanded Sarah to bake unleavened cakes. And Abraham took the calf and slaughtered it.[89] He prepared the calf and brought (it) before them, but he did not break any of the calf's bones. And he brought the unleavened cakes and butter. Christ ate; he truly took food in his mouth and chewed, but he did not swallow.[90] Since (i.e., he was) of the 4 elements, Christ ate of the elements. And he said, "Abraham, next year on this day I (will) come; Sarah (will) have a child,[91] Sahak will be his name."

26. Sarah heard this and laughed[92] and said, "I am 90 years old and Abraham is 100 years old. While we were young we had no children, now will there be (children) when we have grown old?"

---

84. This is reminiscent of Gen 31:48–49 and also of Judah's staff left in Tamar's possession: Gen 38:25–26.
85. See text no. 2.4 note.
86. Or, more literally: "when."
87. This is much more developed in text no. 11A.23–24.
88. Gen 18:3–5.
89. Gen 18:6–7. Observe that here Abraham prepares the calf himself. The detail about the calf's bones is connected with the story of the calf's resurrection in this text (§29) and in text no. 15.29. The tradition is much older. Compare Exod 12:46, where the breaking of the bones of the paschal lamb is forbidden. This commandment is applied messianically to Christ in John 19:33–36.
90. Literally: "make a swallow." կուլ տալ ("to swallow," literally: "give, cause a swallow") is a normal compound verb in modern Armenian. As the next sentence makes clear, Christ was incarnated in the guest.
91. Literally: "seed"; cf. Gen 15:3. For the naming, see Gen 18:10 and 18:12–15.
92. Or "mocked."

8. STORY OF ABRAHAM, ISAAC, AND MAMRĒ

27. Christ said, "Abraham, behold Sarah your wife did not believe and she laughed (mocked)." And Abraham said, "No, Lord, she smiled."
28. Again Christ said, "A child is to be born to you. Then for 400 and 40 years he will be in slavery in *msr*,[93] which (is) Egypt." And according to that speech they were in slavery.[94]
29. Night fell, the cows came and one cow was lowing. Christ asked, "Abraham, why does that cow low?" "Behold," Abraham said, "it was that cow's calf that I slaughtered." Our Lord Jesus Christ commanded Abraham and said, "Gather the calf's bones and cast (them) into (its) skin and bring (them)." And Abraham did that which the Savior commanded, and Christ made the sign of the cross and he resurrected the calf.[95] And then Abraham realized that he is Christ. And Jesus, having gone forth with the angels, went (i.e., away).[96] And Christ looked at the Sodomites' faces and he called out to Abraham and said, "The sin of the Sodomites has become great and has multiplied exceedingly before me. We wish to burn them with fire and I will annihilate them upon the earth, from great to small." And Lot was Abraham's sister's son, and he was in Sodom.[97] And Abraham felt pity for him. He said, "Far be it, Lord, that you destroy the righteous with the sinner." And Christ said, "No."
30. Abraham said to the Lord, "[O] my Lord and my God, if this sinful servant of yours has found favor before you, if there will be 50 righteous people there, will you destroy (i.e., the city) for the sake of the 50?" He said, "No." "And if there are 40, will you destroy (it)?" He said, "No." "And if there are 30, will you destroy (it)?" He said, "No." "And if there are 20?" He said, "No." "And if there are 10?" He said, "No." "If there are 5?" He said, "No." And Abraham stopped and he saw Christ no longer. Abraham returned to his tent and he told Sarah.[98]

---

93. Armenian մսր. A name for Egypt found in medieval texts.
94. Gen 15:13. This chapter is otherwise not mentioned in the Armenian Abraham saga, though it occurs in Stepʻanos Siwnecʻi's *Commentary on Genesis* §87. Stepʻanos Siwnecʻi has four hundred years in accordance with the biblical text in Gen 15:13.
95. The raising up of the calf is found already in *T. Ab.* A 6:5. This incident serves here as a promise of the resurrection of Christ. The cow lowed and the calf arose and followed it according to *Palaea* 215, but the text does not mention the author of the miracle. In *4 Bar.* 7:17 a corpse was resurrected so the people might believe.
96. Ephrem, *Commentary on Genesis* 15 (Mathews and Amar 1994, 158) says that, "the Lord ... appeared to Abraham clearly in one of the three." Note the discussion in the texts here over whether it was God or not.
97. Most texts say that he was the son of Abraham's brother Nahor: cf. Gen 12:5. No sister of Abraham is mentioned in the Bible.
98. Strikingly, the story of Lot is not included, and the text continues on with the Binding of Isaac, which story has its own heading.

Concerning Sahak, Son of Abraham

31. When Sahak was 30 years old,[99] Abraham promised to sacrifice (his) son Sahak to God.[100] And he said, "(My) son Sahak, go, bring a donkey so that we may go (and) make an offering to God." Sahak indeed brought <a donkey>. He loaded wood and he placed the sword[101] and fire upon (it).[102] He took Sahak and two servants and went to the Tree of Sabek. As soon as they went to the bottom of the mountain, Abraham took the wood down and the knife and they said to the servant, "You remain here. I and Sahak are going under the tree. We will make an offering to God and come." And Sahak said, "Father, behold wood, knife, and fire, and where is the sheep?"[103] And Abraham said, "Son, God will make the sheep apparent for himself." [104] And Abraham said, "Son, I have promised that I will make you a sacrifice to God.[105] Lie down on the ground." Behold, Sahak sat down on the ground and said to (his) father, "The flesh and body of man is sensitive. Take a rope, bind my hands and feet. When you slaughter (me), behold, my hands and feet will not move, so that you can slaughter me fittingly."[106]

32. And Sahak was thirty years old.[107] Abraham bound him hand and foot; he laid him down on a millstone under the tree; he took the knife in his hand and he directed it to his neck.[108] As he brought it to the flesh, behold a voice came from heaven and said, "Abraham, Abraham," twice. While it was call-

---

99. On the significance of the age of thirty, see note on text no. 7:2. This age is given also in the *Epistle* by Aram printed in *MH* 9th century, 760.

100. Contrast the biblical formulation, which stresses Abraham's obedience to God's command: Gen 22:1–2. The biblical story is strikingly concise, and the Armenian expands it and adds much circumstantial detail.

101. Or: "scimitar." The instrument is also a sword in *Palaea* 221.

102. Here, after they reached the indicated place, Isaac loads onto the donkey the objects that Gen 12:6 has Abraham load onto Isaac or carries himself. The Armenian apocrypha put the site of the Binding at the Tree of Sabek, as here and in texts nos. 4.22, 6.9.1, and 14.14; it is "Golgotha" in text no. 7.15, and "place of the covenant" in text no. 11.44.

103. Gen 22:7.

104. Gen 22:8.

105. No such promise or vow is mentioned in Genesis. It is assumed in several texts of the Armenian Abraham saga, but the incident is never made explicit.

106. This last interchange is not biblical. Compare the dialogue of Isaac and Abraham in 4Q225, frg. 2, col. 2. See *Gen. Rab.* 56:8; and Kessler 2004, 116, 123. Isaac's willingness to be sacrificed is also to be found in *LAB* 32:3; *Tanḥuma Vayera'* 46, *PRE* 30, *Yalqut Shim'oni Lek Lěka* ad loc., §101. See text no. 15.46.

107. The same statement was made above, in §31.

108. Gen 22:9–10. The location of the place of sacrifice, not called an altar by the Armenian text, is on a millstone, thus a flat stone, underneath the Tree of Sabek; see this text and text no. 6.9.3. There is a repeated biblical prohibition of associating trees with sacrifice; see Deut 12:2 and elsewhere. The understanding of the place of the sacrifice here, therefore, is Christian.

ing fearsomely, he was slaughtering. It said, "Abraham!" Abraham looked up and saw the angel. The angel said, "Do not kill your son. God was pleased at your offering. For (instead of) Sahak, take the ram that is hanging under the tree and slaughter (it) and make a sacrifice to God." He took the ram and he slaughtered it instead of Sahak.[109] This offering was accepted. The marrow of this ram is the sweet oil with which they anointed you.[110] And this ram was Abel's ram that the Lord accepted as Abel's offering, and Cain's (offering) He did not accept.[111] And Heaven accepted the ram whole and it was preserved until Sahak's birth,[112] whom Abraham has promised to God, as is written (above).

33. From Abraham until Isaac, 100 years.
From Isaac until Jacob, 60.
From Jacob until Joseph, 93.
From taking Joseph to Egypt 110 years.
They were in Egypt[113] 144 years.
The complete total from Abraham to Moses, when they went out of Egypt is 567 years.[114]

---

109. This is based on Gen 22:11–13.
110. It is not clear which event this refers to. On the marrow as sweet oil, see the General Introduction, p. 14. The following material about Abel's ram is perhaps connected with Abel and Isaac as sacrificial forerunners of Christ. See also text no. 6.7.4–6.9.4. That is discussed in the General Introduction, p. 13.
111. Gen 4:3–5.
112. The idea is similar to *2 Enoch*'s statements about Melchizedek; see *2 En.* 72.
113. Or: "From their staying in Egypt."
114. Other sources give this total differently, from 430 to 507; see Stone 1996a, 88.

9. Story of Father Abraham: Recension B

M3411 is a *Tałaran* (*Collection of Poems*) of the seventeenth century, written in *notrgir*. It contains a considerable number of poems by medieval Armenian poets as well as two prose documents. One is calendrical in character, while the last text listed is Պատմութիւն հօրն Աբրահամու "Story of Father Abraham." The manuscript is 182 folios long and, of them, we have at our disposal photographs of three pages, fols 176r–v and 177r.[1] These photographs contain part of the Abraham text and are edited here. The title listed is "Story of Father Abraham," but the title is not contained on the pages that are available to us. This text is not the same as the texts nos. 2 and 11 published here, which have very similar titles. On examination, however, this text proved to be a different recension of *The Story of Holy Father Abraham*, text no. 8, immediately preceding this text. However, it varies enough to justify its publication as a separate document. The language has many mediaeval features and the orthography is fairly standard.

We have divided the text into paragraphs that coincide with those of text no. 8. Most general remarks are included in the introduction to and notes on that text.

Story of Father Abraham – Text

6. ... թագաւոր երկնի եւ երկրի. դու ես ճշմարիտ Աստուած. ‹մ›ինչ որ զիաղղոն կթեցին՝ ճահեքն այլ ոչ եստան ի նորա այցին՝ եւ այլ այցեպանքն գոր տեսին. որ ի Թարայի այցին. մեկ ձագ մի ոչ իջանէր այլ կու զարմային թէ այս ինչ է. Եւ Աբրահամ ի յայն տեղն հաւատաց զճշմարիտ զՔրիստոս Աստուած:

7. Եւ երեւեցաւ Աստուած Աբրահամու եւ ասաց՝ ել երկրէդ քումմէ. թող զհայր քո եւ զմայր՝ եւ եկ զկնի իմ որ տեղ որ ես ցուցանեմ քեզ եւ էցոյց նմա Տէր որ տեղ որ երթալոյ էր։ Հէ տարու էր. Աբրահամ երբ գնաց ի մոր Սարային. հետ ոչ մալ ոչ զանձ ոչ ոսկի եւ ոչ արծաթի հետ չի բարձան: դատարկ ելաւ ի հաւրն տանէն: բայց Ա.Ա. հալալ ունէին որ կու հագէին. եւ Ա. էշ մի ունէր Աբրահամ. իդիր զկինն Սառայ ի վերայ իշուն. եւ ինքն հետեւ/ fol. 178 r /ակ. եւ գնացին հասին ի Մըսըր։

---

1. The manuscript is described in a summary fashion in Ēganyan, Zeyt'unyan, and Ant'abyan 1965, col. 1006.

9. STORY OF FATHER ABRAHAM: RECENSION B

8. Պատկերաւք էր Սառայ. ո՞ւաց² որ ի քաղաքն մտան. նա տեսան Մարքցիքն որ Ա կին մի նստեալ էր ի վերայ իշուն. եւ Ա մանուկ մի քաշէր զպախուրցն.³ իշուն: Գնաց իջաւ ի քարվասառան. ասաց եւ Աբրահամ պատուէր ետ Սառայի թէ⁴ մի ասասցես թէ այր իմ է. այլ ասա թէ եղբայր է իմ. եւ իմացուցին փարաունի թագաւորին. թէ Ա մարդ մի տեսաք որ եկն եւ կին մի գեղեցիկ ընդ իւր է հետեալ է ի վերայ իշոյ եմուտ ի քաղաքս. ջեմք⁵ զիտակ թէ յորմէ երկրէ եկն կամ որ իշեւականս եղեւ: ասաց փարաունն. շուտով գնացէք եւ յռշտապով ի մէջ քաղաքիս եւ զըտանիցէք. եւ յորժամ հարցին եւ գտին. ի մէջ քաղաքին ի բարձրաւանդակ⁶ տեղի այսինքն ի քարվասառան. թէ ինչ մարդ ես. որ յաշխարհէ ես: / fol. 178r /

9. եւ նա ասաց ի Բաբիլոնէ եմ. եւ ինչս պիտոյ եկեալ ես աստ. յուր կամիս երթալ. եւ նա ասաց թէ դարիպ մարդ եմ եկեալ՝ եւ աստ բնակիլ կամիմ.⁷ ի քաղաքս. եւ ասացին եկ կոչէ զքեզ փարաունն թագաւորն. եւ ինքն միայն գնաց՝ բարեւ երետու՝ եւ զգլուխն ի գետին եդիր. եւ տեսեալ փարաունի զշարժուվացքն. ասաց ի մտան թէ մեծ մարդ երեւի դայ. զարմացաւ յոյժ թէ զինչպէս եկեալ է. եւ հարցաւ թէ յուր աշխարհէ ես.

10. կամ զինչ է արհեստդ. եւ Ասաց թէ շինական եմ լուծր վարել գիտեմ. եւ ոչխարս արածել՝ եւ ասաց փարաունն ինչ է ան կինն որ հետ քեզ՝ եւ ասաց թէ քոյր է իմ. եւ ասաց փարաունն թէ տուր զնա ինձ ի կունթիւն եւ պատասխանի ետ Աբրահամ եւ ասէ. թագաւոր՝ հրամանք քոյ է. եւ գնաց ի տուն առ Սառայ եւ ասաց՝ Սառայ կուզէ զքեզ փարաուն. առնու<լ> եւ իւր կին արասցէ / fol. 178v /...

Story of Father Abraham – Translation

6. ... king of heaven and earth. You are a true God." <U>ntil the grapes were harvested, the ravens perched no more in his vineyard. And the other guardians of the vineyards, when they saw that in Terah's vineyard not one single nestling ever descended, wondered[8] what this is.[9] And Abraham in that place came to believe in the true Christ God.

7. And God appeared to Abraham and he said, "Go forth from your land. Leave your father and mother and come after me to the place which I will show

---

2. Presumably an abbreviation mark has been lost.
3. Conventional spelling would be պախուրց.
4. Here is a space with some erased letters.
5. The sign is unclear, resembling a q to some extent. The context demands a negative.
6. *Sic!*
7. A second occurrence of բնա at the beginning of this word is dotted: corrupt by dittography.
8. Literally: "but they were wondering."
9. This part of the text is incomplete at the beginning, and so the first two verses, being the end of an incident, are rather unclear as they stand. Compare Recension A.

you." And the Lord showed him the place to which he was to go. Abraham was 75 years old when he went to Egypt with Sarah. With (them) they took no belongings, no treasure, no gold, and no silver[10] with (them). Empty he went forth from (his) father's house. But each had one garment, which they wore, and Abraham had a donkey. He put his wife Sarah upon the donkey, and he himself was on foot. And they went (and) reached Egypt.[11]

8. Sarah was very beautiful[12] {to those}. When they entered the city, behold, the Egyptians saw a[13] woman seated upon a donkey and a young man was drawing the bridle of the donkey. He went, descended at a caravanserai. Abraham said and gave a command to Sarah, "Do not say, 'He is my husband.' but say, 'He is my brother.'" And they informed King Pharaoh, "We saw a man who came and a beautiful woman was with him mounted upon a donkey. He entered the city. We do not know from which land he came or in which lodging he is." Pharaoh said, "Go quickly and promptly within this city and find (him)." And when they asked, they found (him) in the midst of the city on a hilly place, that is, in a caravanserai. (They asked him), "What (sort of) man are you? From which land are you?"

9. And he said, "I am from Babylon, and lacking goods, I have come here." "Where do you wish to go?" And he said, "I came as a stranger and I wish to live here in this city." And they said, "Come, King Pharaoh summons you." And he went alone. He gave a greeting and made obeisance.[14] And Pharaoh, having seen the gesture, said to himself, "This seems to be a great man." He wondered greatly how he had come and asked, "From which land are you

10. and what is your craft?" And he said, "I am a country man; I know how to plough and to pasture sheep." And Pharaoh said, "Who is that woman who is with you?" And he said, "She is my sister."And Pharaoh said, "Give her to me in marriage." And Abraham replied and said, "King, it is your command." And he went home to Sarah and said, "Sarah, Pharaoh wants to take you and he will make (you) a wife for him / . . . ."

---

10. Literally: "and not of silver."

11. Note the late form Měsěr for "Egypt," which is not usual in literary texts associated with the Bible. It is found also in text no. 8.28. The emphasis on Abraham's going forth empty-handed makes his subsequent enrichment the more striking.

12. Literally: "by/with appearance."

13. Throughout, the manuscript expresses the indefinite article by ս (rendered Ա in the edited text) or մէկ + noun + մի as in text no. 8.

14. Literally, "put his head on the ground."

10. Abraham in an Elenchic Text

Manuscript Matenadaran M10200 is a Miscellany written in 1624, 1634, and 1666. The scribes were Sargis and Amiras of Erznka. Previously, we have published texts from it relating to the antediluvian generations, as well as a more detailed description of the manuscript.[1] We named the text relating to the antediluvian generations "Abel and Other Pieces." It occurs on p. 384 of the manuscript. The further section published here is separated from "Abel and Other Pieces" by a passage on the Tower of Babel.

These antediluvian traditions seem, in turn, to be related to material in *Book of Questions* by Vanakan *vardapet* (1181–1251 C.E.), the sources of whose apocryphal traditions are themselves unclear.[2] The passage that is published here refers to postdiluvian events, enumerated by centuries, and the centuries we have given, the twentieth and the twenty-first, refer to Abraham. The traditions differ in a number of points from those of the narrative texts here, nos. 2, 4, 7, 8, 9, and 15, for example.

The paragraph numbering continues that introduced into our previous publication from this manuscript in Stone 1996a.

Elenchic Text (M10200) – Text

9. Ի դարուն վասն անօրէն[3] խառնիցն որդին մերօ առաջի հօրն ի Թարայի աւուրքն[4]. որ զէշն ընդ ձի խառնեաց.[5] Առան. եւ մեռաւ առաջի Թարայի հօրն իւրոյ. ահա Պետրոս վկա է. ումանք աստի ասեն զպատկերապաշտութիւն. Սոդոմն ասէ հայր թագցեալ տարածման սգով ի վերայ որդոց արար պատկեր եւ պատուէր զնա. եւ զկնի եկելոցն. աստուած կարծէցօ.

10. ԻԱ. դարուն զԱստուած ծանեաւ Աբրահամ: Սա զամենայն աշխարհի ապրեցոյց ի յայրեցմանէ Սոդոմա. զի կամէցօ Աստուած զամենայն երկիր այրել եւ Աբրահամ աղաչեաց թէ Ժ այր գտվի. Ա գտօ զՂովտ եւ էհան յայլ աշխարհս գտօ եւ ապրեցան:

11. Աբրահամու որդի մի ասեն. Եղիեստրոս. որ է հայր Արաբացոց. եւ Իսմաէլ հայր Պարսից.

---

1. See Stone 1996a, 140–57.
2. Ervine (2000, 417–28) discusses the sources of this passage. I am preparing the passage on the Tower of Babel for future publication.
3. An additional sign follows the o.
4. The classical nominative plural is strange here.
5. Note this spelling, for խառնեաց.

Elenchic Text (M10200) – Translation

9. In the 20th century. On account of the illegal mixings, the son died before the father in Terah's days, since Achan cross-bred the donkey with a horse. And he died before Terah his father,[6] behold Petros is a witness.[7] Some say[8] that image-worship (is) from this: Solomon says that a father, having buried his sons untimely with mourning, made an image and command(ed) < >,[9] and it was thought to be a god by those who came after.[10]

10. In the 21st century Abraham recognized God. He saved the whole land (earth) from the burning of Sodom, for God wished to burn everything,[11] but Abraham beseeched, "If 10 men be found ..." One was found, Lot, and he brought him forth to other lands. He was found and they were saved.

11. They say that Abraham had one son, Eliestros[12] who is father of the Arabs, and Ishmael, father of the Persians.[13]

---

6. Gen 11:28. This explanation of Achan's early demise is found in a number of texts in the present volume; see texts nos. 2.6, 4.1, 4.6, 6.2.4, etc.

7. This source remains mysterious, as does the identity of Petros.

8. A phrase often used in scholastic documents.

9. Apparently a word such as "to worship" has been omitted.

10. See Wis 14:15: "For a father, consumed with grief at an untimely bereavement, made an image of his child, who had been suddenly taken from him; he now honored as a god what was once a dead human being, and handed on to his dependents secret rites and initiations" (NRSV). This is quoted in a similar context also by John Malalas 57.1 (Jeffreys et al. 1986, 28).

11. This tradition is not found in the other Armenian Abraham texts.

12. That is, Eliezer; see Gen 15:2.

13. See Gen 15:2, where Eliezer is described as "of Damascus." In the other texts published here, Ishmael is not the ancestor of the Persians. In text no. 4.26 Ishmael is father of the Ishmaelites, while the Persians were descended from Keturah. See the notes there.

11. The Story of Terah and of Father Abraham

We are familiar with this writing in three versions. We know the first version, text no. 11 from two manuscripts and we present them in a synoptic edition. The two manuscripts are of the same work, though a number of variations between them occur, including omission and addition of text. The second version, text no. 11A, is rather different and is presented in a diplomatic edition following text no. 11. The third version is printed in this volume as text no. 15. It has basically the same material, but there are quite extensive additions and expansions.

Manuscripts of Text 11

Matenadaran M6340 fols. 21r–29r, a Ճառընտիր or *Collection of Homilies* was written in Łazvin in the region of Erznka in 1651. It includes a corpus of *Stories* or *Histories* (պատմութիւն), among which are two tales relating to Abraham.[1] One is *Story of Terah and of Father Abraham* and the other is *Concerning the Birth of Sahak (Isaac)*. They follow one another in the manuscript and are both edited here. They are two parts of a single composition.

The same two tales are to be found manuscript British Library Harl 5459, fols. 12v–20r, which is no. 89 in Conybeare's catalogue of the Armenian manuscripts in the British Museum. It is a Miscellany dubbed "Hagiological Tales and Apocrypha" (p. 215), of a type called Ոսկեփորիկ *Oskep'orik*. Conybeare suggests an eighteenth-century date for the manuscript on the basis of its language. It is certainly characterized by a very inconsistent orthography and late linguistic features.[2]

Harl 5459 tends, but not consistently, to use single dots as word separators, as well as punctuation marks. We have preserved only those that seem to function as punctuation marks. The spelling of M6340 is not as wildly variant from the norm as that of Harl 5459, but it too diverges from standard orthography.

Text no. 11 contains the following narrative incidents:
- Flood to Abraham (1, 1A–1B only in Harl 5459)
- Terah and Abraham's recognition of God (3)
- The birds or ravens and Abraham's prayer (4–6)

---

1. Ēganyan, Zeyt'unyan and Ant'abyan 1970, 2:298–99.
2. Conybeare 1913, 215–18.

- Abraham refuses to bring idolatrous sacrifice (7)
- Abraham and Sarah in Egypt (8–11)
- Story of Mamrē (12–21)
- Abraham's hospitality and the three guests (26–30)
- Sodom and Lot's escape (30–41)
- Birth of Isaac (43)
- Binding of Isaac (44–46)
- Story of Melchizedek (47–55)

Պատմութիւն Թարայ եւ հօրն Աբրահամու

M6340	Harl 5459
Title omitted	Պատմութիւն Թարայ եւ հօրն Աբրահամու:
1. Չի յորժամ վաղճանեցաւ Նոյ: Որդիքն նորա եւ թոռունք նորա մոռացան զԱստուած եւ պաշտեցին կուռք: Չի գիրք եւ աւրէնք ոչ կայր բնաւ բնաւին: Մոռացան զԱստուած. որ մարդ մի ոչ կայր որ յիշէր կամ գիտէր թէ Աստուած կա թէ ոչ:	Չի յորժամ վաղճանեցաւ Նոյ եւ որդիք նորայ եւ թոռունք նորայ մոռացան զԱստուած եւ պաշտեցին ըզկուռսն. չի գիրք եւ օրէնք ոչ կար բնաւին:
	1Ա. ջրհեղեղէն մինչեւ ի Թարայ ԳՌՃԼՇ տարի եւ Աբրահամ ամս ունէր ԹՃԺ. Ադամայ եկանելու դրախտէն մինչ ի Թարայ յեշվի նախահար Ի այսինքն յառաջ Ադամ: Աբէլ: Սէթ: Ենով: Կանան: Մաղաղիէլ: Յարէտ: Ենովք: Մաթուսաղայ: Ղամէք: Նոյ: Սեմ: Առփաքսաթ: Սաղայ: Եբեր: Փաղէք: Ռագաւ: Սերույք: Նաքովր: Թարայ: որ էր հայր Աբրահամայ մինչ ի ասւոյ նախահարց օրէնքն են. որ կոչի օրէն բնական որ է նախահարց:
Այս է պատմութիւնն Աբրահամայ նախապետին Աստուած ճանաչութիւնն. Ցիւրասիրութիւնն Աբրահամու:	1Բ Այուլ յետոյ օրէն նահապետաց փոխվի որ կոչի օրէն երկրորդ Աստուած ճանանչութեանն:

11. THE STORY OF TERAH AND OF FATHER ABRAHAM   129

2. Իսկ հայրն Աբրահամու Թարայ. կռապաշտ էր եւ կուռք շինող: Զրհեղեղէն մինչ ի Թարայ ԹՃ տարի էր որ կուռք պաշտէին եւ զԱստուած ոչ ճանաչէին: Իսկ Թարայ ասաց Աբրահամու ուսանալ զկուռք շինելն: Իսկ Աբրահամ ասաց. հայր ես [......].ութիւն ի ձեռին իմ լինէր խորտակէի զնոսա զի գործք մարդկան ինչպէս աստուած լինի:	Իսկ Թարայ որ է հայր Աբրահամու. {Աբրահամ}³ որ էր կռապաշտ եւ կուռք շինող. զի Զրհեղեղէն մինչեւ Թարայ կուռք կու պաշտէին. եւ զԱստուած ոչ ճանաչէին իսկ յետոյն կռոցին⁴ Թարա ասաց որդին իւրոյ Աբրահամու. ուսանել եւ կուռք շինել. իսկ Աբրայհամ ասաց. հայր զի է իշխանութիւն. իմ ձեռս լինէր խորտակէի. զամենայն կուռքն զի[ ] ձեռաց մարդքայն. ինչպէս լինի. Աստուած մարդոյ:
3. Ջայս իմանայր Աբրահամ, բայց զԱստուած ոչ ճանաչէր. հանապազ ի միտ ածէր եւ քննէր թէ ով իցէ Աստուած: Եւ ի ժամանակին յայնմիկ թոչնց պատուհաս եկն բազմութիւն եւ ազռաւաց. որ քաղէին զեղմա աշնանային. եւ զկանաչ արտերուն:⁵ այլ ո չ էր եղեալ այնպէս: Իսկ ամենայն մարդ քշէր զնաւսն եւ պահէր կամէին զարտսն եւ ո՛չ կարէին փրկել զարտսն:	ցայս իմանայր Աբրահամ զԱստուած ոչ. ճանաչէր. հանայպազ ի միտ ածէր եւ քնրնէր. թէ ով իցէ Աստուած. յետ այնորիկ ամունսայցաւ. Աբրահամ. էառ զՍառայ եւ ազզականքն իւր ի կնութիւն. այն տարին որ ամունսայցաւ Աբրահամ եւ եկ թոչուն Աբրահամու նմանութիւն սեւ ազռավոց որ քաղէին զաշնայն սերմա ուտէին այլ ոչ կանանչ էր իսկ ամենեքեայն գնացին քշեալ զթոչունսն զատտէն եւ ոչ կարէին. փրկել զարտն.
4. Իբրեւ գնաց. եւ տեսաւ զբազմութիւն թոչնցն. զարմացաւ եւ հիացաւ. քննեալ ընդ միտս իւր թէ մինչեւ այսաւր այլ ոչ եղեւ այսպէս: Չի մեծ Աստուած կա որ զայս առնէ: Հայեցաւ ի արեզակն եւ լուսինն թէ սոքա իցեն Աստուած. այլ ոչ հաւաեցաւ միտքն. Աստուած ասել նցա: / fol. 22v / Վասն զի փոփոխական	Աբրահամ գնաց եւ պահէր զատուս իւրեանց. իբրեւ տեսաւ զբազմութիւն թոչնցն. հայեցաւ յերկինս քնրնէր. զմիտս. իւր թէ մինչեւ ցայս օր այլ ոչ եղեւ այսպէս. զի մեծ արարող կայ որ զայս առնէ. հայեցաւ ի արեզակն եւ զլուսինքրն թէ սոքայ են աստուածք այլ ոչ հավանեցաւ ի միտս իւր թէ աստուած իցէ. զի

---
3. Dittography.
4. A bizarre form. The word is not in *NBHL*; we take it to mean "idolater."
5. This is a non-classical form.

են. երբեմս մեծանան եւ երբեմս փոքրանան։ երբեմս տաքանան եւ երբեմս ցրտանան; Վասն այն ոչ հաւանեցաւ նոցա Աստուած ասել:	փոփականն են։ երբեմս մեծանան երբեմս փոքրանայն. երբեմս տաքանան երբեմս ցրտանան. վասն այն ոչ հավանեցաւ նոցա Աստուած ասեն:
5. Եւ բարձրաձայն գոչեաց երկինքն եւ ասաց։ Է՛ անձանաւթ Աստուած որ բազմեալ կաս ի վերայ աթոռոյն երկնից։ Զի դու ես արարիչ երկնի եւ երկրի. լուսնի եւ արեգական, եւ ստեղծաւղ ամենայն կենդանեաց։ Որպէս առաքեցեր զթռչունս զայս խլել զվաստակս մեր։ Նոյնպէս ողորմեա մեզ. եւ դու պահեա զվաստակս մեր:	5. Եւ բարձրաձայն ասեր. կոչելով Ով վեր է այնձանօթ Աստուած որ բազմեալ կաս ի վերայ աթոռոյ յերկնից. զի դու արարիչ ես աշխարհի արեգակայն եւ լուսնի. ըստեղծող ամենայն կենդայնեաց որպէս առաքեցեր զթչուոնս զի եւ ծանիցուք զքեզ վասն մեղաց մերոց ողորմեայ մեզ զի վաստակա մեր այնպէս արասցես եւ դու պահեայ զվաստակա մեր ամենակարող եւ լցուցանող դու ես:
6. Իբրեւ զայս ասաց ելան ամենայն թռչունքն եւ փախեան. այլ ոչ ունէին զսերմ⁶ եւ զարտոս նորա։ Զի հայէր եւ տեսանէր Աբրահամ ամենայնի վաստակն ունէին թռչունքն. եւ իր վաստակն ոչ մերձենային զոհանայր Աստուծոյ։ Ուրախութեամբ գնաց եւ պատմեաց հաւրն. զքանչելիսն։ Իսկ հայրն ասեր զզաւրութենէ կռոցն եդեւ ա[յս] զի մեր կուռք շատ ունիմք վասն այն ոչ ունեն թռչունք[ն] զարտոսն մեր:	եւ զայս ասացեալ ելայն թռչունքն եւ փախեցայն. այլ ոչ ունէին զարտն Աբրահամույ. զի հայէր եւ տեսանէր որ զայլոց զարտն ունէին եւ զիւր արտն ոչ ունէին. եւ մերձենայն թռչունքն զոհանայր զԱստուծոյ եւ ուրախութեամբ գնայր զտունըն եւ պատմէր ծնողաց իւրոց սիրելեայց եւ բարեկամաց. եւ ըքանչանային որք լսէին ամենեքեան. Իսկ հայրն նորայ Թարայ ասաց ի զօրութեամբ կռոցն եդեւ այտ զի մեր կուռք շատ ունեմք վասն այն ոչ ունեն թռչունքն զարտն մեր
7. Ո՛չ հաւանեցաւ խրատու որդույն այլ[յ]⁷ հ[ր]ամայեաց գնալ ի նախիր[ր] եզն եւ արջառ բերել. եւ զեն[ել] գոհ կռոց: իսկ Աբրահամ առեալ կրակ. եւ գնաց ի տո[ւն]	ոչ հավատացաւ խորհրդոյն որդոյն. այլ հրամայեայց Աբրահամոյ ի նախիրն եզն եւ ամառ բերել զենել զոհս կռոցն. Աբրայհամ առեայլ կրակ. եւ գնաց

---

6. Here the birds eat the seed; compare the other Armenian texts, which are not uniform on this point. See also *Jub.* 11:18–22.

7. այ is also partly unclear in photograph.

11. THE STORY OF TERAH AND OF FATHER ABRAHAM   131

կռօցն եւ կրակ վառեաց ի ն[մա]։ Եւ հօր եղբայրն եկն զի շիջուցանէ զկրակն. եւ նա այրեցաւ ընդ կռօցն։ Իսկ հայր [եւ] ազգ եւ ազինք Աբրահամու կամեցան սպանանել զԱբրահամ։	ի տուն կռօցն. եւ կրակ վառեայց ի նմայ. եւ հայրն եւ եխբարքն գնացին շիջուցէն զկրակն. եւ նոքայ արեցայն ընդ կռօցն. իսկ հայրն եւ ամենայն ազզականքն կամէին ըզպայնանել զԱբրահամ. վասն այնօրիկ պատուհասեցան.
8. Իսկ Աբրահամ առեալ զՍառայ փախեաւ եւ գնաց յԵզիպտոս։ Եւ գովեցին զգեղեցկութիւնն Սառայի. առաջի փարաւոնի։ Եւ տարեալ տեսաւ եւ հաւանեցաւ։ Եւ եհարց զԱբրահամ թէ զինչ լինի քեզ Սառայ։ եւ նա վասն ահէ սպանանելոյն ասաց թէ իմ քոյր է։ Եւ փարաւոն կամեցաւ առնուլ զՍառայ իւրն ի կնութիւն։	Իսկ Աբրահամ առաւ զկինըն իր Սառայ փախաւ եւ գնաց յԵկեպտոս. գովեցին զգեղեցկութիւն կնօջն Աբրայհամոյ. եւ տարեայլ տեսաւ հայեցաւ զՍառայ եւ եհարց զԱբրահամոյ. զի է քեզ զՍառայ. եւ նայ վասն ըսպանելոյ սրոյ եւ ասէ Աբրահամ քրօչս / fol. 13v / իմ է. եւ փարաւոն կամեցաւ առնուլ զՍառայ իւր կնութիւն.
9. Եւ ի գիշերին երբ կամէր մերձենալ ի Սառայ. Երեւեցաւ նմա հրեշտակ հրեղէն զաւագանաւ եւ ասաց։ Մի մերձենար ի Սառայ. զի կին է Աբրահամու. Այլ տուր նմա բազում ինչս. վասն զի հայեցար ի տեսութիւնն Սառայի։ Եւ թէ ոչ առնես այտպէս. հրեղէն զաւագանաւ սատակեմ զքեզ. եւ պակեմ զթազաւորութիւնդ։	ի գիշերին կամէր մերձենայլ զՍառայ երեւեցաւ նմայ հրեշտակն հրեղէն. զաւազանով. եւ ասէ սատակեցանեմ զքեզ. եւ պակեմ զաթօռըն քոյ.
10. Իսկ ահէ հրեշտակին ահ եւ դող անկաւ ի վերայ փարաւոնի։ Եւ կոչեաց զԱբրահամու եւ ասաց. երբ Սառայ քոյ կին էր ընդէ՞ր ասացեր թէ քոյր իմ է։ Ասէ Աբրահամ վասն այն ասացի թէ իմ քոյր է զի մի սպանանես զիս վասն կնօջս։ Իսկ փարայոն ետ Սառայի Խ ծառայս եւ Խ աղախնեայս եւ ՂԾ ուղտս։ բազում կովս եւ ոչխարս. բազում ոսկիս եւ արծաթս։	իսկ ահէն հրեշտակին ահ եւ դողումա. անկաւ ի վերայ փարաւոնի. եւ կոչեայց զԱբրայհամ եւ ասէ. յերբ Սառայ քոյ կին է եւ ընդէր ասես քուր իմ է. ասէ Աբրահամ. վասն այն ասացի թէ քուր իմ է. զի մի ըսպաներ զիս վասն կնօջս. Իսկ փարայյուէնն ընդ Սառային ետ Ռ ծառայս եւ Խ աղախինս ՂԾ ուղտ բազում. կովս ոչխարս. ոսկի եւ արծաթս. եւ ետ Սառայի եւ Աբրահամոյ.

11. Եւ արձակեաց զնոսա[8] եւ ասէ. երկիրս իմ ամենայն առաջի ձեր կա . որ տեղ որ կամիք անդ բնակեցջիք։ Եւ բազմացան ուղտք եւ ոչխարք անասունք եւ ամենայն ինչք Աբրահամու: Վրանով շրջէր եւ արածէր զանասունս իւր ուր եւ / fol. 23v / կամէր: Իսկ ի մաւտ վրանին Ռ ոչխար պահէր վասն ունէր զկաթինն եւ զմածունն. զի մաւտ լիցի իւրն:	Եւ արձակեայց զնոսայ եւ ասէ յերկիրս. իմ առաջի ձեր կայ. յոր տեղ որ կամէք. անդ բնակեցէք. եւ բնակեցային անդ եւ բազմացան անասունքն եւ ամենայն ինչս Աբրահամոյ. եւ վրանով շրջէր Աբրահամ յերկիրն այն. ուր կամէր: Իսկ ի մտոյ վարնին պահէր Ռ խաշինս վասն կաթոյն եւ մածունին. եւ զզատինքն զի մօտ լիցին:
12. Եւ հովիւ մի ունէր անունն Մամրէ. խիստ ողորմած էր ի տուրս աղքատաց եւ հիւրոց: Եւ ի միում աւուր երբ ելանէր ոչխարս արածել Գ հաց տուին իւրն եւ շանն ասաց Աբրահամ. առ զայտ հացտ եւ զնա մինչ որ հացք թխեն. զամ հաց բերեմ քեզ. զի այն Գ հացն պաղարձ էր.	ունէր եւ մին սեւ ծառայ անունրն նորայ Մամրէ. խիստ ողորմած էր եւ աղքատայսէր եւ յալուր միում յերբ ելանէր. ոչխարս արածացանելոյ եւ ասաց Աբրահամ առ նայ մինչեւ հաց թխեն. եւ հաց սակաւ ունեն եւ ես բերեմ քեզ հաց զի այն օրն Գ հաց առաւ եւ գնաց.
13. Իբրեւ էլ ի տանէն Մամրէ սակաւ մի հեռացաւ. եկն աղքատ մի եւ ասաց սոված եմ. վասն սիրոյն Աստուծոյ տուր ինձ ունէլո : Իսկ Մամրէ կթեաց ոչխար. եւ բրդեաց հաց մի. կերաւ եւ աւրհնեաց զՄամրէ եւ գնաց: Իբրեւ ճաշու ժամ եղեւ եկն այր մի աղաչեաց եւ ասէ ճանպորդ ե ս. վասն Աստուծոյ սիրոյն տուր ինձ ունէլ ն՞ զի սոված եմ:	Իբրեւ էլ ի տանէն սակաւ մի հեռացաւ եկն / fol. 14v / աղքատ մի եւ ասէ. Վասն Աստուծոյ սիրոյն տուր ինձ հաց ունէլոյ զի սոված եմ. Իսկ Մամրէն կթայց զոչխարսն եւ բրթաց հաց մի եւ ետ աղքատին. աղքատն եկեր եւ աւրհնեաց եւ գնաչատ զԱստուծոյ եւ գնաց. իբրեւ ճաշու ժամ եղեւ եկն այլ մի աղաչէր, եւ ասէր. Ճանապարհորդ եմ եւ ոսվայծ վասն Աստուծոյ սիրոյն. տուր ինձ ունէլոյ
14. Եւ կթեաց Մամրէ զոչխարս. եւ բրդեաց հաց մի եւ կերակրեաց զնա: Իսկ կերաւ մարդ այն. աւրհնեաց զՄամրէ եւ զոչխարսն թողեալ գնաց: Իսկ Մամրէ կամէր	Եւ Մամրէն կթաց ոչխարս եւ բրթեաց հաց մի եւ կերակրեայց գնայ. եւ նայ կերաւ. եւ աւրհնէր Մամրէի եւ ոչխարացն. գնաց. Իսկ մաց հաց մի. կամեցաւ Մամրէ

---

8. Probably corrupt for the accusative զնոսա; cf. Harl 5439.

11. THE STORY OF TERAH AND OF FATHER ABRAHAM   133

հաց ուտել. բայց ասաց ի մյուս իւր. գուցէ այլ մի ոք զա խնդրէ հաց վասն Աստուծոյ այլ ոչ լինի. վասն այն ոչ ճաշակեաց։ Իսկ յետ ուրն եւեա եկն ծեր մի. աղաչէր եւ ասէր. զի յոյժ սովաձ եմ վասն Աստուծոյ սիրոյն ունիս. ինչ (ուտե)լ. տուր ինձ.	ճաշակել բայց ասաց ի մյուսի իւր. միթէ այլ ոք զայ խնդրէ հացզ. վասն սիրոյն Աստուծոյ. վասն այն ոչ ճաշակեայց: Իսկ յետ սակաւ մի. զնաց եկն այր մի մերձ աղաչէր եւ ասէր. սովաձէմ վասն Աստուծոյ տուր ինձ ուտելոյ
15. Եւ Մամրէ կթեալ կաթն եւ բրդեալ զպաղատճն. եւ ետ նմա ուտել: Իսկ նայ եկեր եւ աւհինեաց / fol. 24r / զՄամրէ ասելով այսպէս: Մամրէ. դու եղիցիս գլուխ ողորմածաց. եւ զեւսն քո` սպիտակ եղիցի: Եւ անուն [ք]ո բարի լիշատակ եղիցի ի վերայ աշխարհի. Եւ զեւ ողխարսն քո սպիտակ եղիցի:	Եւ Մամրէ կթեայց զոչխարսն բրթայց հայցն եւ ետ նրաւ⁹ ուտել. իսկ նա ուտէր եւ օհնէր Մամրէ եւ ասէր. դու եղիցիս գլուխ ողորմածաց եւ եղիցի քեզ ն շան. արդարութեան եւ սեւութիւներն քոյ եղիցի{ու}¹⁰ սպիտակ եւ անուներն քոյ բարի լիշատակ եղիցի մինչեւ ի կատարած աշխարհի ոչխարացն քոյ սեւովա ըսպիտակ եղիցի.
16. Առեալ զկաղենի զաւազանն ի ծեռացն Մամրէի տնկեաց. եւ ասաց. Այս զաւազանս եղիցի նշան ի մէջ իմ եւ քո: Իբրեւ աւհինեաց ծերն եւ ելեալ զնայր։ Ի յետ հայեցաւ Մամրէ եւ տեսաւ զզավազանն կանանչել եւ արմատացեալ: Դարձեալ հայեցաւ ի ծերն զի տեսցէ եւ աւելի աւհնութիւնս առցէ. այլ ոչ երեւեցաւ ծերն:	եւ առեալ զկաղենի զավազաներն ի ծեռաց. Մամրէ ցցցեաց ի հողին եւ ասաց. այս զավազանս եղիցի նշան. ի մէջ իմ եւ ի մէջ քոյ. Իբրեւ աւհինեաց այսպէս եւ ելեայլ զնաց եւ յետ հայեց/ fol. 15r /աւ Մամրէն եւ տեսաւ զզավազանն կանանչնացեայլ. եւ արմատացեայլ մինչեւ հայեցաւ թէ տեսցէ զծերն որ աւելի օհնութիւն առցէ. ի նմանէ զի այլ ոչ երեւեցաւ ծերն.
17. Հայեցաւ ի ոչխարսն եւ տեսաւ զի զամենայն սպտակացեալ էին: Եւ հայեցաւ ի վերայ ծեռացն եւ ոտիցն եւ տեսո զամենայն մարմինն սպիտակացեալ. քանզի սեւ ծառայ էր Մամրէ:	հայեցաւ ոչխարն որ սեւ էին ըսպիտակացեայլ էին. եւ հայեցաւ ի վերայ ծեռացն եւ ոտիցն իւր այլ եւ մարմույն. եւ տեսեայլ ըսպիտակացեայլ քանզի սեւ ծառէն¹¹ էր Մամրէն

---

9. The form is odd and a dative would be expected.
10. Corrupt.
11. Note this spelling of ծառայն.

18. Դարձեալ հայեցաւ ի զաւազանն եւ տեսաւ զաւազանն մեծ ծառ էր եղեալ. եւ աղբիւր մի ջուր բղխեալ ի յատակա ծառին։ Իսկ ոչխարքն ամենայն եկին արբին ի ջրէն։ Եւ նստան ընդ հովանեաւս ծառին։	Դարձեալ ի զավազանն հայեցաւ եւ տեսաւ զի զավազանըն մեծ ծառ. եւ ախբիւր մի բխեցյց ի ներքոյ ծառոյն. իսկ ոչխարքն ամենայն եկին աղբիւրն եւ նստային ընդ յովանեավի ծառոյն.
19. Իսկ Շ ժամու աւուրն եկ Աբրահամ առեալ հաց եւ բերէր Մամրէի։ Հայեցաւ եւ տեսանէր ի դաշտին բարձր ծառ երեւէր։ Զարմանայր թէ ոչ կայր ծառս այս ուստի եղեւ։ Երբեմս երթայր եւ երբեմս կանկներ. քններ եւ այջն սրբեր. [ե]ւ հայեր եւ զարմանայր։	իսկ Ժ ժամոյն աւուրն եկ Աբրայհամ եւ բերեալլ հաց Մամրէի. հայեցաւ Աբրայհամ եւ տեսանէր ի դաշտին բայցր¹² ծայր երեւէր. զարմանայր ի միսա իւր թէ ոչ կայր աստ ծառ այս, ուստի եղեւ. երբեմա երթայր եւ երբեմա կանգներ եւ քններ եւ այջն սրբեր լիաներ զարմանայր.
20. Եւ գնացեալ եհաս ի ծառն եւ տեսեալ զոչխարսն զամենայն / fol. 24v / սպիտակեալ եւ ոչ ծանեաւ եւ հարցանէր թէ ուր իցէ Աբրահամու ոչխարսն. եւ Մամրէ հովիւն։ Իսկ Մամրէ ընդ առաջ եկ եւ ասէ. հայր Աբրահամ արի եւ տես զզօրութիւն եւ զքանչելիսն Աստուծոյ։ Իբրեւ եկն Աբրահամ. եւ տեսո զծառն եւ զոչխարսն սպիտակեալ. եւ զաղբիւրն բղխեալ զՄամրէ սպիտակեալ. զարմացաւ եւ հարցանէր վասն սքանչելեացս թէ որպես եղեւ։	Եւ գնացեալ եհաս ի ծառն. եւտես ոչխարսն ամենայն ճարմակեալ եւ ոչ ճանանչեայց. եւ հարցանէր թէ ուր իցէ Աբրայհամույ յովիվա Մամրայ. Իսկ Մամրէ էլ ընդ յառաջ եւ ասէ. հայր Աբրայհամ. արի եւ տես քսբայնցելիս Աստուծոյ. իբրեւ եկն Աբրայհամ եւտես գծառ այն եւ զաղբիուրն եւ գոչխարսն սպիտակացեալ եւ Մամրէն սպիտակացեայլ. եւտես եւ զարմացաւ վասն ըսբունցելիեայցն եւ հարցան/ fol. 15v /էր թէ որպես եղեւ։
21. Իսկ Մամրէ պատմեաց նմա զամենայն սքանչելեացն թէ Գ աղքատք եկին հանդիպեցան կերակրեցի։ Իսկ յետինն ծեր էր կերակրեցի. եւ նա աւրինեաց զիս եւ զզաւազանս առեալ ի ձեռաց իմոց. եւ ցրցեալ ի տեղիչ¹³ եւ արմատացաւ։ Եւ այս ամենայն	Իսկ Մամրէ պատմեցույց նմայ զամենայն կարզավ. մի ըստ միոչէ. եկ Աբրայհամ անկեայլ գօտն եւ զձեռն համբուրեր ծառային եւ ասէր. դու իմ հայր ես եւ ես քո ծառայ.

---

12. Note this spelling of բարձր.
13. A locative would be expected.

11. THE STORY OF TERAH AND OF FATHER ABRAHAM

սքանչելիքս եղեւ. Իսկ Աբրահամ անկեալ համբուրէր զոտս եւ գձեռս ծառային եւ ասեր դու իմ տղայ. ես քեզ ծառա:	
22. Արդ ուխտեցեր Աբրահամ Աստուծոյ թէ քանի ապ[ր]- իմ մինչ որ հիւր ոչ հանդիպի ոչ ճաշակեմ: Մամրէ եղ[եւ] պատճառ հիւրընկալութ[եան] եւ աղքատասիրութեան Աբրահամու: Իբրեւ ետես Աբրահամ զայս ամենայն սքանչելիքս. եւ ուխտեցաւ ուխտ ընդ Աստուծոյ այլ ոչ կերակրել առանց հիւրի:	անդ ուխտեցայց Աբրայհամ ի սրտի իւրում. թէ քանի ապրեմ եւ կենդանի լինեմ. մինչեւ եւր ոչ հանդիպի հաց ոչ ճաշակեմ. Իսկ Մամրէն եղեւ պատճառ եւրընկալութեանն Աբրահամու եւ աղքատսիրութեանն: Իբրեւ ետես Աբրահամ զայս ամենայն
23. Եւ բերեալ վրան իւր եւ կանգնեցաւ ներքեւ կաղնի ծառոյն. եւ անդ բնակեցաւ ի վերայ ճանապարհին զի անցաւորք կերիցէ ի սեղանոյն եւ ապա գնասցեն: զի [ ]¹⁴ սեղան հացին ոչ վերա/ fol. 24v /ցուցանէր: թէ մէկ օրն Խ [......] հետ հիւր գայր Խ հետ հաց ճաշակէր ընդ հիւրոցն վասն սիրոյ նոցա:	եւ բերեալ զվրան իւր կանկնեաց ներքեւույն ի կողմս ծառոյն եւ անդ բնակեցաւ ի վերայ ճանապարհին զի անցաւորք կերիցէ ի սեղանոյ Աբրահամու եւ ապայ գնասցեն. օթեւանս իւրեանց սեղանս հացին ոչ վերացուցանէն. եւ թէ մի օր անցաներ եւյր ոչ գաիր. Աբրայհամ ոչ ճաշակէ.
24. թէ Ե աւրն մի անգամ հանդիպէր.Ե աւր ծոմ կենայր. թէ Ժ աւրէն Ա անգամ հանդիպէր. Ժ օր ոչ ճաշակեր. մինչեւ որ հիւր չկայր ոչ ճաշակեր. Իբրեւ ետես Սատանայ¹⁵ այսպիսի բարեգործութիւն եւ զհիւրընկալութիւնն Աբրահամու: Նախանձեցաւ եւ պահեր ամենայն ճանապարհիս որ շուրջ գնովալ էին:	եւ թէ Ե օր ոչ գայր եւր եւ ոչ ճաշակէր վասն սիրոյն իրոյ¹⁶ մինչեւ չգայր խուր.¹⁷ եւ ոչ ճաշակէր եւ շատ էր եղեայլ որ Ժ օրով. Ի օրով. Լ օրով ոչ հանդիպէր եւր. եւ ինքն մայր այն սովայդ ոչ ուտէր եւ ոչ ըմպեր. եւ իբրեւ ետես բարիատեացց Սատանայ այսպիսի բարի գործութիւն եւ յուրընկալութիւն Աբրայհամոյ նախանձեցաւ եւ դարնացաւ ընդ բարոյն եւ պահեր զամենայն ճանայպարս որ շուրջ նովալ էին.

---

14. See note 95 below.
15. An infralinear stroke marks "Satan," as often.
16. This is to be taken as a genitive of հուր (հիւր).
17. This is an alternative spelling of հուր < հիւր.

25. Ո՛վ որ զայր յետ դարձուցաներ եւ ցուց տայր այլ ճանապարհի։ Եւ կապեաց գճանապարհն այն որ մինչեւ խ օր հիւր ոչ հանդիպեցաւ. Աբրահամու։ Իսկ յոյժ նուաղեցաւ Աբրահամ։ Ասէ Սառա՛ այր դու սովամահ մեռար։ սակաւ մի ճաշակեա։	ով որ զայր յետ դաղցուց/ fol. 26r /աներ եւ ցուց տայր ընդ այլ ճանայպարսն մինչեւ Խ օր ոչ հանդիպեցաւ տուր Աբրայհամոյ. Իսկ յուժ նուաղեցաւ Աբրայհամ. ասէ Սառէն այր դու սովամահ մեռանես։
26. Ասէ Աբրահամ կենդանի Տէր. մինչ որ հիւր ոչ հանդիպի ոչ ճաշակեմ. ոչ կարեմ ստել Աստուծոյ. բայց ակն ունիմ Աստուծոյ որ ինձ այսաւր հիւր ողարկէ։ Չի անդ շինեալ էր Աբրահամ բարձր տեղ մի՝ զի ելաներ Սառա նստեր անդ եւ հայեր ընդ ճանապարհսն վասն հիւրոց։	ասէ Աբրայհամ. կենդանի է Տէր Աստուածն որ մինչեւ յուր ոչ գոյ ոչ ճաշակեմ եւ ոչ կարեմ ստել ուխտիս առաջի Աստուծոյ բայց ակն ունիմ Աստուծէ որ այսօրին հուր ողարկէ եւ անդի շինեայլ էր. բայցը տեղ մի զի ելաներ Սառայ անդ նստեր եւ հայեր ընդ ճանապրիսն վասն յուրոյ յուսոյ եւ հավատու.
27. Իբրեւ նուաղեաց Աբրահամ. ասաց Սառայ ելի տեղին հայեաց. իբրեւ ելի տեսաներ Գ զային։ Իսկ Աբրահամ հրամայեաց գյորքն զենուլ վասն հիւրոցն. զի որք մի ձնեալ էր յոյժ պատուական. եւ նմանութիւն ուներ զատինն Աբելի։ Ջայն յորքն զենել ետ / fol. 25v / Աբրահամ։	եւ իբրեւ նուաղեցաւ Աբրայհամ ասաց Սառայն ել տեղին եւ յայեայ ի հեռստանէ. եւ իբրեւ ել Սառայ ի տեղին. հայեր եւ եւեւ Գ հոգի զային իսկ Աբրայհամ հրամայեաց զորք զենուլ վասն յուրոցին, զի պատվականյն որք մի ձնեալ էր նմանութիւն զառոյն Աբէլի ուներ. այն որքն զենել ետ Աբրայհամ.
28. իսկ եկաւ Տէրն Բ հրեշտկաւք։ բայց ոչ գիտեր Աբրահամ թէ Տէրն է. եւ ի տեսանելն ուժովացաւ եւ ընդ առաջ ել նմա. իբրեւ նստան եւ կերակրեցան. Աբրահամ ականջ դներ եւ լսեր բազում բան զարմանալի եւ հիանայր։ Իսկ Տէրն ասաց Աբրահամու աւրհնելով աւրհնեցից զքեզ. եւ բազմացուցանելով բազմացուցից զզաւակ քո՝ որպէս զաստեղս երկնից. եւ իբրեւ զաւաղ առ ափն ծովուն։	Իսկ Տէրն եկաւ Բ հրեշտակօբ. բայց ոչ գիտեր Աբրայհամ թէ Տէրն է. զի յուժ ուրախացաւ ի տեսանելն զնայ. եւ ընդ յառաջ ել ռիշունեայց զնոսայ. իբրեւ նստայն եւ կերակրեցայն եւ Աբրայհամ լսեր ի նոցանէ բան զարմաց մս եւ հիանայր։ Իսկ Տէրն ասաց Աբրայհամոյ. օրհնելով օրէնեցից զքեզ բազմացուցից զավակն քոյ որպէս զաստեղս յերկնից եւ որպէս / fol. 16r / զաւաղ առ ափն ծովու։

11. THE STORY OF TERAH AND OF FATHER ABRAHAM 137

29. Դարձեալ ասէ եղիցի քեզ զաւակ Սառայէ՛. անուն նորա կոչեցցի Սահակ: Իբրեւ լուո Սառայ ի ներքեւ ծածկոյթին ծիծաղեր եւ ասեր. ե՞րբ լինի ինձ այդ. զի աւուրք իմ անցեալ է: Իսկ Տէրն ասաց Աբրահամու. Սառա զի ժպտեաց վասն աւետեացն. Սահակայ զի սուտ համարեաց զբանս իմ: Վասն այդմ ծիծաղելուն: ՂՃԿ տարի ազգն քո գերի մաացէ ի ձեռն այլազգաց:	Դարձեալ ասէ եղիցի քեզ զաւակ. անունն նորայ կոչեցես զԻսահակ. իբրեւ լուաւ Սառայ ի ներքեւ ի ծածկոցին ծիծաղեր եւ ասեր. երբ լինի ինձ զաւակ զի աւուրքն իմ անցեալ է. իսկ Տէրն ասէր Աբրայհամոյ թէ Սառայ ժպտեցաւ վասն աւետեացն Սահակայ. զի սուտ համարեցայ զբանս իմ վասն այդ. ծիծաղելուդ. ՂՃԿ տարի ազգն քոյ գերի մացեն ի ձեռն այլազգայց.
30. Եւ աղքնեաց զտունն եւ զերանն. եւ ասեր. Աբրահամ ել ընդ իս մինչ ի լեառն Սողոմայ: Եւ [յ]ահեն ոչ իշխէր հարցանել Աբրահամ թէ դու ո՞ ես: Իբրեւ հասին ի լեառն եր[լ]եաց Սողոմ: հրամայեաց Աստուած[18] Բ հրեշտակաց իւրոց եւ ասէ մտէք ի քաղաքդ ի դուրս. հանէք զՂովտ. զի արդար է եւ հիւրընկալ:	Եւ աղքնեաց զտուներն եւ զեղանն. եւ ասէ Տէր Աբրայհամոյ. ել ընդ իս մինչ ի լեառն Ադամ.[19] եւ ահեն ոչ իշխէր հարցանել Աբրայհամ թէ դու ով ես. իբրեւ հասին ի լեառն հրամայեացգ Աստուած Բ հրեշտակին եւրոյ ասէ. քաղաքէդ ի դուրս հանել զՂովտ. զի արդար է. եւ յուրանկալ.
31. Եւ ասացէք նմա. ելցէ ի Սողոմայ այլ մի դարձցի յետս հայել. զի ոք որ յետ հայի քարանայ: Իբր զայս ասաց Տէրն զիստաց Աբրահամ որ Տէրն է: Ասէ Աբրահամ որպէս կամիս առնել զքաղաքս Տէր: Ասէ Տէրն. կամիմ կորձանել զի մեղք դոցա բազմացեալ են:	Եւ ասէք նմա զի ելցէ ի Սոդոմ եւ այլ մի դառցի յետ հայել. զի ով որ յետ հայէ քարանայ. Իբրեւ զայս ասաց Տէրն եւ Աբրայհամ զիտաց որ Տէրն էր. ասէ Աբրայհամ. Տէր որպէս կամիս կամիս կորձանել զդոսաց: զի մեղք դոցայ բազմացեայլ է:
32. Ասէ Աբրահամ. Տէր ոչ իցէ այդչափի քաղաքդ Ռ մարդ առանց մեղաց: Ասէ Տէրն թէ իցեն ԵՃ այր արդար ոչ կորուսից զդոցա:[20]	Ասէ Աբրայհամ. ոչ իցէ քաղաքիդ մարդ յառանց մեղաց. Ասէ Տէր. եւ թէ իցէ Ճ արդար ոչ կամեմ դոցայ մահ. / fol. 17a / Ասէ Աբրայհամ. եւ

---

18. The abbreviation mark is omitted.
19. This is corrupt for Սողոմ "Sodom".
20. There is confusion of cases here.

Ասէ Աբրահամ եւ թէ իցէ ԹՁ այր արդար ոչ խնայես զդոցա։ Ասէ Տէրն. եւ թէ գտանիցի Ձ արդար ոչ կամիմ զմահ դոցա։ Ասէ Աբրահամ Տէր թէ իցէ Ծ արդար ոչ խնայես ի նոսա։ Ասէ Տէրն թէ գտանիցի. Ի արդար խնայեմ ի նոսա։	թէ իցէ Ծ արդար ոչ խնայես. ասէ Տէրն. թէ իցէ Ի արդար խնայեմ ի դոսայ. Ասաց Տէրն։
33. Ասէ Աբրահամ. Տէր զի ես. հող եմ եւ մոխիր որպէս կարեմ կրկին խաւսել ընդ քեզ. բայց ե՞րբ արժանի արարեր խօսել ընդ քեզ։ Վասն Ժ արդարոցն խնայեայ։	
34. Յայնժամ վերացաւ Տէրն երկինքն. եւ ձայն լսելի եղեւ որ ասաց. Երբ ի քաղաքիդ ոչ գտաւ արդար. Աբրահամ դու կաց ի տեղիդ եւ տես զկատարած դոցա։ Իբրեւ հրեշտակքն գնացին ի քաղաքն. ԺԵ տարեկանի նման ցուց տուին։	եւ վերացաւ ձայն լսելի եղեւ. յերբ քաղաքիդ արդար ոչ գտաւ. Աբրայամ դու կաց ի տեղիդ. տես զկատարածն դոցայ. իբրեւ Բ հրեշտակն գնացին քաղաքն ԺԵ տարեկանի նման. ցուց տվին զի յուրիանքն։
35. Իսկ Ղովտ յոյժ հիւրընկալ էր. Իբրեւ եւտես զնոսա մեծարեալ տարաւ զնոսա ի տուն իւր։ Իբրեւ գնացին հրեշտակքն ի տունն նորա. ասեն հրեշտակ ել ի քաղաքս. զի Տէր կամի կորձանել զսայ. զի մեզ առաքեաց ի դուրս հանել զքեզ / fol. 26v / Ասէ Ղովտ. Նստէք բազմեցէք եւ ճաշակեցուք. եւ տեսանեմ թէ զինչ հրամայէք. զի Ղովդ մարդ գիտէր զնոսա։	Իսկ Ղովդ յուրանկեալ էր. իբրեւ տեսաւ զնոսայ մեծարեայլ տարաւ զնոսայ. ի տունն իւր. իբրեւ գնացին ի տունն նորայ. Ա{ա}սեն²¹ հրեշտակն ել ի քաղաքսու զի Տէր կամի կորձանել զսայ. զի զմեզ Աստուած առաքեաց զի դուրս հանել զձեզ. Ասէ Ղովդ. նստէք ճաշակեցէք եւ տեցուք զինչ հրամայէք զի Ղովտ Բ մարդ գիտեր զնոսայ.
36. Մեղադրէր զնոսա եւ ասէր. Դուք նորահասակ մանուկ էք ընդէ՞ր մտաք այս չար եւ պղծագործ քաղաքս։ Ասեն հրեշտակն. Մեք վասն քոյ եկաք զի հանցուք զքեզ ի քաղաքս։ Իսկ կինն Ղովտայ ոչ հաւատայր խաւսից նոցա։	եւ մեղայդրեր թէ դուք նորայհաս մանկունք էք. ընդէր մտանէք այս չարայգործ պեղծ քաղաքս. Ասեն հրեշտակն. մեք վասն քոյ եկայք հանեցուք զձեզ ի քաղաքսու. իսկ կինն Ղովտայ ոչ հաւատաց խօսից նոցայ.

---

21. Dittography.

11. THE STORY OF TERAH AND OF FATHER ABRAHAM   139

37. Գնաց երաց գթոնիրն թէ հանցէ կերակուր վասն հիւրոցն. եւ տեսաւ գթոնիրն լցեալ չրով: Իբրեւ գիտաց Ղովտ ելանելն չրոյն. հաւատաց զանցումս քաղաքին: Յայնժամ եկին Սոդոմայեցիքն եւ կալան զդուռն Ղովտայ եւ ասացին. տուր մեզ որք եկեալ են ի տուն քո:	գնաց երաց գթունիրն զի հանիցէ զկերայկուրն վասն հրոցն. եւ եւեւս գթոնիրն չրով լցեայլ. եւ ապայ գիտաց զՂովտ²² զջուրն ելանելն. հաւատաց զանցումս քաղաքին. յայնժամ ելին Սոթումայեցիքն եւ կալան զդու/ fol. 17v /րն Ղովտայ. եւ ասեն. տուր մեզ զքոյ տունրն եկեայլ հուրն.
38. Իսկ Ղովտ վասն չարութեան նոցա փակել ետ զդուռն: ի ներքուստ ասէր Ղովտ. ունիմ Բ դուստր գեղեցիկս ի ձեզ տա[մ] եւ մի ձեռն աձէք զհիւրոցն իմ. Եւ նոքա ոչ հաւանեցան. Սկսան խրտակել զդուռն: Իսկ հրեշտակքն ասեն Ղովտա. դու մի հոգար վասն մեր. զի մեք կարող եմք փրկել զմեզ: Ահա ել ի դուրս ի տանէ քումմէ որ այժմ կորձանի քաղաք:	Իսկ Ղովտ չարութիւն նոցա գիտեր. փակեայլ էր զդուռս տանն ներքսուստ. ասէր ունեմ Բ դուստր գեղեցիկ ձեզ տաց եւ մի ձեռն այձէք զհրոցն իմ. եւ նոքայ ոչ հաւանեցան. ըսկսան խրտակել զդրունես նոցա. Իսկ հրեշտակն ասացին Ղովտոյ. թէ դու մի հոգար վասն մեր. մեք կարող եմք փրկել զմեզ. այս ժամոյս դու<ր>ս²³ ելէք ի տանեւ քումմէ. որ այժմ կորձանել իցէ քաղաքս:
39. Իբրեւ Սոդոմայեցիքն խրտակեցին²⁴ զդուռն. ելին հրեշտակք հարին եւ կուրացուցին զնոսա. եւ ինքեանք վերացան: Իսկ Ղովտ եւ ի քաղաքէն ինքն կինն եւ զդուստրն իւր: Չի կինն նորա առաքեաց զումս զի փեսայիցն զիտակ առնել նոցա / fol. 26v / զանցումն: Իբրեւ հասին ի ստորոտ լերինն: Իսկ կինն Ղովտայ յետ նայեցաւ վասն փեսայիցն առ ժամայն քարացաւ:	Իբրեւ Սոդոմայեցիքն խրտակեցին զդուռն, ելին հրեշտակքն. հասին եւ կուրացուցին զնոսայ. եւ ինքնայն վերացան. իսկ Ղովտ եւ ի քաղաքէն ինքն եւ կինքն եւ Բ դուստրն. զի կինքն նորայ առաքեաց զոմս վասն փեսայիս գիտակ առնել զնցայ զանցումս քաղաքին. իբրեւ հասին լեռին զերդումս իսկ Ղովտայ կինրն. յետ հայեցաւ վասն փեսայիս առ ժամայն քարացաւ.

---

22. As elsewhere, the prefixed q- has lost its "classical" function as *nota accusativi* and is often used on a nominative.
23. So we have emended դու.u.
24. This is preceded by խրտակն surmounted by delete marks.

40. Քանզի հրեշտակը ասացեալ էր նոցա ոչ նայել ի յետս. Որք ի յետ նային քարանան։ Իբրեւ ել Ղովտ հուր վառեցաւ շուրջ զՍոդոմայ իբրեւ զպարիսպ քարեա. հուր եւ ծծումբ կարկուտ ի միասին ի վայր թափէին յերկնից։ Մինչեւ է այր է գիշեր։ այնպէս տեղեաց ի վերայ Սոդոմայ. մինչ որ այրեցաւ գիողն զքարն. եւ սեւ ջուր ելաւ եւ ծովացո զտեղին²⁵ Սոդոմայ. եւ է մինչեւ ցայսաւր։	Քանզի հրեշտակ ասացեայլ է նոցայ ոչ նայել ի յետս. եւ որք ի յետու յայեցեն քարանային. իբրեւ ել Ղովդ հուր վառեցաւ շուրջ Սոդումայ. իբրեւ պարիսպ յուր եւ ծրծումբ. եւ կարկուտ ի միասին. եւ վայր թափէր յերկնից. մինչեւ է օր է գիշեր այն/ fol. 18r /պէս տեղեաց ի վերայ նոցայ մինչեւ ամենեսեայն արեցայն. գիոդ եւ զքարն. սեւ ջուր ելաւ եւ ծովացաւ ի տեղոյն. մինչեւ ցայսօր։
41. Եւ տեսեալ Աբրահամ զայս ամենայն փառս տայր Աստուծոյ. որ այնպէս մարդասէր է Աստուած որ միայն Ղովտ էր աղքատասէր եւ հիւրընկալ. մինչ որ ոչ հանեց Ղովտ եւ ոչ անցոյց զքաղաքն։	Եւ տեսաւ Աբրայհամ զայս ամենայն եւ փառս տայր Աստուծոյ եւ զուաներ որ մին²⁶վտ աղքատայ{տ}էր²⁷ էր եւ զեղծաւ ի չարէ Տէր Աստուած հանեց Ղովտ ի Սոդումայից. եւ ապայ անցուց եւ պատուհասեց զքաղաքն ամենայն։
42. Աղաչեմ զձեզ եղբարք առէք ձեզ օրինակ զՄամրէ որ հացով եբեր զԱստուած ի ոչխարս իւր. եւ Աստուծոյ աւրհնութեանցն եւ արքայութեանն արժանացաւ։ Եւ Աբրահամ որ հատով. ծնմով եւ աղաւթիւք հիւրընկալութեամբ եւ սեղանով զՏէրն երկնից իջուց ի տունն իւր. եւ ի սեղանն իւր բազմեցոյց. կերաւ եւ նստաւ խաւսեցաւ ընդ Աստուծոյ. եւ զաւետիսն Իսահակա ընկալաւ։ Եւ խառն զաւրհնութիւնն Աստուծոյ. որ աւրհնեաց զԱբրահամ եւ ասաց. աւրհնելով աւրհնեցից զքեզ. եւ բազմացուցանելով	

---

25. There is an erasure of one word here.
26. Unclear letter.
27. This is probably corrupt for աղքատասէր.

11. THE STORY OF TERAH AND OF FATHER ABRAHAM 141

բազմացուցից զզօակ քո: Եւ զայս տեսեալ / fol. 27v / եւ ուսարութ առնել ողորմութիւն[28] աղքատաց. եւ զհիւրասիրութիւն աւտարաց եւ թէ կամիք զարքայութիւն Աստուծոյ մտանել:	
colophon continues for 17 more lines.	
Title: *microfilm illegible here*	վասն ծընունդեայերն Սահակայ
43. Ի [ ]ալ Աբրահամ ի Սառայ յղացաւ եւ ծնաւ զԻսահակ: յոյժ գեղեցիկ եւ պատուական սիրական էր: Այնպէս սիրէին զնա ծնաւղքն որ գիշեր զցրագն ոչ շիջուցանէին վասն տեսութեանն Սահակայ: Իբրեւ զարգացաւ. առաքեաց Աստուած զհրէշտակ իւր եւ ասաց Աբրահամու զենել զորդին իւր մատաղ եւ պատարագ Աստուծոյ:	Տէր Աստուածն ամենայնի եւ մարդայսերն. երեւեցաւ Աբրայհամոյ ի Սարայի որ աւետեաց եւ հղացաւ զի ծնաւ զԻսահակ յոյժ գեղեցիկ եւ պատուական ծնողացն: Այնպէս սիրէին ծնօղքն նորայ որ գիշերն ճրակն որ ոչ շիջուցանէին վասն տեսութեան Սահակայ. եւ իբրեւ զարգացաւ զՍահակ առաքեայց Տէր զհրեշտակս եւ ասէ ընդ Աբրայհամու զենել զորդին իւրն մատաղ եւ պատարագ Աստուծոյ.
44. Զի փորձեց զնա Աստուած զի տեսցէ թէ զորդին իւր մատաղ եւ պատարագ Աստուծոյ տա թէ ոչ. Իբրեւ լուաւ Աբրահամ ի հրէշատակին համեւտեաց զեշն: Եւ առեալ ընդ իւր հուր եւ փայտ եւ Սահակ. եւ գնաց ի տեղի ուխտին: հարցան[էր] Սահակ զհայրնսն[29] եւ ասէր. / fol. 28r /ա . հայր. ահա հուր եւ սուր ուր իցէ ողշակէզն:	զի փորձեցգ զնոսայ Աստուած զի տեսցէ առնէ Աբրայհամ սիրելի որդին իւր մատադ. իբրեւ լուաւ Աբրայհամ համետեացգ զէշն եւ առեայլ ընդ իւրն փայտ եւ հուր եւ Սահակ. եւ գնայր ի տեղին ուխտին. հարցաներ զՍահակ հօրն եւ ասէր. հայր հայր այայ հուր եւ փատ. ուր է ոխչակէզս:
45. Ասէ Աբրահամ. որդի Աստուած պատրաստէ ողշակէզ: Զի Աբրահամ զայս գիտեր թէ խաբէ զորդին. բայց բերանն մարգարէնն մարգարէանայր: Իբրեւ հասաւ ի տեղի ուխտին. կապեաց զորդին իւր զԻսահակ:	Ասէ Աբրայհամ. որդի Աստուած պատրաստէ մեզ ողջայկէզս. զի Աբրայհամ զայս ասէր զի որդին խաբեր Աբրահամ զայս ասելով. գիտեր թէ / fol. 18v / խաբեր զորդին. բայց բերանովս մարգարէանայր: Իբրեւ գնաց

---

28. An erased word follows.
29. This appears to be corrupt.

Եւ առ սուրն իւր զի կոտրեսցէ q<զլուխ>[30] որդոյն: Իսկ հրեշտակ ճայնեալ ասաց մի մերձենար ի պատանեակտ զի առաքեաց Աստուած քեզ խոյ որջակէզի: Իբրեւ ի վեր հայեցաւ եւ ետես զխոյ ողջակէզի կախեալ ի ծառոյն եւ եղջերուացն:	հասաւ տեղին ուխտին. կայպեայց զորդին իւր զՍահակ եւ առաւ զսուրն զի կոտրեսցէ զզլուխն որդոյն. Իսկ հրեշտակ ճայնեայլ ասաց. մի մեռանեայլ ի պատանակդ զի առաքեաց Աստուած քեզ խոյ ողջայկէզ. իբրեւ ի վեր հայեցաւ ետեւ զխոյ ողջայկէզ կապեայլ ի ծառոյն ի յերջերվացն.
46. Իբրեւ իջոյց զխոյն եւ զենաւ: Եւ ճայն եղեւ առ նայ եւ ասաց: Աբրահամ, որպէս ոչ խնայեցեր զորդին քո՛ վասն իմ: Նոյնպէս եւ ես ոչ խնայեմ զորդին իմ վասն քո. եւ ուրախութեամբ դարձաւ Աբրահամ ի տունն: Եւ յաւուր միում մինչ աղօթէր էջ հրեշտակ{էր}[31] առ նայ եւ ասէ: Աբրահամ. հրամայեաց քեզ Աստուած երթալ Երուսաղէմ. զուցես անդ զծառայն Աստուծոյ Մելքիսեդեկ. գեղձեա զզլուխ նորա եւ հերք զեղջնկունս նորա. եւ բեր ի տուն քո: զինով եւ հացիւ պատարաց մատուցէ վասն քո:	իբրեւ իջոյց զխոյն եւ զենեայց եւ ճայն եղեւ առ նայ եւ ասէ. Աբրայհամ Աբրայհամ. որպէս ոչ խնայեցեր զորդի քոյ վասն իմ անուանն որպէս եւ ես ոչ խնայեցից զորդին իմ վասն քոյ եւ ուրախութեամբ դարձաւ Աբրայհամ ի տուներն իւր. եւ յաւուր միում մինչ աղօթէր էջ հրեշտակն առ նայ եւ ասէ. Աբրայհամ. հրամայեայց քեզ Աստուած զի գնասցես յԵրուսաղէմ եւ զուցես ծառայն Աստուծոյ Մելիքսէք. գերծեայլ զեղունկն նորայ եւ հերք զզլուխն նորայ եւ բեր ի տունն քոյ. զինով եւ հացիւ պատարզ մատուցէ
47. Նայ եղիցի քահանայ եւ աստուածակոյս կողմանէ վասն քո եւ ընդանեաց քոց քահայնայութիւն գործեսցէ: Ասէ Աբրահամ յոր տեղ գտանեմ զնա: Ասէ հրեշտակն ի յանսարին գտանես զնա: Իբրեւ գնաց Աբրահամ յԵրուսաղէմ ի գիշերին տեսանէր զսիւն լուսոյ ի յանտարին. գիտաց Աբրահամ որ անդ է: Իբրեւ տիւ եղեւ էլ գնաց ի տեղ/ fol. 28v /ին եւ գտաւ. զի ոչ էր տեսիլ նորա իբրեւ զտեսիլ մարդոյ:	վասն քոյ եւ վասն ընտանեաց քոց քահանայութիւն գործեցուցէ: Ասէ Աբրայհամ յոր տեղ գտանեմ զնայ. ասէ հրեշտակն ի յայնտարին գուցես զնայ. իբրեւ գնաց Աբրայհամ յԵրուսաղէմ ի գիշերին տեսանէր զսյուն լուսոյ ի յայնտարին. յիմացավ Աբրայհամ որ անդ էր Մելիսէք. իբրեւ տիւ եղեւ էլ եւ գնաց ի տեղին. յերբ տեսաւ Մելիքսէք զԱբրայհամ զի ոչ էր տեսեայլ նորայ իբրեւ տեսիլայնէրն մարդի.

---

30. This is written over another word.
31. Here the text is apparently corrupt.

11. THE STORY OF TERAH AND OF FATHER ABRAHAM

48. Այլ ազունեալ էր եւ զհեր գլխոյ նորա իջաներ մինչեւ[32] ի ծունկն: Եւ քամակ նորա որպէս էր քամակ կրայի: Եւ զեղրնկունս նորա թզայցափ: Ողջունեալ զնա Աբրահամ խաւսեցաւ ընդ նմա եւ ասաց․ քանի՛ ժամանակ է որ աստ կաս: Ասէ մելքիսեդ. Ը. տարի է որ աստ ճզնիմ անտես ի մարդկանէ․ այլ մարդ ոչ է տեսեալ զիս բայց ի քէն: Ասէ Աբրահամ. պատմեա ինձ զհաւատալն քո թէ որպէս եղեւ: Ասէ Մելքիսեդ. Ես եմ որդի Մելքեայ թագաւորին. որդոյ Սադիմ թագաւորին որ շինեաց զքաղաքս: Ի միում աւուր առաքեաց զիս հայր իմ ի նախիրն եւ բեր պատուական [եւ] գէր երինջք գի զոհս մատուցից կռոց:	այլ այ/ fol. 19r /զոյնեալ էր եւ զհեր գլուխն նորայ հերսն մինչեւ ի ծունկն. եւ գեղունկն թզայցափ. եւ ողջունեալյ զնայ. Աբրայհամ եւ խօսեցաւ ընդ նմայ եւ ասէ. քանի ժամանակ է որ աստ ես. Ասէ Մելիքսեդէք Ը տարհայ որ աստ ճքնիմ[33] այնպէս ի մարդկանէ. այլ մարդ ոչ է տեսեալյ զիս բայց ի քէն. Ասէ Աբրայհամ. պատմեայ ինձ զհաւատալդ քոյ թէ ինչպէս եղեւ. ասէ Մելիքսեդէք ես եմ որդի Մելքի թագաւորհին որ են որդի Սադէմ. թագաւորհին. որ շինեայց զքաղաքս. միում աւուր առաքեայց զիս հայրն իմ թէ զնայ նախիրն բեր գէր երինչք մի.
49. Եւ ես գնամ ի նախիրն եւ ջոկեցի զգէր երինջք եւ արշաոք: Եւ ծգեաց գշնորհս աստուածային սիրտս իմ. քնեցի եւ ոչ հաւանեցա կենդանիքն սպանանել․ թող կենդանասունն որ վասն անշարժ ձեռագործաց պատկերին կամէի տանել յետ դարձուցի: Հայեցա ի յերկինս եւ լուսաւորս եւ ամենայն արարածս արարչին․ եւ արարի քնութիւն շնորհօքն Աստուծոյ ծանեա արարիչն Աստուած. թողի անասունս եւ եկի առ հայրն իմ առանց ողջակիզի:	Եւ ծագեայց Աստուած լոյս ի սիրտս իմ․ քնրնեցի եւ ոչ հավանեցայ կենդանի անասուն տանել վասն այնշարժ ձեռայզորժ պատկերին. կամէի տանել ի յետս դարցուցի հայեցայ ի յերկինս․ եւ ի լուավորս {արարչին}[34] զամենայն արարածս արարչին. եւ շնորհիքն Աստուծոյ ծանեայ զարարիչն․ Աստուած եւ թողի անասունս. եւ եկի առ հայրն իմ առանց ողջայկիզի․

---

32. An abbreviation mark missing.
33. This is corrupt for ճզնիմ.
34. This word is dotted in the manuscript.

50. Եւ եհարց հայրն իմ թէ ուր է երինչք եւ / fol. 29r / առջարք քո։ Եւ ես ասացի հայր իմ ինձ դժուար թուի զկենդանին զոհ մատուցանել վասն անշարժ ձեռագործած մարդկան. որ ոչ են Աստուած այլ սուտ չասատուածք։[35] Վասն այն ոչ բերի։ Եւ հայրն իմ նխեցաւ ընդ իս եւ մտեալ ասաց մօրն իմ. զի այսաւր Բ որդոցս զմիւսն զոհ մատուցանեմ կռոց։ Եւ մայրն իմ իմացաւ որ նխացաւ ընդ իս հայրն իմ։ լայր մայրն իմ եւ ողբայր. երեսն ճանկէր եւ զգլուխն ծեծէր։	եւ եհարց զիս հայրն իմ թէ ուր է երինչն. եւ ես ասացի թէ ինձ դժվայր թվեցաւ զկենդայնին զոհ մատուցանել. վասն անշարժ ձեռայգործ մարդքայն որ ոչ է Աստուած. Այլ սուտ չասաւածք. վասն այն ոչ բերի. եւ հայրն իմ նիսացաւ ընդ իս եւ ‹ի› մտի իւր ասաց եւ ի մօրն իմ. զի այսօր Բ որդի ունիմք մինն զոյ մատուցանեմ ի կռոց. եւ մայրն իմ զիտաց որ ոխացեայլ էր ընդ իս. {Եւ մայրն իմ զիտաց որ ոխացեայլ / fol. 19v / էր} լայր եւ ոխպայր զերեսն ճանկէր եւ զգլուխն ծեծէր։
51. Չի մայր իմ զիս սիրէր. եւ հայրն իմ եղբայրն իմ. սիրէր։ Իսկ հայրն իմ իբրեւ ետես զսուգ մաւրն իմո որ լայր դառնապէս։ Ասէ հայրն իմ ընդէ՛ր լաս. զի վիճակ արկցուք ի վերայ Բ որդոց մերոց. ում ելցէ վիճակն զնա զենցուք։	զի մայրն իմ զիս սիրէր. Եւ հայրն իմ զեղբայր իմ սիրէր. իսկ հայրն իմ ետես զսուքն մօր իմոյ. որ լայր դառնայպէս. ասէ հայրն իմ ընդ մօրն իմու ընդէր լայս. եկ վիճակ արկցուք ի վերայ {որ}[36] զորդոց մերոց. ում ելցէ վիճակն. նա զենցուք։
52. Իսկ վիճակ արկին Գ անգամ. վիճակն անկաւ ի վերայ եղբօրն իմ։ Եւ ել հայրն իմ. եւ առեալ զեղբայրն իմ կապեալ տանէր։ Իսկ մարն իմ լայր եւ ասէր. ոչ ողորմիս քոյ եղբօրն։ Եւ մայրն իմ լալով գնաց զի տեցց զկատարումա որդոյն իւրոյ։ Իբրեւ լսեցին իշխանք եւ մեծամեծք թագաւորին. տարան զորդիս եւ զդուստրս իւրեանց զենումա կռոց։	Գ անգամ վիճակս արկցին եւ ել վիճակս եխբօրն իմոյ. Իբրեւ ել հայրն իմ. առեալ եխբարն իմ. կապեայլ. տանէր. Իսկ մարն իմ լայր եւ ասէր. ոչ ողորմեա քոյ եղբօրն. եւ մարն իմ լալով գնաց զի տեսցէ զկատարումն որդոյն իւրոյ. իբրեւ լսեցին իշխանքն եւ մեծայմեծքն եւ թագաւորն. տարան զորդիսն եւ զդուստրսն իւրեանց զոհ զենել կռոցն։
53. Եւ ես լալով վասն եղբաւրն իմ փախեայ եւ ելի ի յանտառս։ Յորժամ տեսի որ նորա	Եւ ես լալով վասն եղբօրս իմ փախեայ եւ ելայ անտառն. յորժամ տեսի որ նորա

---

35. A infralinear line marks negative divine force.
36. This word is dotted in the manuscript.

11. THE STORY OF TERAH AND OF FATHER ABRAHAM

ձեռնարին[37] զենումա եղբօրն իմ. խնդրեցի ի Տեառնէ թէ բացցեն դրունք անդընդոց. եւ կլանեցեն զնոսա: Նոյն ժամայն պատառեցօ տեղին եւ կալաւ զնոսա ընդ տաճարին զհայրն իմ եւ զմայրն իմ ամենայն ժողովրդովա: եւ ես միայն մաացի աստ: Բայց այս Շ տարի է որ չէ տեսեալ զիս մարդ.	ձեռնարկեն ի զենումա եխբօրն իմոյ. Եւ ես խնդրեցի ի Տեառնէ թէ բացցեն դրունք անդունդոց եւ կլանիցէ զնոսայ. Նոյն ժամայն պատառեցաւ տեղին եւ կլաւ զնոսա ի տաճարին եւ ընդ կռոցն զհայրն եւ զմայրն իմ եւ ամենայն ժողովուրդն որ ի տաճարին էին. Եւ ես միայն մաացի աստ այս Շ տարի է. որ չէ տեսեայլ զիս մարդ.
54. Իսկ Աբրահամ գերձեաց զհեր զլխտ նորա. եւ հարթեաց զերընկունքն նորա. լուաց եւ մաբրեաց զնա. եւ շուրջառով պատեաց եւ զարդարեաց զնա: Եւ տարեալ ի տուն իւր հացի եւ զինով պատրաստ մատոյց. եւ ճաշակեցան ընդանիքն որդիքն եւ աղախնեայքն եւ ծառայք նորա ի նմանէ. Եւ եղեւ քահանայ ի տանն Աբրահամու աստուածակոյա կողմանէ. զի այն եղեւ առաջին պատարագն հացի եւ զինով: Չի Մելքիսեղ եղեւ առաջին քահանայն որ աւրինակ էր Քրիստոսի:	Իսկ Աբրայհամ գերձեաց զեղունկն նորայ զերթ զզլուխն նորայ լուաց եւ մաբրեաց. եւ շուրջառով ապըրշմեդենվա զարդարեաց եւ տարեայլ ի տունն իւր. Պատարաց մատուց հացիւ եւ զինով եւ ճաշակեցայն ընտանիք / fol. 20r / որդիքն ծառայքն եւ աղադինքն նորայ ի նմանէ եղեւ քահանայութեամք տանրն Աբրայհամոյ պարոնայկուա կողմանէ. զի այն եղեւ առաջին քահայնայութիւնն եւ պատարագ զի Մելքիսէթովա եղեն.
55. Եւ Աբրահամ բարեգործութեամք ծերացաւ. եւ խաղաղութեամք հանգեաւ ի [ ]. Եւ եթող Բ որդիս Սահակ ի Սառայէ. եւ Իսմայէլ ի Հագարու: Սահակայ ծնաւ Եսաւ եւ Յակոբ.	Աբրայհամ բարի գործութեամք ծերացաւ. եւ հանգաւ ի խաղաղութեամք.[38] Եւ եթող Բ որդի զՍահակ Սառայեն Իմայէլ ի Յագար. աղադինեէն. եւ ի Սահակէ ծնաւ Յեսոյ եւ Յակոբ:
56. Եւ ոչ գրեցաք զլիակատար պատմութիւնն զի աւրինակն այս էր: Ողորմի ստացողի գրոցս. Կարապետին: եւ իւր ծնողացն հօրն Ամիրվելուն. եւ մօրն Գուլումին. եւ որդւոյն Անդրն:	

---

37. Corrupt here for ձեռարկին.
38. The case usage is odd.

This Is the Story of Terah, and of Father Abraham.

M6340 omits title	**Harl 5459**
1. For when Noah died, his sons and his grandsons forgot God and revered idols. For there was no book or law at all.[39] They forgot God, so that there was not one man who remembered or knew whether there is a God or not.[40]	For when Noah died both his sons and his grandsons forgot God and revered idols. For there was no book or law at all.
	1A. From the flood to Terah was 3,138 years and Abraham lived for 940 years.[41] From Adam's going forth from the Garden until Terah 20 forefathers are mentioned, they are, first Adam, Abel, Seth, Eno<s>,[42] Kainan, Mahalalel, Jared, Enoch, Methuselah, Lamech, Noah, Shem, Arpachshad, Sela, Eber, Peleg, Reu, Serug, Nahor, Terah who was Abraham's father. Up to here is the law of the forefathers, which is called natural law, which is of the forefathers.
Title: This is the history of Abraham the patriarch's recognition of God. The hospitality of Abraham.	1B. Hereafter the law of the patriarchs is changed, which is called the second law[43] of the recognition of God.

Q51

---

39. Cf. *Biblical Paraphrases, Story of Moses* §10: Stone 1982a, 115 (re Moses).

40. Other sources for this forgetting include *Biblical Paraphrases: Story of Noah* 11 (Stone 1982a, 93). See Maimonides, *Mishneh Torah*, "Idolatry" 1.1.

41. Such chronological details are quite frequently introduced into the texts. They are closely related to a genre of chronologies found in Armenian and other traditions. See the introduction to text no. 1 above for discussion and references. The number 940 for Abraham's age is surely wrong.

42. Enoch and Enosh are frequently confused. See Stone 1982a, 13; Stone 1996a, 84, 151; and Stone 2010, 522–23, 525, 528.

43. Observe that Deuteronomy (Armenian Գիրք երկրորդ օրինաց) means "Second Law," though at this point clearly a different idea is involved. This is the only place in the Abraham material that we have gathered where the idea of a series of laws or levels of revelation of law occurs. Compare the rabbinic concept of the Noachic laws.

11. THE STORY OF TERAH AND OF FATHER ABRAHAM 147

2. Then Abraham's father Terah was an idolater and a builder of idols. From the Flood up to Terah were 900 years,[44] that they revered idols and did not recognize God. Then Terah said to Abraham to learn the building of idols.[45] Then Abraham said, "Father I [...pow]er was in my hand, I broke them, for how can human works be God?"[46]	Then Terah, who was Abraham's father {Abraham} who was an idolater and builder of idols. For from the Flood up to Terah they revered idols and did not recognize God. Then later Terah the idolater said to his son Abraham to learn and build idols. Then Abraham said, "Father, why is it that there was power through my hands? I was breaking all the idols, for they are works of human hands,[47] how can it be[48] a god for mankind?
3. Abraham discerned this, but he did not recognize God. Continually he considered and questioned, who is God.[49] And at that time a multitude of birds and of ravens came as a punishment. They gathered up the autumn seed and the green of the fields.[50] This had never happened before. Then all everybody chased the birds and desired to guard the fields and were unable to save the fields.	Abraham discerned this; he did not recognize God. Continually he considered and questioned, who God is. After that Abraham married. He took Sarah, also his relative,[51] in marriage. In that year in which Abraham married, bird(s) also came to Abraham, in the likeness of black ravens who were gathering up the autumn seed, they were eating (it), and there was no more green. Then all went to chase away the birds from the field and they were unable to save the field.
4. When he went and saw the multitude of the birds, he wondered and marveled, examining in his mind that up to this day such a thing has never happened. For there is a great	Abraham went also to guard their field.[52] When he saw the multitude of the birds, he looked at the heavens. He examined his mind that up to this day such a thing has never happened.

---

44. This figure fits in general with the dates in Stone 1982a, 82–83.
45. Terah as builder of idols is discussed in text no. 8.1 note.
46. This incident resembles text no. 8.2–3 but is simplified. Abraham's breaking of idols occurs also in *Apocalypse of Abraham* chaps. 1–3.
47. Both recensions have lacunae in this sentence, but the sense is clear.
48. That is, "they be".
49. Abraham rejects idols before he recognizes God. This sequence occurs otherwise in text no. 8 and its parallel in text no. 9.
50. The identity of the fruit is unclear. In texts nos. 2.3 and 4.2 produce is mentioned, while in 8.4–5 grapes are specified. See p. 64, n. 24 on text no. 4.2.
51. This formulation probably reflects discomfort with the incestuous implications of Gen 20:12.
52. In other versions of the story Abraham is sent by his father (see, e.g., text no. 2.3).

God who does this. He looked at the sun and the moon, whether they might be god,[53] but his mind was not persuaded to say "God" to them,[54] because they are mutable, sometimes they wax and sometimes they wane; sometimes they are hotter and sometimes they are cooler. Because of that, he was not persuaded to say "God" to them.[55]	For there is a great Maker who does this. He looked at the sun and the moon, whether they are gods, but was not persuaded in his mind, that they were god, for they are mutable. Sometimes they wax, sometimes they wane; sometimes they are hotter, sometimes they are cooler. Because of that he was not persuaded to say "God" to them.
5. And he cried loudly to the heavens and said, "HE IS;[56] unknown God who are seated upon a heavenly throne. For you are Maker of heaven and earth, of moon and of sun, and Creator of all living beings. Just as you sent these birds to pluck up our labors, so have mercy on us and preserve our labors."	And he said loudly, crying, "Who is on high, unknown God who are seated upon a heavenly throne. For you are Maker of the world, of the sun and moon, Creator of all living beings. Just as you sent the birds so that we may recognize you,[57] have mercy on account of our sins for you will thus do to our labors and preserve our labors, you are omnipotent one and fulfiller."
6. When he said this all the birds rose up and fled. They no longer were eating his seed and field. Since Abraham looked and saw that the birds were eating (the fruit of) everybody's labor and they did not draw close to (the fruit of) his labor, he praised God.[58] Joyously he went and related the miracle to his father. But his father said, "Through the power of the idols this took place, for our (we)[59] have many idols. On account of that, the birds do not eat our fields."	And he having said this, the birds rose up and fled. They no longer were eating the field of Abraham. Since he looked and saw that they were eating others' field and the birds were not eating his field and (not) approaching it, he praised God and joyously went home and related (it) to his parents and loved ones and friends. And all who heard marveled. But his father Terah said, "This took place through the power of the idols, for we have many idols. On account of that, the birds do not eat our field."

---

53. See note 20 on text no. 2.3.
54. Or: "call them God".
55. The resolution of the plague of birds is not given until §6 and the shift to the astronomical recognition of God is rather rough.
56. Է "HE IS" is a divine name in Armenian, derived from Exod 3:14.
57. Here the birds are the instrument of Abraham's recognition of God. See also texts nos. 2.4, 4.3–4, etc.
58. The singling out of Abraham's field is to be found also in other texts
59. Perhaps մեր is erroneous for մեք, which is also the reading of Harl 5459.

11. THE STORY OF TERAH AND OF FATHER ABRAHAM

7. He was not persuaded by (his) son's counsel, bu[t] he commanded (him) to go to the flock, to bring an ox and a bull and offer a sacrifice to idols.⁶⁰ Then Abraham took fire and went to the idolatrous temple and set fire to i[t]. And his father's brother⁶¹ came to extinguish the fire and he was burnt up together with the idols. Then Abraham's father (and) family and relatives wished to kill Abraham.⁶²	He was not persuaded by (his) son's counsel, but commanded Abraham to the flock, to bring an ox and a bull to slaughter as a sacrifice to the idols. Abraham, taking fire, went to the idolatrous temple and set fire to it. And his father and brothers went to extinguish the fire and they were burnt with the idols.⁶³ Then his father and all (his) relatives wished to kill Abraham. On account of that they were punished.⁶⁴
8. Then Abraham took Sarah and fled and went to Egypt.⁶⁵ And they praised Sarah's beauty before Pharaoh.⁶⁶ And having brought (her), he saw and he was pleased, and he asked Abraham. "What is Sarah to you?" And he on account of fear⁶⁷ of being killed said, "She is my sister." And Pharaoh wished to take Sarah to himself in marriage.	Then Abraham took his wife Sarah, he fled and went to Egypt. They praised the beauty of Abraham's wife. And having brought (her),⁶⁸ he saw, he looked at Sarah and he asked Abraham, "What is Sarah to you?" And on account of⁶⁹ being killed by the sword, Abraham said, "She is my sister."⁷⁰ And Pharaoh wished to take Sarah to himself in marriage.
9. And in the night, when he wished to draw near to Sarah, a fiery angel with a staff⁷¹ appeared to him and said, "Do not draw near to Sarah, for	In the night he wished to draw near to Sarah; the fiery angel appeared to him with a staff and said, "I will kill you and destroy your throne."

---

60. Apparently as a thanksgiving offering for the sparing of his vineyard. The story is rather abbreviated at this point.
61. Usually specified as Achan (Haran). The name of Abraham's uncle is not mentioned in this text.
62. This element is unique to this document and to text no. 15.7. Concerning anger against Abraham as the reason he left Ur, see the General Introduction," p. 19.
63. Clearly corrupt for "his father's brother"; see the next phrase.
64. This last sentence is not found in M3640.
65. Gen 12:10. The story that is given more fully in other documents is abbreviated here.
66. Gen 12:14.
67. The case here is problematic.
68. That is, to Pharaoh; cf. M6340.
69. Corrupt for "feared."
70. Wrong case.
71. Text no. 8.11, for example, has פנוף "sabre, sword" at this juncture.

she is Abraham's wife. Rather give him many possessions, because you admired Sarah's appearance.[72] And, if you do not act thus I will kill you with a fiery staff and destroy your kingdom.[73]	
10. Then from fear of the angel, fear and trembling fell upon Pharaoh. And he summoned Abraham[74] and said, "When[75] Sarah was your wife, why did you say, 'She is my sister'?"[76] Abraham said, "Because of that I said that she is my sister, lest you kill me on account of[77] (my) wife." Then Pharaoh gave Sarah 40 servants and 40 maidservants and 400 camels, numerous cows and sheep, much gold and silver.	Then from fear of the angel fear and trembling fell upon Pharaoh. And he summoned Abraham and said, "When Sarah is your wife, why do you say, 'She is my sister'?" Abraham said, "Because of that I said that she is my sister, lest you kill me on account of (my) wife." Then Pharaoh gave with Sarah 1,000 servants and 40 maidservants, 400 camels, numerous cows, sheep, gold and silver. And he gave (them) to Sarah and Abraham.
11. And he dispatched them and said, "All this land of mine is before you. Wherever you wish, there shall you dwell." And Abraham's camels and sheep, beasts and all possessions multiplied.[78] And he traveled around with a tent and pastured his beasts wherever he wished. But, he kept 1,000 sheep close to the tent to eat the milk and the buttermilk, so that it might be close to him.	And he dispatched them and said, "My land is before you. Wherever you wish, there dwell." And they dwelt there and Abraham's beasts multiplied and all (his) possessions. And Abraham traveled around in that land with a tent in that land, where he wished. But at the entrance to the tent he kept 1,000 sheep for milk and buttermilk, and lambs, that they might be close.

---

72. This explanation of Pharaoh's gifts to Abraham does not occur elsewhere. See, however, Gen 20:16 on Abimelech's gift to Abraham in a similar context.

73. In text no. 4.10 Pharaoh is stopped by an affliction in his groin, and the appearance of God (not an angel). In text no. 8.11 the angel appears in a dream (Pharaoh mistakenly thinks that the angel is God) and threatens Pharaoh with a sword (no fire is mentioned). See also *Gen. Rab.* 40:17 for rabbinic versions of this story. Compare text no. 8.11: the image of an angel with a sword is common in the Bible. See, e.g., Num 22:23, Josh 5:13–14, and 1 Chr 21:16.

74. The case use is apparently anomalous. Otherwise, translate: "those with Abraham," but that is a translation of a corrupt text.

75. Or: "if"; so both manuscripts.

76. Gen 12:18–19.

77. Or: "in exchange for"; so both manuscripts.

78. Gen 13:2. Compare texts nos. 2.7, 4.12, and 12.14.

11. THE STORY OF TERAH AND OF FATHER ABRAHAM

12. And he had a shepherd Mamrē by name.[79] He was very merciful in gifts to the poor and guests. And one day, when he went out to pasture the sheep 3 loaves of bread were given to him and (his) dog.[80] Abraham said, "Take this bread and go, until they bake bread, I will come (and) bring you bread." For those 3 loaves were unleavened cakes.	He also had a black servant, whose name was Mamrē. He was very merciful and lover of the poor and one day, when he went forth to pasture the sheep, Abraham also said to him, "Until they bake the bread, and they have little bread, and I (will) bring you bread," so that on that day he took 3 loaves and went.
13. When Mamrē went forth from the house, he had gone a little distance. A poor man came and said, "I am famished. For the love of God, give me something to eat." Then Mamrē milked a sheep and he crumbled one loaf. He ate and blessed Mamrē and went. When it was lunch-time, a man came, beseeched (him) and said, "Are you a traveler? For the love of God, give me (something) to eat, for I am famished.	When he went forth from the house, he had gone a little distance. A poor man came and said, "For the love of God, give me 1 bread to eat, for I am famished." Then Mamrē milked the sheep and he crumbled one loaf and gave it to the poor man. And the poor man ate and blessed (Mamrē) and praised God and went. When it was lunch-time, a man came and beseeched (him), and he said, "I am a traveler and famished. For the love of God, give me (something) to eat."
14. And Mamrē milked the sheep and he crumbled one bread and fed him. Then that man ate. He blessed Mamrē and the sheep (and) leaving, he went. Then Mamrē wished to eat bread, but he said to himself,[81] "Perhaps some other person (will) come (and) ask for bread for God's sake (and) there will be no more." On account of that he did not eat. Then, after midday,[82] he saw an old man. He beseeched and said, "I am very famished. For the love of God, (if) you have anything to eat, give (it) to me."	And Mamrē milked the sheep and crumbled one (loaf of) bread and fed him. And he ate and blessed Mamrē and the sheep (and) he went. Then one (loaf of) bread remained. Mamrē wished to eat, but he said to himself, "Perhaps some other (person will) come (and) ask for bread for the love of God." On account of that he did not eat. Then after a little time, a man[83] drew near. He beseeched and said, "I am famished. For the sake of God, give me (something) to eat."

---

79. For the Story of Mamrē, see the General Introduction, 12–13. See also text no. 2.9 notes.
80. The dog is found only in this manuscript and in text no. 15.13.
81. Literally: "in his mind."
82. Literally: "the day."
83. Literally: "went and came close."

15. And Mamrē, having milked the milk and having crumbled the unleavened bread, he also gave him to eat. Then he ate and blessed Mamrē saying thus, "Mamrē, you will be chief of the merciful ones and your black things will be white. And your name will be a good memorial upon the world. And your black sheep will become white."	And Mamrē milked the sheep, crumbled bread and gave him to eat. Then he ate and blessed Mamrē and said, "You will be the chief of the merciful ones and it will be a sign of righteousness for you and your blackness will become white and your name will be a good memorial until the end of the world. Your sheep's black(ness) will become white."
16. Having taken the oaken staff from Mamrē's hands, he planted (it) and he said, "This staff will be a sign between me and you." When the old man had blessed and set forth, he went. Mamrē looked back and saw the staff had greened and struck root. Again he looked at the old man, so that he might see (him) and he might receive more blessing. The old man was no longer visible.[84]	And having taken the oaken staff from (his) hands, Mamrē stuck it into the earth and said, "This staff will be a sign between me and you." When he had blessed thus, he set forth, he went and Mamrē looked back and saw the staff had greened and struck root, while he looked so that he might see the old man, that he might receive more blessing from him. For the old man was no longer visible.
17. He looked at the sheep and saw that all had become white. And he looked upon (his) hands and feet and he saw that all his body had become white, because Mamrē was a black servant (slave).	He looked at the sheep who were black they had become white. And he looked at his hands and his feet also his body, and he saw that it had become white, because Mamrē was a black servant (slave).
18. Again he looked at the staff and he saw that the staff had become a great tree. And a spring of water flowed forth at the base of the tree.[85] Then all the sheep came (and) drank from the water and sat in the shade (or: shelter) of the tree.	Again he looked at the staff and he saw that the staff (had become) a great tree. And a spring flowed forth from under the tree. Then all the sheep came to the spring and were sitting in the shade (or: shelter) of the tree.

---

84. This seems to mean that he disappeared. If so, it would be typical of an angelophany.

85. References to trees and a spring appearing wonderously to ascetic desert fathers are not infrequent. See N. Stone 1997, 57, 75, etc. The appearance of the spring is to be found only in this version of the Abraham story and, presumably, it has entered here from the *topos* in the desert fathers stories. In §20 it is present only in one recension.

19. Then, at the 8th hour of the day, Abraham went forth having taken bread, and was bringing (it) to Mamrē. He looked and saw that a tall tree was visible in the field. He wondered whence this tree had come, for it had not been (there). Sometimes he went and sometimes he stood still. He examined (it) and rubbed his eyes, and he gazed and wondered.[86]	Then, at the 10th hour of the day, Abraham went forth, and brought[87] bread to Mamrē. Abraham looked and saw in the field a tall[88] tree was visible. He wondered to himself that this tree had not been there: whence did it come? Sometimes he went and sometimes he stood still and examined (it) and rubbed[89] his eyes. He was surprised, he wondered.
20. And having gone, he reached the tree and saw all the sheep whitened and did not recognize (them) and asked, "Where are Abraham's sheep and the shepherd Mamrē?" Then Mamrē met (him) and said, "Father Abraham, come and see the power and the wonders of God." When Abraham came and saw the tree and the whitened sheep and the spring flowing forth (and) Mamrē whitened, he wondered and asked concerning the miracle, how it had taken place.	And having gone, he reached the tree. He saw all the whitened sheep and he did not recognize (them) and asked, "Where is Mamray, Abraham's shepherd?" Then Mamrē met (him) and said, "Father Abraham, come and see God's wonders." When Abraham came he saw that tree and the spring and the whitened sheep and Mamrē whitened. He saw and wondered at the miracle and asked how it had taken place.
21. Then Mamrē told him about all the wonders, "3 poor people came; they encountered (me); I fed (them). Then the last one was an old man. I fed (him) and he blessed me and he took this staff from my hands. And having stuck (it) <in this place>[90] and it took root. And all this was a miracle (wonder)." Then Abraham, having fallen down, kissed the feet and hands of the slave and said, "You are my child, I am your slave."	Then Mamrē told him everything in order, one by one. Abraham came, having fallen down, kissed the foot and the hand of (his) servant and said, "You are my father and I am your servant."

---

86. The way Abraham recognized Mamrē is unlike the other versions of this story.
87. Literally: "having brought."
88. Reading բարձր for բայցր.
89. Literally: "cleaned."
90. Literally: "from the places."

22. Now Abraham swore to God that as long as I li[v]e, before a guest happens by I shall not eat."[91] Mamrē w[as] the cause of Abraham's hospitali[ty] and love of the poor.[92] When Abraham saw all these miracles, he made an oath to God not to eat again without a guest.[93]	Then Abraham swore in his heart, "As long as I live and am alive, I (will) not eat bread until a guest happens by." Indeed, Mamrē was a cause of Abraham's hospitality and love of the poor. When Abraham saw this all
23. And having brought his tent, he set it up beneath the oak tree. And he dwelt there by the way so that the passersby might eat[94] of the table and then go. For [ ][95] did not set up a table of bread. If on one day 40 [ ] times a guest came, 40 times he would eat with the guests on account of his love of them.	and having brought his tent, he set it up underneath, in the area of the tree. And he dwelt there by the way so that the passersby might eat of Abraham's table and then go. Their lodgings did not set up tables of bread. And if for one day a passing guest did not come, Abraham did not eat.
24. If in 5 days, he encountered (one) once, he fasted for 5 days. If after 10 days one happened by (only) once, he would not eat for 10 days; until a guest came he did not eat. When Satan saw such beneficence and hospitality of Abraham's, he was envious and watched all the roads that were around him.	And if for 5 days no guest came, he too did not eat because of (his) love of a guest. Until a guest came he did not eat. And it often happened that for 10 days, for 20 days, for 30 days a guest did not happen by. And he remained hungry (for) that (i.e., period); he did not eat and he did not drink. And when Satan, hater of the good, saw such beneficence and hospitality of Abraham's, he was envious and turned against the good man, and he watched all the roads that were around him.

---

91. See text no. 3.11 on this story.
92. Eznik 4.12.1 speaks of Abraham's զաւտարան եւ զաղքատս ընդունելոյ "reception of the strangers and the poor." Though the qualities are those taken up by the Abraham narratives, the actual terminology varies.
93. Abraham's hospitality is highlighted in *Gen. Rab.* 48:1.
94. Observe the odd number of the verb.
95. Apparently a word like "lodgings" (cf. the other manuscript) has been lost.

11. THE STORY OF TERAH AND OF FATHER ABRAHAM

25. Whoever came he turned back and guided on another path. And he bound[96] that path so that for 40 days a guest did not happen by Abraham. Then Abraham became very faint. Sarah said, "Husband, you are dying[97] of hunger. Eat a little."	Whoever came, he turned back and guided on other paths. For 40 days a guest did not happen by Abraham. Then Abraham became very faint. Sarah said, "Husband, you too will die of hunger."
26. Abraham said, "(By the) living Lord. As long as a guest does not happen by, I will not eat. I cannot lie to God, but I hope in God that he (will) send me a guest today." For there Abraham had built a high place, so that Sarah would go up, sit there and look at the ways for guests.	Abraham said, "(As) the Lord God lives, until there is a guest I (will) not eat and I cannot belie this[98] oath before God, but I hope in God that he sends a guest this day." And outside he had built a place so that Sarah would go up, sit, and look at the ways for guests with hope and faith.
27. When Abraham grew faint, he said, "Sarah, go out to the place, look." When she went out she saw 3 (i.e., travelers) coming. Then, Abraham ordered to slaughter the calf for the guests.[99] For an exceptionally magnificent[100] calf had been born, and it had the likeness of Abel's lamb. Abraham caused the calf to be slaughtered.[101]	And when Abraham grew faint, he said to Sarah, "Go forth (to) the place and look into the distance." And when Sarah went forth to the place, she looked and saw 3 persons coming. Then Abraham ordered to slaughter the calf for the guests, for a magnificent calf had been born, it had a likeness to Abel's lamb. Abraham caused that calf to be slaughtered.
28. Then the Lord came with 2 angels, but Abraham did not know that it was the Lord. And when he saw (him) he was strengthened and he went to meet him.[102] When they sat down and they ate, Abraham listened and he heard much wondrous discourse and he was amazed. Then the Lord said to	Then the Lord came with 2 angels, but Abraham did not know that it was the Lord. For he rejoiced exceedingly when he saw him and he went to meet them (and) he greeted them. When they sat down and they ate, Abraham also heard a wondrous discourse from them and he was amazed. Then the

---

96. This is a magical term meaning "to bind, to compel by magical means." This magical term occurs in this context in text no. 2.12.
97. Literally: "have died"; similarly in text no. 15.35; cf. *Palaea* 214.
98. Or: "my."
99. Gen 18:7.
100. Or: "honorable."
101. See text no. 6.9.4 and note there.
102. Gen 18:2.

Abraham, "I will indeed bless you. I will indeed increase your seed like the stars of heaven and like the sand by the shore of the sea."[103]	Lord said to Abraham, "I will indeed bless you. I will increase your seed like the stars of heaven and like the sand by the shore of the sea."
29. Again he said, "You will have seed from Sarah.[104] His name will be called Sahak." When Sarah heard (this) underneath (her) hiding,[105] she scoffed and said, "When will this happen to me, for my days have passed?" Then the Lord said to Abraham, "Sarah sneered on account of the good news of Sahak. Why did she reckon my words false? On account of this sneering, your people will remain under the control of others for 460 years."[106]	Again he said, "You will have seed. You will call his name Isaac." When Sarah heard (this) underneath in her hiding, she scoffed and said, "When will I have seed? For my days have passed." Then the Lord said to Abraham, "Sarah sneered on account of the good news of Sahak. Why did she reckon my words false? On account of this sneering your people will remain captive under the control of others for 460 years."
30. And he blessed the house and the table and he said, "Abraham go forth with me as far as Mount Sodom." And from fear Abraham did not dare ask, "Who are you?" When they reached the mountain of [ ] Sodom, God commanded his 2 angels and said, "Enter inside the city, bring Lot forth, for he is righteous and hospitable.	And he blessed the house and the table and the Lord said to Abraham, "Go forth with me as far as Mount Adam." And from fear Abraham did not dare ask, "Who are you?" When they reached the mountain, God commanded his 2 angel(s); he said to bring Lot forth outside the city, for he is righteous and hospitable.
31. And say to him (that) he should go forth from Sodom, but let him not turn around to look back for whoever looks back (will) turn into stone." When the Lord said this, Abraham realized that he was the Lord. Abraham said, "Lord, in which fashion do you wish to do to this city?	And say to him (that) he should go forth from Sodom, but also let him not turn around again to look back, for whoever looks back (will) turn into stone." When the Lord said this, Abraham realized that he was the Lord. Abraham said, "Lord, in which fashion do you wish to do to this city?

---

103. Gen 27:17, cited by both recensions.
104. Gen 18:10.
105. Or: "concealment"; so both manuscripts.
106. Gen 15:13 has four hundred years; text no. 8.28 has 440 years, as does text no. 11A.29. This is an unusual tradition.

11. THE STORY OF TERAH AND OF FATHER ABRAHAM

The Lord said, "I wish to destroy (it) for their sins have multiplied."	The Lord said, "I wish to destroy (it) for their sins have multiplied."
32. Abraham said, "Lord, (has) not this great a city 1,000 people without sin?" The Lord said, "If there are 500 just men I will not destroy them." Abraham said, "And if there are 200 righteous men, will you not pity them?" The Lord said, "Even if 100 righteous be found I do not want their death."[107] Abraham said, "Lord if there be 50 righteous will you not have pity on them?" The Lord said, "'If 20 be found, I will have pity upon them.'"[108]	Abraham said, "Is there not in this city a man without sin?" The Lord said, "If there are 100 righteous, I do not want their death." Abraham said, "And if there are 50 righteous, will you not have pity?" The Lord said, "If there are 20 righteous, I (will) have pity on them. The Lord said (this)
33. Abraham said, "Lord, since I am dust and ashes, how can I speak with you again? But if[109] you made me worthy of speaking with you, have pity for the sake of the 10 righteous."	
34. Then the Lord ascended (to) heaven and a voice was heard, which said, "Since[110] in this city no righteous one was found, Abraham, stand in this place. See their ending." When the angels went to the city, they looked as if 15 years old.[111]	and he ascended. A voice was heard, "Since in this city no righteous one was found, Abraham, stand in this place. See their ending." When the 2 angels went (to) the city, they looked like 15 years old themselves.[112]
35. But Lot was very hospitable. When he saw them, having met them, he brought them to his house.[113] When the angels went to his house, the angel(s) said, "Go forth from this city for the Lord wishes to destroy it, for he sent us to bring you (sing.)	But Lot was hospitable. When he saw them, having met them, he brought them to his house. When they went to his house, the angels said, "Go forth from this city for the Lord wishes to destroy it, for God sent us to bring you (plur.) outside." Lot said, "Sit, eat

---

107. The numbers of righteous in this section do not accord with those in the biblical story.
108. Compare Gen 18:24–32.
109. Or: "when."
110. Or "when"; so both manuscripts.
111. On this age, see text no. 2.3 note.
112. The Armenian is unclear.
113. Gen 19:2–3.

outside."[114] Lot said, "Sit, recline and let us eat and I will see what you command." For Lot knew them as human.	and we shall see what you command." For Lot knew them as 2 men.
36. He blamed them and said, "You are of young age, why did you enter this evil and abominably acting city?" The angels said, "We came on your account, that we might bring you out from this city." But Lot's wife did not believe their words.[115]	And he blamed (them), "You are of young age, why do you enter this evil acting, abominable city?" The angel(s) said, "We came on your account. We will bring you out of this city." But Lot's wife did not believe their words.
37. She went, she opened the oven, that he might bring forth food for the guests. And she saw the oven full of water. When Lot learned of the coming forth of the water, he believed in the passing of the city.[116] Then the Sodomites came and seized Lot's door and said, "Give us those who have come to your house."[117]	She went, she opened the oven, that he might bring forth nourishment for the guests. And she saw the oven full of water. And then Lot learned the coming forth of the water, he believed in the passing of the city. Then the Sodomites went forth and seized Lot's door and said, "Give us the guest(s) who came to your house."
38. But Lot, on account of their wickedness, caused the door to be shut from inside. Lot said,[118] "I have 2 beautiful daughters. I am [gi]ving them to you and do not lay hands upon my guests."[119] And they did not agree. They began to break the door down. Then the angels said to Lot, "Do not worry because of us for we can save ourselves. Behold, go out of your house for now the city is being destroyed."	But Lot knew their wickedness. He had shut the doors of the house from inside. He said, "I have 2 beautiful daughters. I will give (them) to you, and do not lay hands upon my guests." And they did not agree. They began to break their door down. Then the angel(s) said to Lot, "Do not worry because of us. We can save ourselves. At this time go out of this house of yours, for now he is going to destroy this city."

---

114. Gen 19:12–13.
115. Lot's wife doubted the angelic pronouncement, just as Sarah had done. This may also have been suggested by her later disobedience, which ended up in her turning into a pillar of salt. His sons-in-law also disbelieved, according to the biblical account; see Gen 19:14.
116. It is not clear why the oven being full of water was a sign that confirmed the angelic announcement. Perhaps it suggests the creation of a sea on the spot of Sodom.
117. Gen 19:9.
118. Alternatively, "From inside, Lot said, etc."
119. Gen 19:8.

11. THE STORY OF TERAH AND OF FATHER ABRAHAM

39. When the Sodomites broke down the door, the angels went out, smote and blinded them. And they themselves ascended (i.e., to heaven). Then Lot went out of the city, he himself, (his) wife and his daughter(s). Because his wife had sent someone to her sons-in-law to inform them of the passing. When they reached the foot of the mountain,[120] then Lot's wife looked back on account of (her) sons-in-law. At once she turned into stone.[121]	When the Sodomites broke down the door, the angels went out, came[122] and blinded them. And they themselves ascended (i.e., to heaven). Then Lot went out of the city, he himself and (his) wife and (his) 2 daughters. Because his wife had sent someone to inform the son-in-law[123] of the passing of the city. When they reached the path of the mountain then Lot's wife looked back on account of (her) son-in-law. At once she turned into stone.
40. Because the angels had said to them not to look back; those who will look back turn into stone. When Lot went forth, fire burned around Sodom like a stone wall. Fire and sulphurous hail together dripped down from the heavens. During 7 days (and) 7 nights thus it rained upon Sodom,[124] until the ground, the stone of the city was burnt. And black water[125] went forth and made a sea of the place of Sodom and it is (it exists) until today.	Because the angel had said to them not to look back; those who will look back turn into stone. When Lot went forth fire burned around Sodom like a wall. Fire and sulphur and hail together also dripped down from the heavens, during 7 days (and) 7 nights thus it rained upon them, until they burnt everything, the ground and the stone. Black water went forth and made a sea in the place until today.
41. And Abraham, having seen all this, gave glory to God, who is such a philanthropic God, for Lot alone was loving of the poor and hospitable. Before he brought Lot out, he also did not make the city pass away.	And Abraham saw all this and gave glory to God and praised him who [ ][126] was so loving of the poor, and delivers from evil. The Lord God brought Lot forth from Sodom. And then he made pass away and punished the whole city.

---

120. The Armenian is unclear.
121. Gen 19:26. Note that it is salt in the Bible, not stone. See text no. 15.41 note.
122. Or: "arrived," perhaps corrupt for հարհու "smote"; cf. M6340.
123. The sense demands that this be plural, as it is in the other recension, but it is singular in both instances in this paragraph.
124. Gen 19:24.
125. This idea is derived from the ancient name of the Dead Sea as "Bitumen Sea."
126. Unclear letter.

42. I beg you, brothers take Mamrē as your example, who brought God to his sheep by bread and was worthy of the blessings and kingdom of God. And Abraham who by faith, fast, and prayers, by hospitality and feast brought God down from heaven to his house; he seated him at his table, ate and sat. He talked with God and received the good news about Isaac. And he received[127] God's blessing, with which he blessed Abraham, and he said, "I will surely bless you and I will surely multiply your seed."[128] And having seen this, learn too to do mercy to the poor and hospitality to strangers, if you wish to enter the kingdom of God.	
colophon continues for 17 more lines.	
Illegible in microfilm	CONCERNING THE BIRTH OF SAHAK
43. In [ ].. Abraham from Sarah. She conceived and bore Isaac. He was very handsome and honored, lovable. His parents so loved him, that they did not extinguish the lamp(s) at night on account of the vision of Isaac.[129] When he grew, God sent his angel[130] and he said to Abraham to slaughter his son as an offering and a sacrifice to God.	The Lord God of all and lover of humans appeared to Abraham in Sarah, in that he gave good news and she conceived. For she bore Isaac, very handsome and honored (by) his parents. His parents so loved him that they did not extinguish the lamp(s) at night, on account of the vision of Sahak. And when Sahak grew up, the Lord sent the angels and he said to Abraham to slaughter his son as an offering and a sacrifice to God.
44. For God tested him, so that he might see whether he would give his son as an offering and a sacrifice to	So that God might test him, so that he might see (whether) Abraham makes[131] his beloved son into an

---

127. Perhaps it should read "receive," an imperative.
128. Gen 22:17.
129. That is, "so that they might see Isaac."
130. In the Bible, it is God himself who gives the command.
131. The tenses of the verbs in this section lack coordination.

11. THE STORY OF TERAH AND OF FATHER ABRAHAM   161

God or not.[132] When Abraham heard (this) <from> the angel he saddled the donkey, and taking with him fire and wood[133] and Isaac and he went to the place of the covenant.[134] Sahak asked (his) father and said, "[ ]Father, here is fire and knife, where is the sacrifice?"[135]	offering. When Abraham heard (this) he saddled the donkey and, taking with him wood and fire and Isaac, he went to the place of the covenant. Isaac asked (his) father and said, "Father, here is fire and wood, where is this sacrifice?"
45. Abraham said, "Son, God is preparing a sacrifice."[136] For Abraham knew this that he was deceiving (his) son, but the mouth (of the) prophet was prophesying.[137] When he reached the site of the covenant, he bound his son Isaac, and he took his sword (knife), so that he might cut off (his) son's head. Then an angel called out saying, "Draw not near to the youth, for God has sent you a sacrificial ram." When he looked up, he saw the sacrificial ram hanging from the tree[138] and by its horns.[139]	Abraham said, "Son, God is preparing this sacrifice for us." For Abraham by saying this was, for Abraham was deceiving his son. He knew that he was deceiving his son, but he was[140] prophesying with (his) mouth. When he went and reached the site of the covenant, he bound his son Sahak, and he took the sword (knife), so that he might cut off (his) son's head. Then an angel calling out said, "Do not die[141] to the youth, for the Lord has sent you a sacrificial ram." When he looked up, he saw the sacrificial ram hanging from the tree by its horns.

---

132. Gen 22:1–2.
133. The fire and wood are introduced only at a later point of the story in Gen 22:6.
134. Gen 22:9 describes this as "the place that God had shown him." The name "place of the covenant" here may come from an identification of Moriah (Gen 22:2) with the Temple Mount based on 2 Chr 3:1. This identification may also be reflected in the mention of "the mountain of the Lord" in Gen 22:14. Throughout these texts, we observe the tendency to collapse different holy places into a single one.
135. Gen 22:7.
136. Gen 22:8.
137. By attributing Abraham's deception of Isaac to the power of prophecy, the text obviates Abraham's culpability. Note that the word մարգարէին "(of the) prophet" does not have its case ending.
138. The name of the tree, Tree of Sabek, is not mentioned here. See text no. 4.22 note.
139. Gen 22:9–13.
140. That is, actually.
141. The reading of M6340, "draw not near," is original.

46. When he got the ram down and slaughtered (it), a voice spoke to him and said, "Abraham, just as you did not withhold[142] your son for my sake, in the same way I too will not withhold my Son for your sake." And Abraham returned home joyously. And one day, while he was praying, an angel descended to him and said, "Abraham, God commanded you to go to Jerusalem.[143] You will find there Melchizedek, the servant of God. Trim his head (i.e., hair) and straighten his nails and bring (him) to your house. With wine and bread he will offer a sacrifice on your account.	When he got the ram down and slaughtered (it), a voice also spoke to him and said, "Abraham, Abraham, just as you did not withhold your son for my name's sake, just so I too will not withhold[144] my Son for your sake." And Abraham returned to his home joyously. And one day, while he was praying, the angel descended to him and said, "Abraham, God commanded you that you should go to Jerusalem and find Mēlik'sēt' the servant of God. Trim his nails and straighten his head (i.e., hair) and bring (him) to your house. With wine and bread he will offer a sacrifice.
47. He will be a priest also from the divine side for your sake and your family's he will perform the priestly actions." Abraham said, "In which place do I find him?" The angel said, "You find him in the forest." When Abraham went to Jerusalem, in the night he saw a pillar of light in the forest. Abraham knew that he was there. When day came, he set forth and proceeded to the place and found (him), that his appearance was unlike a human appearance.	For your sake and your family's he will perform priestly actions." Abraham said, "In which place do I find him?" The angel said, "You will find him in the forest." When Abraham went to Jerusalem, in the night he saw a pillar of light in the forest. Abraham realized that Mēlik'sēt' was there. When day came, he set forth and proceeded[145] to the place. When Mēlik'sēt' saw Abraham,[146] for his appearance was unlike a human appearance.
48. But he was dressed and the hair of his head descended as far as (his) knees. And his spine was like a tortoise's spine[147] and his nails were	But he was dressed and because the hair of his head was knee-length, and his nails were a span long. And Abraham, greeting him, spoke with

---

142. Literally: "pity"; so both manuscripts. Compare Gen 22:16. Notice the chistological ending substitued for that of the biblical verse here.

143. See p. 11, n. 32 above.

144. Literally: "pity."

145. This is a case of hendiadys.

146. The sense demands, "when Abraham saw Mēlik'sēt'."

147. Compare Adam covered with fingernail, as mentioned in *Gen. Rab.* 20:21.

11. THE STORY OF TERAH AND OF FATHER ABRAHAM

a span long.[148] Abraham, greeting him, spoke with him and said, "How long is it that you have been here?" Melk'isēt' said, "I have lived the ascetic life here for 8 years,[149] unseen by men. No other man has seen me but you." Abraham said, "Tell me how you came to be believe." Melk'iset' said, "I am the son of King Melk'i, son of King Sałim who built this city.[150] One day my father sent me to the herd, 'Bring a honorable[151] and fat heifer so that I might offer sacrifice to idols.'"[152]	him and said, "How long is it that you are here?" Melik'set' said, "It is 8 years that I have lived the ascetic life here thus, away from men. No other man has seen me but you." Abraham said, "Tell me how it was that you came to be believe." Melik'sēt' said, "I am the son of King Melk'i, who is[153] son of King Sałim who built this city. One day my father sent me, 'Go to the herd, bring a fat heifer.'
49. And I went to the flock and I separated the fat heifer and oxen. And my heart shone with divine grace. I considered and I was unwilling to kill the animals. I left the living animals that I had wanted to bring for the sake of the immobile, artifactual image. I turned back. I looked at the heavens and luminaries and all of the Creator's creations and I considered (them). By God's grace I recognized the Creator, God. I left the animals and came to my father without a sacrifice."[154]	And God shone light in my heart. I considered and I was unwilling to bring a living beast for the sake of the immobile, artifactual image. I wished to bring it back. I turned and regarded the heavens and the luminaries, all the Creator's creations. And <by> the grace[155] of God I recognized the Creator, God, and I left the beasts. And I came to my father without a sacrifice.
50. And my father asked, "Where are the heifer and your oxen?" And I said, "My father, it seems to me difficult to	And my father asked me, "Where is the heifer?" And I said, "It seems to me difficult to offer the living beast

---

148. Compare the description in *Palaea* 206. This is a description of Melchizedek as a wild man; see p. 11, n. 28 above.
149. Usually the number is 7, and once, 40.
150. Jerusalem, also called Horeb, was built by Melchizedek (Michael the Syrian, Chabot 1899, 17).
151. Cf. text no. 15.49. The calf that Abraham slaughtered for the Three Men was also described as "honorable." See text no. 15.28.
152. Note the overall similarity of the story of Melchizedek's conversion with that of Abraham. This story is discussed in the General Introduction above.
153. The verb is plural.
154. Structurally, this story is very like that of Abraham's recognition of God.
155. An instrumental case would be expected.

offer the living beast as sacrifice for the sake of immobile, human artifacts, which are not God but false gods. For that reason I did not bring (them)." And my father was resentful of me and having entered, he said to my mother, "Today I will sacrifice one of these 2 sons to idols." And my mother realized that he was resentful of me. My mother wept and lamented, she scratched her face and beat her head.	as sacrifice for the sake of immobile, human artefacts, which are not God but false gods. For that reason I did not bring (them)." And my father was resentful of me also <in> his mind, and said to my mother, "Today we have 2 sons. One I will sacrifice to idols." And my mother knew that he was resentful. She wept and lamented, she scratched her face and beat her head.
51. For my mother loved me and my father loved my brother.[156] Then my father, when he saw my mother's mourning, who was weeping bitterly, my father said, "Why are you weeping, for let us cast lots for our 2 sons. Him on whom the lot falls, let us slaughter."	For my mother loved me and my father loved my brother. Then my father saw my mother's mourning, who was weeping bitterly. My father said to my mother, "Why are you weeping? Come let us cast lots for our 2 sons. Him on whom the lot falls, him let us slaughter."
52. Then thrice they cast the lots. The lot fell upon my brother. And my father went forth, and having taken my brother bound, brought (him). Then my mother wept and said, "Do you not pity your brother?" And my mother weeping went so that she might see the end of her son. When the princes and the notables of the king heard, they brought their sons and daughters to slaughter to the idols.	Thrice they cast the lots and the lots fell upon my brother. When it fell (i.e., thus) my father, having taken my brother bound, brought (him). Then my mother wept and said, "Do you not pity your brother?" And my mother weeping went so that she might see the end of her son. When the princes and the notables and the king[157] heard, they brought their sons and daughter to slaughter as a sacrifice to the idols.
53. And I, weeping on account of my brother, fled and went forth to this forest. When I saw (that) they laid hands to slaughter my brother, I asked from the Lord that the gates of the abyss open and it swallow them. At that very time, that place was	And I, weeping on account of this brother of mine, fled and went forth to the forest. When I saw that they laid hands to slaughter my brother, I asked from the Lord that the gates of the abyss open and it swallow them. At that very time, the place was

---

156. Reminiscent of Jacob and Esau (Gen 27); cf. Mal 1:2–3.

157. This word should probably be in the genitive, as in the other manuscript, so "of the king."

11. THE STORY OF TERAH AND OF FATHER ABRAHAM

split open and it seized them with the temple, my father and my mother with all the people. And I alone remained here. But it is these 8 years, that no man has seen me.	split open and it swallowed them in the temple, and with the idols, my father and mother and all the people who were in the temple. And I alone remained here. It is 8 years, that no man has seen me.
54. Then Abraham clipped the hair of his head and straightened his nails. He washed and cleaned him. And he wrapped him with a chasuble and adorned him. And having brought (him) to his house, he offered a sacrifice of bread and wine.[158] And the household ate of it, his sons and his maidservants and servants. And he became a priest in Abraham's house from the divine side, for that was the first offering with bread and wine. For Melk'isēd was the first priest, who was a type of Christ.	Then Abraham clipped his nails as well as his head, washing and cleaning (him). And he adorned (him) with a silk chasuble and having brought him to his house, he offered a sacrifice of bread and wine and the household ate of it, his sons, servants and maidservants. The priestly acts of Abraham's house took place through him, from the lordly side. For that was the first priesthood and offering, which took place through Melk'isēt'
55. And Abraham grew old with good deeds and he rested in peace in [ ]. And he left 2 sons, Sahak from Sarah and Ishmael from Hagar. To Sahak were born Esau and Jacob.	Abraham grew old with good deeds and he rested in peace. And he left 2 sons, Sahak from Sarah, Ishmael from H(Y)akar the maidservant. And from Sahak was born Esau[159] and Jacob.
56. And we did not write the full story, for the exemplar was this (i.e., what is here). Mercy upon the commissioner of this book, Karapet, and his parents, (his) father Amirvel and (his) mother Gulum and (his) son Anton.	

---

158. This is, of course, a hint at the Eucharist.
159. Յեսու "Joshua" corrupt for Եսաւ "Esau."

11A. Concerning Abraham's Hospitality

H. Anasyan drew attention to this work in 1959.[1] It occurs in a printed book published in Constantinople in 1730.[2] The extracts I succeeded in getting of this book, taken from pages 50-60, show that in the same context it also publishes the stories of Jacob and Joseph. We give here the sections O*n Abraham's Hospitality* and *On Isaac's Birth* transcribed from the printed edition. These two sections constitute another recension of part of text no. 11 *Story of Terah and Father Abraham*, presented here immediately preceding. *Abraham's Hospitality* varies more, however, from both forms of text no. 11 than those differ from each other. It adds and omits whole sentences and changes the elements of the text. I have introduced paragraph breaks in accordance with the synoptic text no. 11, but not all of its paragraphs are present.

Վասն Հիւրընկալութեան Աբրահամու
ի վերայ ճանապարհին

23. Իբրեւ եւտես Աբրահամ զայս մեծ ըպբանչելիսն, բերեալ զվրա/ p. 51 / են ցրցեալ ի ներքեւ կաղնի ծառոյն եւ արկ սեղան խաշածել ի վերայ ճանապարհին. եւ ուխտեաց ընդ Աստուծոյ թէ առանց հիւրի ոչ ճաշակեմ. եւ անցաւորք ճանապարհին որք հանդիպէին, զեղեան լի եւ պատրաստութեամբ տեսանէին. կերակրէին եւ անցեալ գնային. թէ Ա օրն Խ անգամ հիւր հանդիպէր, նա Խ անգամ ճաշակէր Աբրահամ վասն հիւրին.

24. եւ թէ Է օր կամ Ժ օր կամ Ի օր ոչ հանդիպէր, ոչ ճաշակէր առանց հիւր. Իբրեւ եւտես Սատանայ յայնպէս բարէգործութեան, նախանձեցաւ ընդ Աբրահամու. եւ կապեաց զճանապարհին, զի ոչ ոք անցանէր եւ զայր ի նոյն ճանապարհին.

25. զի թէ զայր յետ դարձուցանէր. եւ ցուցանէր այլ ճանապարհ. մինչեւ Խ օր ամենեին հիւր ոչ հանդիպեցաւ։ Իսկ յոյժ նուազեցաւ Աբրահամ.

---

1. Anasyan 1959, col. 138, no. 4.
2. Ակիզբն գրոց որ կոչի Ժողովածու (*Book which is called Miscellany*).

11A: CONCERNING ABRAHAM'S HOSPITALITY

եւ Սառա աղաչեաց զտէրն Աբրահամ եւ ասէ՝ ահա սովամահ կու մեռանիս. սակաւ մի հաց կեր.
26. եւ Աբրահամ ասէ՝ ուխտ եղեալ եմ հետ Աստուծոյ, ոչ կարեմ ուտել. զի մինչ իմ վկայ է, որ այսօր հիւր կը հանդիպի մեզ, եթէ ոչ հանդիպի, նա մեռանիմ ի սէրն Աստուծոյ։ զի փոքրիկ պատուհան մի շինեալ էր Աբրահամ. զի միշտ հայէր վասն հիւրի եւ էր բարձրութիւն նորա երեք մարդաչափի.
27. եւ ասաց Սառայի Աբրահամ թէ հայեա ի դիտակն.[3] իբրեւ հայեցաւ, ետես ի հեռաստանէ որ Գ / p. 52 / մարդ կու գայր։ Աւետիս ետ Սառա Աբրահամու եւ ասէ. Տէր ողորմեցաւ քեզ, եւ ահա երեք մարդ գան առ քեզ.
28. եւ ասէ Աբրահամ. շուտով զենէք զհորթն եւ եփեցէք. զի հորթ մի ծնեալ էր Աբրահամու որ նման էր գառին Աբելայ. զայն զենեաց վասն հիւրոց։ Իբրեւ մօտեցան մարդիկք, զօրացաւ Աբրահամ եւ ել ընդ առաջ նոցա. եւ նորա եկին բազմեցան. իսկ մինն յերից խոսէր զբանս զարմանալիս. ականչ դնէր Աբրահամ եւ հիանայր. բայց ոչ գիտէր որ Տէրն է։
29. Իբրեւ կերան եւ լիացան, ասէ Տէրն, եղիցի զաւակ ի Սառայէ, եւ անուն նորա կոչեսցի Իսահակ. եւ նա եղիցի մեծ նահապետ։ Իբրեւ լուաւ Սառա ընդ յետոյս վրանին, նա ժպտեցաւ, զի ասէր ընդ միտս իւր. թէ ես ծերացեր եմ որպէս կարեմ ծնանիլ զաւակ. զի ստեալ էր Սառա ծածուկ ի նոցանէ առ յետոյ վրանին։ Իսկ Տէրն ասէ՝ Սառա զիա՞րդ ծիծաղեցաւ. եւ ոչ հաւատացեր ինձ. զի սուտ համարեցար զբանս իմ։ Վասն այդ ծիծաղելոյդ չորեքհարիւր տարի անկցի ազգդ քո գերի ի ձեռն այլազգեաց. զայս ամենայն լսէր Աբրահամ եւ զարմացայր. բայց ոչ իշխէր հարցանել թէ դու ով ես. եւ դարձեալ ասէ՝ օրհնելով օրհնեցից զքեզ Աբրահամ. եւ բազմացուցանելով բազմացուցից զզաւակ քո որպէս զաստեղս երկնից. եւ որպէս զաւազ առ ափին / p. 53 / ծովու.
30. եւ օրհնեաց զտունն եւ զսեղանն։ Իբրեւ ել ասէ արի ընդ իս մինչեւ ի լեառն Սոդոմայ. եւ ի ճանապարհին առաքեաց զերկու հրեշտակն եւ ասէ. գնացէք ի Սոդոմ. եւ անդ կայ այր մի հիւրընկալ անուն նորա Ղովտ եւ հանէք զնա անտի. զի կամիմ պատուհասել զքաղաքն։
31. Իբրեւ գնացին հրեշտակքն, գիտաց Աբրահամ զի Տէրն է. ի յահէն դողալով երթայր ընդ նմա. բայց ոչ իշխէր հարցանել բան ինչ. իբրեւ եկին ի լեառն, երեւեցաւ Սոդոմ. ասէ Տէրն gԱբրահամ, կամիմ կործանել զքաղաքս զի յոյժ բազմացեալ են մեղք նոցա.
32. Ասէ Աբրահամ, Տէր ոչ իցէ ի նմա Ծ արդար գոր ոչ խնայես։ Ասէ Տէրն՝ եթէ լինիցի Խ արդար՝ ոչ կորուսից զնա.
33. Ասէ Աբրահամ ես հող եմ եւ մոխիր. եթէ իցեն անդ Լ. կամ Ի, ոչ խնայես ի նա։ Ասէ Տէրն եթէ լինիցի անդ Ժ արդար ոչ կորուսից։

---

3. The word դիտակ "watchtower" should be in the ablative case.

34. Ապա կրկնեալ Աբրահամու ասէ, Տէր երբ արժանի արարեր զիս խօսիլ ընդ քեզ. ադաչեմ զքեզ. եթէ լինիցի ե արդար ոչ խնայես զնոսա: Յայնժամ վերացաւ Տեառն ձայն եղեւ Աբրահամու եւ ասաց. ոչ կայ ի նմա արդար եւ ոչ մի. բայց դու կաց ի տեղիդ մինչեւ տեսցես զկարարածն Սոդոմայ: Իբրեւ զնացին երկու հրեշտակքն ի Սոդում, մտին ի քաղաքն եւ ընդ երեկս էր իբրեւ ժէ տարեկան / p. 54 / տղայի նման.

36. Եւ տեսեալ Ղովտ զնոսա, մեծարեալ տարաւ ի տուն իւր ասելով, թէ դուք նորահաս մանկունք՝ եւ քաղաքացիքս չարագործ մարդիկ՝ ընդէր մտիք ի քաղաքս: Ասեն հրեշտակքն մեք վասն քոյ եմք եկեալ. զի բարկացեալ է Աստուած. եւ կամի կործանել զքաղաքս. ել շուտով ի սմանէ. զի մի կորնչիս դու ընդ ոսային: Իսկ Ղովտ ադաչէր բազմիլ ի սեղան եւ կերակրիլ ի գիշերի անդ:

37. Ապա մինչդեռ կային անդ, յանկարծ եկեալ պղծագործքն կալան զդուռն Ղովտայ եւ ասացին. տուր մեզ զայն օտար մարդիկքն որ եկեալ են ի տուն քո:

38. Իսկ Ղովտ ադաչէր զնոսա ասելով, թէ մի մեղանչէք նոցա. այլ զերկու կոյս ադջկունս իմ տամ ձեզ. նորա սկսան զդուռն խորտակել: Իսկ հրեշտակքն ասեն ց'Ղովտ, մեք հրեշտակ եմք Աստուծոյ դու մի հոգար վասն մեր, այլ փութապէս ել ի քաղաքս մինչեւ ի գլուխ լերինն.

39. Իբրեւ խորտակեցին զդուռն Ղովտայ, ելին հրեշտակք եւ կուրացուցին զաչս նոցա եւ ասացին Ղովտայ ելէք եւ փախերուք ի լեառն եւ մի յետս հայիք. իսկ Ղովտ ել ի քաղաքէն ինքն եւ երկու դստերքն եւ կինն: Իբրեւ հասին ի կէս լերինն, նա կինն դարձաւ յետս հայելով թէ փեսայքս պիտի զան. քանզի նշանած էին ադջկունքն. նա առ ժամայն յաղի դարձեալ եւ է մինչեւ ցայսոր: / p. 55 / Ապա հուրն շրջապատեաց զքաղաքն իբրեւ պարիսպ. եւ ծծումբն տեղացեալ իբրեւ անձրեւ. քար եւ կարկուտ. կրակ եւ կայծակ ի միասին վայր թափեր յերկուց մինչեւ է օր. որ այրեցաւ քար եւ թուփ.[4] այլ եւ սեւ չուր ելաւ ի գետէն որ դեռեւս երեւի ի սքանչացումա տեսողացն, եւ ծով եղեւ մինչեւ ցայսոր:

42. Ապա Աբրահամ տեսեալ զանցումա նորա,[5] փարք տայր Աստուծոյ եւ գոհանայր. քանզի Ղովտ որ հիւրասէր եւ ադքատասէր էր. գնա ազատեաց ի Սոդումայ. եւ ապա կորույս զնոսա:

Ադաչեմ զձեզ եղբարք ուսարուք զտուրս ադքատաց. եւ հիւրընկալութիւն. զմեծարել զոտարսն. զի յորինակ առէք զՄամբրէ եւ տեսէք թէ ադքատաց ողորմելով որպիսի փառաց արժանաւորեցաւ։ Եւ կամ Աբրահամ որ հիւրընկալութեամբն, պաշոր եւ ծմոր որչափ մեծութեան հասաւ. եւ Աստուած ընդ նմա կերակրեցաւ. եւ խոսակցեցաւ. եւ օրհնեաց զնա եւ հայր ազգաց կացոյց զնա:

42A. Ըստ նմին օրինակի պարտիք ողորմութիւն տալ ադքատաց եւ

---

4. See n. 24 below.
5. We might expect նցա.

կարօտելոց. տայ հաց քաղցելոց եւ ջուր ծարաւելոց. որով գովաբանիք ի գործըս ձեր. եւ ուրախական առաքեալք եւ մարգարէք եւ ամենայն արդարք, հրեշտակք եւ երկնաւոր զօրք ամենայն։ Որ ինքն բարերար Աստուած օրհնէ եւ փառօք փառաւորէ զձեզ։

42B. Աստ յամենայն պատահարցին փրկէ. եւ անդ ընդ սուրբս / p. 56 / դասէ եւ պսակէ։ Եւ արժանացուցէ զձեզ նոցին փառաց եւ իւր օրհնեալ տեսուն. որ է օրհնեալ յաւիտեանս Ամէն։

Concerning Abraham's Hospitality on the Way

23. When Abraham saw this great wonder,[6] he brought (his) tent, he erected it under the oak tree and set a cruciform table upon the way. And he made an oath to God, "Without a guest I will not dine."[7] And passersby on the road who would happen by the table would see it full and ready. They would eat and passing on, they went. If on one day he encountered 40 guests, behold, Abraham ate 40 times for the sake of the guest.
24. And if for 5 days or 10 days or 20 days he did not encounter (i.e., a guest), he did not eat without a guest. When Satan saw this beneficence, he was envious of Abraham and he bound[8] the way, so that nobody passed by and came on that same road.
25. For if one came, he (Satan) caused him to turn back and showed (him) another road, until he (Abraham) encountered no one at all for 40 days. Then Abraham became very faint, and Sarah beseeched her lord, Abraham, and said, "Behold you will die of hunger, eat a little bread."
26. And Abraham said, "I made an oath with God, I cannot eat, for my mind is a witness that today a guest will happen by[9] us. If one does not happen by (us), then I will die for the love of God." For Abraham had built a small window[10] so that he might always look out for a guest, and its height was that of three human heights.
27. And Abraham said to Sarah, "Look <from> the watchtower." When she looked, she saw in the distance that 3 men were coming. Sarah gave the news to Abraham and said, "The Lord has had mercy upon you, and, behold, three men are coming to you."

---

6. This first phrase actually parallels material in text no. 11.22–23. That section refers both to Mamrē's whitened complexion and the growth of his staff into an oak tree. The cruciform shape of the table is unique to text 11A.

7. This is very like the story of Abraham's hospitality in *Palaea* 47.1. There, however, Abraham fasts only for three days and then the Three Men appear, interpreted as the Holy Trinity.

8. Or: "ensorcelled"; this is a magical term.

9. Or: "encounter."

10. Or: "niche." This seems to be something like a watchtower; see §27.

28. And Abraham said, "Quickly slaughter the calf and cook (it)."[11] For a calf had been born to Abraham that resembled Abel's lamb: he cooked that calf for the guests.[12] When the men drew near, Abraham grew stronger and went forth to meet them. They came (and) sat down. Then one of the three spoke wondrous words. Abraham attended and was amazed but he did not know that he was the Lord.

29. When they had eaten and were sated, the Lord said, "There will be seed from Sarah, and his name will be called Isaac, and he will be a great patriarch." When Sarah heard behind the rear of the tent, she scoffed for she said to herself, "I have grown old, how can I bear seed?" For Sarah had sat hidden from them at the rear of the tent. Then the Lord said, "Sarah, how did you laugh and not believe me? For you thought my words to be a lie. Because of this laughing, your family will fall captive in the hands of foreigners for four hundred years."[13] Abraham heard all this and wondered, but he did not dare to ask, "Who are you?" And again he said, "I will indeed bless you Abraham, and I will surely multiply your seed like the stars of heaven and like the sand on the seashore."[14]

30. And he blessed the house and the table. When he went forth, he said, "Rise up, (come) with me as far the mountain of Sodom." And on the way, he dispatched the two angels and said, "Go to Sodom, and there there is a hospitable man named Lot, and bring him forth from there, for I wish to punish the city."

31. When the angels went, Abraham realized that he was the Lord, and he went with him, shaking from fear, but he did not dare to ask anything. When they came to a mountain, Sodom became visible. The Lord said to Abraham, "I wish to destroy this city, for their sins have multiplied greatly."[15]

32. Abraham said, "Lord, are there not 50 righteous in it, that you will not have pity upon them?" The Lord said, "If there will be 40 righteous, I will not destroy it."

33. Abraham said, "I am dust and ashes: if there are 30 or 20 there, will you not have pity upon it?" The Lord said, "If there are 10 righteous there, I will not destroy (it)."

34. Then Abraham said again, "Lord, if you have made me worthy to speak with you, I beseech you, if there are 5 righteous, will you not pity them?" Then

---

11. These two imperatives are in the plural.

12. Observe that the other food described in the Bible is not mentioned here. This includes bread, which in some readings was supplemented by wine and turned into a sacramental meal.

13. This is based on Gen 15:13–14, a chapter not usually incorporated into the Abraham saga. In text no. 11.29 and in the present text, the period of captivity is 460 years; in text no. 8.28 it is 440 years.

14. Gen 22:17. This biblical context of this phrase is that of the Binding of Isaac and not the angelic visitors.

15. Gen 18:20.

the Lord rose up and there was a voice to Abraham, and he said, "There is not even one just one in it.[16] But you, remain in this place until you see that which is done to Sodom.[17] When the two angels went to Sodom, they entered the city and it was towards evening. They resembled 15-years old boys. [18]

36. And when Lot saw them, having paid respects (to them), he brought them to his house saying, "You (are) young boys and these citizens (are) evildoing men. Why did you enter the city?" The angels said, "We have come for your sake, for the Lord is angry and wishes to destroy this city. Go out of it quickly lest you be destroyed with these." But Lot beseeched (them) to sit to table and to eat on that night.[19]
37. Then while they were there, suddenly the doers of abominations came. They seized Lot's door and said, "Give us these foreigner men who have come to your house."
38. But Lot beseeched them saying, "Do not sin against them, but I will give you my two virgin girls."[20] They began to break down the door. Then the angels said to Lot, "We are God's angels. You, have not worry on our account, but leave this city quickly, as far as the top of the mountain."
39. When they broke down Lot's door, the angels went forth and smote their eyes with blindness[21] and said to Lot, "Go forth and flee to the mountain and do not look back." Then Lot went forth from the city, he and (his) two daughters and (his) wife. When they reached halfway up the mountain, then (his) wife turned around, to see whether the sons-in-law would come, [22] for the girls were affianced. She at that moment, turned into salt[23] and it exists up to this day. Behold, fire surrounded the city, like a wall, and sulphur dripped down like rain, stone and hail, fire and lightning together. They dripped on the place from the heavens for 7 days and burnt stone and bush.[24] Also, black water issued from the river, which still seems to be a wonder to the viewers, and it became a sea to this day.[25]

---

16. §§31–34 relate the incidents in Gen 18:26–32, but the biblical dialogue reaches only ten righteous, while the apocryphal text descends to one righteous in addition to Lot and his family.
17. Or: "the end of Sodom."
18. See Gen 19:1. On the age of fifteen years, see the note on text no. 2.3.
19. Gen 19:2–3.
20. Or: "daughters." See Gen 19:8. On the breaking down of the door, see Gen 19:9.
21. Gen 19:11.
22. Inferred from Gen 19:14.
23. Gen 19:26.
24. The word is uncertain and is not in Malxaseanc' 1944. We translate as if from փնւի "bush" in modern Armenian (Th. M. van Lint).
25. This might be a reference to the name of the Dead Sea as "Sea of Bitumen." Compare the remarks of Sextus Iulius Africanus, F26 8 (Walraff and Adler, 2007, 58–61).

42. Then Abraham, having seen (their) transgression,[26] gave praise to God and lauded, because He freed from Sodom Lot who was hospitable and lover of the poor. And then he destroyed them.

I beseech you, brothers, learn (about) gifts to the poor and hospitality, honoring the strangers, for you take Mambrē as an example, and see of what glory he was worthy through being merciful to the poor, and what a measure of greatness through hospitality, fast and abstinence Abraham achieved. God ate with him and conversed and blessed him and made him a father of nations.

42A. By the same example you should give mercy to the poor and needy. Give bread to the hungry and water to the thirsty, through which you will be praised for your deeds. And the prophets and Apostles and all the righteous, angels and all heavenly hosts rejoice. He who is himself a benefactor, God blesses and makes you glorious with glory.

42B. Here (i.e., in this world) he saves from all catastrophes, and there (i.e., in that world) he classes him with the saints and crowns him. And he reckons you worthy of that glory and of a blessed vision of him, who is blessed for even. Amen.

Վասն ծնընդեան Իսահակայ

43. Իբրեւ մերձեցաւ Աբրահամ առ Սառա կին իւր, յղացաւ եւ ծնաւ զԻսահակ որդին գեղեցիկ եւ պատուականագոյն քան զամենեսին: Իսկ ծնօղքն սիրեին յոյժ. եւ ոչ շիջուցանեին զճրագ ի գիշերի՝ վասն նորա պայծառ երեսույն: Իբրեւ զարգացաւ Իսահակ, որք տեսանեին զգեղեցկութիւնն եւ զճարտարախօս անուշ լեզուն, զարմանային եւ ապուշ մնային: Ապա առաքեաց Աստուած գիրեշտակ իւր եւ ասաց Աբրահամու թէ, զորդին քո խնդրէ Աստուած պատարագ զԻսահակ:

44. Իբրեւ լուաւ Աբրահամ զբանն ի հրեշտակէն. համոզեաց զէշ իւր եւ բարձեալ զիւր եւ գիայտ՝ եւ զԻսահակ ընդ իւր եւ երթայր ի տեղի ուխտին: Եւ ի ճանապարհին հարցանէր Իսահակ թէ հայր ահա կրակ եւ ահա փայտ. ուր է ողջակէզ եւ մատաղ քո:

45. Ասէ Աբրահամ, Աստուած պատրաստեսցէ մատաղ ողջակիզաց. քանզի այնպէս խաբէր Աբրահամ զԻսահակ. բայց մարգարէանայր Աստուծով: Իբրեւ գնացին ի տեղի ուխտին, կապեաց զորդին իւր զԻսահակ եւ եառ զսուրն զի զենցէ զորդին իւր: / p. 57 / Իսկ հրեշտակ ձայնեաց ասաց թէ, մի մերձենար ի պատանեակդ զի առաքեաց Աստուած քեզ խոյ մի ողջակէզ կախեալ զեղջերէն ի Սաբեկայ ծառէն:

---

26. Or: "(its) passing."

11A: CONCERNING ABRAHAM'S HOSPITALITY 173

46. Եւ առեալ Աբրահամու գինոյն եզեն փոխանակ Իսահակայ. եւ արձակեաց զԻսահակ. ձայն եղեւ յերկնից եւ ասէ՝ Աբրահամ, Աբրահամ. որպէս ոչ խնայեցեր դու զորդին քո վասն իմ. նոյնպէս եւ ես ոչ խնայեցի զորդի իմ վասն քոյ: Եւ ուրախութեամբ դարձաւ Աբրահամ ի տուն իւր։ Եւ յաւուր միում աղօթեր մինչ²⁷ Աբրահամ երեւեցաւ նմա հրեշտակ եւ ասէ. հրամայեաց քեզ Աստուած զի գնասցես ի կողմ Երուսաղէմայ. եւ գտանիցես ի յանտառին այր մի Աստուծոյ ծառայ անուն նորա Մելքիսեդեկ. ըզգլուխն գերծեա եւ զղրնկունսն հարբեա. եւ զզեցո նմա հանդերձս. զի նա վասն քո մատուցէ պատարագս գինւով եւ հացով.
47. Եւ նա եղիցի տան քոյ քահանայ, եւ ամենայն ընտանեաց քոց յաստուածակոյս կողմանէ։ Ասէ Աբրահամ ուր տեղ գտանեմ գնա. ասէ հրեշտակն յերուսաղէմ ի յանտառին. իբրեւ գնաց Աբրահամ ի յանտառն, տեսանէր, զի սիւն լուսոյ յերկնից իջանէր ի վերայ անտառին. գիտաց Աբրահամ զտեղին. Իբրեւ տիւ եղեւ, գնացեալ եզիտ զՄելքիսեդէկ ահեղակերպ եւ գոյնն փոխեալ. եւ դէմքն այլակերպեալ.
48. Եւ մազն գլխոյն մինչեւ ի ծունկն իջեալ. / p. 58 / եւ ողնկունքն թզաւ չափ. եւ քամակ նորա իբրեւ կրիայի։ Եւ ողջունեալ գնա Աբրահամ, խօսեցաւ ընդ նմա եւ ասէ. քանի՞ ժամանակ է որ դու աստ կաս. եւ կամ որպէս ճանաչեցեր զԱստուած. ասէ Մելքիսեդէկ, զի է տարի է որ աստ ճգնիմ անտես ի մարդկանէ. այլ ոչ ոք է տեսեալ զիս բաց ի քէն։ Ասէ Աբրահամ՝ պատմեա ինձ ըզհաւատալն քո թէ, որպէս եղեւ. ասէ Մելքիսեդէկ. ես եմ որդի Մելքեայ թագաւորին որդւոյ Սաղիմ թագաւորին որ զքաղաքս շինեաց։ Եւ յաւուր միում ի տօնի կռոցն առաքեաց զիս հայր իմ թէ գնա ի նախիրն եւ բեր պարարտ երինչ առջառ զի զոհեցուցուք կռոցն:
49. իբրեւ գնացի ի նախիրն, չոկեցի զեր եւ ըստուար երինջք եւ առջառք. եւ ծագեաց լոյս շնորհացն Աստուծոյ ի սիրտս իմ. քննեցի եւ ոչ հաւանեցայ զկենդանիքս ըսպանանել վասն մեռեալ պատկերի. թողի զանասունքն եւ դարձեալ հայեցայ յերկինս եւ յարեգակն եւ ի լուսին եւ յամենայն արարածս. եւ արարչին շնորհօք ի քննութենէ այսոցիկ ծանեայ զարարիչն Աստուած. թողի զանասունքն եւ գնացի առ հայրն իմ.
50. թէ ուր է երինջքն. եւ ես ասացի հայր իմ դժուար թուեաց ինձ զկենդանիքն ըսպանանել վասն մեռեալ եւ անշունչ եւ ձեռագործ պատկերաց որ ոչ են Աստուած. այլ սուտ չաստուածք վասն այն ոչ բե/ p. 59 /րի։ Եւ հայրն իմ ոխացաւ ընդ իս. եւ մտեալ ասաց մօրն իմ. թէ այսօր երկու որդւոցս մինն զոհ մատուցանեմ կռոցն. եւ մայրն իմ գիտաց որ ոխացաւ ընդ իս հայրն իմ. ապա ողբայր մայրն իմ եւ ճանկեր զերեսն իւր եւ զարնէր զլխոյն.
51. քանզի սիրեր զիս մայրն իմ. եւ հայրս սիրէր զեղբայրն իմ։ Իսկ հայրն

---

27. · Note the inversion of verb and conjunction.

իմ տեսեալ զզուգ մօրն իմոյ որ լայր դառնապէս, ասաց հայրն իմ մօր իմոյ. ընդէր սուք առնես եւ լաս. արկցուք վիճակ ի վերայ երկու որդւոցս. ում եւ ելցէ վիճակն զնա զենցուք. զի հայրն իմ այնպէս կարծէր թէ վիճակն ինձ ելցէ եւ մեռանիմ վասն կռոցն.

52. երեք անգամ վիճակ արկին. նա երեք անգամ անկաւ յեղբօրս վերայ, եւ պիտէր որ վասն կռոցն մեռանէր: Իբրեւ եղեւ այս. առեալ հայրն իմ տանէր կապեալ զեղբայրն իմ. իսկ մայրն իմ լայր եւ ասէր ընդ իս. ո՛չ ողորմիս եղբօրն քոյ. եւ մայրն իմ լալով զնաց զհետ նորա զի տեսցէ զկատարումա որդւոյն իւրոյ: Իբրեւ լսեցին իշխանքն եւ մեծամեծքն թագաւորին իւր որդին մատուցանէ զոհ կռոցն, բազումք առեալ զդուստր եւ զորդիս իւրեանց տարան ի զենումա.

53. եւ ես յոյժ լացի վասն եղբօրն իմոյ փախեայ եւ ելայ ի յանդաստ եւ հայեի ի յանտառէն, զի արկին ձեռն յեղբայրն իմ ըսպանանել. եւ ես խնդրեցի ի Տեառնէ եւ ասացի, եթէ բացցին դրունք անդնդող եւ կլա/p. 60 /նեցեն զդոսա: Իսկոյն պատառեցաւ երկիր եւ եկուլ զնոսա ընդ կուրսն եւ ընդ տաճարսն, զհայրն իմ եւ զմայրն իմ ամենայն ժողովրդով եւ ես միայն մնացի ասա: Բայց աւա, է տարի է որ ոչ տեսեալ զիս մարդ:

54. Իսկ Աբրահամ զերծաւ զզլուխ նորա. եւ կտրեաց զզեկունս նորա լուաց եւ մաքրեաց եւ զզեցոյց զնա եւ տարեալ ի տուն իւր. եւ պատարագ մատոյց զհինով եւ հացիւ. եւ ճաշակեաց Աբրահամ համան ընտանեօքն. եւ եղեւ քահանայ տանն Աբրահամու յաստուածակոյս կողմանէ: Չի այն եղեւ առաջին պատարագ հացով եւ գինւով. զի Մելքիսէք եղեւ առաջին քահանայ. որ օրինակ էր Քրիստոս{ի}:

55. 55. Եւ Աբրահամ բարեզործութեամբ ծերացաւ եւ հանգեաւ խաղաղութեամբ. եւ եթող Բ որդիս, զԻսահակ ի Սառայէ. եւ զԻսմայէլ ի Հազարայ. եւ Իսահակայ որդիքն Եսաւ եւ Յակոբ. եւ Յակոբայ ԺԲ նահապետքն յորոց օրինեցան ազգ եւ ազինք ի ոցանէ: Նոյն օրինութիւն ի վերայ ձեր եղիցի հանդերձ տամբ եւ տեղօք ձերով. Ամէն:

Concerning Isaac's Birth

43. When Abraham drew near to his wife Sarah, she conceived and bore (his) son Isaac, handsome and more honored[28] than all. Then (his) parents loved (him) greatly and did not extinguish the candle at night,[29] because of his brilliant countenance. When Isaac developed, those who saw (his) beauty and his eloquent, sweet tongue were amazed and were left astounded. Then

---

28. This is the same adjective that is used of the divinely designated heifer in the Annunciation description: see the General Introduction" p. 21, n. 20 and p. 155, n. 100.

29. One might expect that they did not kindle a candle.

God sent his angel and he said to Abraham, "God seeks your son Isaac as an offering."[30]

44. When Abraham heard that word from the angel, he persuaded (i.e., saddled) his donkey and took the fire and the wood and Isaac with him and he went to the place of the covenant.[31] And on the way Isaac asked, "Father, behold fire and behold wood, where is your sacrifice and offering?"[32]

45. Abraham said, "God will prepare the sacrificial offering,"[33] for in that way Abraham deceived Isaac, but (in fact) he prophesied through God.[34] When they went to the place of the covenant, he bound his son Isaac and took the sword,[35] so that he might slaughter his son. But the angel called out (and) said, "Do not draw near to this youth, for God sent you a ram as sacrifice, hung by its horns from the Tree of Sabek."[36]

46. And Abraham took the ram, slaughtered (it) instead of Isaac[37] and released Isaac. There was a voice from the heavens and it said, "Abraham, Abraham, just as you did not spare your son for my sake, in the same way I did not spare My son for your sake." And Abraham returned joyously to his home. And one day,[38] while Abraham was praying, the angel appeared to him and said, "God commands you to go towards Jerusalem, and you will find in the forest a man, servant of God, whose name is Melchizedek. Groom his head and straighten his nails and clothe him with garments, for he will offer sacrifice of wine and bread on your behalf.

47. And he will become a priest for your house and all your family from the divine side." Abraham said, "In which place[39] do I find him?" The angel said, "In Jerusalem, in the forest." When Abraham went to the forest he saw that a pillar of light was descending from the heavens upon the forest. Abraham knew the place. When it was day, having gone, he found Melchizedek with frightening aspect and having changed color, and his face was transformed,[40]

48. and the hair of his head descended to his knees, and his nails were a span long and his back was like a turtle's. And Abraham having greeted him,

---

30. In Gen 22:2, God himself speaks, and not an angel.
31. See Gen 22:3. The fire and wood are drawn from a later point in the story, Gen 22:6.
32. Gen 22:7.
33. Gen 22:8.
34. See text no. 4.17 note. Compare Irenaeus, *Adv. haer.* 4.5.5.
35. This is the same word that is used in Armenian Genesis. It may also signify a long knife.
36. Gen 22:12–13. See the notes on text no. 4:22.
37. Gen 22:13.
38. Here the Story of Melchizedek starts. On it, see the General Introduction, 8–12.
39. Reading ուր as if it were որ.
40. On transformation of the face, see the information gathered by Orlov 2009, 180–82; 2007, 327–32, 337–39.

spoke with him and said, "How long is it that you remained here and how did you recognize God?" Melchizedek said, "It is seven years that I am living here ascetically unseen by men and no one has seen me but you." Abraham said, "Tell me how you came to believe?" Melchizedek said, "I am the son of king Melk'i, son of king Saḷim, who built this city. And one day on an idolatrous festival, my father sent me, 'Go to the herd of black cattle and bring a fat heifer (and) an ox so that we might sacrifice to the idols.'"

49. When I went to the flock, I separated fat and strong heifers and oxen. And the light of God's grace shone in my heart. I examined (the matter) and I was not persuaded to kill the living beasts for the sake of dead images. I left the beasts and again I looked at the heavens and at the sun and at the moon and at all creations. And, by the grace of the Creator, through examination of these, I recognized the Creator, God. I left the beasts and went to my father.

50. "Where are the heifers?" And I said, "My father, it seemed hard to me to kill the living animals for the sake of dead and unbreathing and handmade images, which are not God, but false not-gods. For this reason I did not bring (the heifers). And my father bore a grudge against me and, going in, he said to my mother, "Today, of (our) two sons, one I will offer as a sacrifice to the idols." And my mother knew that my father bore a grudge against me. Then my mother lamented and scratched her face, and smote her head,

51. because my mother loved me and my father loved my brother. Then my father, saw my mother's mourning, that she was weeping bitterly. My father said to my mother. "Why are you mourning and weeping. Let us cast lots for (our) two sons and we will slaughter him upon whom the lot falls." For my father thought thus, that the lot would fall upon me and I would die on account of the idols.

52. Thrice they cast the lots. Lo, three times it fell upon my brother, and he was to have died for the sake of the idols. When it happened thus, my father took my brother and brought (him) tied up. Then my mother wept and said to me, "Do you not have mercy upon your brother?" And my mother, weeping, went after him, so that she might see the end of her son. When the princes and nobles heard that the king was offering his own son as a sacrifice to the idols, many, having taken their daughters and sons, brought them to slaughter.

53. And I wept exceedingly on account of my brother. I fled and went forth to the forest and looked[41] from the forest, that they laid hand upon my brother to kill (him). And I sought from the Lord and said, "Let the gates of the deeps be opened and let them swallow them." Indeed, the earth split open and swallowed them with the idols and with the temples, my father and my mother and all the people, and I remained alone here. But, behold, it is 7 years that no man has seen me.

54. Then Abraham groomed his head, and cut his nails, washed and cleaned

---

41. Or: "watched."

11A: CONCERNING ABRAHAM'S HOSPITALITY

(him) and dressed him and brought him to his (Abraham's) house.[42] And he (Melchizedek) made an offering of wine and bread, and Abraham ate together with his household, and he became Abraham's priest from the divine side. For that was the first offering of bread and wine, for Melchizedek was the first priest, who was a type {of} Christ.[43]

55. And Abraham through good deeds, grew old and fell asleep in peace. And he left 2 sons, Isaac from Sarah and Ishmael from Hagar. And Isaac's sons (were) Esau and Jacob. And from Jacob were the 12 patriarchs, by whom people and family were blessed. May the same blessing be upon you with your house and place. Amen.

---

42. See the General Introduction, note 11.
43. See the similar remarks in George Syncellus 111 (Adler and Tuffin 2002, 139).

12. SERMON CONCERNING THE SODOMITES

This text occurs in manuscript M5571 fols. 206v–212r, which was copied in 1657–59 in Smyrna and Surat' (India).[1] A second copy of the document is to be found in M2242, fols. 18r–31r. That manuscript is a Miscellany copied in the seventeenth century.[2] The variants of M2242 are noted in the apparatus following the text. On occasion, its readings are preferable to those of M5571 and have been included in the text. Such instances are clearly marked. In addition, M2242 has several pages of additional text at the end, following §55, and these have been included in this edition. On the whole, M5571 has less "classical" or "normative" spellings and morphology than does M2242. Whether such classicizing readings are original or a subsequent correction by a zealous scribe is impossible to determine. Each manuscript has lacunae not present in the other, so it does not seem that one is copied from the other.

The document presented here, then, is based primarily on M5571 as default manuscript and M2242 is put in the text when it is either patently preferable or where M5571 does not exist. In manuscript M5571, the present work occurs after *Sermon Concerning the Flood,* which has been published elsewhere.[3] Another text from this manuscript has been published as well, *Adam, Eve and the Incarnation,* and a quite detailed description of the manuscript is to be found in connection with that publication.[4] Notable is a developed didactic and theological dimension and certain sections may be observed in which it departs from the narrative line to make a theological point. This seems to indicate that the text was used in some sort of instruction; see especially notes on §§9, 24, and 25–27 and less prominently elsewhere throughout. This character coheres with its title "Sermon" and with *Sermon Concerning the Flood* and perhaps other, still unpublished works in this manuscript.

Following the document published here, both manuscripts have a detailed homily dealing with Lot, his hospitality and its aftermath, his family's flight from Sodom, and his wife's transformation into a pillar of salt. This text, which is not presented in detail here, is for the most part homiletic and moral in charac-

---

1. Ēganyan, Zeyt'unyan, and Ant'abyan 1970, 2:210.
2. See Ēganyan et al. 1965, 1:753–754.
3. Stone 1996a, 174–83.
4. Stone 1996a, 8–9.

12. SERMON CONCERNING THE SODOMITES

ter, with limited narrative sections. In M5571, it is given a separate title, while in M2242 it is presented as a continuation of the *Sermon Concerning the Sodomites*. It contrasts quite strongly with the material published here, in that the homiletic element greatly outweighs the narrative.[5]

Sermon Concerning the Sodomites has many medieval Armenian forms of which only the most usual are noted. Both manuscripts mix medieval forms with ancient ("classical") Armenian forms. The style of the document is quite often somewhat obscure. In some sections the language differs, especially in the heightened use of medieval and modern Armenian verb forms. It is conceivable that this indicates that it is a composition drawing on diverse sources. Its orthography is generally fairly standard, but the following instances should be observed in M5571.

Variant spellings in M5571 apart from voiced/unvoiced stops:

a. *Confusion* հ / յ
հերկիւդէ <յերկիւդէ   §1
գյաւատոյ <գհաւատոյ   §3
b. հ / -
աշխարին   §10 §13
c. ձ / g
բարցրացեալ   §21
d. *Variation* ոյ / ու
յարուց <յարոյց   §5
դարձուց <դարձոյց   §17
e. *Superfluous use of* nota accusativi   §15 and note
f. In our notes numerous instances of strange case usage are observed and these instances noted, but not exhaustively.

Ełišē, *Commentary on Genesis* (Khachikyan and Papazian 2002), served as a source in §41, and is cited verbatim in §§43–44a. The author draws upon it, but rewrites it, again in §44b–46.

---

5. See M2242, fols. 24v–31v and M5571, fols. 212r–218r.

/fol. 206v / Քարոզ ի բան վասն Սոդոմաեցոցն ի բանն որ ասէ աղաղակ Սոդոմաեցոց ելաւ առաջի իմ.

1. Յորժամ ել Նոյ ի տապանէն եւ բաժանեաց Գ բաժին աշխարհս ի վերայ երիցորդոցն. զԱսիայ <զԱրաբիա> եւ զԼիբիա եւ Շխամ լցաւ աշխարհս ծնընդօք նոցա եւ ապա շինեցին զաշտարակն յերկիւղէ ջրհեղեղին եւ յետ կործանման աշտարակին. <եւ բաժանման> երկուտասան լեզուացն մոլորեցան մարդիկք եւ անկան ի կռապաշտութիւն.
2. ումանք ասեն թէ զԲէլ որ սպան Հայկ որդիքն արարին զպատկերն եւ յետոյ աստուած կարծեցաւ բայց Սոդոմն ասէ հայր թաղեալ ի վերայ տարաժամ մահուան որդոյ Կայեն անուն արար զպատկերս եւ յետոյ մոլորեալ աստուած պաշտեցին: Եւ ի Բաբելոնէ սկսաւ կռապաշտութիւն եւ ի ՉԾ ամս բոլորեալ զաշխարհս մոռացան զԱստուած եւ փոխանակ զարարչին զարարծս աստուած պաշտեցին:
3. / fol. 207a / Եւ եհաս ժամանակն ի Աբրահամ որ նա ծանեաւ զճշմարիտն Աստուած եւ հայր եղեւ <հաւատոյ>. զի անուն հօր նորա Թարայ էր եւ ինքն կռապաշտ առաջն եւ որդի կռապաշտի եւ իւր <ծննդեան> տեղիքն Բաբելոն էր եւ այսպէս <ծանեաւ>[6] զԱստուած երկիրն Բաբելացոց պարարտ էր եւ բարին շատ բնակիչքն ունէին եւ ըմպէին եւ բտին զմարմինն կերակուր անմահ որդանցն:
4. Եւ փափկացեալ եւ որ կլա մոլութեան. եւ արբեցութեան. եւ վատեցին զհոյր ցանգութեան ի հոգիս իւրեանց. եւ ոչ դատարկին ի մեղաց եւ ի պոռնկութենէ: Բարկացաւ Աստուած եւ սով եւ <աղութիւն> ետ նոցա զի սովամաշ մարմին դարձին ի մեղաց. եւ գերամս ճայէկ հալուցն յարուց ի վերայ նոցա որ ունէին զվաստակս նոցա եւ զբերս երկրին:
5. Եւ Աբրահամ է ՁԵ ամաց առաքեաց հայրն <պահել զարտորայս> զի մի սովամաշ լինիցին. եւ նա գնացեալ շատ ջանաց եւ ոչ կարաց հալածել զնոսա այլ նեղեցեալ անկաւ երկիր. եւ նայեցաւ ի վեր եւ եւտես շրջագաութիւնս երկնից եւ զդիրս աստեղաց եւ զթաց արեգական եւ լուսնի. եւ ինքն իմաստուն եւ ճարտար աստղագէտ էր:
6. Եւ նոյն ժամայն ծագեաց լոյս մարդասիրութեան ի սիրտն Աբրահամու եւ միտս իւր եկեալ ծանո զմոլորութեան[7] իւրեանց: Եւ յարուցեալ եկաց ի վերայ ծնկաց. եւ զբազուկս տարածեալ առ Աստուած աղօթս եւ ասաց. Անծանօթից Աստուած եւ արարիչ ամենայնի. եւ ստեղծիչ այս թոչնցս դու տուր հրաման զի հեռասցեն եւ մի կերիցեն զվաստակս:
7. Եւ նոյն ժամայն չիք դարձան. եւ ուրախացաւ Աբրահամ զի եգիտ զճշմարիտն Աստուած եւ եկեալ պատմեաց հօրն եւ ասաց թէ. շատ աղաչեցի զպաշտելիս ձեր եւ ոչ եղեւ լսելի. եւ ապա ճանեաւ զճշմարիտն Աստուած եւ նորա հրամանաւն հալածեցան թռչունքն: / fol. 207v /

---

6. Compare ծանեօ in §6 below.
7. This word has the *nota accusativi* q- together with an oblique case. Other instances may be noted where classical case usage is not preserved.

8. Եվ ի լուսանալ առաւատուն առանձացեալ⁸ Աբրահամ եւ եկաց աղօթս. եւ երեւեցաւ նմա Աստուած եւ ասէ. ել յերկրէ քումմէ եւ ազգէ. եւ եկ երկիր զոր ցուցից քեզ. վասն այսորիկ երեւեցաւ քեզ։ Ասաց Աստուած զի ճշմարիտ եւ հաստատ ճանաչել տամ զիս քեզ. որովհետեւ հաւատացիր զիս. մի բնակեր ընդ անհաւատան. զի ոչ կա բաժին հաւատացելոց ընդ անհաւատին. եւ ոչ է միաբանութիւն լուտ եւ խաւարի։

9. <Եւ առին իւրեանց կանայս Նաքվոր եւ Աբրահամ. անուն կնոջն Աբրահամու Սառայ. եւ Նաքովրայն Յեսք եւ երկոքին դստերք Առանայ։> Եւ էառ Թարա զորդիս իւր եւ ել յաշխարհէն Քաղդեացոց գնալ յերկիրն Քանանացոց. բարեխորհուրդ Աստուծոյ. <ազդեալ> Թարայի գնա ի Միջագետս. եւ բնակեր ի Խառան. վասն բ պատճառի. մի գ<ի ի>⁹ Քաղդեացոց աշխարհին բազմացաւ կախարդութիւն եւ ոչ տար պտուղ երկրին. եւ բ զի Աբրահամ կամեցաւ գնալ յետ Աստուծոյ. հրամանին. եւ հայրն եւ եղբարքն ոչ թողին գնա։

10. Եւ ելեալ ի Բաբելոնէ բնակեցաւ ի Խառան եւ շինեաց Թարա տուն կոչ ի Խառան. Եւ բարկացեալ Աբրահամ կամեցաւ այրել հրով. եւ Առան եղբարն¹⁰ Աբրահամու հայրն Ղովտա կամեցաւ շիջուցանել զհուրն եւ անկեալ ի տաճարն այրեցաւ եւ մեռաւ. եւ առաջի հօրն յայտնի է զհետ ջրհեղեղին այլ չէր մեռեալ որդի առաջի հօրն. եւ պատճառ պատժին ասեն զի իմացաւ զձուննդն ջորոյ հակառակ աստուածութեան. եւ արարչութեան

11. զի Աստուծոյ կամքն այն է որ ամէն ազգ իւր ազգէն ծնանի. մարդէն մարդ, ոչխարէն ոչխար. եւ շանէն շուն. արտաքո <բնութենէ>¹¹ եւ հակառակ Աստուծոյ արարչութեան, ծնունդն ջորոյ. զի Աստուած զամենայն ազգ ծերընդական արար եւ ջորին վասն այն չունի ծնունդ. զի չէ արարած Աստուծոյ։

12. Այլ մարդիկ իմացան ի հնարից Սատանայէ եւ թեպետ կորեաւ Առ<ա>ն այլ չար յիշատակն մնաց աշխարհի. եւ մեռաւ Թարա / fol. 208r / ի Խառան։ Եւ ասէ Աստուած գԱբրահամ. ել յերկրէ եւ ազգէ քումմէ. եւ ունկնդիր. ելեալ գնաց յետ հրամանին Աստուծոյ եւ եկին ի Սեքիմ եւ ի կաղնին բարձր սինք իմա սիւ քարն է որ է Սամարիայ.¹² Եւ կաղնին բարձր թերեւս զոր յետտ Մամր<էի> կոչէ.

13. Եւ զի ժ ազգ որդոցն Քանանի դառնալն աշտարակէն առեալ էին գերկիրն որդոցն Սիմա զրկանոք Քանանու, կոչէ գնա որում տեղւոչ

---

8. This is a late spelling of առանձնացեալ.
9. So basically M2242. We have added the extra ի. Manuscript M5571 reads qՔաղդեացոց, which makes no sense here. We regard this as an instance of the common corruption of q- / զի (see Stone and Hillel 2012, Index of Variants, s.v.) and a haplography.
10. Note the spelling; see Stone and Hillel 2012, Index of Variants, s.v.
11. բնակութենէ "dwelling" and the graphically similar բնութենէ "nature" are confounded. The variant is known elsewhere; see Stone and Hillel 2012, Index of Variants, s.v.
12. The grammar of սիւ քարն է is odd.

երևեցաւ Աստուած Աբրահամու եւ ասէ. զաւակի քում տաց զերկիրս
զայս:

14. Եւ եղեւ սով եւ էջ Աբրահամ յ<Ե>գիպտոս եւ արին զՍառայ ի տունն փարաւոնի եւ պատժեաց Աստուած զփարաւոն դարձուց տուկանօք զկինն առ Աբրահամ. Եւ եղեւ ի բազմանալ խաշանցն եւ անասնոց Աբրահամու. եւ Ղովտա. եւ երկիրն ոչ կարէր տանել եւ կարգէին հովիւքն. եւ ասէ {ի}[13] Աբրահամ գՂովտ. եղբար եւ մարսին իմ ես դու. ոչ է պարտ խռովութեան ի միջի մերում քանց կրտող միատեղ կացայց սիրով բաժանած լա՜ւ եմք.

15. եւ բաժանեցաւ Ղովտ Աբրահամէ եւ մեկն բնակեցաւ ի Սոտոմ եւ առ իւր կինն: Եւ Աբրահամ բնակեցաւ ի Քեբրոն. եւ մինչ կար յաղօթս խօսելով ընդ Աստուծոյ <աստ եղեւ> նմա թէ եկին Դ թագաւոր յարեւելից եւ արին զհին<գ> թագաւորութիւնս Սոդոմացոց. եւ զՂովտ եղբօր որդի նորա.

16. եւ պնդեցաւ Աբրահամ ՅԱ եւ ԺԸ հեծելօք կոտորեաց զնոսա. եւ դարձուց զգերին. եւ Մելքիսեթեկ թագաւոր Սադիմա ել ընդ յառաջ Աբրահամու. եւ էօծ զնա թագաւոր. եւ հաց եւ գինի պատարագ մատուց նմա եւ տասանորդաց.

17. <եւ եղեւ> Աբրահամ[14] Հ ամաց եւ Սառա Ղ ամաց: Եւ Սառա ամուլ էր ոչ ծնանէր զաւակ:
Եւ երեւեցաւ նմա Աստուած առ կաղնեան Մամրէի մինչդեռ նստէր ի խորանի անդ զի Մամրէի սեւ ծառայ եւ հովիւ էր Աբրահամու եւ ոչխարք Աբրահամու սեւք էին / fol. 208v / վասն ջերմութեան աշխարհի Բաբելացոց:

18. Եւ եղեւ սով ի ժամանակին եւ ետ Աբրահամ Մամրէի հաց մի եւ ասաց արուտ տանել գոչխարն. եւ տեսեալ Մամրէի աղքատ մի նուազեալ ի սովու: եւ անկեալ ի վերայ ճանապարհին. եւ ասէ աղքատն գ<Մ>ամրէի.[15] քո Աստուծոյ սիրուն համար թէ ունիս հաց պատառ մի տուր զի նուազեալ եմ ի սովու եւ ոչ կարեմ գնալ:

19. Եւ նա վասն Աստուծոյ սիրուն համար[16] հանեալ զհացն ետ աղքատին. եւ աղքատն զհաց կերաւ եւ զօրացաւ եւ գնաց. եւ Մամրէ մաաց քաղցած եւ ջերմացեալ ուլուրն. ցրցեալ զկաղնին հովակն[17] ցուպն եւ արկ զվերարկուն. եւ շուք արար. եւ ինքն նստեալ ի հովանին ննջեաց.

---

13. The ի appears to be superfluous and might be a corruption of a final ր of an imperfect ասէր. M2242 does not have it. The combination ի noun համար is found elsewhere (Th. M. van Lint).

14. The superfluous use of *nota accusativi* as in M5571 has been remarked upon on pp. 179–80 above. See Stone and Hillel 2012, Index of Variants, s.v.

15. Corrupt: the first men is omitted in the manuscript.

16. Note the use both of the preposition վասն and of the postposition համար, which occurs elsewhere in Middle Armenian.

17. There are two difficulties in this phrase. The declined forms of կարնի "oak" are odd throughout this text and here it must be a genitive governing ցուպն. Second, the word հովակ

20. Եւ իբրեւ զարթեաւ եւեա արմատացեալ կաղնին եւ բար<ձ>գրացեալ[18] եւ եղեալ ծառ մեծ եւ շուք էր արարեալ ի վերայ իւրեան եւ ոչխարին.[19] եւ ուրախացաւ եւ գոհացաւ Աստուծոյ։ Եւ սպիտակացեալ էր ինքն եւ ոչխարքն. եւ յերեկուին յորժամ դարձաւ ի տունն եւ զնաց Աբրահամ ընդ յառաջ նորա. եւ հարցանէր թէ ով ես դու. եւ նա ժմտալ[20] ասաց ես եմ Մամրէ հովիւն քո.
21. Եւ հարցանէր զպատճառն թէ վասն էր ես սպիտակացեալ դու եւ ոչխարքդ։ Եւ նա ասաց թէ քո Աստուածն արար զմէկ հացն որ դու ինձ պաշար տուիր ես նորա սիրուն համար աղքատի տուի. զայս ամենայն բարութիւնս արար Աստուած։
22. Եւ զարմացեալ Աբրահամ գոհացաւ զԱստուծոյ եւ ուխտ եւս անձին իւրոյ զի առանց աղքատի այլ հաց մի կերիցէ. եւ մինչեւ Աբրահամ նահապետնք ամենայն թուլ մուրուոք մեռանէին։ Իսկ հայրն հաւատոյ Աբրահամ ծաղկեցաւ աստուածպաշտութեամբ. ծաղկեցաւ ալեօք.
23. Եւ առաւօտուն առաջնորդեալ Մամրէի <տարեալ> եցոյց Աբրահամ[21] զկաղնին եւ նա տեսեալ ալիքնեաց / fol 209r /Աստուած եւ շրջապատ արար տեղին աղօթից։ Եւ օրն Գ անգամ աղօթէր՝ եւ սստեալ ընդ հովանեաւ ծառուն եւ մօտաւոր ճանապարհի էր անցաւոր զով որ տեսանէր ճանապարհորդ կերակրէր վասն սիրուն Աստուծոյ։ Եւ պատուով ճանապարհի էր:
24. Եւ ասեն թէ Սատանա կապեաց զճանապարհին Խ օր հիւր ոչ եկն Աբրահամու եւ այլազգիքն. զայն բարի սովորութեան[22] Աբրահամէ ունին որ զեվխա շինեն ի վերայ ճանապարհին։ Եւ հաց տան աղքատաց. եւ ճանապարհորդաց. եւ եղեւ զի բազում ժամանակ որ հիւր ոչ եկն Աբրահամու եւ հասեալ աւագ Ե շաբաթի աւուրն.
25. Եւ ի հասակ աւուրն կայր յաղօթս առ կաղնեան Մամրէի։ Եւ երեւեցաւ նմա Աստուած. եւ <երկուս> ընդ իւր ունելով ի կերպարանս արանց։ անփոփոխական բնութենէ Աստուած այլ վասն մարդասիրութեան խոնարհի ձեւանայ եւ թուեցուցանէ թէ փոխի <զոր մի լիցի կարծել. այլ տեսութիւն մարդոյն փոխի. զոր> զօրինակ լեառն մեծ փոքր ձեւանայ թվի եւ բոլոր եւ արծուի մեծ ճիճառն թվի եւ լոյս մի Բ երեւի տեսութեան տկարութենէ այլայլումն եւ ոչ թէ իրացն որքան առաւել անփոփոխ է Աստուած իւրական մալով իսկութեան եւ ոչ ի հեռաստանէ զա Աստուած այլ միշտ մօտ կա եւ ականէ եւ տեսանէ

---

does not appear in the dictionaries but might be related to հով "cool" or հովանի "shadow, shade" and perhaps means "shelter."

18. Note the spelling with գ instead of ձ.
19. A plural would be expected; see the next sentence.
20. A participle would be expected, or else this might be a case of -ալ for –եալ; see Stone and Hillel 2012, Index of Variants, nos. 122–123.
21. A dative case would be expected.
22. The case usage is anomalous.

զզորձս մարդկան. այլ զի մեք ոչ տեսանեմք կարձեմք թէ այլ աշխարհի կա եւ մեք այլ:

26. Եւ յորժամ երեւի թվի եկն ամենայնի թագաւորն ոչ կարապետ յղէ առաջի իւր այլ ազդումա ինչ արկեալ ի սիրտ երեւման Աստուծոյ արարուն: Եղեալ ասէ նստա ձառովա ի տոթոյ ժամու գիրն ասէ ի միում աւուր. այլ ամենայն օր գործ ջան ունէր աղօթս կալ խաղաղական առանձնութեան. եւ ոչ զզալ տոթոյ եւ ցրտոյ կեալ ընդ Աստուծոյ միշտ տեսանէր զԱստուած կամ զպատկեր նորա մարդ գիտելով թէ որ զմարդ հանգուցանէ զկամս Աստուծոյ կատարէ:

27. Ամբարձ Աբրահամ զաչս իւր եւ / fol 209v / {եւ}[23] ետես արս Գ կային ի վերու քան զնա արանց զալուստ ի յերկրի երեւի եւ կամ առաջն կամ յետո կամ ի աջմէ կամ ահեկէ զայսպիսեցաւ ինչ ոչ ասէ. այլ միայն թէ արք Գ կացին ուստի այտէ թէ ընդ զզալի արեզական իմանալի արեզական ձազեցաւ.

28. Եւ Բ կողմանս կատարէին միտքն Աբրահամու. Աստուծոյ զալ երեւումա կամ աշխար<հ>ի կատարած փառաւորեաց. յառաջն տարակուսեցաւ միտս իւր եւ ասէ թէ Աստուած է ընդէր մարդակերպ երեւի. եւ թէ մարդ է մարմաւոր որպէս իշանէ երկնից.

29. Եւ զի իմաստուն էր Աբրահամ խրատեաց զինքն եւ ասաց. վասն էր ես տարակուսեալ. ընդ յառաջ զնա մեծարէ եւ պատուէ. թէ Աստուած է աստուածասէր եղեր. թէ մարդ է մարդասէր եղեր. աստուածասէրն մարդասէրն մի են ճշմարիտ է բանն զի Աստուծոյ սէրն ձածուկ է Աստուծոյ սիրու նշանն ընկերասէրն եւ աղքատասէրն է որպէս ձառն պտղով ձանաչի եւ մարդն կերպարանաւ:

30. Այսպէս աստուածասէր մարդն աղքատի սիրովա ճանաչի թէ մարդն մարդասէր եւ ողորմած տեսանես իմացիր որ ճշմարիտ աստուածասէր է որ Աստուծոյ սիրուն համար[24] կու տա զողորմութիւն. աղքատաց զի սրտի սէրն ի ձեռաց տուրսն երեւի:

31. Ապա[25] թէ զմարդն անողորմ եւ զազանասիրտ տեսանէի եւ պարձենա թէ աստուածասէր եմ, սուտ է: ձեր մէկ դրամ կամ մէկ ստակ չտա աղքատին եւ ապաւր կերեւի թէ Աստուած կու սիրէ սրտով զԱստուած կատէ լեզուան կու խաբէ. Աստուած մարդ չէ թէ խաբուի:

32. Իբրեւ ետես Աբրահամ ընթացաւ ընդ յառաջ նորա իբրեւ երից ուղեւորաց. եւ երկիր եպազ ի վերայ երեսազ որպէս սովոր էր. եւ Տէրն կամեցաւ փորձել զհաւատն եւ զկատարեալ սէրն Աբրահամու առաջն ասէ[26] / fol. 210r / մեք ձանապարհորդենք կու զնանք ի մեր ձանապարհին տեսանենք. ասէ այլ մեծարէ թէ ոչ նոյնպէս մարդ

---
23. Dittography.
24. Observe the postposition.
25. Note the use of medieval present forms with կ or կու, which appear in this and the preceding section and also the late middle-passive form խաբուի. These forms are not found in the preceding parts of this document.
26. In lower margin: վասն հուր զալոյ to combine with titles on other pages.

12. SERMON CONCERNING THE SODOMITES 185

յորժամ գևա մոտ բարեկամն յառաջև որ մեծարէ թէ միանգամ որ մեծարէ դու չե ասեն.

33. թէ սուտ սիրելի է բաց թողու. թէ ճշմարիտ սիրելի է ոչ թողու մինչեւ տանի պատուէ. եւ զի Տէրև թագաւորի ձեւով երեւէր. եւ Բ հրեշտակքև ծառայի. վասև իւրո իբր գմիտ խօսի այլ թէ գոր խևդրէի կարօտիւ զօեսութիւև եւ զողորմութիւն քո:

34. Ապա մի զանձ²⁷ առևեր զիևեւ այլ առցի սակաւ մի ջուրև թէ ումէ ոչ իշխէ եւ լուացեև զոտս ձեր եւ զաս կնօջ ասէ պատկառանօք զի թէ Տէրև է ոչ պիտի նմա ջուր եւ թուի թէ հարցանելով է բանս առցի սակաւ ջուր եւ լուացցի:

35. Համարձակիմք ասէ վտահանամք իշխեմք եւ զով առնեք արժանի սպասաւորելո ձեզ. զի թէ զանևանձև առևուցուս ապա եւ այլ ինչ համարձակեցցի թէ Աստուած է մարդակերպեալ առ իս ուրիք այևպէս ի ուրիցև ջուր արժանէ տալ. զի յերկիրս պանտուխտ անուանե ուրից նորա:

36. Ազարական Մամրէի արքայանիստ եղեւ եւ ծառև կաղնի առաւել քան զդրախտև Ադենա.²⁸ զի անդ է Տէր արարածոց որում չիշխէ ասել թէ նստէք կերաք, զի մի հրամադ ից մինչեւ առնու համարձակութենէ. ասելն այդպէս արա. որպէս ասացերդ. յամօք այնոցիկ որ այլազգ ասեն եւ այլազգան են:²⁹

37. Եւ ապա տարել իջուց գՏէրև ի խորանին. եւ լուաց ջրով զոտս նորա: Եւ Սառայի ասաց փութ արա. ոչ ծառայի եւ ոչ աիսախևու: հրամայէ <արա ևկանակս> երեք որ է բազարձ:

38. Եւ Աբրահամ առեալ հորդ կաթևակեր եւ էգեն. եւ ետ ծառայս եփել եւ հասուցանել. եւ Սառա հասուց գբողարձև եւ էած Աբրահամ սեղան. նախ զկաթև:/ fol 210v / Եւ կոցի որ է կարաք եւ կերան եւ ապա զիորդև մատադ զի այլ ծեր էր Աբրահամ մոռացաւ զիւր ծերութեամբ անձին. սպասաւորէին ինքն եւ Սառա. նախ զի ծառայքև անարժան համարեցան բարի հիւրոց սպասաւորութիւն. եւ Բ պատճառ անձամբ աշխատէին զի վարքև իւրանքև առցեն:

39. Այսպէս պարտ է անձամբ սպասաւորել սրբոց. եւ ադքատաց լուանա<լ> զոտս եւ կերակրել զի վարձս անձամբ առցեն. զի ոչ միայն տանև է զովելի. այլ եւ անձամբ սպասաւորել պարտ է կերակրել եւ զգեցուցանել զաղքատն: Եւ ոչ թէ առ աչօք այլ ճշմարիտ կերան կերակուրն անմարմիք զոլով եւ հրեղէնք ծիսեցին որպէս հուրն ուտէ գձէք ճրագին եւ զվառած մոմին առանձ բերանի ուտէ առանց յորովայնէ ժողովէ եւ ոչ երեւի թէ ուր գևա:

40. Այսպէս կերան զկերակուրև եւ մաքրեցան հուրև աստուածային: Եւ

---

27. Read as if it were զանց.
28. Ադէև is a variant form of "Eden," often found in Armenian texts.
29. The preceding phrase is unclear.

Աբրահամ կանկնեալ կայր եւ սպասաւորէր. եւ դեռ տարակուսէր թէ մարդ է թէ Աստուած:

41. Եւ ապա ատ սակաւ մի ծանօթութեան տա Տէրն. Տէրն խօսելով ասէ ուր է Սառա կին քո. եւ Սառա կայր յետեւ խորանին. եւ ունկն դեր բանից նորա: բայց Աբրահամ ոչ գիտէր:

42. Եւ յօրժամ ասաց զանունն կնոջն. եւ ապա ճշմարիտ գիտաց Աբրահամ թէ Տէրն է որ զանունն գիտէ եւ գիրն եւս քաչ գիտէ այլ հարցանէ վարցս տալ վասատակցն. եւ շնորհակալութեան. եւ սպասաւորութեան. զի որպէս Աբրահամ անդա[30] ընթացաւ եւ Սառա նմանայ երն Աբրահամու թերեւս օգէին ծառայն: իսկ ծառայի եւ ոչ ոք զի ոչ թոյլ տար ադախնեացի. անարժան յամարելով զնոսա.

43. ան որ ոչ դեղ եւ ոչ արմատ. եւ ոչ դիւթող մուտ ի խորան նորա. վասն որդեծնութեան նորա այլ Աստուծոյ մառ / fol. 211r / ասելով Տէր վիրկեաց զիս նմա մառ զի բացցէ փակողն. եւ ասէ Տէրն ուր է Սառա կին քո. ուր է առաքինութիւն քո. ուր է զօրութիւն եւ ձակիցս քո:

44. Պատասխանի ետ Աբրահամ աւանիկ ի խորանին է. չգայի ի դեմս եւ Տէրն գիտէր զի յետ յետտ խորանին է կայր լսելով զբանս նորա հրաշա: Դարձեալ եկից ատ քեզ ի ժամուս յայսմիկ քեզ որդի լինի ի գիրկն Սառայի. յայտնի արար եւ պարզեաց զի Տէրն է. եւ Բ մեծ բարի խոստանա զիր զայն եւ զորդին.

45. Եւ լուաւ Սառայ ծիծաղեցաւ ասելով թէ մինչեւ ցայժմ չեղեւ մեզ որդի այժմ ի ծերութեան ժամանակիս լինի. իբրեւ զԱբրահամ ծիծաղի խնդացեալ չկարելով բերել գհիրոն զուարճութիւն. ասէ Տէրն գԱբրահամ զի է զի ծիծաղեցաւ Սառա ես պատաւեալ եմ արդարեւ ծնանիցեմ մի թէ տկարասցի առ Աստուծոյ ամենայն բան. Մի թէ ես տկար եմ.

46. ասէ մօտ յիս ծեր եւ տղայ մի է յերբ որ կամենամ չոր ծառեն որպէս զդալարէ պտուղ {պտու}[31] բերեմ յառաչ վասն էր ծիծաղեցաւ եւ ժպտեցաւ Սառայ. ուր աստ եկաց երկիւղեն ասաց թէ ոչ ծիծաղեցա:

47. Եւ ասէ Տէրն ոչ այսպէս այլ ծիծարեցար: դարձեալ. հաստատեց գխոստումն գալ տարէ նոյն օրն հուր պիտի գամ եւ լինիցի քեզ գիտելով թէ միայն Աստուած է գործ գտոր փայտն եւ պողաբեր առնելով. վասն որ կացի եւ երկարացի գխոստումն զի Աստուծոյ եւ ոչ բնութեան կարծիցէ տուր գաւակին. զի թէ թերահաւատութեամբ էր ծիծաղեալ դատապարտեալ լինէր իբրեւ Զաքարիա:

48. Եւ ոչ զմօր ծաղր ներ անուն մանկանն. մի տկարասցի Սառա ամենայն բան յիշեցելոցս եւս ցայն եւ եղեւն. զարարածս եւ գնորին

---

30. Անդա is not in the dictionaries. Th. M. van Lint, who has kindly advised me at a number of difficult points in the latter part of this text, suggests that անդա should be compared with ընդու. համար "for that reason" (Sayat' Nova), where ընդ(ու) is a reduced form of անդ; cf. *MHB* 2:163 յանդու, glossed as "երանից". M2242 has յանդեաց, which does not resolve the problem.

31. Dittography.

12. SERMON CONCERNING THE SODOMITES

հաւասար սքանչելիքն. որով անփորձ մնաց ի տուն[32] փարաւոնի. եւ յայտ է զի ծնանելն Իսահակա եկն Աստուած առ Աբրահամ / fol 211v / եւ նորա հրամամաւ[33] կոչեցաւ անուն մանկանն թէպէտ որ ոչ գրեցաւ այլ արդիւնանալ բանին զալուստ է նմա:

49. Եւ որ օրինակ թագաւոր ոմն հիւր հանդիպի իմաստուն մարդոյ եւ նա պատուէ զթագաւորն եւ գնալոյ ժամանակին թագաւորն պարգեւէ տա տանտիրոջն եւ ապա գնա ի տանէն: Այսպէս Աբրահամ պատուեաց զԱստուած գերկնի թագաւորն եւ նա գործին պարգեւեաց նմա բարի պարգեւէ:

50. Եւ զի աստուածասէր եւ ողորմած էր Աբրահամ եւ շատ աղքատաց կարօտութիւն լցեալ էր եւ ինքն կարօտէր զաւակի: Աստուած եկն նմա հուր. Բ. հրեշտակօք եւ նորա սրտի կարօտութեան եւ փափկին ելից. տալով նմա բարի զաւակ որով չափով չափեաց չափեցաւ նմա:

51. Թէ մարմաւոր թագաւոր մարդոյ հիւր հանդիպի ուրախանա մարդ եւ իւրանն մեծ փարք եւ պարծանք համարի. Այսպէս մեծ ամենայն արդարոց մեծ փարք է Աբրահամու Աստուծոյ հիւր գալն եւ ի տան նորա կերակրելն: Եւ ապա ալրինեցաց զտուն եւ զեղան նորա եւ ելեալ երթար ի տանէն խնաելով ի տունն եւ հանգիստ տալով նոցա:

52. Չի իւրմէ յետե յայտնեցաց զինքն կալաւ զնոսա դողումն. թէպէտ եւ անուշահոտութիւն. անձառելի կալաւ զԱբրահամ: Եւ ի գնալն ոչ կարէր հրաժարել հիա{նա}նալի[34] լուսուն քանզի միացաւ փակալ ընդ տեսանելն. եւ երթայր ողորկել զնոսա:

53. Որպէս եւ ասացեալ իսկ է հուրին ընդ յառաջ երթալ. եւ երթայր ողորկէր զի պարտ է հիւրին սիրով ընդ յառաջ գնալ եւ ուրախ սրտով պատուել. եւ սիրով գլեւտն գնալ ճանապարհի դնել. եւ ապա խոսի Տէր ընդ հրեշտակացն եւ ասէ միթէ թագու<ս>տ[35] ինչ իցէ ծառայի իմմէ Աբրահամէ զոր ինչ առնելոց էր աշխարհիս վերայ ասէ այս մեկ մարդ է մեզ բարեկամ եւ ծանօթ եւ մարդ զիւր խորհուրդն / fol. 212r / բարեկամին յայտնէ եւ օտարաց ծածկէ: Թէ մեք մեր բարեկամէս ծածկինք ապա այլումն յայտնենք զմեր խորհուրդ փոխանակ զի ոչ զարշեցաւ:

54. Աբրահամ լինել բարեկամ օտարաց ոչ զարշի Աստուած զալ առ նա եւ լնուլ զքաղցր նորա վասն որդոյն եւ առնել զնոսա խորհրդակից. զի ոչ միայն զզուշանալ անձամբ կամացն Աստուծոյ:[36]

55. Այլ պատուիրելով պատուէ որդոյն եւ տան իւրոյ խոկալ աստուածային նմին էր ի տան նմա որդի եւ շինէ նմա տուն

---

32. The case is anomalous.
33. Corrupt for հրամանաւն.
34. So in text, which has a dittography within հիանալի.
35. We emend թագուտ.
36. In M5571 the sentence continues: զի ոչ միայն Ա..... այլ Բ (in §56) and is about God: "Because not only did he [God] inform him [A.] of God's wish/desire." This does not appear at all in M2242.

ասպնջական լինել Աստուծոյ. եւ պատկեր նորա մարդոյ չի ածզէ Աստուած ի վերայ Աբրահամու. եւ ոչ զմասն ինչ աւետեաց խոստանալ զրողոր բարութիւնս յերկինս եւ յերկրի ասաէն կարող զոլ օտարաց հանգիստ եւ յետ մահու հայր եւ հանգիստ արդարոց. ասա անխտիր բարերար եւ անդ ընդրողութեան արժանաւորացն միայն: փարք եւ"

Here M5571 ends. M2242 continues with much homiletic material and short narrative passages. That text occurs as an independent work in M5571. It is not included here.

Variant Readings

The following are not recorded:
-gng or –nյ, etc.] –ւng, -ւnյ, etc.
+ / - intermediate and final յ
յետ / հետ
- այ / -ա etc.
ու / nյ in endings

Title. ի բան] om | սողմաեցոցն] + եւ զմնրացոց | ի բանն] om | եղաւ] եղ
1. աշխարհուլ°] աշխարհիս | Շխ] շիե | ամա] om : *vacat* | <եւ բաժանման>] 2242 երկոտասան 5571: graphic corruption | լեզուագ] լեզուացն
2. <զԲել>] 2242 զԱբել 5571: graphic corruption | սպան] եսպան | թղծեալ] թաղծեալ | կայեն անուն] կայենան այնու | բլորեալ] բլորեաց | մոռացան] եւ մոռացան | զարարշին] արարչին | աստուած] զաստուած
3. ապրահամ] յաբրահամ | <հաւատոյ>] 2242 գյաւատոյ 5571 | կռապաշտ] + էր | առաջն] յառաջն | <ծնեղեալ>] 2242 ծնընդան 5571 | <ծանեաւ>] ծնաւ 5571
4. եւ որ] որ | կլա] կրա | մոյութեան] մոյութամբ | արբեցութեան] ամբեցութամբ | եւ4°] om | <աղութիւն>] 2242 ադութեան 5571 | զի] զի ի | սովամաշ] սովու մաշեալ | մարմին] մարմինն | հաւցն] հաւուց | որ ուտին ... նոցա] om
5. է] om | ամաց] + էր | <պահել զարտորայս>] 2242 զարտորասն | նեղեցեալ] նեղացեալ | շրջագայութիւնս] գշրջակայութիւնս | արեզական] արեզականն | լուսնի] զլուսնին
6. մարդասիրութեան] + եւ իմաստութեան "and of wisdom" | միտս] ի միտս | ծանօ] ծանեաւ | զմոլորութեան] մոլորութին | աղօս] յաղօթից | անծանօթից] անծանօթ | հեռացեն] հեղացին | զվաստակս] + մեր
7. շիք] ի շիք | ձանեա] ծանեա
8. աղօս] յաղօս | ազզէ] յազզէ | այսրիկ] այնրիկ | հաւատացիր] հաւատացեր | զիս] յիս | բնակեր] բնակիր | անհաւատսն] անհաւատո | անհաւատին] անհաւատից | եւ խաւարի] ընդ խաւարի
9. եւ1° -- առանայ] 2242 om 5571 | էառ] առ | յերկիրն] երկիրն |

12. SERMON CONCERNING THE SODOMITES

բարեխորհուրդ] բարիխորհուդ | <ազդեալ>] 2242 աստեալ 5571 | զնա] զնաց | բնակեր] բնակէ | զ<ի ի> քաղդէացոց] ed. զքաղդէացոց 5571 զի քաղէացոց 2242 | տար] տայր | երկրին] յերկիրն | եղբարքն] եղբայրքն
10. եղբարն] եղբայրն | եւ առաջի] առաջի] յայտնի] յայտէ] զհետ] յետ | պատճառ] պատճառն | իմացաւ] իմացան | զծնունդն] ծնունդն | ջորդյ] ջորդյն | աստուծութեան եւ] աստուածոյ | արարչութեան] արարչութեանն "God's creation"
11. իր] յիր | մարդէն] ի մարդոյն | շանէն] ի շանէն | <բնութենէ>] 2242 բնակութենէ 5571 : corrupt | արարչութեան] արարչութեանն | ջորոյ] ջորոյն | չունի] ոչ ունի
12. սատանաէ] սատանայի | առ<ա>ն] 2242 առն 5571 | յիշատակն] յիշատակ | ազգէ] յազգէ | ելեալ] ելեալ | եկին] եկն | սեփիմ] սիքեէմ | սիքիմ] սիքեէմ | սիւ քարն] սուքարն | մամ<էի>] 2242 մամրիէ 5571
13. քանան] քանանու | աշտարակէն] յաշտարակէն | սիմա] սեմայ | որդում] յորդում | տեղւոյ] տեղւոց
14. յ<ե>զիպտոս] 2242 յիզիպտոս 5571 | տունն] տուն | դարձոց] եւ դարձոյց | տուկանօք] տուգանօք | աբրահամու] աբրահան | կարել] կարեր | եւ6°] om | եղբար] եղբայր | խռովութեան] խռովութեին | կռուող] կռովով | կացայց] կեցած | ենք] ենք
15. աբրահամէ] յաբրահամէ | մէկն] եկն | կինն] կին | կար] կայր | աստ] ազդ | զհին<զ>] 2242 զհին 5571 | թագաւորութիւնս] թագաւորութիւն | զղվտ] յովտ
16. եւ1°] om | աբրահամ] յաբրահամ | հեծելոք] ընդծօքն եւ | զզերին] զզերիսն | էոծ] ոծ | տասանորդաց] տասանորդեաց զաբրահամ "tithed Abraham"
17. <եւ եղեւ> աբրահամ] 2242 զաբրահամ եղեւ 5571 | ամաց2°] om | ոչ] եւ ոչ | զաւակ] om | կաղնան] կեղղնեան | մամրէի] մամբրէի : and so throughout | մամրէի2°] մամբրէն | հովիւ էր] om | ոչխարք] ոչխարքն | սեւք] սեաւք | աչխարհի] աշխարհին
18. եւ1°] om | արօտ] յարօտ | սովու] սովոյն | g<մ>ամրէի] 2242 գմամբրէ 5571 | hաց պատառ մի] մէկ պատառ հաց | ի սովու] om
19. hամար] om | զհաց կերաւ] եկեր | մամրէ] ինքն | քաղցած] սովաց | ջերմացեալ] ի ջերմանալ | ցրցեալ] ցրցեաց | զկաղնին] զկաղնի | հովակն] հովուական
20. կաղնին] զկաղնին | բար<ձ>րացեալ] 2242 բարցրացեալ 5571 | իւրեան] իւրեան | եւ ուրախացաւ – ոչխարքն] om | յերեկուին] յեր/եցն : corrupt | տունն] տուն | հարցանէր] հարցանէ | դու] om | ասաց] + թէ
21. զմէկ] զմէկն | hացն] + առայ | դու] om | տուիր | տրիր | տուի | տրի
22. ուխտ] ուխդ | եւ] եղ | աբրահամ2°] ի յաբրահամ | նահապետք] նահապետքն | մուրուօք] մօրուօք | ծաղկեացաւ2°] եւ ծաղկեցաւ
23. առաւոտուն] յառաւօտուն | մամրէի] մամբրէին | <տարեալ>] 2242 տար [ ]եայլ 5571 | աբրահամ] աբրահամու | շրջապատ] շրջապատեալ

| տեղին] տեղի | նստեալ] նստէր | եւ 6°] եւ ի | ճանապարհի էր]
ճանապարհն էր | գով] եւ գով | սիրուն աստուծոյ] աստուծոյ սիրոյն
| ճանապարհ էր] դրներ ճամփու
24. այլազգիքն] այլազգիքդ | աբրահամէ] յաբրահամէ | ունին] ունէին |
զեվիա] զեւիա | շինեն] շինէին | աւուրն] օրն
25. եւ1°] om | հասակ] հասարակ | կաղնեան] կաղնեւան | մամրէի] 2242°
om 5571 | եւ3°] 2242 om 5571 | բնութենէ] բնութիւն է | խնարիի]
խնարի | թուեցուցանէ] ձեւացուցանի | զոր1° -- զոր2°] om 5571: hmt
| թվի1° & 2°] թուի | տեսութեան] ի տեսութիւն | առաւել] առալել
| անփոփոխ է աստուած] է աստուած եւ անփոփոխ | զգործս]
զամենայն գործս | մարդկան] մեր | այլ1°] նայ այլ | այլ2°] յայլ
26. եկն] թէ եկն | յոէ] յոկէ | եւեալ] եկեալ | նստա] նստաւ | տօթոյ ժամու]
տօթաժամու | միում] միւմ | այլ ամենայն օր] om | զան] զայն |
աղօթս] յաղօթս | առանձնութեան] առանձնութեամբ | զզալ] զալ |
կալ2°] կեալ
27. եւես] տեսաւ + աիս | արս] արք | կային] գային | արանց] առանց
| կամ] եւ կամ | առաջն] յառաջ | աջմէ] յաջմէ | ահեկէ] ի ձախմէ
| գայսպիսեաց] գայսպիսեացս | կացին] գային | այտէ] յայտէ |
արեզական - ծագեաց] om
28. եւ1° – կատարէին] om 2242 | աշխար<հ>ի] 2242 աշխարհի 5571 |
աշխար<հ>ի կատարած] չնաշխարհիկ օտար արանց | միտա] ի մտա
| ասէ] ասաց | երկնից] յերկնից
29. ասաց] թէ | տարակուսեալ] + եմ | գնա մեծարէ] գնամ մեծարեմ |
պատուէ] պատուեմ | եղեր1°] եղիր եւ | եղեր2°] եղիր | բանն] բանս
| ընկերասէր եւ աղքատասէր] ընկերի եւ աղքատի սէրն է | պտղով]
պտղովա | մարդն – մարդն (§30)] om 2242
30. մարդն] զմարդ | որ1°] om | ճշմարիտ] + որ | զողորմութիւն]
զողորմութիւնն | տուրսն] տուրն
31. տեսանեի] տեսանեա | ձեր] երք | ստակ] հաց | եւ ապուր] նաուր |
աստուած] զաստուած | լեզուան] լեզուովա
32. ուղղեւորաց] ուղղաւորաց | որպէս] եւ | առաջն] յառաջն |
ճանապարհորդենք] ճանապարհորդեմք | տեսանենք] տեսանեմք |
միանգամ] մէկանգամ
33. թէ2°] եւ թէ | տանի] + եւ | իւրո իբր զմիո] որոյ իբրեւ ընդ միոյ | այլ]
om | կարօտիւ] կարոտով
34. զանձ] զանց | ջուրն] ջուր | ումէ] յումէ | եւ զաս կնոջ] զոյքն ոչ | զի
եւ զի | բանս] բան | սակաւ] սակաւ մի | լուասցի] լուասցեն
35. իշխենք] յիշխեմք | զանանձն] զայն յանձն | առնուցուս] առնուցուն |
է] + ասէ | առ իս] եկն առ իս | այնպէս ի] այնպիսի | յերկիրս] երկիրս
| պանտուխտ անուանէ] պատու անդանէ
36. արքայանիստ եղեւ] արքայնի տեղ | աղենա] աղսնա | տէր] տէրն
| համարձակութենէ] համարձակութիւն | ասեն] յասեն | այդպէս]
յայդպէս | են] առնեն

12. SERMON CONCERNING THE SODOMITES   191

37. նորա] նոցա | արա] աթթեա | <արա նկանակս>] 2242 ստան կանակս 5571 | որ է] om
38. հորդ] հորթ | եւ2°] om | եզեն] եզէն | ետ] + ի | զբադարձն] զբադարձն | զկաթն] կաթն | կարաք եւ] կարագ | զհորդն] զորթն | ծերութեամբ] ծերութիւնն | անձին] անձամբ | ծառայք] զծառայքն | սպասատրութիւն] սպասատրութեանն | պատճառ] + զի | աշխատին] սպասաւորէին եւ աշխատին | վարցք] վարձք | իւրանք] իւրեանքն | առցեն] առնէին
39. <լուանալ>] 2242 լուանան 5571 | վարձս] զվարձս | ոչ] + թէ | աշօք] + կերան | ծխեցին] ծախեցին | անրանձ] առանց | յորովայնէ] որովայն
40. մաքրեցան] մաքրեաց | կանկնեալ] կանգնեալ
41. ծանօթութեան] ծանօթութիւն | ասէ ուր է] ուր է ասէ | բանից] բանիցն | նորա] աստուծոյ
42. զանունն] զանուն | եւ ապա] ապա | զիւրն] զուրն | քաշ] քաշ | այլ հարցանէ] om | վարցս] վարձս | շնորհակալութեան եւ սպասաւորութեան] շնորհակալութիւն եւ սպասաւորութեանն | անդա] յանդեաց | նմանալ] յամանալ | ծառայի] ծառային | թոյլ տար] տայր թոյն | յամարելով] համարելով
43. ան] այն | ոչ1°] եւ ոչ | դիւթողդ] դիւթող | մուտ] եմուտ | խորան] խորանն | նորա2°] om | փակողն] փակօղն
44. յետ] om | է2°] om | դարձեալ] իսկ տերն ասէ դարձեալ
45. սատայ1°] + եւ | շկարելով] շկարալով | ցսիրտն] զսրտին | ասէ] եւ ասէ | տէրն] տէր | պառաւեալ եմ] պարվել եմ | ծանիցեմ] ծանիցիմ | աստուծոյ] յաստուծոյ
46. ծեր] ծերն | եւ] ու | տղայ] տղայն | յերք] երք | չոր] ի չոր | եւ ժպտեցաւ] om | ուր] որ | եկաց] եկից | երկիւղէն] յերկիւղէն
47. այսպէս] այդպէս | զխսոստումա] զխստումա | տարէ] տարի | հուր քեզ հիւր] քեզ] + որդի | աստուած] աստուծոյ | փայտն եւ] ծառն առնելով] առնել | կացի եւ] կացի | երկարացի] յերկարացի | տուր տուրք | ծեծաղեալ] ծիծաղել
48. մանկանն] մանկան | սարա ամենայն] առ յամենայն | յիշեցոյց] յիշեցելոցս | եւս ցայն] զուցին | տուն] տունն | յայտ է] յայտնէ | զի] զի ի | ծնանելն] ի ծնանին | հրամանու] 2242 հրաման 5517 | թէպետ] թէպէթ | որ] եւ
49. եւ որ] զոր | ոմա] om | իմաստուն] om | գնալոյ] ի գնալոյ | ժամանակն] ժամա | գերկնի] գերկնաւոր
50. լցեալ էր] ~ | եկն] եկ | հուր] հիւր | նորա սրտի] զնորա սիրտին | կարօտութեան] կարօտութիւնն եւ | փափակն] զփափաքն
51. իւրանն] իւրեանն | գալն] գնալն | կերակրելն] կերակրիլն | գտուն] գտունն | եւ զեղան] եւ q/եւ զեղան : dittography | երթար] երթայր
52. իւրմէ] յորմէ | թէպետ] թէպէթ | անուշահոտութիւն] անուշահոտութիւնն | հիանալի] յիանալի | միացա] իմացա | փակա] om | տեսանելն] տեսիլն | ողորկել] ուղարկեր

53. հուրին] հիւրոյն | երթալ] երթ | երթայր] ի գնալն | ողորկէր] յուղարկէր | գնալ] գնայն | գյետն] գհետ | ճանապարհի] ճանապարհաւ] թագու<ա>տ] 2242 թագուտ 5571 | իգէ] է +ի | աբրահամէ] յաբրահամէ | մարդ] մարդա | օտարաց] յօտարաց | մեր] ի մեր | բարեկամէս] բարեկամէն | ծածկինք] ծածկեմք | ապա] om | յայտնենք] յայտնեմք | խորհուրդս] խորհուրդն
54. գբաղցր] գբաղց | գգուշանալ անձամբ] անձամբ գգուշանալ
55. պատուէ] պատուիրէ | որդոյն] որդոց | խոկալ] խոյկալ | աստուածայինս] յաստուածային | էր ի տան] իրի տալ | պատեր] պատկերի | եւ ոչ] ոչ | խոստանալ] խոստանալ այլ | կարող] կարոդ | արդարոց] + արդարոց : dittography | ընդրողութեան] ընդդդութեան end of 5571

Sermon on the Word Concerning the Sodomites, in the Verse That Says, "The cry of the Sodomites went forth before me"*

1. When Noah went forth from the ark and divided this world into three divisions, upon (according to) the three sons—Asia, <Arabia> and Lybia.[37] And for 640 years this world was filled with their descendants.[38] And then they built the tower from fear of the Flood[39] and after the destruction of the tower and the separation, men of twelve tongues[40] wandered[41] and fell into idol worship.[42]

---

* Gen 19:10.

37. Traditionally, this should be Europe, but it is unclear how this name might signify Europe. See, for example, the various texts on the division of the earth, such as *Generations of the Sons of Noah* in Stone 1981, 221–27. See *Jub.* 8:10–9:15 for a detailed, early description of this, and see Scott 1997, 370 n. 8. The relevant biblical verses are in Gen 10. See also Charles 1902, 68; Eshel 2007. In another form this material occurs in Dowsett 1961, 1–2 and in Matenadaran M2679 of 981 C.E., fol. 31r.

38. This span is not found in the other chronological texts that we have published; see, e.g., Stone 1996a, 87, 98 (525 years), 99 (515 years). According to *Jubilees* and biblical chronology, the period is significantly shorter.

39. This differs from the biblical motive for building the tower; see Gen 11:4, which says: "Then they said, 'Come, let us build ourselves a city, and a tower with its top in the heavens, and let us make a name for ourselves; otherwise we shall be scattered abroad upon the face of the whole earth.'"

40. This refers to the same tradition of the list of "Twelve Literate Peoples," published by Stone, 1996a, 159. The text is already attested in Matenadaran M2679 of 981 C.E., 32r, which is, perhaps, drawing on P'ilon Tirakac'i; see *MH* 7th century, 906. See also *Palaea* 201. This text also mentions the seventy-two languages, a list later found in many sources.

41. That is, erred. The meaning "wandered" fits better with Gen 11:8–9.

42. See also Maimonides, *Mishneh Torah*, "Idolatry"; ch. 1 deals with God's being forgotten but puts this before the flood.

2. Some say that the sons (of) Haig, who killed Bel,[43] made an image and afterwards it was considered to be God. But Solomon says, "A father is grieved over the untimely death of a son."[44] Cain[45] made names for the images and afterwards they revered erroneous gods. And idolatry began from Babylon and in 400 years encompassed the world: they forgot God and revered creatures as god instead of the Creator.
3. And the time came to Abraham when he recognized the true God and he became father of faith, for the name of his father was Terah and he was an idolater before and son of an idolater and the place of his birth was Babylon. And thus he recognized the god of the land of the Babylonians. It (i.e., the land) was prosperous and good. The many inhabitants ate, drank, and nourished their bodies as nourishment for the undying worms.[46]
4. And living voluptuously and swallowed up by frenzy and drunkenness,[47] they kindled the fire of desire in their spirits and did not cease sins and promiscuity. God was angry and gave them famine and exiguity so that, with bodies consumed by hunger, they might turn from sin. And he raised up flocks of ravens against them, which were eating their labors and the fruit of the earth.
5. And Abraham was 15 years old.[48] His father sent (him) <to guard the fields>, lest they be consumed by hunger. And he, having gone strove mightily and was unable to chase them[49] away, but being afflicted he fell to the ground. And he looked up and he saw the orbits of the heavens and the stations (or: positions) of the stars and the movement of the sun and moon, and he himself was a wise and proficient astrologer.[50]
6. And at the same time a light of love of humans shone on Abraham's heart[51] and his mind came and recognized its error. And rising up he remained upon his knees and stretching forth his arms he prayed to God,[52] "God of unknown

---

43. The reading "Abel" of M5571 introduces an anomalous confusion of Armenian and biblical traditions. It is to be regarded as a corruption.
44. Wisdom 14:15, also cited in n. 10 on p. 126. This euhemeristic explanation of idolatry was quite popular among the Armenians.
45. The variant reading is Kenan, who is the son of Enosh; see Gen 5:9–14.
46. Standard denizens of the underworld, developed from Isa 66:24. With this description of Babylon, compare text no. 2.2.
47. Literally: "so that he swallowed up frenzy and drunkenness and." The Armenian, as it stands, is both ungrammatical and unclear.
48. See notes to text no. 2.3.
49. That is, the ravens.
50. Or: "astronomer." See note on text no. 2.3 above.
51. Abraham's recognition of God is described as an illumination, as is Melchizedek's in the Story of Melchizedek; see texts nos. 11.49 and 11A.49.
52. Observe that he takes what may be called a "kneeling *orans*" position. See text no. 2.4 above.

things and Maker of all and Creator of these birds, give a command that they become distant[53] and not eat this labor."

7. And at that same time they turned into nothing.[54] And Abraham rejoiced for he found the true God and having come, he related (this) to his father and said, "I greatly begged your objects of worship and nothing was heard. And then I recognized the true God and he, by his command the birds were put to flight."

8. And when the morning grew light, Abraham went off alone and prayed and God appeared to him and said, "Go forth from your land and people (or: family) and come to the land which I will show you. For this reason I appeared to you."[55] God said, "I cause you to recognize me truly and firmly. Because you believed in me, do not dwell with the unbelievers. For the portion of the believers is not with the unbeliever, and there is no harmony of light and darkness."[56]

9. <And Nahor and Abraham took wives for themselves. Abraham's wife's name was Sarai (Sarah) and Nahor's Isk(a), and they were both daughters of Achan.> And Terah took his sons and went forth from the land of the Chaldeans to go to the land of the Canaanites. God's benevolence having impressed[57] Terah, he went to Mesopotamia and he took up his dwelling in Haran, for 2 reasons.[58] One, <that in> the land of the Chaldeans sorcery was rife and it did not give fruit of the earth.[59] Second, because Abraham wished to follow God's commandment, and his father and brothers did not let him.[60]

10. And having gone forth from Babylon, he dwelt in Haran. And Terah built a house of idols in Haran. And Abraham becoming angry, wished to burn (it) with fire. And Abraham's brother Achan, father of Lot, wished to extinguish the fire and having fallen into the temple, was burned up and died, even before his father. It is known (that) after the flood no other son had died before his father. And the reason of the punishment, they say, is because he discovered the begetting of the mule,[61] (a thing) against the Divinity and the creation.[62]

---

53. The verb "make distant" is common in exorcism and apotropaic texts.

54. In other versions of the story the ravens depart (see Michael the Syrian 1871, 22) or even leave only Terah's field untouched.

55. That is, in the revelation of my existence; see Gen 12:1. The second sentence is not biblical. The context here is the move from Chaldea (Ur) to Haran, while the biblical verse is related to Abraham's leaving Haran for Canaan. See §12 below.

56. This sentence is not biblical, and the sentiment is not expressed in Genesis 12.

57. The sentence is unclear.

58. This phrasing reflects a didactic or school context of origin.

59. Note contradiction of the description of Babylonia in §3.

60. It is difficult to see how this sentence makes sense as an explanation of Terah's move to Haran.

61. On this incident, see texts nos. 4.1 and 4.6 and notes there with further references.

62. Observe, once more, the didactic phrasing "they say." This school style continues in the next section, where the contents of the statement are listed in detail.

11. For God's will is that, that every species be born from its own species: human from the human, sheep from the ovine, and dog from the canine. The birth of the mule is outside nature and against God's creation, for God made every species fertile and the mule, for that reason, has no offspring, for it is not a creation of God's.
12. But men discovered (this) by the wiles of Satan and although Achan perished, still the evil memory remained (in) the world. And Terah died in Haran. And God said to Abraham, "Go forth from your land and your family (people) and attend (obey)."[63] Having gone forth he went according to God's command and they came to Sekʻim[64] and on the oak tree (were) high pillars; there is a certain black stone, which is Samaria.[65] And the high oak is perhaps that which afterwards it calls "of Mamrē".[66]
13. And since the 10 families of the sons of Canaan, when they returned from the Tower, had taken the land of the sons of Shem through Canaan's despoiling, he called it, "The place where God appeared to Abraham," and he said, "To your seed I will give this land."[67]
14. And there was famine and Abraham went down to Egypt. And they took Sarah to Pharaoh's house, and God punished Pharaoh. He returned the woman to Abraham with indemnity.[68] And it came to pass when Abraham's and Lot's sheep and cattle increased that the earth was unable to sustain (them) and the shepherds drew up for battle.[69] And {in} Abraham said to Lot, "You are my brother and flesh. There should not be disturbance between us

---

63. This, reflecting Gen 12:1, is the third "Go forth" command in the text, the previous ones being implied in §§8 and 10. This pattern is to be observed in other texts here as well: see texts nos. 2.5, 14.5, and 14.7, though others, such as texts nos. 4 and 9, only have one commandment, to Abraham.

64. That is, Shechem.

65. This geography seems to draw on Gen 12:6: "Abram passed through the land to the place at Shechem, to the oak of Moreh. At that time the Canaanites were in the land." See further in the next note. The didactic tone continues. The reference to the black stone remains obscure and it appears that some geographical tradition is included here. A tradition of the tree, not connected with the Mamrē story found here, occurs in Sextus Iulius Africanus F 30 (Walraff and Adler 2007, 66–67). This includes the planting of a staff by one of Abraham's guests. See also Adler and Tuffin 2002, 153–54 and note there.

66. Gen 12:6 has an "oak of Moreh" at Shechem, while the "oaks of Mamrē" are farther south, at Hebron (Gen 13:18; 14:13; and 18:1). Mamrē is identified as Hebron in Gen 23:19 and 35:27. Of course, the Story of Mamrē discussed above is in part an etiology of the "oaks of Mamrē." Rabbinic speculations on the name are to be found in *Gen. Rab.* 41:13. Is there an etymology from מרום ("high place") implied here?

67. Compare Gen 12:7; 15:18; etc. The conquest of Shem's land by Canaan is mentioned in *Jub.* 10:29–34; compare *Palaea* 203, where Ham is said to seize Palestine.

68. Compare text no. 11.10 and note there. This story is much abbreviated here, but longer in other texts.

69. Gen 13:2 and 13:5–7.

so that I might become a quarreler[70] together. We will be well if we separate amicably."[71]

15. And Lot separated from Abraham, and the one (i.e., Lot) dwelt in Sodom and took a wife for himself. And Abraham dwelt in Hebron. And while he was praying, speaking with God, he learned that four kings had come from the east and had taken the five kingdoms of the Sodomites, and his nephew Lot.[72]

16. And Abraham gathered together[73] 300 and 18[74] cavalry. He cut them down and returned the captive. And Melchizedek king of Salem went forth to meet Abraham and he anointed him as a king. And he made him an offering of bread and wine and he gave a tithe.[75]

17. <And it came to pass> that Abraham was 100 years old and Sarah (was) 90 years ago. And Sarah was barren and did not bear a child.[76] And God appeared to him by the oak of Mamrē,[77] while he was sitting in the tent. For Mamrē (was) a black slave and he was Abraham's shepherd and Abraham's sheep were black on account of the heat of the land of the Babylonians.[78]

18. And there was a famine at that time and Abraham gave one (loaf of) bread to Mamrē and said to take the sheep to pasture. And Mamrē saw[79] a poor man fainting from famine and fallen upon the road. And the poor man said to <M>amrē, "For love of your God, if you have bread, give (me) a piece, for I am fainting from famine and I cannot go on."[80]

19. And he took out the bread for the sake of the love of God. He gave it to the poor man and the poor man ate the bread and was strengthened and went. And Mamrē remained hungry and the day became hot. He planted the stick

---

70. The text is somewhat difficult; the overall sense is: "we will quarrel if we stay together."

71. Gen 12:8–9; cf. 12:19–20.

72. See Gen 14. In the biblical text this is revealed by a refugee. This incident does not commonly occur in the Armenian Abraham stories; see the General Introduction, 11.

73. Or: "gathered tightly."

74. Compare Gen 14:14. See text no. 6.14.3 and note there.

75. It is unclear here who is doing what. Compare Gen 14:18, "And King Melchizedek of Salem brought out bread and wine; he was priest of God Most High." The anointing of Abraham as king is not mentioned in Genesis, but the tithe is recorded in Gen 14:20. The context appears to require that Abraham be regarded as the object of "anointed," not the subject, and anyway, earlier in the sentence, Melchizedek is called "king."

76. Gen 11:30.

77. See §12 and note there.

78. This detail occurs only in this text.

79. Literally: "having seen."

80. Or: "walk." In other texts Mamrē receives three loaves and gives them to three different hungry wayfarers. This story is less complex than other versions, as was true also of the incident of Pharaoh and Sarah.

of the oak as a shelter(?), and cast his cloak on it and made shade. And he having sat down in the shelter fell asleep.

20. And when he woke up, he saw that the oak had taken root and had grown tall and become a great tree and it had made shade over him and the sheep. And he rejoiced and praised God, and he and the sheep had become white. And in the evening when he returned to the house and Abraham went to meet him, he asked, "Who are you?" And smiling, he said, "I am Mamrē your shepherd."

21. And he asked the reason, "On account of which (thing) have you and these sheep become white?" And he said, "Your God did (it). The one (loaf of) bread that you gave me as food, I for love of Him gave to a poor man. God did all this goodness."

22. And Abraham was amazed (and) praised the (deeds) of God and made an oath to himself that he would never again eat bread without a poor man.[81] And up to Abraham the patriarchs all died black bearded. But the father of faith, Abraham, flowered with piety, flowered with grey hair.[82]

23. And in the morning, Mamrē led, <brought>, and showed Abraham the oak tree.[83] And he, having seen (it), blessed God and made an enclosure around the place of prayer.[84] And three times daily he prayed and, seated in the shelter of the tree, he was near the road. Whichever passing traveler he saw, he fed for the sake of the love of God, and the way was honored.

24. And they say[85] that Satan ensorcelled the road. For 40 days no visitor came to Abraham. And the foreigners have this good custom from Abraham, that they build a shelter upon the road and they give bread to the poor and travelers. And it came to pass that for a long time no guest came to Abraham, and the time passed and the Great Thursday[86] arrived.

25. And for the period of a day he prayed by the oak tree of Mamrē. And God appeared to him and with him He had <two beings> in the forms of men.[87] God (is) unchangeable by nature, but for reason of his love of men he descends to take on a form and makes it seem that he is changed <so that it be not thought he changes his appearance to that of a man>. Just like a great mountain seems to take on the form of a small one and a great eagle seems (to be) a swallow and one light appears to be two because of the weakness

---

81. See text no. 2.11 for this story.
82. See the General Introduction, p. 45 and n. 47.
83. Observe, once more, that the narrative is simpler and shorter in this version.
84. This detail is not found in the other texts.
85. This phrase once more indicates a didactic context.
86. This is apparently Maundy Thursday, the Thursday of the week of Easter. On this day the Last Supper is commemorated, so here a typological connection is highlighted.
87. Compare Gen 18:1–2. The continuation of this section is an argument of theological character.

of vision, and it is not changed, inasmuch as God is more unchangeable than things, always remaining his own selfness. And God does not come from afar, but he remains always close and he looks and sees the deeds of humans. But since we do not see (this), we think that he is in one world and we in another.[88]

26. And when the King of all appeared[89] and came, he sent no forerunner before him, but he cast a certain impression, a creation of appearance of God into (Abraham's) heart. Going forth, he said, "Sit by the tree in the hour of heat." Scripture says, "On one day,"[90] but "day" specifically denotes work, that he had been praying peacefully alone, not feeling the heat and the cold. Being with God he always saw God or his image, a man, knowing that he who gives repose to a man does God's will.

27. Abraham raised up his eyes and {and} he saw three men.[91] They were standing above him, without being seen coming on the earth, from forward or behind or right or left. It speaks nothing about such things, but only that the men were present from somewhere, this is as if the noetic sun shone with the sensible sun.[92]

28. And Abraham was of two minds. He was uncertain whether the apparition came (from) God or he had glorified a worldly created thing. At first his mind was uncertain and he said, "If it is God, why does he appear in human form, and if it is fleshly man, how does he descend from the heavens?"[93]

29. And because Abraham was wise, he counseled himself and said, "Why are you uncertain? Go meet (him), praise and pay respects to him. If he is God, you will have been[94] loving of God; if he is human, you will have been loving of humans." The loving of God and the loving of humans are one. True is the saying that love of God is hidden. The sign of love of God is lover of neighbor and lover of the poor man, like a tree that is known by (its) fruit and a man, by (his) form.

30. Thus, the man, loving of God, is known by (his) love of a poor man. If you see a man loving of humans and merciful, realize that he is a true lover of God who for the love of God gives mercy (charity) to the poor, for the love of the heart is evident from the gift of the hands.

---

88. This paragraph, once more, exhibits the domesticating of the narrative, presented as anonymous discourse in a didactic context.

89. Taking երեքի թվի as a hendiadys of two synonyms (Th. M. van Lint).

90. Armenian Gen 18:1 has միջաւրհի "middle of the day." In the next phrase, take զան as "specifically" (Th. M. van Lint).

91. Gen 18:2.

92. This is another exegetical section, dealing with issues arising from the "logic" of the biblical narrative.

93. This was a standard argument for the incarnation. See, e.g., Eusebius, *Hist. eccl.* 1.2.8.

94. Literally an aorist.

31. Then, if I saw[95] a man merciless and cruel-hearted and he boasts, "I am God-loving," it is a lie of yours (plur.). He gives not one dram or one farthing to the poor man and when he appears to love God, with his heart he hates God, with his tongue he deceives. God is not a man that he be deceived.
32. When Abraham saw, he hastened to meet him as three travelers.[96] And he prostrated himself as he was accustomed. And the Lord wished to try Abraham's faith and perfect love.[97] First he said, "We travelers are going on our road. We (shall) see," he said, "if he pays respects to us like a man going to meet a friend or not.[98] If he once pays respects, you say not.
33. If he is a false friend, he (will) leave (us) outside; if he is truly a friend, he (will) not leave (us) until he brings (us) with honor." And because the Lord appeared with the form of a king and the 2 ministering angels, he (i.e., Abraham) spoke concerning him as to one person,[99] "But that which I sought with longing (is) your presence and mercy.
34. But, do not pass by me but let a little water be taken, even if it is by someone who is not authorized (to do so)[100] and let them wash your feet." And he said to his[101] wife respectfully, "If he is the Lord, he has no need of water and it seems that this matter is (i.e., to be resolved) through asking, will a little water be taken and will he be washed?"
35. "We venture," he says, "we have confidence, we take the liberty and (are the one) whom you deem worthy to serve you. For if you accept (me) the non-person[102] (i.e., as the water pourer) then let something else be ventured, that God, having taken on human form (has come) thus to me on foot. Consequently, it is fitting to give water to feet,[103] for he designates his feet sojourner(s) in this land."
36. Mamrē's field became a royal seat and the oak tree more than paradise of Eden.[104] For the Lord of creations is there, to whom it is impossible to say,

---

95. Note that the speaker of the discourse intervenes in the first person singular here, which again must be due to the genre. This whole passage, from §29 to §31, is moralizing discourse, with a theological underpinning. This distinguishes this document from the straightforward narratives about Abraham presented in this volume.
96. That is, the Lord who manifested himself as three travelers.
97. This incident is not biblical.
98. The words յառաջն որ մեծարէ seem corrupt at this point and are not translated.
99. That is, using a second person singular. This is a hint at the incarnation here.
100. That is, is unworthy to do so. This and the next sentence are difficult.
101. Translating as if the text were գում. This is a fairly common variant.
102. This is an expression of humility.
103. The case usage is odd.
104. Observe the central place taken by the oak. It recurs in many of these texts, both in the Story of Mamrē and in the Binding of Isaac. Note also the role of the cypress in the Story of Melchizedek. This point is already made in Ełišē, *Commentary on Genesis*, on Gen 18:4, which says that the field of Mamrē became a place of royal residence and the oak tree "greater than the garden of Eden" (Khachikyan and Papazian 2004, 129).

"Sit, eat," lest he be a giver of command, until through daring he receives (takes) the saying, "Do thus as you said."[105] In shame of those who say foreignly and are foreign.[106]

37. And then bringing (him), he seated[107] the Lord in (his) tent. And he washed his feet with water. And he said, "Hasten, prepare!" — to Sarah, not to a servant and not to a maidservant. He commanded (her), "<Make> three <cakes,> which are unleavened."
38. And Abraham, having taken a suckling calf, slaughtered (it). And he caused the servants to cook (it) and prepare (it). And Sarah prepared the unleavened bread and Abraham brought a feast,[108] first the milk and curdled stuff, which is butter, and they ate, and then the slaughtered calf. Because Abraham was an old man he forgot himself,[109] due to his age. He and Sarah were serving, first since they reckoned the servants to be unworthy of good service to guests,[110] and a second reason, they themselves worked so that they might themselves earn the reward.[111]
39. Thus it is incumbent to serve saints oneself, and <to> wash the feet of the poor, and to feed (them), so that one might onself earn the reward. For not only is giving praiseworthy, but it is also incumbent on oneself to serve, to feed and to clothe the poor. And not just apparently, but truly they ate the food (despite) being bodiless and the fiery ones emitted smoke, just as fire consumes the oil of the lamp and without a mouth it consumes the burning candle, without a belly it gathers (it) in and the place it goes is not visible.[112]
40. Thus they ate the food and were purified (by) the divine fire.[113] And Abraham remained standing and served, and he still doubted whether he was man or God.
41. And then the Lord gave a little knowledge.[114] The Lord, speaking said,

---

105. The preceding, somewhat unclear sections seek to soften the anthropomorphism that resulted from the interpretation that one of Abraham's guests was God.
106. The meaning of this sentence is unclear.
107. Literally: "made descend."
108. Literally: "a table."
109. The same point is made by Ełišē, *Commentary on Genesis* (Khachikyan and Papazian 2004, 129).
110. See ibid.
111. Again, didactic motifs come to the fore. Compare also *b. Qidd.* 32b.
112. This section deals with the anomaly of angels eating. Compare also *T. Ab.* A 4:9 and the note by E. P. Sanders in *OTP* 1:884; and here, text no. 2.14 and note on text no. 8.25. (Pseudo?)-Ełišē, *On the Transfiguration* maintains that the incorporeal ones really ate Abraham's meal: see *MH* 5th century, 1618.
113. The reason for the plural of this verb in Armenian is obscure.
114. Note Ełišē, *Commentary on Genesis* (Khachikyan and Papazian 2004, 131): "Then gradually the one made himself known by saying, 'Where is your wife Sarah?'"

"Where is Sarah your wife?" And Sarah was standing behind the tent and attending to his words,[115] but Abraham did not know.

42. And when He said (his) wife's name, then Abraham truly knew that He is the Lord, because[116] he knew (her) name and his own (name) also he knew well. He also asked (him) to give a reward for his labors and gratefulness and service. For just as Abraham, so also Sarah applied (herself), and Sarah was like Abraham, (in order that) perhaps they might assist as servants. Then there was no servant for (s)he did not permit the maidservants, reckoning them unworthy of it (i.e., service). [117]

43. She into whose tent no potion and no root and no maker of charms entered[118] for the sake of her procreation rather remained God's, saying, "Lord, save me."[119] She remained His so that He who closed (i.e., the womb) might open it. And the Lord said, "Where is Sarah your wife? Where is your virtue? Where is your power and spouse?"

44. Abraham answered, "Behold, she is in the tent."[120] She did not come forward, and the Lord knew that she was (standing) behind the back of the tent, listening to his miraculous words. "I will come to you again in this time. You will have a son for Sarah's bosom."[121] He revealed and made clear that he is the Lord and he promises 2 great benefits, his own coming and the son.

45. And Sarah heard, she laughed saying, "Up to now we had no child, now in this time of our old age, will there be (one)?"[122] Like Abraham, she laughed, rejoicing, her heart being unable to bear the joy.[123] The Lord said to Abraham, "Why is it that Sarah laughs saying, 'I am old. Shall I indeed bear a child?'[124] Is anything impossible for God? Am I powerless?"[125]

46. He said, "With me, an old man and a child are one. When I desire (it), I bring

---

115. Gen 18:10.

116. Here, it seems best to take np as in Modern Armenian, to signify "because" (Th. M. van Lint).

117. So Ełišē, *Commentary on Genesis* (Khachikyan and Papazian 2004, 131).

118. Ełišē, *Commentary on Genesis* (Khachikyan and Papazian 2004, 131) speaks similarly: "neither a potion nor a root nor a sorcerer entered her tent on account of childbirth." This whole section (§§ 43–44a) is drawn word for word from Ełišē (Khachikyan and Papazian 2004, 131).

119. Ełišē has փակեաց "closed," that is, "The Lord closed me," which text is apparently preferable to that of our manuscript (Khachikyan and Papazian 2004, 131).

120. Gen 18:9.

121. Gen 18:10.

122. Gen 18:12.

123. This reading of the text heightens Sarah's virtue; cf. Gen 18:11–12. Other texts here have interpreted her laughter as mocking or doubting; see 8:27 and 11:29. See Ełišē (Khachikyan and Papazian 2004, 131).

124. Gen 18:13.

125. Gen 18:14.

forth fruit from a dry tree as from a green one. Why did Sarah laugh and sneer?"[126] When[127] she came in fear, she said, "I did not laugh."[128]

47. And the Lord said, "To the contrary, but you did laugh." Again, he affirmed the promise, "I will come as a guest next year on the same day, and you will have (i.e., a child), knowing that only God's[129] is the deed, to make the dry wood (tree) fruitful. On account of this I stood and extended the promise so that she might think that the gift of seed is from God and not from nature." For if she was laughing because of little faith, she would be judged guilty like Zechariah.[130]

48. And he did not make the child's name "Laughter of the Mother" lest Sarah be weakened by remembering all things up to that moment and that had taken place, the creations (the things) and the miracles equal to them, by which she remained untested in the house of Pharaoh. And it is evident that (in) the birth of Isaac, God came to Abraham and by his command the child was named. Although it was not written,[131] nonetheless the matter resulted from (His) coming to him.

49. And just as a[132] royal guest happened by a wise man and he honors the king, at the time of going away the king gives gifts to the master of the house and then he goes away from the house. Thus Abraham honored God, the king of heaven, and He gave him the son as a good gift.

50. And since Abraham was God-loving and merciful and he had filled the lacks (needs) of many poor and he himself lacked seed, God came to him as a guest with two angels and filled his lack and his heart's yearning by giving him a good seed. By the measure by which he measured out it was measured out to him.[133]

51. If a bodily king happens by a man as guest, the man rejoices and reckons it to be a great glory and honor for himself thus among all the righteous, God's coming as a guest and eating in his house is a great glory for Abraham. And then he blessed his house and table and going forth, he went from the house, caring for the house and giving it repose.

52. And from the moment He revealed Himself, trembling seized them, even

---

126. Compare note on §45. Also note a narrative form of the statement about dry and green wood in the Story of Mamrē, where his dry staff miraculously becomes green, takes root, and grows. See also the use of this metaphor in Isa 56:3; etc. See the General Introduction, p. 17. This expression is found also in Ełišē, *Commentary on Genesis* (Khachikyan and Papazian 2004, 131) in the same context.

127. In context որ պատ seems to mean "when."

128. Gen 18:15.

129. This word should be in the genitive case.

130. See Luke 1:18–20. See text no. 2.16. This detail in not found in Ełišē.

131. That is, explicitly in the Bible. In Gen 21:3 Abraham gives the name to Isaac.

132. ոմն seems to function here just as an indefinite article, equivalent to Modern West Armenian մը, thus yielding, "just as a royal guest happened by" (Th. M. van Lint).

133. This last sentence reads as if it were a proverbial saying.

though indescribable, sweet fragrance seized Abraham. And when he went away, he (Abraham) was unable to do without the wondrous light, because it united with and stuck to his vision. And he went to smooth (the way) for them.[134]

53. Just as it is said that he went forth to meet the guest, he went and smoothed (the way), for it is incumbent to meet the guest with joyous love and to honor (him) with a joyous heart, and lovingly to go in his footsteps to set the way. And then the Lord spoke with the angels and said, "Will there be anything hidden from my servant Abraham, which is going to be done upon this earth?" He said, "This is one man, our friend and familiar, and a man reveals his plan to his friend and hides it from strangers. If we hid (it) from this friend of ours, then revealed our plan to somebody else instead, how would he not abhor (i.e., us/that)?"[135]

54. Abraham, being a friend of strangers, God did not draw (him) to come to Him and be filled with his sweetness on account of (his) son and to make them fellow-planners, so that not only did He advert him of the will of God,

55. but by commanding, he honors the son and his house, to consider the divine things for him (Abraham). There was a son in (his) house for him and he (God) built a house (i.e., gave a son) for him, to be a receptacle for God and his image (was that of) a man, for God will bring (it) upon Abraham. And he did not promise just a part of the good news, (but) all the good things in heaven and on earth. Hence he is able to be a respite for strangers and after death a father and respite for the righteous, in this world an undifferentiating benefactor and in that world (an intercessor) for election only of the worthy.

---

134. Another meaning is to "console, to soothe"; see *NBHL* 2:509c; however, the following suggests that 'ease their way' is meant (Th. M. van Lint). Abraham receives heavenly or Edenic characteristics, fragrance and luminosity. The whole paragraph closely follows Ełišē, *Commentary on Genesis* (Khachikyan and Papazian 2004, 133).

135. We take qh for qhupn to mean "how," following a suggestion by Th. M. van Lint.

13. The Ten Trials of Abraham, Ms M0717

This document is preserved in Matenadaran M0717, a Miscellany of the eighteenth century.[1] The manuscript is described fully in vol. 3 of the catalogue of the Matenadaran, Institute of Ancient Manuscripts, Erevan.[2] The first 123 folios contain various list texts and other minor works, and on fols. 123v–255 an Infancy Gospel ensues. Our text is among the list texts on 54r. The manuscript is in *notrgir* script in various hands. All numerals are in Armenian letters, with lines above and below them.

The Ten Trials[3] of Abraham also occur as a list in other manuscripts, and one such list, embedded in another document, has been published in text no. 5.2 above. Such trials are to be found in *Jub.* 17:15–18, where there is a passage on the testing of Abraham and a series of tests are mentioned. They are not numbered, however, and the scene is Job-like, with Mastema challenging God to test Abraham by the trial of the Binding of Isaac. This means that, already in *Jubilees*, the tests have been extended from the one explicit biblical one in Gen 22:1, and a series of events in Abraham's life preceding the Aqedah are seen as tests.[4]

Text no. 5.2 lists ten trials, the same as M0717, but with divergences in order and wording. In another text I am publishing in this book, seven + three tests are mentioned (text no. 6.6.1; see note there). Further events are connected with testing; see text no. 2.13 including, of course, the Binding of Isaac (one of the ten) in texts nos. 6.7.2 and 11.44. Satan's blocking the road is another test or trial of Abraham. Of course the theme of Abraham's trials derives from Gen 22:1 and its extension highlights the view of Abraham as a paradigmatic believer and firm and faithful servant of God.[5]

---

1. The text is taken from a hand copy made by the author in the Matenadaran some years ago and is published with permission.

2. Ēganyan et al. 2007, 3:449–54.

3. On ten trials, see Licht 1973, 79–88. The number is common in rabbinic sources, though the actual list differs. See, e.g., *m. 'Abot* 5:3, *ARN* Redaction A 33:2, *ARN* Redaction B 36:4, *Yalquṭ Shim'oni Lek Lĕka* 12, 68, *Midrash Tehillim* on 18:25, and *PRE* 26–30. In *PRE* tests are specified at length, but only three overlap with this list. The role of Mastema in the event is found in 4Q225, frgs. 2.1–2.

4. Licht (1973, 53 n. 6) counts up to nine tests in *Jubilees* and sees this as an indication that the number 10 was stereotypical.

5. See the discussion of Abraham's tests in the General Introduction, p. 16, n. 51 and p. 21. The tradition is old indeed.

13. THE TEN TRIALS OF ABRAHAM

Տասն փորձութիւնք Աբրահամու:

Առաջին ել յերկրէ քումմէ:	ա
Վարեցաւ Սառայ ի տունն փարաւոնի:	բ
Կարգ հովուաց Ղովտա:	գ
թէ ոչ առնուլ յրևշիցն Սոդոմայ:	դ
թէ եղիցի զաւակ քո. իբրև զաստեղս ոչ երկմտեաց:	ե
Չի գձագար էր ի ձեռն Սառայի:	զ
Չի ասաց. ի բաց հան զաղախինդ քո և զորդի իւր:	է
Հրամայեաց նմա թլփատիլ ի ծերութեան:	ը
Չի առաւ Սառայ Աբէմէլէքայ:	թ
Կատարումն ամենայնի այս. զի ասէ առ դու. և զորդիդ քո:	ժ

TEN TRIALS OF ABRAHAM

The first, "Go forth from your land."[6]	1
Sarah was led to the house of Pharaoh.	2
Drawing up of the shepherds of Lot.	3
Not to take possessions from Sodom.	4
He did not doubt, "Your seed will be like the stars."[7]	5
That Hagar was in Sarah's power.	6
That he (God) said, "Expel your maidservant and her son."[8]	7
He commanded him to be circumcised in old age.	8
That Sarah was taken to Abimēlēkʻ.	9
The completion (perfection) of all (was) this: that He said, "Take you . . . and your son."	10

---

6. Gen 12:1.
7. Gen 15:5.
8. Gen 21:10; cf. 21:12.

14. Synaxarium, Constantinople 1730

This text is drawn from the Synaxarium published in Constantinople in 1730, pp. 385–86.[1] This printing of the Synaxarium is that of the edition attributed to Gregory of Xlatʻ (d. 1425). This document is clearly a narrative comprising many incidents that are part of the Armenian Abraham saga. What is unclear is whether it is the holus-bolus incorporation of an anterior document into the Synaxarium, or whether it is composed for hagiographical purposes, drawing on diverse sources. Clearly, the list of ten trials is related to text no. 13 above in the present work, but it has some distinctive elements. Moreover, the emphasis in this document is chiefly on the Binding of Isaac, which is deeply integrated into a unitary Christian perception of the history of salvation. This is done even at the expense of geographical coherence and the detail of the biblical text.[2] Such a perception of history is to be expected, *a fortiori* in a hagiographical work. The chief themes touched upon in this work are the following:

- Abraham's genealogy (§1)
- The ravens (§§2 and 4)
- Abraham as astrologer; he recognizes God through luminaries (§3)
- Abraham moves from Ur to Haran (§5)
- Terah's idolatry; death of Achan in the fire (§6)
- Abraham goes to Canaan (§7)
- Sarah and Pharaoh (§§8-9)
- Abraham has no sons (§10)
- The Ten Trials of Abraham (§§11–12: cf. text no. 5.2, 13) and the Tree of Sabek pericopes.
- The Binding of Isaac (§§13–14)
- Abraham's virtues (§§15–16)

---

1. See Anasyan 1959, 1:137–38. On the various recensions of the Armenian Synaxarium, see Mécérian 1953; and compare also Stone 1969, 59–77. The same text is found in the Constantinople edition of 1706 published by Karapet son of Astuacatur *tpir*. Numerous years ago I transcribed a fragment of what is apparently a variant form of this text from manuscript M0640: see Appendix 1.
2. Stone 1999.

Synaxarium 1730 – Text

1. Յայսմ աւուր յիշատակ է մեծի նահապետին եւ հօրն հաւատոյ Աբրահամու:
   Աբրահամ որդի Թարայի, որդւոյ Նաքովրայ, ԻԱ ազգ էր յԱդամայ. եւ ԺԱ ազգ ի Նոյէ յորդւոցն Սեմայ. եւ բնակէր յերկիրն Քաղդէացւոց: Եւ իբրեւ եղեւ Աբրահամ ՀԵ ամաց, սկսաւ խնդրել զԱստուած այսու պատճառաւ:
2. Երկիրն Քաղդէացւոց պարարտ էր. եւ յօքացեալ մարդիկքն՝ զազիր գործոց պարապէին յանքաւ չարիսն: Վասն որոյ ետ նոցա Աստուած պատուհաս գերամ ճայիցք որ ուտէին զբերս երկրին զարտոյ եւ զայգոյ: Եւ Աբրահամ աղաչեաց գշարագործսն Քաղդէցոց եւ ոչ եղեւ լսելի:
3. Եւ զի քաջ հմուտ էր Աբրահամ աստղագիտութեան, հայեցաւ յարուեստն յայն եւ զմտաւ ածեալ գշարուածս աստեղացն՝ ծանեաւ զարարիչն նոցա. եւ յարուցեալ անկաւ ի վերայ ծնկաց իւրոց եւ տարածեալ զբազուկան իւր եւ ասաց: Անձանօք Աստուած եւ շարժիչ ամենայնի եւ այս թշնոցս ստեղծից. հալածեա զսսա եւ ծանն մեզ զկամս քո:
4. Եւ ընդ ասելն՝ վաղվաղակի տարմն հաւուցն ի շիք դարձան եւ անյայտ եղեն. եւ յարուցեալ գնաց Աբրահամ ի տուն իւր խնդութեամբ: Եւ յայնմ օրէ եղեւ Աբրահամ յարաչաղէմ հաճոյ Աստուծոյ:
5. Եւ յորժամ եղեւ Աբրահամ Կ ամաց, լուաւ Աստուած բազմաժամանակեայ եւ անձանձիր աղօթից նորա եւ աներկբայ հաւատոցն եւ ասաց՝ ել յերկրէ եւ յազգէ քումմէ եւ եկ յերկիր զոր ցուցից քեզ: Եւ անդիմադարձ լեալ Աբրահամու՝ ել ի Բաբելոնէ եւ գնաց ի Խառան՝
6. Եւ անդ ի Խառան կռօցն տուն շինեաց Թարա հայրն Աբրահամու՝ եւ Աբրահամ հուր վառեաց զի այրեցք զտունն եւ զբագինն. եւ Առան եղբայրն Աբրահամու կամեցաւ շիջուցանել զայն զի մի այրեցի մեհեանն. եւ ինքն՝ եւս անկաւ ի հուրն եւ այրեցաւ Առան հայրն Ղովտայ:
7. Եւ ապա յետ ՁԷ ամաց իբրեւ եղեւ Աբրահամ ՀԵ ամաց եւ մեռաւ հայրն նորա ի Խառան եւ եղբայրն նորա Առան: Ասաց Աստուած Աբրահամու ել յերկրէդ յայդմանէ եւ եկ յերկիր զոր ցուցից քեզ. եւ ելեալ գնաց հրամանաւ Աստուծոյ ի Քանան:
8. Եւ եղեւ սով յերկրին Քանանու. եւ էջ Աբրահամ յԵգիպտոս՝ եւ ասաց Սառայի կնոջ իւրոյ, տես զի կին գեղեցիկ ես դու. եւ արք Եգիպտացիք տեսեալ՝ զիս սպանցեն եւ զքեզ առցեն: Եւ ես ասացից վասն քո թէ քոյր իմ է. եւ դու ասա վասն իմ թէ եղբայր իմ է. եւ ասացին այսպես ի մտանելն յԵգիպտոս. եւ փարաւոն խաթ զՍառա ի տուն իւր. եւ բարիս արարին Աբրահամու՝ եւ բազմացան նորա ուղտք եւ ոչխարք եւ ամենայն ինչ:

9. Եւ հրեշտակ Տեառն տանջեաց գիսարաւն եւ զամենայն արս տան նորա եւ ոչ մերձեցան ի Սառա: Կոչեաց փարաւոն զԱբրահամ եւ ասաց, Չի՞ նչ գործեցեր զայդ որ ասացեր թէ քոյր իմ է Սառա: Եւ նա ասաց վախեցայ թէ զիս սպանէիք եւ զդա առնուիք: Եւ ետ ի նա զՍառա եւ ածիկ մի Ագար անուն ընդ նմա առ ի պատիւ երեսացն Սառայի՝ եւ հանին գնաաս խաղաղութեամբ յերկրէն իւրեանց՝ եւ նա դարձեալ եկն յերկիրն Քանանու:
10. Եւ զի Սառա ամուլ էր եւ ոչ ծնանէր. ասաց Աբրահամու անկանիլ ընդ Հագարու, զի լիցի, ասէ, մեզ զաւակ: Եւ յամի ՁՁ կենացն Աբրահամու ծնաւ նմա որդի Իսմայէլ ի Հագարայ աղախնոյն Սառայի: Եւ Սառա առեալ զԻսմայէլ հարկ ի ծոց իւր եւ ասաց, ահա սա ինձ որդի եղիցի: Եւ ի Ճ ամին Աբրահամու Սառա ծնաւ նմա որդի զԻսահակ՝ աւետեօքն Աստուծոյ:
11. Աբրահամ Ճ տարոյ եւ Սառա Ղ ի ծնանին Իսահակայ: Եւ Ժ փորձանաց հանդիպեալ Աբրահամու ընտիր գտաւ եւ հաճոյ կամացն Աստուծոյ:
12. Նախ՝ ելանել յերկրէն. զի գհայրենի եւ զբուն տեղիս թողուլ՝ կարի դժուարին է եւ մեծ փորձանք:
Երկրորդ՝ քաշանքն Սառայի ի տունն փարաւոնի:
Երրորդ՝ կագ եւ կռիւ հովուացն՝ իւրն եւ Ղովտայն՝ եւ բաժանիլն ի միմեանց:
Չորրորդ՝ ոչ առնուլն յլնչից Սոդոմայեցւոց:
Հինգերորդ՝ ասացաւ նմա յԱստուծոյ թէ եղիցի զաւակ քո որպէս զաստեղս՝ եւ յամենայն ոչ երկմտեցաւ:
Վեցերորդ՝ զի ետ զհազար ի ձեռն Սառայի:
Եօթներորդ՝ զի ասաց Սառա թէ ի բաց հան զաղախինդ եւ զորդին դորա:
Ութերորդ՝ զի առաւ Սառա յԱբամելիքայ:
Իններորդ՝ զի ասացաւ նմա յԱստուծոյ թլիփատիլ ի ծերութեան աւուրն:
Տասներորդ՝ զի խնդրեաց զորդին ի զենումն:
13. Այս ահագին եւ մեծ փորձանք քան զամենայն. որ Գ օր շրջեցաւ Աբրահամ մեղմով ի լերինսն Ամուրհացւոց. այն մտօքն զի զվիասօրէն Իսահակ ողջակիզէլ կամէր՝ եւ ոչ թնդաց ի մտածն. մինչեւ եկեալ ի լեառն յեփուսացւոց ի Գողգոթա՝ եւ անդ լի սրտիւ եւ բոլոր հաւատով պատարագէլ կամէր զորդին իւր սիրելի:
14. Մինչեւ որ հայեցաւ Աստուած յանդորդութելի միտս եւ ի հաւատն Աբրահամու: Եւ ետ զխոյն ի ծառոյն Սաբէկայ փխանակ Իսահակայ՝ եւ զնեաց Աստուած խոյին զԻսահակ յաբրահամէ իւր ծառայ:
15. Եւ հայրն Աբրահամ այս ամենայն փորձանագս տարեալ ժուժկալեաց հաւատովա զոր ունէր առ Աստուած: Վասն որոյ յԱստուծոյ պսակեցաւ. հայր բազմաց եղեւ եւ զոգ հոգինգ կոչեցաւ: Եւ հասեալ ի

բարուք ծերութեան ծաղկեցաւ. այեօք որպէս եւ հոգին բարի գործովք եւ հաւատովս Աստուծոյ:

16. Չի մինչ ի սա այլ ումեք ի նախահարցն չէ գրեալ թէ ծաղկեցաւ այեօքն ծերութեան: Եւ յետ Աբրահամ ՃՁԵ ամաց՝ պակասեալ աստի յաւելաւ առ հարս իւր: Եւ եկեալ Իսմայէլ եւ Իսահակ թաղեցին զնա ընդ Սառայի ի Սիկիմ յայրին Քեբրոնի: Զոր ստացաւ Աբրահամ զնց արծաթոյ յորդւոցն Եմովրայ ի գերեզմանն Սառայի եւ իւրն:

Colophon:

Աղերսանոք՝ նահապետին քո Աբրահամու անճառելիդ Քրիստոս Աստուած ողորմեա ըստացողի գրոյս:

SYNAXARIUM 1730 – TRANSLATION

1. On this day is a memorial of the great patriarch and father of the faith, Abraham.
   Abraham (was) son of Terah, son of Nahor, he was the 21st generation from Adam and the 11th generation from Noah, of the sons of Shem, and he lived in the land of the Chaldeans. And when Abraham was 15 years old, he began to seek God, for this reason.[3]
2. The land of the Chaldeans was rich and men were very wealthy, they were occupied with obscene deeds in immeasurable evils. On account of that God punished them with flocks of crows[4] that were eating the produce of the earth, of field and of vineyard.[5] And Abraham beseeched the evildoers[6] of the Chaldeans, and none hearkened.
3. And because Abraham was very well versed in astrology,[7] he consulted that skill and considered the arrangement of the stars (and) came to recognize their Maker. And rising up, he fell upon his knees and spread his arms wide

---

3. The age fifteen for Abraham's recognition of God occurs elsewhere; see text 2.3. Its origins are unclear. Jewish sources put this at various dates, from three years on; see Beer 1859, 103–4.

4. Or: "jays, rooks."

5. Compare *Jub.* 11:11–13. In the Armenian Adam texts, crows are demonic.

6. Literally: "evil ones."

7. Here three themes about Abraham's recognition of God are combined: (1) Abraham as originator of or expert in astrology; see text nos. 2.3 and 12.5. (2) Abraham concluding from contemplation of the luminaries that God is beyond them; see text no. 3:11 and cf. text no. 11:49; (3) Abraham recognizing God through his dispersal of the crows: texts nos. 2.4, 6.1–2, and 8.5–6. Generally, in the Abraham texts the theme of Abraham and the luminaries is neither widespread nor much stressed.

and said,[8] "Unknown God and mover of all[9] and creator of these birds, chase them away and make known your will to us."
4. And at the saying (of this) at once the flock of birds turned into nothing and disappeared. And Abraham arose (and) went joyously to his house. And from that day Abraham was advancing in pleasing God.
5. And when Abraham became 60 years old, God hearkened to his long-standing and indefatigable prayer and his undoubting faith and said, "Go forth from your land and family and come to the land which I will show you." And, Abraham not being opposed, went forth from Babylon and went to Haran.[10]
6. And there in Haran, Terah Abraham's father built a house of idols[11] and Abraham kindled a fire to burn the house and the altar. And Achan, Abraham's brother, wished to extinguish it, so that the temple should not be burnt, and, moreover, he himself fell into the fire and Achan, Lot's father, was burnt up.[12]
7. And then, after fifteen years, when Abraham was 75 years old and his father and his brother Achan died in Haran, God said to Abraham, 'Go forth from this land and come to the land which I will show you."[13] And going forth, he went at God's command to Canaan.
8. And there was a famine in the land of Canaan, and Abraham went down to Egypt.[14] And he said to Sarah his wife, "See that you are a beautiful woman and the Egyptian men, having seen (you), will kill me and take you. And I will say about you, 'She is my sister,' and you, say concerning me, 'He is my brother'." And they said thus when they entered Egypt, and Pharaoh took Sarah to his house. And they did benefits to Abraham, and his camels and sheep and every thing[15] increased.[16]
9. And the Lord's angel afflicted[17] Pharaoh and all the men of his house, and

---

8. See text no. 2.4 and notes there.

9. Here God is celebrated as the originator of movement; see Philo, *Cher.* 2.35 §124; *Post.* 9 §27; cf. Aristotle, *Physics* 3:2 202a; 8:4 255b 29–31 on movement and on the "unmoved mover."

10. The command "Go forth . . ." is drawn from Gen 12:1. Here it is applied to the move from Ur (Babylon) to Haran, and the same use of Gen 12:1 may be observed in text no. 5.1. In §7 below, the verse is used in its biblical context.

11. That is, an idolatrous temple.

12. The usual reason given for Achan's (Haran's) death, the breeding of the mule, is absent from this text, as is the observation, based in a biblical verse, that Achan died before his father.

13. Gen 12:1.

14. This incident is related in Gen 12:10–20.

15. Or: "possession".

16. Here Pharaoh's gifts to Abraham are connected with his taking of Sarah and not, as elsewhere, with his repining his actions.

17. Or: "tortured".

they did not draw near to Sarah. Pharaoh summoned Abraham and said, "Why did you do that, that you said, 'Sarah is my sister'?" And he said, "I was afraid that you would kill me and take her." And he gave Sarah to him and a handmaiden named (H)agar with her, for honor of Sarah's face.[18] And they brought them forth peacefully from their land, and he once more came to the land of Canaan.

10. And because Sarah was barren and did not bear,[19] she said to Abraham to lie with Hagar, "So that we may have a son,"[20] she said. And in the 86th year of Abraham's life a son Ishmael was born to him from Hagar, Sarah's maidservant.[21] And Sarah took Ishmael and embraced him and said, "Behold, he will be a son for me." And in Abraham's 100th year, Sarah bore him a son, Isaac, at the Annunciation[22] of God.[23]

11. Abraham was 100 years old and Sarah 90 at Isaac's birth. And Abraham having encountered 10 trials, was found elect[24] and pleasing to the will of God.[25]

12. First, to go out of (his) land, for to leave one's homeland and original place is very difficult and a great trial.

Second, the sufferings of Sarah in Pharaoh's house.

Third, contention and strife of the shepherds, his own with Lot's, and (their) separation from one another.

Fourth, not taking of the possessions of the Sodomites.[26]

Fifth, it was said to him by God, "Your seed will be like the stars," and in everything he did not doubt.[27]

Sixth, that he gave Hagar into Sarah's hand.[28]

Seventh, that he said to Sarah, "Expel your maidservant and her son".[29]

Eighth, that Sarah was taken to Abimelech.[30]

Ninth, that it was said to him by God to be circumcised in the day of his old age.[31]

Tenth, that He (i.e., God) asked his son as a sacrifice.[32]

---

18. Or: "presence": this is inferred from Gen 16:1.
19. Gen 16:1; cf. 11:20.
20. Or: "seed."
21. Gen 16:16,
22. Or: "announcement."
23. Gen 21:5.
24. Or: "choice."
25. See the introduction to text no. 5 and §2; see also text no. 13.
26. See Gen 14:23.
27. Երկմտեցան is apparently corrupt for the singular երկմտեցաւ. Emended in the translation.
28. Cf. Gen 16:6.
29. Cf. Gen 21:10. In the biblical text Sarah tells Abraham to expel them.
30. Gen 20:2.
31. Gen 17:1; 17:10; 17:24.
32. Gen 22.

13. This (is) a more terrible and greater trial than all of them, that for 3 days[33] Abraham wandered around gently on the mountains of the Amorites,[34] with that thought that he wanted to sacrifice Isaac, only son of his mother, and he did not shake off the thought until he came to the mountains of the Jebusites, to Golgotha,[35] and there with a whole heart and with complete faith, he wished to offer his beloved son.
14. While God regarded the unshakable mind[36] and the faith of Abraham, he gave[37] the ram into the Tree of Sabek[38] in place of Isaac, and God bought Isaac as his servant from Abraham for the ram.[39]
15. And father Abraham bore patiently all these trials by the faith which he had in God. On account of this he was crowned by God.[40] He became father of many[41] and was called bosom of souls.[42] And having reached a good old age, he flowered with grey hair,[43] just as his soul flowered with good deeds and faith in God.
16. For, up to him of no other of the patriarchs is it written that he flowered with the grey hair of old age. And Abraham was 175 years old,[44] having been taken from here he was joined to his fathers. And Ishmael and Isaac came and buried him with Sarah in Shechem, in the cave of Hebron,[45] which Abraham acquired for silver from the sons of Hamor as his and Sarah's tomb.

Colophon:

By the prayers of your forefather Abraham, do you, ineffable Christ God, have mercy on the commissioner of this book.

---

33. Gen 22:4.
34. This is surely a corruption of "the land of Moriah" in Gen 22:22.
35. Concerning Golgotha as Zion, see text no. 2. This is conflated with a tradition identifying the mountain of the Binding of Isaac with Zion and the place of Isaac's sacrifice with that of Christ's crucifixion.
36. Or: "intention."
37. This is probably an error of etu "he gave" for etʻ "he put."
38. That is, the thicket; cf. Gen 22:13. See text no. 4:22 and note on this name.
39. For this idea, see texts nos. 4.22, 7.15, and 8.23.
40. Cf. Rev 2:10.
41. Gen 17:5.
42. Cf. Luke 16:22.
43. For this expression, see text no. 2.11.
44. Gen 25:7.
45. Cf. Gen 25:9–10. There is confusion between Hebron and Shechem, also found in text no. 4.23. This leads to the introduction of Hamor here, in place of Ephron the Hittite as the original owner of the Cave of Machpelah.

15. Sermon Concerning Hospitality

This document, which is a sermon, is found in a *Book of Sermons*, Paris Armenian Museum no. 62, fols. 44v–60v.[1] The date of the manuscript is not recorded, but Dr. Edda Vardanyan, who is cataloguing this collection, opines that it is perhaps of the eighteenth century. The date being based on paleography, a measure of uncertainty persists, especially in this late script type. There were two scribes: Awēt, who copied fols. 2r–145r, and a second scribe, who was responsible for 145v–240v. The commissioner was Nazar, and the manuscript belonged to a Monastery of St. Thomas.[2]

This writing seems to be, in parts, quite similar to text no. 11 but differs enough from it, and particularly by its additions, to be regarded as a separate work. I have preserved the punctuation and capitalization of the original with slight changes for sense. *Sermon Concerning Hospitality* is followed by an untitled text on Jacob.

The text contains a number of unique details that result from its expansionary technique: the milking of the sheep in §12, the dog in §13, the spring of water in §19, and his rubbing his eyes §20.

Քարոզ վասն հիւրընկալութեան.

1. Չի յորժամ վաղճանեցաւ Նոյ. որդիք նորա եւ թոռունքն մոռացան զԱստուած եւ պաշտեցին կուռք: Չի գիրք եւ օրէնք ոչ կայր բնաւ մոռացան զԱստուած: մարդ մի չկայր որ յիշէր կամ գիտէր թէ Աստուած կայ:
2. Իսկ Թարայ հայրն Աբրահամու կռապաշտ էր եւ կուռք շինող. զի ջրհեղեղէն մինչեւ ի Թարայ ԹՃ տարի էր որ կուռք պաշտէին. եւ զԱստուած ոչ ճանաչէին: Իսկ ի տոսի կռոցն՝ Թարայ ասաց որդւոյն իւրոյ Աբրահամու: որդի ուսիր զկուռք շինելու իմ. բազում վարձք է քեզ: Իսկ Աբրահամ ասաց հայր. զի թէ իշխա/ fol. 45r /նութիւնն ի ձեռս

---

1. Here I thank the director, Mr. F. Fringhian for the permission to publish this text and Dr. Edda Vardanyan, who graciously not only drew my attention to it but supplied me with the still unpublished description she had made of the manuscript.
2. According to Thierry 1993, Index s.v. there were a number of monasteries of that name.

իմ լինէր խորտակէի զնոսա: զի գործք մարդկան ինչպէս Աստուած լինի մարդոյ.
3. զայս իմանայր Աբրահամ. բայց զԱստուած ոչ ճանաչէր: հանապազ ի միտ ածէր եւ քննէր թէ ո՞վ իցէ Աստուած: Եւ ի ժամանակին յայնմիկ՝ թռչնոց պատուհաս եկն բազմութեան սեւ ազռաւոյ. որք քաղէին աշնան սերմն. եւ զկանանչ արտերն ուտէին: Այլ ոչ էր եղեալ այնպէս. իսկ ամենայն մարդ քշէր զհաւկն եւ պահէլ կամէր զարտան՝ եւ չկարէին փրկել: Գնաց Աբրահամ եւ կամէր պահել զարտան:
4. Իբրեւ գնաց եւ տեսաւ զբազմութիւն թոչնոցն անհամար. զարմացաւ եւ հիացաւ. քնէր ընդ միտս իւր եւ ասէր. մինչեւ այսաւր այլ ոչ եղեւ այսպէս: Չի մեծ Աստուած կայ որ զայս առնէ. Հայեցաւ ի արեգական եւ ի լուսինն. թէ ո ոք իցեն Աստուած. / fol. 45v / այլ ոչ հաւանեցաւ միտքն Աստուած ասել նոցա. վասն զի փոփոխական են. երբեմս մեծանան եւ երբեմս փոքրանան. երբեմս տաքանան. եւ երբեմս ցրտանան. վասն այն ոչ հաւանեցաւ նոցա Աստուած ասել:
5. Եւ բարձրածայն կոչեաց երկինքն ի վեր եւ ասաց. է՛ անձանօթ Աստուած որ բազմեալ կաս ի վերայ յաթռոյ երկնի եւ յերկրի. լուսնի եւ արեգական եւ ամենայն կենդանեաց ստեղծող. որպէս առաքեցեր զթռչունս զայս. խլել զվաստակս մեր: Նոյնպէս ողորմեա եւ դու պահեա զվաստակս մեր:
6. Իբրեւ զայս ասաց եյան ամենայն թռչունքն եւ փախեան. այլ ոչ ուտէին զսերմն եւ զարտան նորա: զի հայրն եւ տեսանէր Աբրահամ. զի ամենեցուն վաստակն ուտէին թռչունքն՝ եւ իւր վաստակն ոչ մերձենային՝ զոհանայր եւ փառ / fol. 46r / տայր Աստուծոյ. ուրախութեամբ գնաց տուն եւ պատմեաց հաւրն զքանչելիսն: Իսկ հայրն նորա ասաց՝ որդեակ՝ ի զաւրութենէ կռոցն մերոց եղեւ զայդ: զի մեր կուռքն շատ է. վասն այն ոչ ուտեն զարտան մեր.
7. եւ հայրն ոչ հաւանեցաւ խրատոյ որդյն: Այլ հրամայեաց Աբրահամու գնալ ի նախիրն. եզն եւ արջատ բերել. եւ զենել զոհ կռոցն: Իսկ Աբրահամ առեալ կրակ եւ գաղտ գնացեալ ի տուն կռոցն. եւ վառեալ ի նմա կրակն եւ այրեաց զկուռսն: Եւ հաւր եղբայր եկն զի շիջուցէ զկրակն. եւ նայ անկեալ ի հուրն այրեցաւ ընդ կռոցն. իսկ հայրն եւ ամենայն ազգ ու ազինքն Աբրահամու՝ խորհեցան սպանանել զԱբրահամ:
8. Իսկ Աբրահամ իմացեալ առեալ / fol. 46v / զՍառայ կինն իւր. եւ փախեալ գնաց Եգիպտոս. եւ գովեցին առաջի փարաւոնի զգեղեցկութիւնն Սառայի. եւ փարաւոն տարեալ տեսաւ եւ հաւանեցաւ Սառայի: Եւ հարցաւ զԱբրահամու թէ զի՞նչ լինիցի քեզ Սառայ. եւ նա վասն ահի[3] սպանելոյ ասաց թէ իմ քոյր է: Եւ փարաւոն կամեցաւ առնուլ զՍառայ իւրն ի կնութիւն:
9. Եւ ի գիշերն երբ կամէր մերձենալ ի Սառայ՝ երեւեցաւ նմա հրեշտակ

---

3. The case is anomalous. A genitive would be expected.

15. SERMON CONCERNING HOSPITALITY 215

Աստուծոյ հրեղէն զաւագանաւ եւ ասաց. մի մերձենար ի Սառայ զի կին Աբրահամու է։ Այլ եւ տուր նմա բազում ինչս վասն զի հայեցար ի տեսութիւն Սառայի։ եւ թէ ոչ առնես այդպէս. հրեղէն զաւագանաւ սատակեմ զքեզ եւ որդիքն քո. եւ քակեմ զթագաւորութիւնդ քո։

10. Յայն/ fol. 47r /ժամ թագաւորն ահէ հրէշտակին՝ ահ եւ դող անկաւ ի վերայ փարաւոնի եւ կոչեաց զԱբրահամ՝ եւ ասաց. երբ Սառայ քո կին էր, ընդէր ասացեր թէ իմ քոյր է։ Ասաց Աբրահամ վասն այն ասացի թէ իմ քոյր է զի մի սպանանիցէք զիս վասն Սառայի։ Իսկ փարաւոն ետ Սառայի Խ ծառայս եւ Խ աղախինս ՂԾ ուղտս. եւ բազում կովս. եւ ոչխարս՝ ձիս եւ ջորիս՝ ոսկիս եւ արծաթս։

11. արձակեաց զնոսա եւ ասէ երկիրս իմ ամենայն առաջի ձեր կայ՝ որտեղ որ կամիս անդ բնակեաց. եւ երբեալ բազմացաւ ոչխարքն ուղտքն եւ ամենայն անասունքն եւ ամենայն ինչքն Աբրահամու. վրանով շրջէր եւ արածէր զանասունքն իւր ուր եւ կամէր։

12. Իսկ մոտ վրանին Ռ ոչխար պահէր վասն ուտելոյ / fol. 47v / զկաթն զմածուն եւ զդառն զի մատ լիցի իւրն։

13. Եւ հովիւ մի ունէր անուն նորա Մամրէ՝ խիստ ողորմած էր ի տուրս աղքատաց եւ հիւրոց. եւ ի միում յաւուր երբ ելանէր ոչխարս արածել. հաց սակաւ տվին նմա Գ հաց տվին նմա եւ իւր շանն։ Ասաց Աբրահամ. առ զայդ հացդ եւ գնա՝ մինչ որ հաց թխեն. զամ ես եւ բերեմ քեզ հաց։ Չի այն Գ հացն բաղարձ էր.

14. իբրեւ ել ի տանէն Մամրէ՝ եւ սակաւ մի հեռացաւ. եկն աղքատ մի եւ ասաց՝ վասն սիրոյն Աստուծոյ տուր ինձ ուտելոյ՝ զի սոված եմ։ Իսկ Մամրէ կտեց ոչխար. եւ բրբեաց հաց մի կերաւ աղքատն եւ աւրհնեաց զՄամրէ եւ գնաց. իբրեւ ժամ մի անցաւ եկն այր մի աղաչեաց եւ ասէ. ճանապարհորդ եմ եւ սոված։ վասն Աստուծոյ / fol. 48r / սիրոյն տուր ինչ ուտելոյ.

15. եւ կտեաց Մամրէ գոչխարն. եւ ցհաց մի բրբեաց եւ ուտեցոյց զնա։ Իսկ մարդն այն կերաւ եւ աւրհնեաց զՄամրէ եւ գոչխարն նորա. եթող եւ գնաց. իսկ Մամրէ դեռ անօթի էր. մէկ հացն էր մնացեալ. կամէր ուտել զհացն. բայց ասաց ի մտան իւր. միթէ այլ ոք գայ եւ խնդրէ հաց վասն սիրոյն Աստուծոյ. վասն այն ոչ ճաշակեաց։ Իսկ յետ կես աւուրն եկես եկն ձեր մի՝ աղաչէր եւ ասէր. սոված եմ վասն սիրոյն Աստուծոյ տուր ինձ ուտելոյ զինչ ունիս.

16. եւ Մամրէ կտեալ կաթն եւ բրբեաց զբաղարձն. եւ ետ նմա ուտել։ Իսկ նայ եկեր եւ աւրհնեաց զՄամրէ. եւ Մամրէ ասաց. հայր ձեր. օրս տօթ է եւ դու խոնջեալ ես. սակաւ մի ննջեա շոքն անցոյց եւ ապա ելեալ / fol. 48v / գնասցես։ եւ յորժամ ննջեաց ձերն եւ նա ցրցեալ զզաւագանն իւր ի գետինն. եւ արար հովանի ի վերայ նորա զի մի նեղեսցէ զտօթ արեգականն ձերն. եւ յորժամ զարթեաւ ձերն եւտես զի հովանի էր շինեալ ի վերայ իւրն։ Չայնեաց Մամրէի եւ կրկին անգամ աւրհնեաց զՄամրէ ասելով այսպէս. Մամրէ դու եղիցիս գլուխ ողորմածաց. եւ զեւն քո սպիտակ եղիցի. զպակասն եւ զթերատն քո եւ որդոցն քոց

լիակատար եւ լցեալ եղեցի։ Եւ անուն քո բարի յիշատակ եղիցի ի վերայ աշխարհի. զեւ նշխարքն քո ամենայն սպիտակ եղիցի։
17. Չկաղնի զաւազանն Մամրէի գոր ցեալ էր. առեալ տնկեաց ի գետինն եւ ասաց. որդեակ այս զաւազանս եղիցի նշան ի մէջ քո եւ ընդ մէջ իմ։ Իբրեւ աւրհնեաց այսպէս եւ ելեալ գնայր ծերն. եւ Մամրէ ի յետ հայեցաւ եւ տեսաւ զզաւազանն կանանչացեալ էր եւ յարմատացեալ։ Դարձեալ ի ծերն հայեցաւ զի տեսցէ եւ այլ աւելի աւրհնութիւնս առցէ. այլ ոչ երեւեցաւ ծերն։
18. Հայեցաւ ի նշխարսն եւ տեսաւ. զի զամենայն սպիտակացեալ էին. եւ հայեցաւ ի վերայ ոտաց եւ ի ձեռաց իւրոց. եւ այլ մարմնոյն իւրոյ. եւ տեսանէր սպիտակացեալ ՝ քանզի Մամրէ սեւ ծառայ էր Աբրահամու։
19. Եւ դարձեալ ի զաւազանն հայեցաւ եւ տեսաւ զի զաւազանն մեծ ծառ էր եղեալ. եւ արբեւր մի ցուրտ ջուր բխեալ յատակս ծառին. իսկ նշխարքն ամենայն եկին արբին ի ջրէն եւ նստան ընդ հովս ծառին։
20. Իսկ Շ ժամու աւուրն առեալ հաց եւ ելեալ բերդր Մամրէի. հայեցաւ եւ տեսանէր / fol. 49v / ի դաշտին ծառ մի երեւայր։ Զարմանայր Աբրահամ եւ ասէր մինչեւ այս աւր ոչ կայր ծառս այս. ուստի եղեւ ծառս այս. երբեմն երթայր եւ երբեմն կանգնէր. քնէր. եւ գայցն սրբէր. հայէր եւ զարմանայր.
21. եւ գնացեալ եհաս ի ծառն. եւ տեսեալ զամենայն գոյխարսն սպիտակացեալ. եւ զՄամրէի երեսն սպիտակ եւ ոչ ծանեաւ։ Հարցանէր եւ ասէր. այ հովիւ ո՞ւր իցէ Աբրահամու գոյխարսն։[4] Եւ Մամրէ հովիւն եկն ընդ առաջն Աբրահամու եւ ասաց հայր իմ արի եւ տես զօրութիւնն եւ զքանչելիսն Աստուծոյ։ Իբրեւ եկն Աբրահամ տեսաւ զծառն՝ գոյխարսն եւ զՄամրէ սպիտակացեալ։ Զարմացաւ վասն սքանչելեացն։ Հարցանէր թէ որպէս եղեւ զքանչելիսն.
22. իսկ Մամրէ պատմեաց նմա զամենայն եւ ասաց թէ / fol. 50r / հայր իմ այսաւր Գ աղքատ հանդիպեցաւ յիս. եւ ես կերակրեցի զնոսա։ իսկ յետինն պատուական եւ գեղեցիկ ծեր մի էր՝ եւ գնա եւս կերակրեցի։ Եւ նա բազում եւ զանազան աւրհնեաց զիս եւ զնշխարս մեր. եւ առեալ զաւազանն իմ ցցեալ ի տեղիս. առ ժամայն արմատացեալ կանանչացաւ եւ եղեւ ծառս այս ըստ նմին եւ բղխեաց աղբիւրս այս։ Իսկ Աբրահամ անկեալ համբուրէր զծեռն եւ զոտն ծառային իւրոյ՝ եւ ասէր. դու իմ հայր եւ ես քո ծառայ։
23. Անդ ուխտեաց Աբրահամ Աստուծոյ թէ քանի ապրիմ մինչ որ հիւր ոչ հանդիպի հաց ոչ ճաշակեմ։ Մամրէ եղեւ պատճառ հիւրընկալութեանն եւ աղքատասիրութեանն Աբրահամու։ Իբրեւ եւտես Աբրահամ զայս ամենայն սքանչելիս եւ ուխտեաց ուխտ ընդ Աստուծոյ. այլ ոչ կերակրէլ առանց հիւրի.
24. եւ բերեալ վրան իւր կանգնեաց ներքեւ / fol. 50v / կաղնի ծառոյն եւ անդ բնակեցաւ ի վերայ ճանապարհին։ Չի անցաւորք կերիցեն ի

---

4. The accusative case is anomalous. This phenemenon is not unusual.

15. SERMON CONCERNING HOSPITALITY 217

սեղանոյ նորա եւ ապա գնասցեն։ զի սեղան հացին հանապազ ոչ վերացուցանէր. թէ մէկ աւրն խ հետ հիւր հանդիպէր Աբրահամ հետ ամենեցուն ճաշակէր վասն սիրոյ հիւրին.
25. թէ է աւրն հանդիպէր է որ ծոմ կենայր. թէ ժ օրն մէկ հիւր կայր մինչեւ ժ օրն ոչ ճաշակէր. Բազում անգամ այսպէս արար որ[5] առանց հիւր գալոյ ոչ ճաշակէր. Իբրեւ ետես Սատանայ այսպիսի բարեգործութիւնն եւ զհիւրընկալութիւնն Աբրահամու, նախանձեցաւ ընդ նմա եւ պահէր զամենայն ճանապարհսն որ շուրջ զնովաւն էին.
26. ով որ գայր յետ դարձուցանէր. եւ եցոյց տայր ընդ այլ ճանապարհի. եւ կապեաց զճանապարհսն այն. որ մինչեւ խ օրն ոչ հանդիպեցաւ հիւր Աբրահամու. Իսկ Աբրահամ գոյ[6] նուաղեցաւ. ասաց Սառայ՝ այր դու / fol. 51r / Աբրահամ սովամահ եղար. սակաւ մի ճաշակեայ։
27. Ասէ Աբրահամ կենդանի է Տէր՝ մինչեւ հիւր ոչ գայ ոչ ճաշակեմ. ոչ կարեմ ստել Աստուծոյ. բայց ակն ունիմ Աստուծոյ որ այսօր ինձ հիւր ուղարկէ. եւ անդ շինեալ էր Աբրահամ բարձր տեղ մի. զի ելանէր Սառայ եւ նստէր անդ՝ հայէր ընդ ճանապարհսն վասն հիւրոյ։
28. Եւ իբրեւ որ խիստ նուաղեաց Աբրահամ. ասաց Աբրահամ Սառայ՝ ել եւ հայեա. եւ Սառայ իբրեւ ելեալ հայեաց՝ տեսաւ որ ի հեռաստանէ Գ հոգի գային. աւետիս ետ Աբրահամու եւ ասաց՝ տէր իմ. Գ մարդ հիւր է գալիս[7] մեզ. իսկ Աբրահամ հրամայեաց հորթն զենուլ վասն հիւրոցն. զի պատուական հորթ մի ծնեալ էր. նմանութիւն ունէր զարհին Աբէլի։ այն հորթն զենուլ ետուր։
29. յայնժամ տեսան որ եկաւ Տէրն Բ հրեշտակաւ բայց Աբ/ fol. 51v / րահամ ոչ գիտէր թէ Տէրն է. ապա ուժովացաւ ի տեսնուլն[8] զնա։ Եւ ելեալ ընդ առաջ նոցա մեծարեալ եւ բերեալ նստան. եւ բերեալ սեղան կերակրեցին. նոքա խօսին ընդ միմեանս. եւ Աբրահամ ականջ դնէր. բանից նոցա եւ լսէր բազում խօս զարմանելի եւ հիանայր։ Իսկ Տէրն ասաց ժողովեցէք զոսկերս հորթուն. եւ յորժամ ժողովեցին եւ լցին զմորթն հորթին. յայնժամ խաչակնքեալ կենդանացոյց զհորթն. եւ Աբրահամ հիացեալ ոչ կարէր խաւսել ի յետ ճաշակելոյն. Յորժամ աւրհնեաց զսեղանն եւ զԱբրահամ. ասաց Տէրն Աբրահամ աւրհնելով աւրհնեցից զքեզ եւ բազմացուցից զզաւակս քո որպէս զաստեղս երկնից իբրեւ զաւազ ծովու.
30. եւ յետ բազում աւրհնելոյ. դարձեալ ասաց՝ եղիցի քեզ զաւակ ի Սառայէ. անուն նորա կոչեսցի Սահակ. / fol. 52r / իբրեւ լուաւ Սառայ ի ներքեւ ծածկոյթին. ծիծաղեւ եւ ասէր. երբ լինի ինձ այդ՝ զի աւուրք իմ անցեալ են. եւ Տէրն ասաց Աբրահամ.[9] Սառայ ժպտեցաւ վասն աւետիս Սահակայ. զի սուտ համարեաց զբանս իմ. վասն այդմ

---

5. Take this as "so that" in late usage.
6. This is a strange word.
7. Note the late Armenian verb form.
8. This is a late form of the infinitive.
9. Either a prepostion or a dative case would be normal here instead of the nom./acc.

ծիծաղելոյն ի վերայ իմ. ԴՃԿ տարի ազգն քո գերի ՟մասցէ ի ձեռն այլազգաց.
31. Զայս ասաց եւ արհնեաց գտունն եւ զեղանն եւ զամենայն ինչսն Աբրահամու, եւ դարձեալ Տէրն ասաց gԱբրահամու.[10] Աբրահամ ել ընդ իս մինչ ի լեառն Սոդոմայ. եւ ի ահէն ոչ իշխեր հարցանել Աբրահամ թէ դու ով ես Տէր. իբրեւ հասին ի լեառն որ երեւեցաւ Սոդում. հրամայեաց Աստուած. Բ հրեշտակաց իւրոց երթայք մտէք ի քաղաքդ. եւ դուրս հանեցէք զՂովտ զի արդար է եւ հիւրընկալ
32. եւ ասացէք զի ելցէ ի Սոդումէ. եւ այլ մի դարձցէ յետս հայել / fol. 52v / զի ով որ ետ հայի քաղանայ. իբրեւ զայս ասաց իմացաւ որ Տէրն է: Ասէ Աբրահամ. զի՞նչ կամիս առնել քաղաքիդ.
33. Ասէ Տէրն կամիմ կործանել զդայ. զի մեղք դոցա բազմացեալ են. Ասէ Աբրահամ. Տէր ոչ իցէ այդ քաղաքիդ Ռ մարդ առանց մեղաց: Ասէ Տէրն եթէ իցէ ԵՁ արդար ոչ կորուսից զդոսա վասն արդարոցն: Ասէ Աբրահամ եթէ իցէ ԲՁ ոչ խնայես: Ասէ Տէրն եթէ իցէ Ձ արդար ոչ կամիմ զմահ դոցա: Ասէ Աբրահամ. Տէր թէ իցէ Ծ արդար ոչ խնայես վասն նոցա. Ասէ Տէր եթէ գտանիցի Ի արդար խնայեմ ի նոսա:
34. Ասէ Աբրահամ. Տէր զի ես հող եմ եւ մոխիր որպէս կարեմ կրկին խաւսել ընդ քեզ. բայց երբ արժանի արարեր խաւսել ընդ քեզ. վասն Ժ արդա/ fol. 53r /րոցն խնայեաւ.
35. Յայնժամ վերացաւ Տէրն երկինս եւ ձայն լսելի եղեւ որ ասաց. երբ քաղաքդ[11] ոչ գտաւ ի դմա արդար. դու Աբրահամ կաց ի տեղիդ եւ տես զկատարած դոցա. իբրեւ այն Բ հրեշտակքն որ գնացին ի քաղաքն. Ժէ տարեկան տղայի պէս ցոյց տուին զիւրեանքն:[12]
36. Իսկ Ղովտ հիւրընկալ էր եւ աստուածասէր. իբրեւ ետես զնոսա մեծարեալ տարաւ զնոսա ի տուն իւր, իբրեւ գնացին ի տուն նորա. Ասեն հրեշտակքն ել ի քաղաքէս: զի Տէր կամի կործանել զսա. եւ զմեզ առաքեաց ի դուրս հանել զքեզ. Ասէ Ղովտ՝ սստարուք բազմեցէք՝ ճաշակեցուք եւ տեսցուք թէ զի՞նչ հրամայէք: քանզի մարդ գիտէր զնոսա.
37. մեղադրէք զնոսա եւ ասէր. ով որդիք՝ դուք նորահասակ մանուկ էք ընդէր եկիք եւ / fol. 53v /մտաք այս չարագործ եւ պղծագործ քաղաքս: Ասեն հրեշտակքն մեք վասն քո եկաք աստ զի հանցուք զքեզ ի քաղաքէս: Իսկ կինն Ղովտայ ոչ հաւատայր խօսից նոցա.[13]
38. գնաց եւ երաց զթոնիրն թէ կերակուր հանէ վասն հիւրոցն. եւ ետես

---

given in the manuscript. It might also be, conceivably, a vocative. If so, translate ". . . said, "Abraham."

10. Note the conflation of two constructions, the preposition g- and the dative case.

11. քաղաքդ is in an odd case in context. երբ literally means "when." In §34 above it means "if"; here it seems to introduce indirect speech. In both cases, թէ might have been expected.

12. This does not seem to be a complete sentence.

13. g is written over ր.

15. SERMON CONCERNING HOSPITALITY

զթոնիրն ջրով լցած. իբրեւ եւտես Ղովտ գշրոյն ելանելն՝ հաւատաց զանցումա քաղաքին։ Յայնժամ եկին Սողոմայեցիքն եւ կալան զդուռն Ղովտայ. եւ ասեն տուր մեզ որ եկեալ են ի տունս քո։

39. Իսկ Ղովտ վասն չարութեան նոցա փակեալ էր դուռն ի ներգուստ։ Ասէր Ղովտ. ունիմ Բ դուստր կոյս. գեղեցիկ ի ձեզ տաց՝ եւ մի ձեռն աձէք հիւրոց իմոց։ եւ նոքա ոչ հաւանեալ սկսան խորտակել զդուռն. Իսկ հրեշտակքն ասացին Ղովտայ. դու մի հոգալ վասն մեր. մեք կարող եմք փրկել զմեզ։ այսմ ժամու դու<ր>ս¹⁴ ել ի տանէ քումմ[է]. / fol. 54r / որ¹⁵ այժմ կործանի քաղաքս։

40. եւ յորժամ խորտակեցին զդուռն ելին հրեշտակքն եւ կուրացուցին զնոսա եւ ինքնեանք վերացան։ իսկ Ղովտ ել ի քաղաքէն ինքն՝ կինն եւ Բ դուստր իւր. Չի կինն նորա առաքեաց զոմա վասն փեսայիցն. գիտակ առնել նոցա զանցումա քաղաքին. իբրեւ գնացին հասան ի ստորոտ լերինն. իսկ կինն Ղովտայ յետ նայեցաւ վասն փեսայիցն. առ ժամայն քարացաւ.

41. զի հրեշտակն ասացեալ էր ոչ հայիք յետս։ ասաց թէ որք ի յետ հային. քարանան։ Իբրեւ ել Ղովտ՝ հուր վառեցաւ շուրջ զՍոդոմայ՝ իբրեւ զպարիսպ հուր եւ ծծումբ. քար եւ կարկուտ ի միասին ի վայր թափէին յերկնից միեչեւ է օր եւ է գիշեր այնպէս տեղաց ի վերայ նոցա. մինչ որ այրեցաւ գիհոն եւ զքարն. եւ ջուր ելաւ եւ ծովեցաւ գտեղին. եւ է միեչեւ ցայսօր։

42. Եւ տեսեալ Աբրահամ / fol. 54v / զայս ամենայն փառս տայր զԱստուծոյ եւ գոհանայր զՏեառնէ. որ այն մարդասէր է Աստուած. որ մէկ¹⁶ Ղովտ աղքատասէր էր աւտարասէր եւ հիւրընկալ։ մինչ որ հանեց Ղովտ եւ ապա անցոյց զքաղաքն։

43. Ադաչեմ զձեզ եղբարք աւրինակ առէք ձեզ եւ տեսէք զՄամբրէ որ հացով զԱստուած եբեր ի յոչխարսն իւր. Աստուծոյ աւրհնութեննն եւ արքայութեննն արժանեցաւ։ Եւ Աբրահամ որ հաւատով ծմով. աղօքիւք եւ հիւրընկալութեամբսեղանովս գՏէրն էջոյցյերկնից ի տուսն իւր եւ ի սեղանն իւր բազմեցոյց՝ կերաւ եւ խաւսեցաւ ընդ Աստուծոյ։ Եւ ընկալաւ զաւետիսն Սահակայ. եւ ընկալաւ զաւրինութիւնն Աստուծոյ որ աւրհնեաց զԱբրահամ եւ ասաց. աւրհնելով աւրհնեցից զքեզ եւ բազմացուցանելով բազմացուցից զաւակդ. Ձայս տեսեալ / fol. 55r / յուսարուք առնել ողորմութիւն աղքատաց. եւ հիւրասիրութիւն աւտարաց։ եւ թէ կամիք արքայութիւնն մտանել հիւրընկալ եւ սեղանաւդիր կացէք։ զի հացով եւ սեղանով մարդն քահանայքն եւ աղքատքն աւրինէն իշխանքն. եւ պարոնայք գովեն. եւ ամենայն մարդիկք գոհանան. եւ բազում պատուհասէ եւ չարէ փրկէ. եւ անդ դատաստանի աւրն Քրիստոս ինքն աւրինէ եւ գովէ. եւ զզիր

---

14. Corrupt in the manuscript.
15. Note the late use of որ.
16. Above line.

մեղաց չնչէ. եւ ընդ արդարռն պասկէ. եւ գովի բերանով ամենայն
հրեշտակաց. եւ մտանէ ի դրախտն Աստուծոյ։ ընդ Աբրահամու եւ
ընդ այլ ամենայն սրբոցն Աստուծոյ. աղաչեմ լսեցէք զխրատս՝ ի միտ
առէք եւ պահեցէք. եւ ողորմի ասացէք ստացողի գրոցս Նազարին
եւ իւր ծնօղացն Ամիրին եւ Փաշին. եւ եղ/ fol. 55v /բարցն Մէլիքին
եւ Գասպարին. եւ ինձ մեղապարտ Աւետ գծողիս. եւ գթթի կողղղի
սրբին զտէր Ներսէսն. որ բազում փափազանաւք՝ սպասաւորաց
սմա. եւ զհոգեւոր հայրն մեր՝ զտէր Գասպարն. որ պատճառ եղեն՝
եւ ցայակից ներքին մարդոյն. եւ յորդորեցին զգիրքս՝ գրել տվին զի
եւ հայցեմք ի ձեզմէ ով սուրբ հարք եւ ընթերցողք. յորժամ ընթեռնուք
զսակաւ տրակս. յիշեցէք զբազմամեղս՝ եւ Աստուած ողորմի ասացէք։

Վասն ծնընդեանն Սահակայ։

44. Իբրեւ մերձեցաւ Աբրահամ ի Սառայ. յղացաւ եւ ծնաւ զՍահակ. զի
յոյժ գեղեցիկ էր եւ պատուական եւ սիրական ծնօղաց։ Այնպէս սիրէին
զնա ծնօղքն որ գիշերն ամենայն ճրագա/ fol. 56r /նշ շիջուցանէին վասն
տեսութեանն Սահակայ։ իբրեւ մեծացաւ եւ զարգացաւ առաքեաց
զհրեշտակ իւր եւ ասաց Աբրահամու զենել զորդին իւր մատաղ եւ
պատարագ Աստուծոյ.
45. փորձեաց {զնոսա}[17] Աստուած զի տեսցէ թէ առնէ Աբրահամ սիրական
զորդին իւր մատաղ թէ ոչ։ Իբրեւ լուաւ Աբրահամ ի հրեշտակէն.
համետացաւ զէշ իւր. եւ առեալ ընդ իւր հուր եւ փայտ եւ զՍահակ
որդին իւր եւ գնայր ի տեղի ուխտին։ Հարցանէր Սահակ հայրն իւր եւ
ասէր՝ հայր. ահա հուր ահա սուր եւ փայտ՝ ո՞ւր է ողջակէզն.
46. Ասէր Աբրահամ. որդի Աստուած պատրաստէ մեզ ողջակէզ.
զի Աբրահամ զայս ասէր թէ խաբէ զորդին իւր. բայց բերանն
մարգարէանայր. իբրեւ գնաց հասաւ ի տեղի ուխտին որ զենելոցն էր.
ասաց / fol. 56v / Սահակ ընդ հաւրն իւր։ հայր ու՞ր է ողջակէզն։ Ասաց
հայրն լալով որդի՝ ողջակէզն դու ես. զքեզ Աստուած բաշխեաց մեզ.
եւ ես խոստացայ Աստուծոյ որ մատաղ առնեմ զքեզ իւրն՝ որդի մի
ստեր խոստումմ իմ. հնազանդիր որ զենեմ զքեզ։ Ասաց Սահակ. հայր
իմ կամք քո է, հնազանդ ծառայ եմ քեզ։ այս անցաւոր յաշխարհիս
համար չեմ ստեր ուխտն քո. բայց պինդ կապեա զձեռս եւ զոտս իմ. զի
մի ձգեցից զձեռս կամ զոտս իմ եւ անհաճոյ լինիցս մատաղ քո։ Իսկ
Աբրահամ կապեաց զձեռսն եւ զոտսն Սահակայ. եւ Սահակ ասաց
հայր հալալ արա աշխատանքն քո. եւ ասասցես մաւրն իմ զի հալալ
արասցէ ինձ զկաթն եւ զաշխատանքն իւր. եւ հայրն խառ զսուրն՝ եւ
խզեաց զիւր/ fol. 57r /չակն Սահակայ. եւ ոչ մտաւ սուրն եւ ոչ կտրեաց.
եւ սակաւ մի յարիւն ել ի կուլէն. եւ յորժամ կամեցաւ թէ սրեսցէ
զդանակն ի վերայ քարին. եւ առ ժամայն կտրեաց զվէմա իբրեւ միս

---

17. Probably the abbreviation զևս "them" is a misreading of զևա "him."

առանց ոսկրոյ. Յայնժամ հրեշտակն ճայնեալ ասաց մի մխեր սուրդ ի պատանեակդ. զի հածոյ եղեւ Աստուծոյ պատարագ քո։ Չի առաքեաց Աստուած քեզ ողջակէզ փոխանակ Իսահակայ. իբրեւ ի վեր հայեցաւ Աբրահամ եւ ետես խոյ ողջակէզ կախեալ ի ծառէն եղջերացն։

47. Եւ առեալ Աբրահամ իջոյց զխոյն եւ զՍահակ արձակեաց. եւ զենել զխոյն մատոյց մատաղն. եւ իբրեւ կրկնեաց ձունր. ձայն եղեւ երկնից որ ասէ՝ Աբրահամ Աբրահամ. որպէս որ դու ոչ խնայեցիր զսիրելի զորդին քո վասն իմ։ Նոյնպէս / fol. 57v / եւ ես ոչ խնայեցից զսիրելի զորդին իմ վասն քո. որ եկեալ ազատեսցէ ի դժոխոցն զամենայն զորդիսն Ադամայ վասն բարութեանդ քո։ Յայնժամ Աբրահամ ուրախութեամբ առեալ զորդին եւ դարձաւ ի տուն իւր։ Եւ յաւուր միում մինչ ազօթէր Աբրահամ ի խորանին. էջ հրեշտակ Աստուծոյ առ նա եւ ասէ. Աբրահամ Աբրահամ հրամայեաց Աստուած քեզ՝ զի զնասցես Երուսաղէմ եւ զոցես անդ զծառայն Աստուծոյ Մելքիսեդէկ։ գերձեա զզլուխ նորա. եւ հերք զեղունկ նորա. եւ բեր ի տուն քո. եւ պատուեա զնա. եւ նայ զինով եւ հացիւ պատարագ մատուսցէ վասն քո.

48. նա քեզ քահանայ աստուածակոյս կողմանէ վասն քո եւ ամենայն ընտանեաց քոց. քահանայութիւն գործեսցէ։ Ասէ Աբրահամ որ տեղ գտանեմ զնա։ Ասէ հրեշտակն ի / fol. 58r / յանտառին գտանես զնա։ Իբրեւ զնաց Աբրահամ յԵրուսաղէմ. հայեցաւ ընդդէմ անտառին՝ ի գիշերին տեսանէր զսիւն լուսոյ ի անտառին. գիտաց Աբրահամ որ անդ է։ Իբրեւ տիւ եղեւ ել զնաց ի տեղին զտաւ զնա. երբ տեսաւ զՄելքիսեդէկ Աբրահամ զի ոչ էր տեսիլ նորա իբրեւ զտեսիլ մարդոյ.

49. այլ ազունեալ էր եւ հեր զլխոյ նորա իջանէր մինչեւ ի ծունկն. եւ քամակ նորա որպէս թէ քամակ կրիայի. եւ եղունկն նորա թզաչափ էր եղեալ. եւ ողջունեալ զնա Աբրահամ խաւսեցաւ ընդ նմա եւ ասաց. քանի ժամանակ է որ աստ կաս։ Ասէ Մելքիսեդ՝ Շ տարի է որ աստ ճզնիմ անտես ի մարդկանէ։ Այլ մարդ ոչ է տեսեալ զիս բայց ի քէն։ Ասէ Աբրահամ պատմեա ինձ զիաւ/ fol. 58v /ատաղ քո թէ ինչպէս եղեւ։ Ասէ Մելքիսեդ՝ ես եմ որդի Մելքթեա թագաւորին որդուն Սադիմա որ շինեց զքաղաքն Երուսաղէմ. Ի միում աւուր առաքեաց զիս հայր իմ թէ զնա նախիրն եւ բեր պատուական եւ զեր հերինչք եւ արջառք. զի զոհս մատուցից կռոցս.

50. եւ ես զնացի նախիրն. եւ ժողեցի զզեր երինչքն եւ արջառք։ Եւ ծագեաց Աստուած զլոյս շնորհաց ի սիրտս իմ. քննեցի եւ ոչ հաւանեցայ զկենդանիքս սպանանել վասն անկենդանին չաստուածոցն. եւ դարձեալ ետ, դարձուցի զկենդանիսն եւ ես թողի եւ զնացի. եւ ի զնալն իմում հայեցայ յերկինս. զլուսաւորս եւ զամենայն արարածս արարչին մտոք քննեցի. եւ շնորհաւքն Աստուծոյ ծանեայ զարարիչն Աստուած. եւ զնացի առ հայրն իմ առանց մատաղի.

51. Եհարց զիս հայրն իմ եւ ասաց. ո՞ւր եր[18] երինջք եւ արջառք քո։ Եւ ես ասացի հայր իմ ինձ դժար[19] թուի զկենդանին գոհ / fol. 59r / մատուցանել. վասն անշարժ ձեռագործաց մարդկան որ ոչ են աստուածք՝ այլ սուտ չաստուածք. վասն այն ոչ բերի. եւ հայրն իմ ոխացաւ ընդ իս եւ մտաւ տունն իմ ասաց մօրն իմում. զի ես այսօր Բ որդւոցս մէկն գոհ մատուցանեմ կռոցս։ Եւ մայրն իմ գիտաց որ ոխացաւ ընդ իս հայրն իմ. լայր մայր իմ ողբայր եւ ճանկեր գերեսս իւր. ծեծեր զգլուխ իւր եւ ասեր այդ զի՞նչ բան է որ դու կասես։
52. զի մայրն իմ զիս սիրեր. եւ հայրն իմ գեղբայրն իմ սիրեր. Իսկ հայր իմ յորժամ ետ<ես>[20] զսուզ մօրն իմոյ որ լայր դառնապէս։ ասէ հայրն իմ ընդ մօրն իմոյ ընդէ՞ր լաս, զի վիճակ արկցուք ի վերայ Բ որդոց մերոց. ում ելցէ վիճակն գնա գեսցուք։
53. Երբ որ վիճակ արկաներ հայրն իմ. այսպէս թվեր թէ վիճակն ինձ անկաներ ի մեռանիլ վասն կռոցն. Դարձեալ Գ անգամ վիճակ արկին. վիճակ ան/ fol. 59v /կաներ եղբաւրն իմ մեռանիլ կռոցն. իբրեւ եւ հայրն իմ եւ առեալ գեղբայրն իմ զի կապեալ տաներ զենումի կռոցն. իսկ մայրն իմ լայր եւ ասեր ոչ ողորմիս քո եղբօրն. եւ լալով գնաց զի տեսցէ զկատարումն որդոյ իւրոյ։ Իբրեւ լսեցին իշխանքն եւ մեծամեծք թագաւորին՝ տարան գորդիս եւ գդուստրս իւրեանց ի զենումի կռոց։
54. Եւ ես լալով վասն եղբաւր իմ փախեայ եկի եւ ելի անտառս. Յորժամ տեսի որ նորա ձեռն արկին ի զենումի եղբաւրն իմ. եւ ես խնդրեցի ի Տառնէ թէ[21] բացցեն դրունք անդնդոց. եւ կլանեցցեն գնոսա. նոյնժամայն պատառեցաւ տեղին եւ կլաւ գնոսա ընդ տաճարն եւ ընդ կռոցն. զհայր իմ եւ զմայր, եւ զամենայն ժողովուրդքն ընդ նոսա. Եւ ես միայն մացի աստ. եւ ես տեսանեմ զամենայն մարդիկք. բայց այս Շ տարի է որ բնաւ չէ տեսեալ զիս մարդ։ / fol. 60r /
55. Իսկ Աբրահամ գերծեաց զհեր գլխոյ նորա. եւ հերթեաց զեղունկ նորա. լուաց եւ մաքրեաց գնա. եւ ապրշմով շուրջառով զարդարեաց գնա. եւ տարեալ ի տուն իւր պատարագ մատոյց հացիւ եւ գինեաւ եւ ճաշակեցին ընտանիքն եւ որդիքն՝ ճառայք եւ աղախնայք նորա ի նմանէ։ Եւ եղեւ նա քահանայ ի տունն Աբրահամու աստուածակոյս կողմանէ. Զի այս եղեւ առաջի քահանայ եւ առաջի պատարագող հացիւ եւ գինով. զի Մելքիսէդ եղեւ առաջին քահանայն որ օրինակ էր Քրիստոսի. Զի Ադամայ մինչեւ Աբրահամ քահանայ հրէշտակ էր. այլ մարմնաւոր քահանայ ոչ կար. Ադամայ եւ Աբելի Եւայի՝ եւ այլոցն իրիցութիւնն հրէշտակք արարին։
56. Եւ Աբրահամ բարեգործութեամբ մեծացաւ եւ ծերացաւ եւ

---

18. The singular verb is anomalous; it should be plural.
19. This is an alternative spelling of դժուար.
20. So we emend the text ետ "he gave."
21. *Inter lineas* զի.

15. SERMON CONCERNING HOSPITALITY 223

հանգեաւ խաղաղութեամբ ի հանգիստն արքայութեան մէջն։ որ զոք արքայութեան կոչեցաւ. եւ եթող Բ որդիս. զՍահակ ի Սառայէ որ աւետաւոր էր. եւ Իսմայէլ ի Յագարոյ որ / fol. 60v / ադախին ետ փարաւոն ի տեսութեանն Սառայի. եւ Իսահակայ ծնաւ այլվի Բ որդի. զՅեսոււ եւ զՅակոբ

57. եւ ոչ լիակատար գրեցաք զպատմութիւնս. զի օրինակն այս էր. ադայեմ զձեզ եղբարք յորժամ կարդայք եւ լսէք զպատմութիւնս զայս. լի սրտիւ ողորմի ասացէք Նազարին. եւ ծնողացն Ամիրին եւ Փաշին. եւ եղբարցն՝ Մէլէքին եւ Գասպարին. եւ ինձ անարժան Աւետ գծողիս եւ կարդացողաց եւ լսողաց։

An untitled text on Jacob follows.

SERMON CONCERNING HOSPITALITY

1. For when Noah died,[22] his sons and grandsons forgot God and served idols. Because books and laws did not exist at all,[23] they forgot God. There was not one man who remembered or discerned that God exists.

2. But Terah, Abraham's father, was an idolater and builder of idols. For, from the Flood up to Terah it was for 900 years[24] that they worshiped idols, and did not know God. Then on the idols' feast Terah said to his son Abraham, "Son, learn my (profession) of idol-building.[25] It will be very rewarding for you." Then Abraham said, "Father, if I had the authority in my hands (power), I would break them, for how can human works be god for humans?"

3. Abraham understood this, but he did not know God. He continually considered and investigated who is God.[26] And in that time, a punishment of birds came, of a multitude of black ravens which were gathering up the autumn seed and eating the green fields.[27] It had not ever been like this. Then every man chased off the birds and wished to protect his fields, and they were not able to save (them). Abraham went and wished to guard his fields.[28]

4. When he went and saw the innumerable multitude of birds, he wondered

---

22. Text no. 2.1 in an equivalent place, reads "After the Tower."
23. The idea of books and laws embodying God's will is unique to this text and text no. 11.1, 1A and 1B.
24. See text no. 12.2.
25. Terah as builder of idols is discussed in notes on texts nos. 8.1 and 11.2.
26. Abraham rejects idols before he recognizes God. This occurs otherwise in text no. 8 and its parallel in text no. 9. See also text no. 11.3 note.
27. Note that here the ravens attack fields and seed, not vineyards. See notes on text no. 4.2.
28. In other versions of the story (see note on text no. 4.2) Abraham is sent by his father. See also text no. 11.4 note.

and stared. He investigated in his mind and said, "Until this day there has never been (anything) like this. For there is a great God who does this." He stared at the sun and the moon, (considering) which one of these was God,[29] but his mind was not convinced to say God to them (i.e. to call them God), because they are changeable. Sometimes they wax and sometimes they wane; sometimes they become hot and sometimes they become cool. Therefore he was not persuaded to say God to them.[30]

5. And he called out aloud <to> the heavens above, and said, "HE WHO IS,[31] unknown God who are seated upon a throne of heaven and earth, Creator of moon and sun and all living animals, just as you sent these birds to uproot our labors, so have mercy and preserve our labors."[32]

6. When he said this all the birds went forth and fled. They no longer ate his seed and field. For Abraham looked and saw that the birds were eating everybody's labor and they did not approach his labor.[33] He praised and glorified God. Joyfully he went home and told the wonder to his father. Then his father said, "Son, this happened through the power of our idols, for our idols are many. Therefore, they do not eat our field."

7. And the father was not convinced to (his) son's counsel. Moreover, he commanded Abraham to go to the flock, to bring an ox and a bull[34] and to slaughter (them) as a sacrifice to the idols. Then Abraham took fire and going secretly to the temple[35] of the idols, he set a fire in it and burnt up the idols. And his father's brother[36] came in order to extinguish the fire, and he fell into the fire (and) was burned up with the idols. Then Abraham's father and all his family and relatives planned to kill Abraham.[37]

8. Then Abraham apprehending (this), took Sarah (his) wife and fleeing, he went to Egypt.[38] And they lauded Sarah's beauty before Pharaoh and Pharaoh brought (her)[39] and he saw her and he was pleased by Sarah. And he asked Abraham, "What might Sarah be to you?" And he said on account of

---

29. See texts nos. 2.3 and 8.4.

30. The resolution of the plague of birds is not given until §8, and the shift to the "astronomical" recognition of God is rather rough.

31. This is a name of God current in Armenian usage. It derives from Exod 3:14. Compare *NBHL* 1:758.

32. The word "labors" implies "fruit of our labors."

33. The singling out of Abraham's field is to be found also in text no. 11.6.

34. The difference of designation between the two words is not clear. Both are bovine animals.

35. Literally: "house."

36. Usually specified as Achan (Haran); see also text no. 11.7.

37. This element is unique to this document and text no. 11.7 among the Armenian texts. It is similar to *Jub.* 12:6–8, in which passage Terah is presented as an unwilling idolater.

38. The form of the story as given in other documents is abbreviated here.

39. That is, had her brought.

fear of being killed, "She is my sister." And Pharaoh wished to take Sarah in marriage.

9. And in the night, when he wished to draw near to Sarah, an angel of God appeared to him with a fiery staff and said, "Do not approach Sarah for she is Abraham's wife.[40] Moreover, also give him many things because you gazed upon Sarah's appearance. And, if you do not do thus, I will kill you and your sons with a fiery staff, and I will destroy your kingdom."[41]

10. Then the king due to fear of the angel—fear and trembling fell upon Pharaoh and he summoned Abraham and said, "When (if) Sarah was your wife, why did you say, 'She is my sister'?" Abraham said, "Because of that I said that she is my sister, lest you kill me for the sake of Sarah." But Pharaoh gave 40 servants and 40 maidservants to Sarah, 400 camels and many cattle and sheep, horses and mules, gold and silver.

11. He sent them off and said, "All this land of mine lies before you. Wherever you wish, dwell there." And Abraham having gone, (his) sheep, camels and all beasts and all possessions increased.[42] With a tent he wandered and pastured his beasts wherever he wished.

12. Then he kept 1,000 sheep close to the tent so as to eat milk and yoghurt and sour (probably a cultured milk product), so that they might be close to him.

13. And he had a shepherd named Mamrē.[43] He was particularly merciful in gifts to the poor and to guests. And one day, when he went out to pasture the sheep, they gave him little bread. They gave him and his dog[44] three loaves. Abraham said, "Take this bread and go, while the bread is being baked. I will come and bring you bread," for those 3 loaves were unleavened (i.e., had not risen).

14. When Mamrē went forth from the house and had gone a little distance, a poor man came and said, "For the love of God, give me to eat, for I am famished." Then Mamrē milked a sheep and crumbled one loaf. The poor man ate and blessed Mamrē and went. When one hour had passed a man came, beseeched and said," I am a traveler and famished. For the love of God, give me to eat."

15. Then Mamrē milked the sheep and crumbled a loaf and fed him. Then that man ate and blessed Mamrē and his sheep. He left and went. But Mamrē was still hungry. One loaf[45] remained; he wished to eat the bread, but he said to himself,[46] "Perhaps someone else will come and ask for bread for the love of God." Therefore, he did not eat. Then after midday he saw (that) an old man

---

40. In other texts Pharaoh is stopped by other means. See text no. 11.9 note.
41. Compare *Gen. Rab.* 40:7; 52.18, for an angel with a sword.
42. Compare texts nos. 2.7, 4.12, and 12.14; cf. Gen 13:2.
43. For the Story of Mamrē, see the General Introduction, 12–13. See also text no. 2.9.
44. The occurrence of the dog is unique here and this is another recension of text no. 11.12.
45. Literally: "bread."
46. Literally: "in his mind."

came, he beseeched and said, "I am famished. For the love of God, give me what you have to eat."
16. And Mamrē milked milk and crumbled the unleavened bread and gave to him to eat. Then he ate and blessed Mamrē, and Mamrē said, "Aged father, this day is hot and you are tired. Sleep a little, the heat will pass and then setting forth you will go. And when the old man fell asleep, he stuck his staff into the ground and he made shade over him so that the heat of the sun might not distress the old man. And when the old man awoke he saw that he had constructed a shelter over him. He called Mamrē and blessed Mamrē a second time saying thus, "Mamrē, you will be chief of the merciful and your black will become white. Your lack and your incompletion and that of your sons will be complete and filled.[47] And your name will be a good memory in the world. All your black sheep will become white."
17. He took Mamrē's oaken staff, which he had stuck and planted in the ground and said, "Son, this staff will be a sign between you and me." When he had blessed thus, the old man went forth and went. And Mamrē looked back and saw that the staff had greened and taken root. He regarded the old man once again, so that he might see (him) and receive yet a further blessing, but the old man was not visible.[48]
18. He looked at the sheep and saw that all of them had become white. And he looked upon his own hands and feet and the rest of his body and he saw that (it had become) white, for Mamrē was Abraham's black servant.
19. And again he looked at the staff and saw that the staff had become a great tree and a spring of cold water welled up at the base of the tree. Then all the sheep came, drank from the water and settled[49] under the shade of the tree.
20. Then, at the 8th hour of the day, (Abraham) having taken bread and having set forth, brought (it) to Mamrē. He looked and saw in the field that a tree was visible. Abraham was amazed and said, "This tree was not there until today. Whence did this tree come into being?" Sometimes he went and sometimes he stood still, investigated; and he cleaned[50] his eyes, looked and wondered.[51]
21. And going on he reached the tree. And having seen all the whitened sheep and Mamrē's face white, he did not recognize (him). He asked and said, "O, shepherd! Where might Abraham's sheep be?" And Mamrē the shepherd greeted Abraham and said, "My father, come and see God's power[52] and miracles." When Abraham came, he saw the tree, the sheep and Mamrē

---

47. The language of this blessing is not paralleled in the other narratives except text no. 11.
48. Does this mean he disappeared? If so, this would be typical of an angelophany.
49. Literally: "sat."
50. Or: "rubbed."
51. The way Abraham recognized Mamrē is unlike the other versions of this story.
52. Or: "wonder."

15. SERMON CONCERNING HOSPITALITY

whitened. He was amazed on account of the miracle. He asked, "How did the miracle come about?"

22. Then Mamrē told him everything and said, "My father, today 3 paupers encountered me and I fed them. But the last was an honorable and handsome old man and him also I fed. And he blessed me and our sheep greatly and variously. And he took my staff and stuck it into this place. At once it took root, greened and became this tree and this spring welled up with it." Then Abraham fell down, kissed his servant's hand and foot and said, "You are my father and I (am) your servant."

23. There Abraham swore to God,[53] "As long as I live, until a guest does not happen by, I will not break bread." Mamrē was the cause of Abraham's hospitality and love of the poor. When Abraham saw all these miracles he swore an oath with God, not to eat without a guest.

24. And he brought his tent and set it up under the oak tree and dwelt there by the way, so that passersby might eat of his table and then go on. For he never removed the table of food (bread). If on one day Abraham encountered forty guests, he ate with them all because of his hospitality.

25. If he encountered (one) in 7 days, he fasted for 7 days. If there was one guest in 10 days, he did not eat for 10 days. He did this often, so that he did not eat without a guest. When Satan saw such benefaction and hospitality of Abraham, he was jealous of him and guarded all the ways that were about him.

26. Whoever came he turned back and showed him (and) caused (him to go)[54] another way. And he ensorcelled that way,[55] so that for 40 days no guest happened by Abraham. Then Abraham was weakened. Sarah said, "You, husband Abraham, have become starved to death. Eat a little."

27. Abraham said, "As the Lord lives, I will not eat until a guest comes. I cannot be false to God, but I hope in God that today he will send me a guest." And there Abraham had built a high place, so that Sarah used to go up and sit there; she looked at the ways for a guest.

28. And when Abraham was greatly weakened, Abraham said, "Sarah, go up and look." And when Sarah, having gone up, looked, she saw 3 persons[56] who were in the distance. Sarah gave news to Abraham and said, "My lord, three guests have come to us." Then Abraham commanded to slaughter the calf for the guests, for an honorable calf had been born. It bore likeness to Abel's lamb. He caused that calf to be slaughtered.[57]

29. Then they saw that the Lord came with two angels, but Abraham did not

---

53. See note on text no. 3.11 concerning this story and see also text no. 11A.23.
54. The phrase "showed him (and) caused (him to go)" is perhaps a scribal error for gnjg ունայր "showed" (Th. M. van Lint).
55. This magical term occurs in this context in text no. 2.12.
56. Literally, "souls"; "person" is a common later usage.
57. See text no. 6.5.3 and note there.

discern that he was the Lord. Then he was strengthened in seeing him. And having gone forth to meet them paying respects and having (brought) them, they sat down and (he) having brought a meal,[58] they ate. They spoke with one another, and Abraham listened to their words and he heard much wondrous speech and he was amazed. Then the Lord said, "Gather the bones of the calf." And when they had gathered (them) and filled the hide of the calf, then having signed the cross, he revived the calf.[59] And Abraham, being amazed, was unable to talk in the postprandial (talk). When He blessed the meal (table) and Abraham, the Lord said, "Abraham! I will surely bless you and increase your seed like the stars of the heaven and like the sand of (the) sea."

30. And after much blessing, again he said, "You will have seed from Sarah. His name will be called Sahak." When Sarah heard inside (her) hiding place, she laughed and said, "When will this happen to me, for my days have passed?" And the Lord said to Abraham, "Sarah mocked because of the good news (the Annunciation) of Isaac, for she reckoned my words to be false. On account of that laughing at me, your family will remain in exile for 460 years in the power of strangers."[60]

31. He said this and he blessed the house and the meal and all Abraham's possessions. And the Lord said again to Abraham, "Abraham, come forth with me as far as Mount Sodom." And from fear Abraham could not ask, "Who are you, Lord?" When they reached the mountain where Sodom was visible, God commanded his two angels, "Go, enter this city and bring out Lot, for he is righteous and hospitable.

32. And say that he should go forth from Sodom. And let him not turn around to look back again, for he who looks back turns into stone." When He said this, he (Abraham) realized that He is the Lord. Abraham said, "What do you wish to do to this city?"

33. The Lord said, "I wish to destroy it, for their sins have multiplied." Abraham said, "Lord, might this city not have 1,000 sinless men?" The Lord said, "If there be 500 righteous ones, I will not destroy them for the sake of the righteous." Abraham said, "If there be 200, will you not pity (the city)?" The Lord said, "If there be 100 righteous ones, I would not wish for their death."[61] Abraham said, "Lord, if there be 50 righteous, will you not have pity for their sake?" The Lord said, "If 20 righteous be found, I will have pity upon them."

34. Abraham said, "Lord, since I am dust and ashes, how can I speak again with

---

58. Or: "table."

59. See above text no. 8.25 and 8.29 and see the General Introduction, on Step'anos Siwnec'i, 20–21 above.

60. Cf. Gen 15:13, but in a different context; see text no. 8.28, which has 440 years and text no. 11A.29 note.

61. The numbers of righteous in this section are not in the biblical story. Those commence in the continuation of this section.

15. SERMON CONCERNING HOSPITALITY

you? But, if[62] you made (me) worthy of speaking with you, for the sake of the 10 righteous ones, have pity!"

35. Then the Lord ascended to the heavens and a voice was heard which said, "Since[63] a righteous one was not found in the city, you, Abraham, remain in this place and see that done to them." When those 2 angels who went to the city gave an appearance of 15 years old youths.

36. Indeed, Lot was hospitable and God-loving. When he saw them, having paid his respects, he brought them to his house. When they went to his house the angels said, "Go forth from this city, for the Lord wishes to destroy it and He sent us to lead you out." Lot said, "Sit down, recline at table, dine and we will see what you command." Since a man discerned them,

37. he (i.e., Lot) blamed them and said, "O, sons, you are tender youths. Why did you come and enter this evildoing and abomination-doing city?" The angels said, "We came here on your account so that we might bring you forth from this city." But Lot's wife did not believe their discourse.

38. She (or: he) went and opened the stove to get out food for the guests, and she (or: he) saw the stove full of water. When Lot saw the coming forth of the water he believed in the passing of the city.[64] Then the Sodomites came and seized Lot's door and said, "Give us those who have come to this house of yours."

39. But Lot had closed the door from within on account of their wickedness. Lot said, "I have two beautiful virgin daughters. I will give (them) to you, and do not lay hand upon my guests." And they were not persuaded. They began to break the door down. Then the angels said to Lot, "Do not worry about us. We can save ourselves. At this hour go forth from your house, for now this city is perishing."

40. And when they broke the door down, the angels went forth and blinded them, and themselves ascended (i.e., on high). Then Lot went forth from the city, he, his wife and his 2 daughters. For his wife had sent somebody on account of (her) sons-in-law, to apprise them of the passing of the city.[65] When they went, they reached the lower part of the mountain, then Lot's wife looked back because of the sons-in-law. At once she turned into stone,

41. for the angel had said, "Do not look back!" He said, "Those who look back turn into stone."[66] When Lot went forth, fire burnt around Sodom, like a wall

---

62. Here ḥpp functions with the meaning of ḥpṭ, and also in the next clause. Literally it means "when".

63. Literally: "when."

64. Just how this sign convinced Lot remains somewhat unclear.

65. The sons-in-law doubted the angels' prediction; see Gen 19:14.

66. In the Bible (Gen 19:26), Lot's wife looks back and is turned into a pillar of salt. In the angelic prohibition in Gen 19:17 no specific punishment for looking back is mentioned. Petrification as a punishment is not mentioned there, but it is in other Abraham texts; see texts nos. 11.39–40 and 11A.41.

of fire and sulphur. Rock and hail rained down together from the heavens for 7 days and 7 nights. Thus it rained upon them, until the ground and stone was burnt and water filled the place and turned it into a sea. And it is (exists) until today.

42. And Abraham having seen all this, gave glory to God and glorified the Lord, who is that human-loving God, for Lot was a lover of the poor and the stranger, and hospitable, to such an extent that He brought Lot forth and then made the city pass away.

43. I beg you, O brothers, make Mamrē an example and see (him) who through bread brought God to his sheep. He was rendered worthy through the blessing and kingdom of God, and Abraham who by faith, by fast, by prayer and by table hospitality caused God to descend from heaven to his house and caused him to recline at his table. He ate and he spoke with God. And he received the good news (the Annunciation) of Isaac, and he received God's blessing, with which He blessed Abraham and said, "I will surely bless you and I will surely increase (your) seed."[67] Having seen this, hope to do mercy to the poor and hospitality to strangers. And if you wish to enter the kingdom, be hospitable and set a table, for priests and paupers bless a man at bread and meal, princes and householders laud, and all men praise. And it (i.e., hospitality) saves from many punishments and from evil. And there, on the day of judgment Christ himself blesses and praises and deletes the book of sins.[68] And he is crowned with the righteous and is praised by the mouth of all angels and enters into the Garden of God with Abraham and with all God's other saints. I beseech, attend to this counsel, take it to mind and observe (it) and say "Have mercy" for the commissioner of this book, Nazar and his parents, Amir and Pʻaš, and (his) brothers Mēlikʻ and Gaspar, and for me, sinful Awēt, the scribe. And Rev. Nersēs the polisher of its paper, who with great desire served it, and our spiritual father Rev. Gaspar, who were the causes of it (i.e., were instrumental in making this book) and sharers of pain of the inner man and they encouraged (i.e., me). They caused this book to be written and we ask from you, O holy fathers and readers, when you read this small booklet, remember me, great sinner, and say "God have mercy."

Concerning the Birth of Sahak

44. When Abraham drew near to Sarah, she conceived and bore Sahak. Since he was very beautiful and honorable and beloved of (his) parents, (his) parents loved him so that all night they did not extinguish a candle,[69] for the sake of

---

67. Gen 22:17.
68. Col 2:14.
69. See also text no. 11.43.

the visibility of Sahak. When he grew and developed, He sent his angel[70] and said to Abraham to slaughter his son as an offering and a sacrifice to God.

45. God tested <him>,[71] so that he might see whether Abraham would make his beloved son a sacrifice, or not. When Abraham heard (this) from the angel, he saddled his ass and having taken fire and wood[72] and his son Sahak, he went to the place of the covenant.[73] Sahak asked his father and said, "Father, here (is) fire, here (is) a knife and wood. Where is the sacrifice?"[74]

46. Abraham said, "Son, God is preparing a sacrifice for us,"[75] for Abraham said this so that he might deceive his son, but (his) mouth was prophesying. When he went (and) arrived at the place of the covenant, where the slaughter was going to take place, Sahak said to his father, "Father, where is the sacrifice?" (His) father said, weeping, "Son, you are the sacrifice. God gave you to us (i.e., shared you with us) and I promised God that I will make you his sacrifice. Son, do not give the lie to my promise.[76] Obey, so I may slaughter you."[77] Sahak said, "My father, it is your will. I am your obedient servant. I will not give the lie to your oath for this transient world. But, tie my hands and feet firmly, lest I draw back hands or feet and your sacrifice shall be unpleasing."[78] Then Abraham bound Sahak's hands and feet.[79] And Sahak said, "Father, do this work of yours righteously (properly) and say to my mother that she should make for me her milk and her work righteous."[80] And (his) father took the knife and he cut Sahak's throat. And the knife did not enter and did not cut, and a little blood came out of the neck.[81] And when he wished to sharpen the knife upon the stone, at once it cut the rock like boneless meat.[82] Then the angel calling said, "Do not plunge your knife into this youth, for your sacrifice was pleasing to God. For God has sent you a

---

70. In the Bible, it is God who gives the command.
71. The association of testing with Abraham here derives from Gen 22:1.
72. In Gen 22:6, the fire and wood are introduced only at a later point in the story.
73. Gen 22:9 describes this as "the place that God had shown him". The name "place of the covenant" here may come from an identification of Moriah in Gen 22:2 with the Temple Mount based on 2 Chr 3:1.
74. Gen 22:7.
75. Gen 22:8.
76. This promise or covenant is not mentioned in the Bible or in the preceding narrative. Some Islamic sources know an oath that Abraham made to God relating to his son; see Firestone 1990, 108.
77. Cf. Gen 22:7-8. In the biblical story Abraham avoids telling Isaac the truth.
78. See above text no. 8:32.
79. Gen 22:9.
80. This last phrase is unclear as it stands, but it means that Sarah's care of him served a fitting end.
81. Note the miracle here. The knife would not cut Sahak's neck.
82. This detail is not found in the other Abraham stories.

sacrifice instead of Isaac." When Abraham looked up, he saw a sacrificial ram hanging from the tree[83] by the horns.[84]

47. And Abraham, having taken (it) brought the ram down and set Sahak free, and having slaughtered the ram, he offered the offering. And when he bent (his) knee, there was a voice from the heavens that said, "Abraham, Abraham. Just as you did not pity your beloved son for my sake, in the same way I too will not pity my beloved Son for your sake, who, having come, will free all the children of Adam from Hell because of your goodness."[85] Then Abraham joyously having taken (his) son, returned to his house. And one day while Abraham was praying in the tent, an angel of God descended to him and said, "Abraham, Abraham! God commanded you to go to Jerusalem and there you will find Melchizedek, God's servant. Dress his head and clip his nails straight and bring (him) to your house and honor him. And he will offer a sacrifice for you with wine and bread."[86]

48. He (will be) a priest for you from the godly side, for your sake and all your family he will perform priestly actions. Abraham said, "Where do I find him?" The angel said, "You (will) find him in the forest." When Abraham went to Jerusalem, he looked toward the forest. In the night he saw the column of light in the forest. Abraham realized that he was there. When day broke, he went forth, he went to the place, he found him. When Abraham saw Melchizedek, (he saw) that his appearance was not like a human appearance,

49. but he was attired and the hair of his head came down to (his) knee. And his back was like a tortoise's back[87] and his nails had become a span long and Abraham, greeting him, spoke with him and said, "How long is it that you have remained here?" Melchizedek (Melk'ised) said, "It is 8 years that I am in ascesis here, unseen by men. No other man has seen me but you." Abraham said, "Tell me how your believing came about." Melchizedek (Melk'ised) said, "I am son of king Melk'i, son of Salim, who built the city of Jerusalem.[88] One day my father sent me, 'Go to the flock and bring honorable and fat heifers and oxen, for I will offer sacrifices to my idols.'

50. And I went to the flock and I set apart fat heifers and oxen. And God shone the light of grace in my heart. I considered[89] and I was not persuaded to kill

---

83. The name of the tree, "Tree of Sabek," is not mentioned here or in 11.45. See text no. 4.22 note.

84. Gen 22:11–13.

85. Compare Irenaeus, *Adv. haer.* 4.5.5.

86. Here the series of sacrifices is spelled out. Abraham offers his son, God offers His, and Melchizedek offers the first eucharistic sacrifice (which is proleptic). For notes on this text, see the relevant sections of text no. 11.

87. Compare Adam's covering, smooth as fingernail in *Gen. Rab.*20:21. See also 11.48.

88. In *Cave of Treasures* (Budge 1927, 152) Melchizedek is associated with the building of Jerusalem, but in a quite different narrative.

89. That is, "investigated, thought about it." The language here is very like that in the

15. SERMON CONCERNING HOSPITALITY

animals for the sake of unliving non-gods. And turning back, I returned the animals and I left and went. And as I went, I regarded the heavens, I examined in my mind the luminaries and all the creations of the Creator.[90] And by God's grace, I recognized God, the Creator. And I went to my father without the sacrifice.

51. My father asked me and said, 'Where are your heifers and oxen?' And I said, 'My father, it seems difficult to me to offer a living animal as a sacrifice for the sake of unmoving things, made by human hands, which are not gods, but false non-gods. For that reason, I did not bring (them).' And my father bore a grudge against me and entered my house. He said to my mother, 'Today I am offering one of these two sons as a sacrifice to my idols.' And my mother knew that my father bore a grudge against me. My mother wept, lamented and scratched her face. She tore her hair[91] and said, 'What is this thing that you say?'

52. For my mother loved me, and my father loved my brother. Then my father, when he <saw> my mother's mourning, who was weeping bitterly, my father said to my mother, 'Why do you weep? For let us cast lots for our two sons. He on whom the lot falls, him shall we slaughter.'

53. When my father cast a lot, thus he reckoned that the lot would fall upon me to die for the sake of the idols. Again, three times they cast the lot. The lot fell on my brother to die for the idols. When my father went forth and, having taken my brother, so that he might bring him bound as a sacrifice to the idols, then my mother was weeping and saying, "Will you not have mercy on your brother?" And she went weeping for she would see the end of her son. When the king's princes and nobles heard, they brought their sons and daughters as a sacrifice to idols.

54. And I, weeping on account of my brother, fled. I came and went forth to this forest. When I saw that they laid hand for sacrifice of my brother, I besought of the Lord that the gates of the abyss open and swallow them. Immediately, the place was split and swallowed them with the temple and with the idols, my father and mother and all the people with them. And I alone remained here and I see all men but for these 8 years no man has seen me at all."

55. Then Abraham trimmed the hair of his head and clipped his nail(s). He washed and cleaned him and he ornamented (him) with a silk chasuble and he brought (him) to his house. He offered a sacrifice of bread and wine, and the family and children ate of it, his servants and maidservants. And he became a priest in Abraham's house from the divine side. For this one became a first priest and first offerer with bread and wine. For Melchizedek

---

variant text no. 11A.49, including also the verb հաւանէցի. This is similar to the story about Abraham's refusal to bring beasts for idolatrous sacrifice, which may have formed the basis of this incident in the Story of Melchizedek.

90. Observe the evocation of the story of Abraham's astronomical discovery of God.

91. Literally, "head."

(Melk'ised) became the first priest who was a type of Christ. For from Adam to Abraham the priest was an angel,[92] but there was no corporeal priest. For Adam and Abel, Eve and the others angels did priestly service.

56. And Abraham increased in doing good and grew old and lay peacefully in rest, in the kingdom, which was called the bosom of the kingdom. And he left two sons, Sahak from Sarah, who was bearer of the tidings, and Ishmael from Hagar the handmaiden whom Pharaoh gave when he saw Sarah. And Isaac begot another 2 sons, Esau and Jacob.[93]

57. And we have not written the story fully, for this was the examplar.[94] I beseech you brothers, when you read and hear these stories, say, "Have mercy" with full heart for Nazar and (his) parents Amir and P'aš, and (his) brothers, Mēlik' and Gaspar and for me the unworthy Awēt the scribe and for the readers and hearers.

---

92. Compare the list of antediluvian priests, including Melchizedek, in *Synagogal Prayers* 9:10; compare *2 En.* 69–71 (*OTP*) and *Cave of Treasures* (Bezold 1883, 11–13). In these cases the patriarchs of each generation were the priests.

93. Both forms of the name Isaac are used.

94. That is, as much as we have written was in the examplar.

Appendix 1

Other Abraham Works and Fragments

There are a number of other documents relating to Abraham mentioned in manuscript catalogues and in other source works, that were not included among the preceding texts, either because they were not available to me or because they did not contain primarily narrative content. In the perspective of the present book, this Appendix contains information on works that, though associated with Abraham, do not signally enrich our knowledge of the Abraham saga. Here I also mention further copies of works that are edited above, but which I have not been able to collate or whose collation seems unlikely to add to the relevant data in a significant way.[1] Those writings that I have examined are described briefly below, their character is set forth, and where appropriate, samples of texts or sample collations are given. Under this head I also list works I have encountered in manuscript catalogues but have not been able to autopsy. I do not aspire to make these listings exhaustive.

M1425 H. Anasyan mentions a work called Սակս Աբրահամու "Concerning Abraham".[2] It occurs on fols. 204r–211r of M1425, a Miscellany copied in Ejmiacin in 1690. Samples of the text follow.

սակս Աբրահամու
Լուայք առաքելական ընթերցուածոյն զԱբրահամէ պատմութեան սակաւուք ճառեալս. յորս ասեն: Բայց Աբրահամու խոստացեալ աստուծոյ զի ոչ յոք ունէր ի մեծագոյն երդնուլ յինքն երդուաւ ասելով զոր ինչ ասացն: Եւ արդ՝ զի ի դեպ է անզիտելի բազմաց պատմութեան իրք. սակաւուք ձեզ տանի զաբրահամ յլնտանեզոյն ազգակցութենէն եւ ի տեղացն հրամանաւ Աստուծոյ. եւ էր յատար երկրի հայրապետն ժուժկալեալ յուսով խոտրմանն:[3]

---

1. When I had access to the manuscripts, I collated samples against the text published above. This is noted in the introductions to the various documents.
2. Anasyan 1959, 138 no. 3, found on fols. 204r–211r.
3. Apparently corrupt. խոտրումն means "depravity." Presumably some form of a word meaning "promise" խոստան- would be appropriate.

Listen to the apostolic reading of a story about Abraham, a few things related, in which they say: But Abraham, having promised to God, for he had no-one greater to whom to swear, he swore to the same, saying that which he said.[4] And now, since some of the things (details) of the story are incomprehensible to many, for you it (i.e., Scripture) adduces that Abraham went forth from the place of the most familial relationship at God's command, and the patriarch was suffering in a foreign land by the hope of the promise.

fol 211r *Explicit* / Քանզի այս էր մեզ առաջի կացուցանել զառաքեալ վկայելով բանս երէ մեծ քան գործի հայր ոչ է. զի աստանաւր հրեշտակ կարգելով զիրք բանի Աստուծոյ ի վերայ աճէ ձայնն: վասն զի ձայնեաց(ես) զնա հրեշտակն Տեառն եւ ասաց. յաղագս որոյ արարեր զբանդ զայդ եւ ոչ խնայեցեր զորդիդ քո միածին. յանձն իմ երդուայ առնել որ ինչ յաւետիսն է ուսանել. ասէ. արդ ո՞ է որ կոչեացն զԱբրաամ մի արդեւք հայր. այլ ոչ եւս ասեմ հրեշտակ ուրուք լիեալ զհայր: ապա յուրումն միածինն Աստուած. յաղագս որոյ ասէ մարգարէն. կոչի անուն նորա մեծաց խորհրդոյ հրեշտակ:
այսքան գրեցի եւ վճարեցի:

Because he was the first apostle established for us, witnessing this matter, that a father is not greater than his son. For here an angel ordering a book of God's word raises up his voice. Because the angel of the Lord called him and said, "On account of this thing that you did and you did not spare your only-begotten son, I swore to myself to do what is to be learned in the Gospels." He said, "Now, who is it that called Abraham, was it not a father? but I no longer say that some angel is the father, (but) then (it was) the only-begotten God, on whose account the prophet says, 'His name is called angel of the secret of the great ones.'"
I have written thus far and I have finished.

M10561 This manuscript contains excerpts of text no. 8 and the text of the Abraham entry in the *Synaxarium* (text no. 14). It is a Miscellany of the seventeenth century, described briefly in Malxasyan 2007.[5]

1. Պատմութիւն հօրն Աբրահամու: Աբրահամու հօրն Թարայ էր "Story of Father Abraham. Abraham's father was Terah." This starts on fol. 133v and continues to the text corresponding to the end of section 6 of text no. 8.

---

4. Or perhaps: "it [i.e., Scripture] said."
5. Malxasyan 2007, 3:115–18.

APPENDIX 1: OTHER ABRAHAM WORKS AND FRAGMENTS 237

2. On fol. 134v we find Պատմութիւն Սահակայ որդոյ Աբրահամու զոր խոստացեալ էր Աստուծոյ մատաղ առնել "Story of Sahak, son of Abraham, whom he promised to make an offering to God," which corresponds to text no. 8.31–32.

3. The text of the Abraham entry in the *Yaysmaurk'* or *Synaxarium* occurs on fols. 98v–100v of this manuscript; compare text no. 14.

4. Some years ago, I copied a fragment of a variant of the *Synaxarium* text from a Matenadaran manuscript. My notes attribute it to M640, 467 col. i, but in the catalogue of the Matenadaran, M640 does not have 467 pages or folios, nor does it, apparently, contain any Abraham text. I transcribe here the information I have, in the hope that in the future it may be possible to identify this text more precisely. It is attributed to a *Commentary on Genesis*.

Title: Բան շահաւէտ. եւ աղտակար ի մեկնութենէ արարածոց ասացեալ:

A profitable and helpful discourse pronounced from a commentary on Genesis.

Incipit: Աբրահամ եալ ժԵ ամաց. եւ գտաւ զԱստուած այսու պատճառաւ՝ Աշխարհն բաբելացւոց պարարտ էր, եւ մարդիկքն յոիացեալ պարպէին զազիր գործոց ...

Abraham being 15 years old, and he found God for this reason. The land of the Babylonians was rich and men being very wealthy, were occupied with obscene deeds . . .

Compare text no. 14.1–2.

M4618 The script of this manuscript is extremely small and was illegible in the photographs at my disposal. I was able to autopsy it in the Matenadaran in October 2010 and on fols. 53v–55r it contains another copy of text no. 2 Պատմութիւն վասն Աբրահամու *Story Concerning Abraham*, in a form very close to that in M8351 (see text no. 2, above),[6] on which the text published above is based. I collated the beginning, a section from the middle and the last section (with some difficulties of decipherment) and I give below the variants that were apparent. The manuscript is a Miscellany in various hands, dating between 1569 and 1714. It contains many patristic texts as well as apocryphal works, including *Assumption of the Virgin*, the *Cycle of Four Works*, and others.[7]

---

6. This is true except for the colophon of the text.

7. Ēganyan et al. 1965, 1:1247–48. The *Cycle of Four Works* is the Armenian Adam cycle described in Stone 1992, 101–4 and published by Lipscomb 1990.

Collation of Selected Sections:

1 եհան] եհաս – a better reading
3 որ1°] որք
զմոլորութիւն] զմոլորութիւնն
14 զԱ] զայն
աբրահամ] + եւ
մամրէ] մամբրէ
21 այզի] + ամէն ինչ
ի գետի] գետի

Another fragment from this manuscript is in a second hand. It is probably a filler. It deals with Abraham, and I transcribe and translate it below. Following the segment of text that I copied, the fragment continues with certain details of John the Baptist's birthplace and certain other incidents. All these are dealt in brief compass, since the fragment altogether covers about one third of a page.

Թարա հայրն Աբրահամու՝ կուռք կու շինէր. եւ Աբրահամ ծախ էր եւ օր մի տարաւ ի շուկայն իշարբեր մի կուռք։ եւ յանկարծակի անկաւ էշն ի շամուռն.[8] եւ կուռքն ամենայն չարդեցան։ Եւ Աբրահամ փախեաւ ի հօրէն.

Terah, Abraham's father, built idols. And Abraham was [ ][9] and one day he brought idols loaded on a donkey to the market. And suddenly the donkey fell in the mud and all the idols were broken. And Abraham fled from his father.

M10720 In this eighteenth-century Miscellany[10] there occurs an anonymous elenchic text that includes one little fragment of Abraham material (fol. 194v), followed by a passage on the New Testament. This reads as follows:

Հարց։ Յաբրահամէ մինչեւ ի Մովսէս քանի ազգ է։
Պատասխանի։ է ազգ է այսպէս. Աբրահամ. Իսահակ. Յակոբ. Ղեւի. Կահաթ. Ամրամ. Մովսէս.
Հայրն Մովսէսի Ամրամ է. եւ մայրն Յոքաբեթբ

Question: From Abraham up to Moses, how many generations were there?
Answer: There were 7 generations as follows: Abraham, Isaac, Jacob, Levi, Kohath, Amram, Moses.
Moses' father is Amram and (his) mother Jochebed.[11]

---

8. A dialect word, meaning "mud" (G. Muradyan), deriving from Turkish but which occurs also in Middle Armenian.

9. This is an obscure word, not appearing in the chief dictionaries.

10. Malxasyan 2007, 3:175–77.

11. The Armenian is corrupt, reading "Yokʻatʻetʻ" by a common graphic error.

APPENDIX 1: OTHER ABRAHAM WORKS AND FRAGMENTS

M6514 This is a Miscellany dated 1830–1862 written in a cursive script on blue paper.[12] On fols. 162–165v this manuscript contains a copy of a discussion of Melchizedek taken from Գիրք Հարցմանց *The Book of Questions* of Grigor Tatʻewacʻi (ca. 1344–1409). Grigor's learned text combines various traditions both Armenian and Western.[13] I give here a transcription and translation of the first of these sections as printed in the *Book of Questions*, p. 300. M6514 does not seem superior to it in these sections. Following this passage are two more pages of a discussion of Melchizedek, showing the same learned combination of traditions as may be observed in the passage given here.[14]

Վասն Մելքիսեդեկի հարցումն։ Ուստի՞ է Մելքիսեդեկ։
Պատասխան. Հօրն անունն Մելքի, եւ մօրն Սաղա. եւ քաղաքին Սաղիմ։ Ի մանկութենէ կռոց նուիրեցաւ, եւ հրեշտակ Աստուծոյ յափշտակեալ սնցոյց զնա յանապատի մինչեւ հասոյց ի կատարումն։
Ապա ի Թաբոր լերինն ամպ խոնարհեալ եւ ձեռն կարկառեալ ձեռնադրեաց զնա ասելով, այս Մելքիսետեկ անհայր անմայր չհամարեալ յազգս՝ նմանեալ որդւոյն Աստուծոյ։
Զի տղայ մանուկ երթեալ ոչ ոք գիտէր զնա. եւ ոչ նա զոք ճանաչէր զի քանանացի էր եւ աննման վարուց նոցա։ Բնակէր ի ներքոյ գողգոթային ուր ադամայ գերեզմանն էր։ Իւր ձեռօք ցանէր եւ որթ վաստակէր իւր բաւական։
Ուր եկեալ Աբրահամ, եւ նա էլ ընդ առաջ նորա ջերմ բաղարջ հացով եւ գինեաւ օրհնակ տերունեան խորհրդոյն։
Եւ անդ օրհնեալ զԱբրահամ, եւ տասանորդ էառ յաւարէ անտի։

Question Concerning Melchizedek: Whence is Melchizedek?
Answer: His father's name was Melkʻi and his mother's Saɫa, and the city's Saɫim. From (his) youth he was devoted to idols and an angel of God snatched (him) away, nurtured him in the forest until he reached the fulfillment.
Then, on Mount Tabor,[15] a cloud descended and having stretched forth an arm ordained him saying. "This Melchizedek, without father, without mother, was not reckoned to this people,[16] being like the Son of God."
For, since he went as a child, no one knew him, and he did not recognize anyone for he was a Canaanite and was unlike their customs. He lived inside Golgotha, where Adam's tomb was. With his hands he sowed and cultivated a vine (which was) enough for him.

---

12. Ēganyan et al. 2:335–36.
13. Compare the discussion of these issues in Stone 2009b.
14. This Melchizedek material is worthy of separate attention, in the context of Grigor's work and its compilatory character.
15. This is the only place in the texts we have examined that situates Melchizedek on Mount Tabor, which is his usual location in the Greek tradition.
16. See Heb 7:3.

When Abraham came there, and he went forth to meet him with warm, unleavened bread and wine like[17] the Dominical Sacrament.
And there he blessed Abraham and took a tithe of the booty.

---

17. Or: "in a pattern of."

Appendix 2

Further Abraham Notes: Literary and Iconographic

It is of interest to mention a number of sources down to and including the tenth century, which include Abrahamic traditions specifically linked to those in the sources we publish here. These have been accessed through the Indexes of *MH* down to the tenth century. Above, in the General Introduction, the chief implications of these sources for dating have been drawn out (see pp. 16–18). Here we add some further details to that information, not including the Genesis commentaries of Ełišē and Stepʻanos Siwnecʻi.

1. Abraham's hospitality is an early and widespread tradition, not distinctive enough to be used for dating. So Anania Catholicos (900?–965) refers to it (*MH* 10th century, 255 col. i), noting that God sat with Abraham (§§297–98) while Isaac is taken as an example of Christ's passion (ibid.). A different view of the Three Men is exhibited by Anania Narekacʻi (910?–985?), who regarded them as the Trinity. Both views of the Three Men are not unique, and these interpretations, like viewing the sacrifice of Isaac as a foreshadowing of Christ's passion, are far from distinctive, although they appear in our texts.
2. Anania (*MH* 10th century, 450) also calls circumcision on the eighth day "a seal," an old Jewish usage reflected, e.g., in Rom 4:11. He stresses Abraham's faith, also an old, biblical theme (ibid., 509).
3. As we noted above, the issue of Christ's truly (ճշմարտապէս) eating the calf is a source of worry to our stories. Anania (p. 528) cites Chrysostom about Christ really ճշմարտապէս eating: compare also p. 545, col. ii. This issue becomes associated with aspects of the incarnation.
4. Samuel Kamrǰajorecʻi (940?–1010) says որպէս երեւեցաւ Աբրահամու իբրեւ զմարդ երկու հրեշտակաւք առ կաղնեաւ Մամբրէի, եւ ի խորանի նորա կերակրեցաւ. "just as He appeared to Abraham as a man with two angels by the oak of Mamrē and he ate in his tent"; cf. p. 736 on the same subject. This coincides with Anania Catholicos, cited above.
5. On p. 740 Samuel mentions the Annunciation to Abraham, parallel to that to the Virgin. This is a common tradition also reflected in art (see below). More distinctive in his statement that Խ տիւ եւ Խ գիշեր պահեաց Աբրահամ, զի որպէս եղ անձին իւրոյ՝ ոչ ճաշակել առանց հիւրոյ. զի ողորմած էր. "for 40 days and 40 nights Abraham fasted, as he had taken upon himself not to eat without a guest, for he was compassionate" (see p. 742). This feature

parallels the Story of Mamrē and is the most distinctive found outside the Step'anos Siwnec'i's *Commentary on Genesis.*

6. Grigor Narekac'i (951–1003), Մատեան ողբերգութեան *Book of Lamentations*, ed. P.M. Xač'atryan and A.A. Łazinyan (Erevan: Academy of Sciences, 1985), 622 (ՂԳ, Ե: (93.5) apparently shows some familiarity with the Melchizedek material,

Ո՞չ ապա Մելքիսեդեկ յարինակ ճշմարտիդ ահաւորութեան ի Չիթաստանեաց լերինն, ուր յետոյ ոտք մարմնացելոյդ աստուծոյ գետեղեալ կացին, ի վերնոց անտի հրեշտակաց ի պտղոց տեղույն իւղեցաւ. ուստի շիրմի սկզբնահաւրն պաշտպան եպիսկոպոսական արքայապատիւ ճոխութեամբ ի քէն հանդերձեալ նստաւ...

Was not Melchisedek anointed as a type of your true fearsomeness on the Mount of Olives where afterwards the feet of God incarnate stood, by the celestial angels in the place of fruits (i.e., olives), where by the power put on You from the grave of forefather, protector through episcopal royal power, he sat...

Bibliography

Abełean, Manuk
1955　Հայ հին մատենագրութեան պատմութիւն *History of Ancient Armenian Literature.* 2 vols. Beirut: Sevan Press.
Ačaṙyan, Hṙč'ea
1972　Հայոց անձնանունների բառարան *Dictionary of Armenian Proper Names.* 5 vols. Beirut: Sevan Press.
Adler, William
2008　"Jewish Pseudepigrapha in Jacob of Edessa's Letters and Historical Writings." Pages 49–65 in *Jacob of Edessa and the Syriac Culture of His Day.* Edited by Bas ter Haar Romeny. Monographs of the Peshitta Institute, 18. Leiden/Boston: Brill.
Adler, William, and Paul Tuffin
2002　*The Chronography of George Synkellos.* Oxford: Oxford University Press.
Anasyan, Hakob S.
1959　Հայկական մատենագիտութիւն (Ե-ԺԸ դդ.) *Armenian Bibliology, 5–18th Centuries.* Vol. 1. Erevan: Academy of Sciences.
Assfalg, J., and J. Molitor
1962　*Armenische Handschriften.* Verzeichnis der orientalischen Handschriften in Deutschland 4. Wiesbaden: F. Steiner.
Auerbach, Erich
1957　*Mimesis: The Representation of Reality in Western Literature.* New York: Doubleday.
Awetik'ean, G., X. Siwrmēlean, and M. Awk'erean
1836–37　Նոր բառգիրք հայկազեան լեզուի *New Dictionary of the Armenian Language.* 2 vols. Venice: St. Lazzaro.
Bardakjian, Kevork B.
2000　*A Reference Guide to Modern Armenian Literature 1500–1920.* Detroit: Wayne State University Press.
Baronian, Sukias, and Frederick C. Conybeare
1918　*Catalogue of the Armenian Manuscripts in the Bodleian Library.* Catalogi codd. mss. Bibliothecae Bodleianae, Pars XIV. Oxford: Clarendon Press.
Beer, Bernhard
1859　*Leben Abrahams nach Auffassung der jüdischen Sagen.* Leipzig: Oskar Leiner.

Bezold, Carl
1888   *Die Schatzhöhle, syrisch und deutsch herausgegeben.* Leipzig: Hinrichs.

Böttrich, Christfried
2010   *Geschichte Melchizedeks.* JSHRZ n.s. 1. Gütersloh: Gütersloher Verlagshaus.

Bowley, James E.
1994   "The Compositions of Abraham." Pages 215–38 in *Tracing the Threads: Studies in the Vitality of Jewish Pseudepigrapha.* Edited by John C. Reeves. SBLELJ 6. Atlanta: Scholars Press.

Brock, Sebastian P.
1978   "Abraham and the Ravens: A Syriac Counterpart to *Jubilees* 11–12 and Its Implications." *JSJ* 9:135–52.

Brunschvig, R.
2011   "'Abd." *Encyclopaedia of Islam, Second Edition.* Edited by P. Bearman et al. Brill Online

Budge, E. A. Wallis
1886   *The Book of the Bee.* Anecdota Oxoniensia 1.2. Oxford: Clarendon Press.
1927   *The Book of the Cave of Treasures: A History of the Patriarchs and the Kings, Their Successors, from the Creation to the Crucifixion of Christ: Translated from the Syriac Text of the British Museum Ms. Add. 25875.* London: Religious Tract Society.

Čemčian (Jemjemian), Sahak
1996   Մայր ցուցակ հայերէն ձեռագրաց մատենադարանին Մխիթարեանց ի Վենետիկ *Grand Catalogue of the Armenian Manuscripts of the Mekhitarist Library in Venice.* Vol. 7. Venice: S. Lazzaro.

Chabot, Jean-Baptist.
1899   *Chronique de Michel le Syrien.* 4 vols. Paris: Ernest Leroux.

Charles, Robert H.
1902   *The Book of Jubilees or The Little Genesis.* London: Black.

Conybeare, F. C.
1913   *A Catalogue of the Armenian Manuscripts in the British Museum.* London: British Museum.

Coulie, Bernard
1994   *Répertoire de manuscrits arméniens.* Leiden: AIEA.

Denis, A.-M., and J.-C. Haelewyck
2000   *Introduction à la littérature religieuse judéo-hellénistique.* Turnhout: Brepols.

Der Nersessian, S.
1973   *Armenian Manuscripts in the Walters Art Gallery.* Baltimore: Walters Art Gallery.

Dochhorn, Jan
   2004   "Die Historia de Melchisedech (Hist Melch)—Einführung, editorischer Vorbericht und editiones Praeliminares." *Le Muséon* 117:7–48.
Durnovo, L.
   1961   *Armenian Miniatures*. New York: Abrams.
Dowsett, C. J. F.
   1961   *The History of the Caucasian Albanians, by Movses Dasxuranci*. London Oriental Series 8. London/New York: Oxford University Press.
Dudley, Martin, and Geoffrey Rowell
   1993   *The Oil of Gladness: Anointing in the Christian Traditions*. London/ Collegeville, Minn.: SPCK.
Ēganyan, Onik, Andranik Zeytʻunyan, and Pʻaylak Antʻabyan
   1965   Յուցակ ձեռագրաց Մաշտոցի անվան Մատենադարանի *Catalogue of Manuscripts of the Maštocʻ Matenadaran*. vol. 1. Erevan: Academy of Sciences.
   1970   Յուցակ ձեռագրաց Մաշտոցի անվան Մատենադարանի *Catalogue of Manuscripts of the Maštocʻ Matenadaran*. vol. 2. Erevan: Academy of Sciences.
Ēganyan, Onik, et al.
   2004   Մայր ցուցակ հայերէն ձեռագրաց Մաշտոցի անուան Մատենադարանի *General Catalogue of Armenian Manuscripts of the Maštocʻ Matenadaran*. vol. 2. Erevan: Nairi.
   2007   Մայր ցուցակ հայերէն ձեռագրաց Մաշտոցի անուան Մատենադարանի *General Catalogue of Armenian Manuscripts of the Maštocʻ Matenadaran*. vol. 3. Erevan: Magałat Publishing House.
Ervine, Roberta R.
   2000   "Antecedents and Parallels to Some Questions and Answers on Genesis in Vanakan Vardapet's *Book of Questions*." *Le Muséon* 113:417–28.
Eshel, Esther
   2007   "The *Imago Mundi* of the *Genesis Apocryphon*." Pages 111–31 in *Heavenly Tablets: Interpretation, Identity and Tradition in Ancient Judaism*. JSJSup 119. Leiden/Boston: Brill.
Fabricius, Johannes A.
   1713   *Codex Pseudepigraphus Veteris Testamenti*. Hamburg/Leipzig: Liebezeit.
Firestone, Reuven
   1990   *Journeys in Holy Lands: The Evolution of the Abraham-Ishmael Legends in Islamic Exegesis*. Albany: State University of New York Press.

Friedlander, Gerald
  1981   *Pirke de Rabbi Eliezer: The Chapters of Rabbi Eliezer the Great.* 4th ed. New York: Sepher-Hermon Press.
Gafni, Isaiah M.
  1987   "'Pre-Histories' of Jerusalem in Hellenistic Jewish and Christian Literature." *JSP* 1:5–22.
Ginzberg, Louis
  1909–38   *The Legends of the Jews.* 7 vols. Philadelphia: Jewish Publication Society of America.
Greenfield, J. C., E. Eshel, and M. E. Stone
  2004   *The Aramaic Levi Document: Edition, Translation, Commentary.* SVTP 19. Leiden/Boston: Brill.
Grigor Narekacʻi
  1985   Մատեան ողբերգութեան *Book of Lamentations*. Edited by P. M. Xačʻatryan and A. A. Łazinyan. Erevan: Academy of Sciences.
Grigor Tatʻewacʻi
  1993   Գիրք Հարցմանց *Book of Questions*. Reprinted, Jerusalem: St. James Press.
Grypeou, Emmanouela, and Helen Spurling
  2009a   "Abraham's Angels: Jewish and Christian Exegesis of Genesis 18–19." Pages 181–203 in *The Exegetical Encounter between Jews and Christians in Late Antiquity.* Edited by Emmanouela Grypeou and Helen Spurling. Jewish and Christian Perspectives Series 18. Leiden/Boston: Brill.
  2009b, eds.   *The Exegetical Encounter between Jews and Christians in Late Antiquity.* Jewish and Christian Perspectives 18. Leiden/Boston: Brill.
Haase, F.
  1915   "Die armenischen Rezensionen der syrischen Chronik Michael des Grossen." *Oriens Christianus* n.s. 5:60–82, 271–84.
Harl, Marguerite
  1986   *La Bible d'Alexandrie: La Genèse.* Paris: Cerf.
Hay, David M.
  1973   *Glory at the Right Hand: Psalm 110 in Early Christianity.* SBLMS 18. Nashville/New York: Abingdon.
Jeffreys, E., et al.
  1986   *The Chronicle of John Malalas.* Byzantina Australiensia 4. Sydney: Australian Association for Byzantine Studies.
Jellinek, Adolph
  1938   *Bet ha-Midrasch.* Reprinted, Jerusalem: Bamberger & Wahrmann.
Kʻēosēyan, Yakob, and Šahē Hayrapetean
  1988   Վարդան Այգեկցի. Գիրք հաստատութեան եւ արմատ հաւատոյ *Vardan Aygekcʻi: Book of the Establishment and Root of Faith.* Erevan: Erevan State University.

Kessler, Edward
  2004   *Bound by the Bible: Jews, Christians and the Sacrifice of Isaac.*
          Cambridge: Cambridge University Press.
Kévorkian, Raymond H., and Armèn Ter-Stépanian
  1998   *Manuscrits arméniens de la Bibliothèque nationale de France:
          Catalogue.* Paris: Bibliothèque nationale de France and Fondation
          Calouste Gulbenkian.
Khachikyan (Xač'ikyan), Levon, and Papazian, Michael
  2004   *Commentary on Genesis by Eghishe.* Introduction by Hakob
          Kyoseyan. Erevan: Magaghat Publishing House.
Kister, Menahem
  1994   "Observations on Aspects of Exegesis, Tradition, and Theology in
          Midrash, Pseudepigrapha, and Other Jewish Writings." In *Tracing
          the Threads: Studies in the Vitality of the Jewish Pseudepigrapha.*
          Edited by John C. Reeves. SBLEJL 6. Atlanta: Scholars Press.
Kiwleserean, Babgen Coadj. Catholicos
  1961   Ցուցակ ձեռագրաց Ղալաթիոյ Ազգային Մատենադարանի
          Հայոց *Catalogue of the Manuscripts of the Armenian National
          Library of Galata.* Calouste Gulbenkian Armenian Library. Antelias:
          Armenian Catholicossate.
Kulik, Alexander
  2010   *3 Baruch: Greek-Slavonic Apocalypse of Baruch.* Commentaries on
          Early Jewish Literature. Berlin/New York: de Gruyter.
Łazaryan, Ṙ. S., and H. M. Avetisyan
  1987–92 Միջին հայերենի բառարան *Mediaeval Armenian Dictionary.* 2
          vols. Erevan: Erevan State University Press.
Leslau, Wolf
  1951   *Falasha Anthology: The Black Jews of Ethiopia.* New York:
          Schocken.
Licht, Jacob
  1973   *Trial in the Bible and in Second Temple Judaism.* In Hebrew.
          Jerusalem: Magnes Press.
Lipscomb, W. L.
  1978   "A Tradition from the Book of Jubilees in Armenian." *JJS* 29:149–
          63.
  1990   *The Armenian Apocryphal Adam Literature.* University of Pennsylvania Armenian Texts and Studies 8. Atlanta: Scholars Press.
Lowin, Shari L.
  2006   *The Making of a Forefather: Abraham in Islamic and Jewish
          Exegetical Narratives.* Islamic History and Civilization: Studies &
          Texts 65. Leiden/Boston: Brill.
Malxaseanc', St.
  1944   Հայերեն Բացատրական Բառարան *Armenian Explanatory
          Dictionary.* 4 vols. Erevan: Armenian SSR State Press.

Malxasyan, Armen
2007   Ցուցակ ձեռագրաց Մաշտոցի անուան Մատենադարանի *Catalogue of Manuscripts of the Maštocʻ Matenadaran.* Vol. 3. Erevan: Erevan State University Press.

Martirosyan, A. A.
1969–72   Պատմութիւն եւ խրատք Խիկարայ իմաստնոյ *The Story and Counsels of Xikar the Wise.* 2 vols. Erevan: Academy of Sciences.

Matʻevosyan, Artašes S.
1995   Մատեան Գիտութեան եւ Հաւատոյ. Հայերէն թղթեա հնագոյն ձեռագիրը 981 *A Book of Knowledge and Belief by Priest David; The Oldest Armenian Manuscript on Paper, 981.* Vol. 1, Facsimile. Erevan: Matenadaran-Nairi.

1997   Մատեան Գիտութեան եւ Հաւատոյ. Հայերէն թղթեա հնագոյն ձեռագիրը 981 *A Book of Knowledge and Belief by the Priest David: The Oldest Armenian Manuscript on Paper.* Vol. 2, Transcription, Notes and Indexes. Erevan: Nairi.

Mathews, E. G., Jr., and J. P. Amar
1994   *Selected Prose Works of Ephrem the Syrian.* Fathers of the Church 91. Washington, D.C.: Catholic University of America Press.

Mathews, Thomas F., and Roger S. Wieck
1994   *Treasures in Heaven: Armenian Illuminated Manuscripts.* New York: The Pierpont Morgan Library.

Mécérian, Jean
1953   "Introduction à l'étude des synaxaires arméniens." *Bulletin arménologique, Mélanges de l'Université de S. Joseph* 43:99–128.

Meillet, A.
1913   *Altarmenische Elementarbuch.* Indogermanische Bibliothek, 1. Reihe 10. Heidelberg: Carl Winters Universitäts-Buchhandlung.

Michael the Syrian
1871   Ժամանակագրութիւն Տեառն Միքայէլի Ասորւոց Պատրիարքի *Chronicle of Rev. Michael, Patriarch of the Syrians.* Jerusalem: St. James Press.

Murdoch, Brian O.
2000   *Adam's Grace: Fall and Redemption in Medieval Literature.* Cambridge: D. S. Brewer.

Napier, A. S.
1894   *History of the Holy Rood Tree.* London: Kegan Paul.

Orlov, Andrei A.
2000   "Melchizedek Legend of 2 (Slavonic) Enoch." *JSJ* 31:23–38.
2007   *From Apocalypticism to Merkabah Mysticism: Studies on the Slavonic Pseudepigrapha.* JSJSup 114. Leiden/Boston: Brill.
2009   *Selected Studies in the Slavonic Pseudepigrapha.* SVTP 23. Leiden/Boston: Brill.

Petit, Françoise
    1991–96 *La Chaine sur la Genèse: édition intégrale.* 4 vols. Tradition exegetica graeca 1-4. Leuven: Peeters.
Petit, Françoise, Lucas van Rompay, and J. J. S. Weitenberg
    2011   *Eusèbe d'Emèse: Commentaire de la Genèse.* Traditio Exegetica Graeca. Leuven/Walpole, Mass.: Peeters.
Petrosyan, Eznik, and Armen Ter-Stepanyan
    2002   Ս. Գրքերի հայերէն մեկնութիւնների մատենագիտութիւն *Bibiliography of Armenian Commentaries on the Bible.* Armenian Bible Society Biblical Studies Series 2. Erevan: Bible Society of Armenia.
Piovanelli, Pierluigi
    In press "Much to Say and Hard to Explain—Melchizedek in Early Christian Literature, Theology, and Controversy."
Quinn, E. C.
    1962   *The Quest of Seth for the Oil of Life.* Chicago: University of Chicago Press.
Reeves, John C.
    1999   "Exploring the Afterlife of Jewish Pseudepigrapha in Medieval Near Eastern Religious Traditions: Some Initial Soundings." *JSJ* 30:148–77.
    2005   *Trajectories in Near Eastern Apocalyptic: A Postrabbinic Jewish Apocalypse Reader.* SBLRBS 45. Atlanta: Society of Biblical Literature.
Satran, David
    1985   "Early Jewish and Christian Interpretation of the Fourth Chapter of the Book of Daniel." PhD. thesis. Jerusalem: Hebrew University.
Scott, James M.
    1997   "The Division of the Earth in Jubilees 8:11–9:15 and Early Christian Chronography." Pages 295–319 in *Studies in the Book of Jubilees.* Edited by Matthias Albani, Jörg Frey, and Armin Lange. TSAJ 65. Tübingen: Mohr Siebeck.
Shulman, David D.
    1993   *The Hungry God: Hindu Tales of Filicide and Devotion.* Chicago: University of Chicago Press.
Sprengling, M., and W. C. Graham
    1931   *Barhebraeus' Scholia on the Old Testament.* Vol. 1, *Genesis–II Samuel* OIP 13. Chicago: University of Chicago Press.
Stählin, Otto
    1960   *Clemens Alexandrinus, Bd. 2.* Revised by Ludwig Früchtel. GCS 52. Berlin: Akademie-Verlag.
Steudel, Annette
    2000   "Melchizedek." Pages 535–37 in vol. 1 of *Encyclopedia of the Dead*

Sea Scrolls. Edited by In Lawrence H. Schiffman and James C. VanderKam. New York: Oxford University Press.

Stone, M. E.

1969   "The Apocryphal Literature in the Armenian Tradition." *The Israel Academy of Sciences and Humanities Proceedings*, 4.4:59–77.

1981   *Signs of the Judgment, Onomastica Sacra and The Generations from Adam.* University of Pennsylvania Armenian Texts and Studies 3. Chico, Calif.: Scholars Press.

1982a   *Armenian Apocrypha Relating to Patriarchs and Prophets.* Jerusalem: Israel Academy of Sciences.

1982b   *The Armenian Inscriptions from the Sinai with Appendixes on the Georgian and Latin Inscriptions by Michel van Esbroeck and William Adler.* Harvard Armenian Texts and Studies 6. Cambridge, Mass.: Harvard University Press.

1988   "The Months of the Hebrews." *Le Muséon* 101:5–11.

1990   *Fourth Ezra: A Commentary on the Book of Fourth Ezra*. Hermeneia. Minneapolis: Fortress.

1992   *A History of the Literature of Adam and Eve*. SBLEJL 3. Atlanta: Scholars Press.

1996a   *Armenian Apocrypha: Relating to Adam and Eve*. SVTP 14. Leiden: Brill.

1996b   "The Armenian Apocryphal Literature: Translation and Creation." Pages 611–46 in *Il Caucaso: Cerniera fra Culture dal Mediterraneo alla Persia (Secoli IV–XI)*. Spoleto: Presso la Sede del Centro. = Stone 2006, 105–37.

1998   "The Mixed Erkat'agir-Bolorgir Script in Armenian Manuscripts." *Le Muséon* 111:293–317 = Stone 2006, 503–27.

1999   "Two Armenian Manuscripts and the Historia Sacra." Pages 21–31 in *Apocryphes arméniens: transmission – traduction – création – iconographie*. Edited by Valentina Calzolari Bouvier, Jean-Daniel Kaestli, and Bernard Outtier. Prahins, Switzerland: Zèbre.

2000a   "The Bones of Adam and Eve." Pages 241–45 in *For a Later Generation: The Transformation of Tradition in Israel, Early Judaism, and Early Christianity*. Edited by Randal A. Argall, Beverly A. Bow, and Rodney A. Werline. Harrisburg, Pa.: Trinity Press International.

2000b   "The Angelic Prediction in the Primary Adam Books." Pages 111–32 in *Literature on Adam and Eve: Collected Essays*. Edited by Gary A. Anderson, Michael E. Stone, and Johannes Tromp. SVTP 15. Leiden: Brill.

2002   *Adam's Contract with Satan: The Legend of the Cheirograph of Adam*. Bloomington: Indiana University Press.

2004   "Armenian Pilgrimage to the Mountain of the Transfiguration and the Galilee." *St. Nersess Theological Review* 9:79–89.

2006	*Apocrypha, Pseudepigrapha and Armenian Studies: Collected Papers.* 2 vols. OLA 144–45. Leuven: Peeters.
2007	*Adamgirkʻ: The Adam Book of Aṙakʻel of Siwnikʻ.* Oxford: Oxford University Press.
2009 a	"Biblical Figures in the Armenian Tradition." Pages 629–46 in *Yearbook 2008: Biblical Figures in Deuterocanonical and Cognate Literature.* Edited by Hermann Lichtenberger and Ulrike Mittman-Reichert. Berlin/New York: de Gruyter.
2009b	"Two Unpublished Eschatological Texts." *JSP* 18:293–302.
2010	"Some Texts on Enoch in the Armenian Traditions." Pages 517–30 in *Gazing on the Deep: Ancient Near Eastern and Other Studies in Honor of Tzvi Abusch.* Edited by Jeffery Stackert, Barbara N. Porter, and David P. Wright. Bethesda: CDL.
2011	*Ancient Judaism: New Visions and Views.* Grand Rapids: Eerdmans.

Stone, Michael E., with Vered Hillel
2012	*The Armenian Version of the Testaments of the Twelve Patriarchs: Edition, Apparatus, Translation and Commentary.* Hebrew University Armenian Series 14. Leuven: Peeters.
In press A	"The Cedar in Jewish Antiquity." In *Proceedings of Conference on Talmudic Archaeology, London, June 2009.*
In press B	"Biblical and Apocryphal Themes in Armenian Culture." In *Proceedings of Strasbourg NT Apocrypha Conference of January 2010.* Edited by R. Gounelle.

Stone, Michael E., Dickran Kouymjian, and Henning Lehmann
2002	*Album of Armenian Paleography.* Aarhus: Aarhus University Press.

Stone, Nira
1997	*The Kaffa Lives of the Desert Fathers: A Study in Armenian Manuscript Illumination.* Corpus Scriptorum Christianorum Orientalium, Subsidia 94. Louvain: Peeters.

Stordalen, Terje
2000	*Echoes of Eden: Genesis 2–3 and Symbolism of the Eden Garden in Biblical Hebrew Literature.* CBET 25. Leuven: Peeters.

Thierry, Michel
1993	*Répertoire des monastères arméniens.* Corpus Christianorum. Turnhout: Brepols.

Thomsen, Peter
1907	*Loca Sancta: Verzeichnis der im 1. bis 6. Jahrhundert n. Chr. erwähnten Ortschaften Palästinas.* Halle: Rudolf Haupt.

Thomson, Robert W.
1995	*A Bibliography of Classical Armenian Literature to 1500 AD.* Corpus Christianorum. Turnhout: Brepols.
2006	*Movses Khorenatsʻi History of the Armenians.* Rev. ed. Ann Arbor: Caravan Books.

Toorn, Karel van der, Bob Becking, and Piet van der Horst
1995   *Dictionary of Deities and Demons in the Bible (DDD)*. Leiden/New York: Brill.

VanderKam, James C.
1989   *The Book of Jubilees*. CSCO 510–11. Leuven: Peeters.

van Rompay, L.
1997   "Antiochene Biblical Interpretation: Greek and Syriac." Pages 1–23 in *The Book of Genesis in Jewish and Oriental Christian Interpretation*. Edited by Judith Frishman and Lucas van Rompay. Traditio exegetica graeca 5. Leuven: Peeters.

Vassiliev, A.
1893   *Anecdota Graeco-Byzantina*. Moscow: Imperial University Press.

Vosté, Jacques-Marie, and Ceslas van den Eynde
1950–55 *Commentaire d'Iso'dadh de Merv sur l'Ancien Testament: Genèse*. CSCO 126, 156. Louvain: L. Dubecq.

Wahlgren, S.
2006   *Symeonis magistri et logothetae Chronicon*. Corpus fontium historiae Byzantinae; Series Berolinensis 44/1. Berlin/New York: de Gruyter.

Wallraff, Martin, and William Adler
2007   *Sextus Iulius Chronographiae: The Extant Fragments*. GCS n.F. 15. Berlin/New York: de Gruyter.

Wilkinson, J.
1977   *Jerusalem Pilgrims before the Crusades*. Jerusalem: Ariel.

Wutz, F. X.
1914–15 *Onomastica Sacra*. TU 40–41. Leipzig: Hinrichs.

Xač'ikyan (Khachikyan), Levon
1992   Եղիշէի *"Արարածոց մեկնութիւնը"* Etišē's *"Commentary on Genesis."* Erevan: Zvart'noc'.

Yassif, Eli
2001   *The Book of Memory, that is The Chronicles of Jerahme'el* [*Sefer Ha-Zikronot hu Divrei ha-yamim le-yerahmeel*]. Tel-Aviv: Tel Aviv University (in Hebrew).

Zekiyan, Boghos Levon
1997   "Quelques observations critiques sur le 'Corpus Elisaeanum.'" Pages 71–123 in *The Armenian Christian Tradition*. Edited by Robert F. Taft. OrChrAn 254. Rome: Pontifico Istituto Orientale.

Index of Sources

HEBREW BIBLE

Genesis
Reference	Pages
4:3–5	121
5:9–14	193
10	192
10:31–32	98
11:4	192
11:8	32
11:8–9	192
11:10	51, 97
11:12	97
11:20	32, 211
11:22	51
11:22–23	34
11:24	32, 51
11:24–25	34
11:26	33, 51
11:26–27	64
11:28	43, 64, 126
11:28–29	34
11:29	51, 65
11:30	51, 66 196
11:31	43, 65
11:32	20, 34
12	194
12:1	44, 52, 65, 113 194, 195, 205, 210
12:4	19, 65, 81
12:5	44, 65, 119, 120, 195
12:7	15, 52, 53, 195
12:8	66
12:8–9	196
12:10	44, 65, 149
12:10–20	210
12:11–12	65
12:11–13	114
12:13	65
12:14	149
12:14–15	66
12:15	44, 66
12:16	66
12:17	66
12:17–20	44
12:18–20	66
12:19–20	196
12:20	115
13:1	66
13:1–2	44
13:2	66, 116, 150, 195, 225
13:3	66, 116
13:5–7	195
13:12	44
13:18	13, 44, 45, 195
14	9, 10, 16, 98, 99, 196
14:1–7	44
14:13	13, 45, 116, 195
14:14	44, 196
14:18	9, 196
14:18–20	44
14:21–24	44
14:23	211
14:24	45
15	15, 16
15:2	45, 126
15:5	205
15:13	83, 119, 156
15:13–14	170
15:15	70
15:18	195
16:1	66, 211
16:2	66, 116
16:5	66
16:6	211

Genesis (*continued*)		19:1	171
16:13–14	66	19:1a	49
16:14	82	19:1b	49
16:16	66, 82, 211	19:2–3	157, 171
17:1	67, 211	19:3–9	93
17:5	69, 212	19:4–8	49
17:10	211	19:8	171
17:10–13	67	19:9	158
17:15	69	19:11	49, 171
17:17	82	19:12	49, 93
17:24	82, 211	19:12–13	158
17:24–25	67	19:14	49, 171, 229
18:1	13, 99, 195	19:15	93
18:1 (Arm)	198	19:16	49
18:1–2	197	19:17	229
18:1–16	47	19:24	50, 93, 159
18:2	53, 155, 198	19:25	50
18:2–3	46	19:26	49, 93, 171, 159, 229
18:3	53	19:28	93
18:3–5	118	20:1	67
18:4	53	20:2	67, 211
18:6–7	118	20:3	67
18:7	155	20:4	67
18:7a	53	20:4b–5	67
18:8	53, 90	20:6	67
18:9	53, 201	20:7	67
18:10	53, 118, 156, 201	20:7b	68
18:11–12	201	20:8	68
18:12	201	20:9–10	68
18:12–15	118	20:11	68, 147
18:13	201	20:12	68
18:13–15	48	20:13	68
18:14	53, 201	20:14–15	68
18:15	202	20:16	68, 150
18:16	48	20:17–18	68
18:17–18	15	21:2	68
18:18	53	21:3	202, 203
18:20	53, 92, 170	21:4	67
18:20–23	48	21:5	33, 34, 82, 211
18:21	53	21:10	205, 211
18:23	53	21:12	205
18:23–32	92	22	91, 211
18:24	53	22:1	204, 231
18:24–32	157	22:1–2	120, 161
18:26	53	22:2	69, 161, 175, 231
18:26–32	171	22:3	175
18:33	49	22:4	212

INDEX OF SOURCES

22:6	175, 231	31:48–49	118		
22:7	120, 161, 175, 231	32	77		
22:7–8	231	32:10	77		
22:8	120, 161, 175, 231	33:18–19	69		
22:9	161, 231	35:28	35, 82		
22:9–10	120	37:2	83		
22:9–13	161	38:18–19	69		
22:11–13	121, 232	41:46	83		
22:12	90	42–44	102		
22:12–13	175	42:6	114		
22:13	69, 212	46:26–27	83		
22:14	161	47:2–4	114		
22:15	91	47:9	83		
22:16	162	47:28	35		
22:17	160, 170, 230	49:30	69		
22:22	212	50:13–14	69		
23:1	69, 82				
23:8–18	69	Exodus			
23:19	195	1:5	83		
23:19–20	69	2:1	35		
24:62	82	3:14	148, 224		
25:1–4	70, 82	4:20	91		
25:7	34, 70, 82, 212	6:16	35		
25:8	70	6:18	35		
25:9	116	6:20	35		
25:9–10	212	7:7	33, 35		
25:11	82	12:41	34, 83		
25:12	69	12:46	118		
25:12–18	15	14:7	83		
25:20	69	16:32–34	84		
25:22	70	16:35	35		
25:23	70	20	84		
25:25	33, 35, 69, 70, 74, 83	23:23	85		
		25:10	84		
25:27	74	25:21	84		
25:29–34	82	26:2	84		
26:1–11	74	26:31	84		
26:27–34	75	26:36	84		
27	75, 163	32:28	83		
27:1	75	34:6	84		
27:17	156	40:2	84		
27:36	76				
28–31	76	Numbers			
28:12	82	16:20–21	11		
28:13	82	16:31–33	11		
28:17–19	82	17:5–10	48		
30:35–36	76	17:25	84		

Numbers (*continued*)
22:23 — 150

Deuteronomy — 146
5:12 — 84
7:1 — 85
12:2 — 120
23:3 — 15

Joshua
5:13–14 — 150
10:1 — 97
24:2 — 41
24:32 — 69

1 Chronicles
16:22 — 66
21:16 — 150

2 Chronicles
3:1 — 161, 231

Job
21:24 — 14

Psalms
63:5 — 14
80:8–9 — 99
110:4 — 8, 98

Isaiah
25:6 — 14
56:3 — 202
66:24 — 193

Ezekiel
17:24 — 48

Daniel
6:10 — 46

Malachi
1:2–3 — 82, 163

NEW TESTAMENT
Matthew
2:13–14 — 114

Luke
1:18–20 — 48, 202
1:26–38 — 99
3:24 — 97
3:28 — 97
16:3 — 6
16:22 — 52, 212

John
19:33–36 — 118

Acts
7:3–4 — 43

Romans
4:11 — 241
4:16 — 7, 52
9:13 — 82

Galatians
3:17 — 34

Colossians
2:14 — 230

Hebrews
7:3 — 94, 97
9:4 — 84

Revelation
2:10 — 212

DEAD SEA SCROLLS

1QapGen
20 — 65
20:16–17 — 44, 66
20.32 — 66
21–22 — 12

4Q225
frg. 2, col. 2 — 120
frgs. 2.1–2 — 204

4Q389a
frg. 3.7 — 113

INDEX OF SOURCES

11QMelchizedek	9	11–12	18
		11:11–13	209
		11:18–22	130
APOCRYPHA AND		12:6–8	224
PSEUDEPIGRAPHA AND		12:12	43
SECOND TEMPLE SOURCES		12:12–14	44
		12:16–18	42
2 Baruch		13:13	66
57:2	8	17:15–18	204
		18:13	90
3 Baruch		39:2	83
15:1–2	14	40:11	83
		46:3	83
4 Baruch			
7:17	119	*Liber Antiquitatum Biblicarum*	
		18:5	42
2 Enoch		26:7	42
22:8–9	14	32:3	120
56:2	14		
69–71	234	Orphica A. 26–28	42
71–72	9		
72	10, 121	Philo	
		De Abrahamo	
4 Ezra		69–70	42
3:14–15	15	71, 77–79	42
3:16	82	94–95	44, 66
		107–18	46
Aramaic Levi Document		113	48
11:14	35	118	47
		De cherubim	
Apocalypse of Abraham	113, 147	2.35, §124	210
1–3	112, 147	*De posteritate Caini*	
5–6	112	9, §27	210
7:2	43		
7:7–9	42	Synagogal Prayers	
9	15	2:14	42
		9:10	234
Baruch			
1:4	113	*Testament of Abraham*	
		A 3:7–12	47
Josephus		A 4:9	200
Antiquities		A 4:9–10	47
1.176–78	42	A 6:5	119
		A 6:6	47
Jubilees	20, 24, 42, 47	B 2:10	48
8:10–9:15	192	B 3:6–10	47
10:29–34	195	B 6:13	47

258 INDEX OF SOURCES

Testament of Levi
11:4   35

Wisdom
14:15   126, 193

NEW TESTAMENT APOCRYPHA

Acts of Pilate   52

Infancy Gospel   204

OTHER APOCRYPHAL WORKS

Adam Fragment
2   98
2 §8   94
2 §§9–11   100

Adam, Eve and the Incarnation   178

Ahikar, Wisdom of   101

Biblical Paraphrases
Story of Noah   146

Biblical Paraphrases
Story of Moses
10   146

Cycle of Four Works   37, 237

Sermon Concerning the Flood   178

Sons of Noah
§1   98

Story of Melchizedek
1.1   97

Words of Adam to Seth
6.13   100

ARMENIAN SOURCES

Agathangelos
Teaching
28.4   48

Aṙakʻel Siwnecʻi
Adamgirkʻ
1.22.35   97

Eɫišē
Commentary on Genesis   17, 20, 47, 48, 200, 202, 203
as source   179, 201
17:6   70
18:4   199
74.45   44
74.47   65
95.21   69
97.42   70

Eɫišē, Pseudo–,
On the Transfiguration   12, 200

Eznik
3.15.2   8
22.19   48

Generations of the Sons of Noah   192

Grigor Magistros
Aṙ Manučʻē 125   14

Grigor Narekacʻi,
Book of Lamentation
93.5   17, 242

Homily concerning Lot   178

Movsēs Xorenacʻi
1.5   32, 32, 34
1.15–16   34
2.2   70
2.68   70

Pʻilon Tirakacʻi
§140   32

Stepanos Siwnecʻi,
Commentary on Genesis   15, 20–21, 22, 242
49   23
87   119
112   69

INDEX OF SOURCES

Vanakan *vardapet*
Book of Questions   125

Vardan Arewelc'i,
Commentary on Genesis   17

RABBINIC SOURCES

Aggadat Berešit
19	46
31	2
34	45
37	42
40	45

Abot de Rabbi Nathan
A 33:2	204
B.37	91

b. Baba Meṣi`a
86b	46, 47

b. Nedarim
32b	9

b. Qiddušin
32b	200

Genesis Rabbah
20:21	162, 232
26:3	8
38:13	112
38:28	64, 112
40:7	225
41:13	44, 195
44:5	42
48:1	46, 154
48:2	46
48:3	47
48:5	46, 47
48:8	47
51:2	13
52:18	67, 225
56:8	120
56:13	69
66:13	91

Leviticus Rabbah
25	9

m. Abot
5:3	204

Ma'aseh Abraham   42, 112

Maimonides
Mishneh Torah	146
"Idolatry" 1	192
"Idolatry" 1.1	146

Pirqe de Rabbi Eliezer
20	97
26	66
26–30	204
27	9
28	46
30	91, 120

Seder Eliyahu Rabbah   112

Tanḥuma Lek Lĕka
2.2	112

Tanḥuma Vayera'
1	46
15	49
22	81
23	91
46	120

Yalqut Shim'oni Lek Lĕka
12.62	14
14:74	9
15.77	46
17.81	9
101	120

Yerahmeel
4.5	112

INDEX OF SOURCES

PATRISTIC AND OTHER ANCIENT SOURCES

Anonymous
Commentary on Genesis 237
Aram
Epistle 120

Aristotle
Physics
3:2, 202a 210
8:4, 255b 29–31 210

Athanasius,
Ad Afros epistola synodica
2 92

bar Hebraeus, Gregory
(Budge) 10 18
Scholia to Gen 9:22 45

Barnabas
9 92

Book of the Bee
(Budge) 65
(Budge 33–34) 94
(Budge 34) 97

Cave of Treasures
(Bezold 11–13) 234
(Budge 126–27) 12, 97
(Budge 148) 10, 66, 68
(Budge 151) 11
(Budge 152) 232
(Budge 154) 70
(Budge 224) 12

Cyril of Alexandria
Glaphyra 69, 90

Didymus the Blind
On Genesis 209 41

Ephrem
Commentary on Genesis 90
11 70

11.9 9
12 15
13 66
15 119
16.7 50
20.2 68
20.3 69

Eusebius of Emesa
on Gen 25:22 70

Eusebius
Demonstratio evangelica
5:3 10
Historia ecclesiastica
1.2.8 198
1.14.11 15
Praeparatio evangelica
9.18.1 42

George Monachus
1.93.16–94.16 19

George Syncellus
106–7 41
111 19, 42, 177
112 10, 19
113 66

Ibn Qutayba
Kitab al-ma'ārif 45

Irenaeus
Adversus haereses
4.5.5 175, 232

John Chrysostom
Commentary on Genesis
32.7 66
32.21 66
Homily on Genesis
47.14 69, 90

John Malalas
Chronicle 97
55 41
57 41
57.1 19, 126

INDEX OF SOURCES

Justin		
Dialogues		
56	48	
57	47	

Michael the Syrian		
2.6	18	

OnaV 152	97	

Origen		
on Matt 27:33	98	
Homiliae in Genesim		
8.6–9	69, 90	

Palaea	8, 12, 24	
	201–202, 210, 214	
201	192	
202	43	
203	43, 195	
204	44	
206	98, 163	
210	91	
214	46, 155	
217	49, 50	
218	100	
221	69, 120	
229	90	
47.1	169	

Procopius of Gaza		
Commentary on Genesis		
col 320	41	

Protoevangelium of James		
17:2	114	

Qur'an		
6:76–80	42	
6:98–105	42	
11:67–69	47	
51:24–29	47	
51:24–30	91	

Sextus Iulius Africanus		
F26.8	171	
F30	13, 195	

Symeon Metaphrastes		
32.27–29	41	
33	19	

Te'ĕzāza Sanbat	91	

Theodoret of Cyrrhus,		
Ad quaestiones magorum		
63	66	

Index of Names and Select Subjects

This index includes ancient sources, modern authors and select subjects. The simple occurrences of names Abraham, Isaac and Sarah are not included. The index covers the whole book except for the Armenian texts.

Aaron, 33, 84
   staff of, 48, 84
Abel, 13, 146, 193, 234
   ram of or lamb of, 91, 121, 155
Abelian, M., 86
Abimelech the Philistine, 24, 66, 67, 74, 85, 90, 149, 205, 211
Ableman, O., 30, 102
Abraham, passim
   and idols, 7
   and Lot, separation of, 195–96
Abraham
   age of, 146
   aged, served Three Men, 200
   as astronomer or astrologer, 19, 51, 52, 53, 193, 206, 209
   blessed by God, 160, 170
   blessing of table of, 48
   bosom of, 52, 212
   breaks idols, 102, 112, 147
   brings idols to market, 238
   burial of, 116, 212
   burns idolatrous temple, 19, 65, 89, 149, 194, 210, 224, 234
   change of name, 69
   children of or descendants of, 70, 81, 149, 165, 177
   circumcision of, 67, 81, 205
   death of, 7, 70
   Edenic characteristics of, 203
   father of all believers, 1, 8, 52
   father of faith, 41, 45, 90, 193

fear of God, 156
field of, 148
genealogy of, 209
grey hair of, 45, 46, 70, 89, 197, 212
honored God, 202
hospitality of, 6, 13, 22, 36, 46–47, 52, 103, 118, 146, 154, 169, 172, 198, 227, 241
and idols, 112–13, 128, 149
oath to God, 154
Pharaoh's estimation of, 124
poverty of, 114, 124
praises God, 159
prayer of, 193
priest, 8
promise to, 15
promised sacrifice of Isaac, 120
promised to God, 236
prophetic role, 67, 68, 161, 175, 231
recognition of God, 1, 6, 7, 8, 41, 51–53, 127, 148, 156, 193
recognition of God, astronomical, 42, 51–53, 148, 206, 209
recognition of God, birds, 43, 65, 113, 123, 147–48, 209, 224
recognition of God, by wisdom, 53
and Sodom, 157
summoned to Pharaoh, 150
ten trials of, 23, 78, 81. *See* Ten trials
testing of, 46, 160, 161, 199
virtues of, 206
visited by angels, 155–56

-263-

Abraham (*continued*)
  visited by God, 160
  washes men's feet, 199
  wealth of, 225
  welcomes Three Men, 200
  with Mamrē, 151–53
Abraham saga
  Christian character of, 16
  embroidered, 3, 5, 86
  incidents of omitted, 56
  non-biblical episodes in, 15
Abraham, Sarah and the Tyrant, Islamic legend, 3
Abraham's seed, increase of, 15
Abram. *See* Abraham, 64
Ačaṙyan, H., 86
Achan (Haran, person), 6, 36, 65, 81, 149, 194, 210
Achan (Haran), burned in temple, 125, 149, 194, 206, 210, 224
Adam, 34, 35, 37, 146, 209, 234
  buried on Mount Zion, 98
  covered with fingernail, 162
  head of, buried on Golgotha, 98
Adam and Eve, burial of, 11, 94, 97, 239
Adam books, 4
Adler, William, 10, 13, 19, 41–43, 66, 171, 177, 195
Adoni-Zedek, 97
Adonia, archangel, 83
al-Tabari, 47–48
Amar, J., 9, 15, 66, 68–70, 90, 101, 119
Ammonites, 15
Amorite, Amorites, 69, 85, 116
Amorites, mountains of, 212
Amram (Amran), 33, 35, 238
Anania Catholicos, 13, 241
Anania Širakacʻi, 13, 42
Anasyan, H., 36, 206, 235
Angel, angels, 23, 121, 172
Angel
  afflicts Pharaoh and his men, 210
  commands Abraham, 160
  epiphany of, 225
  fiery, 149
  orders book of God's word, 236
  as priest, 234

Angels
  blind Sodomites, 49
  eat, 14, 47
Angels of Presence, 83
Annunciation, 14
  to Abraham, 6, 13–14, 21, 34–36, 90, 99, 103, 118, 156, 211, 241
  to Virgin, 13
Antʻabyan, P., 36, 37, 122, 128, 178
Apostles, 172
Aqedah, 1–2, 6, 11, 13, 23, 42, 67, 90, 99, 103, 120–21, 128, 147, 160–62, 170, 199, 204, 206, 211–12, 231–32
  place of, 94
  story of, 175
Arabia, 192
Ark, Noah's, 36–37
Ark of the Covenant, measures of, 84
Armenian learned literature, 16
Armenization, 7, 14, 70, 82
Aṙna, Terah's wife, 34
Arpachshad, 94, 97, 146
Arsacids, 70
Aršak, 82
Aršakunis. *See* Arsacids, 82
Asher, 76, 82
Asia, 192
Asians, 34
Assfalg, J., 86
Astuac, popular etymology of, 83
Auerbuch, E., 1
Ayiay, archangel, 83

Babel, Tower of, 125, 192
Babylon, 41, 43, 193–94, 210
Babylonians, 237
  sins of, 193
Bardakjian, K., 86
Bathuel, son of Nahor, 69
Beastiality, 48
Beer, B., 8, 41, 66, 112, 209
Beer-lahai-roi, 82
Beer-Sheba, etymology of, 83
Bel, 193
Benjamin, 76, 82
Bethel, 66
Bethlehem, 98
  grotto, 94

INDEX OF NAMES AND SELECT SUBJECTS 265

Bilhah, 76, 82
Binding, magical term, 155
Birds, eat seed, 130
Birthright, blessing of, 75
Black stone in Samaria, 195
Böttrich, C., 8–9, 11, 92, 94, 97
Bowley, J., 42
Branch, from Eden, 100
Bread and wine, 9–11, 90, 92, 99–100, 162, 165, 170, 175, 177, 196, 232
Brock, S. P., 18, 24, 42
Brunschvig, R., 45
Butter, 200

Cain, 193
Calf, 14, 22, 47, 118, 155, 193, 200, 227
    bones of not broken, 118
    honorable, 163
    resembles Abel's lamb, 170
    resurrection of, 23, 103, 119, 228
Canaan, Canaanites, 33, 35–36, 43, 45, 65, 77, 85, 194, 206, 210–11, 239
    conquers Shem's land, 195
    sons of, 195
Caravanserai, 114
Cave of Machpelah, 212
Cedar trees, 98
Čemčemian, S., 36
Chabot, J.-B., 18, 35, 42–43, 70, 114, 163
Chaldea, 194
Chaldeans, 65, 194, 209
Charles, R. H., 192
Chrism, 14
Christian history of salvation, 206
Christian understanding, 2, 52
Chronological text, 83, 101, 121, 146
Chronology, of patriarchs, 103
Circumcision, 6, 23–24, 54, 67
    a seal, 241
Clement of Alexandria, 10
Conybeare, F. C., 94, 127
Cross, 100
    wood of, 100
Crows. *See* ravens
Curtains of Tent of Meeting, 84
Cypress, Melchizedek plants, 94, 98
Cypress trees, 98

Daily Prayer, 46, 76, 82
Dead Sea, 50
Denis, A.-M., 10
Der Nersessian, S., 114
Didactic writing, 178
Dinah, 76, 82
Divine fire, 200
Dochhorn, J., 8
Dog, 151, 213
Donkey, Abraham's and Moses', 91
Dowsett, C. J. F., 192
Dry wood, metaphor of, 17, 48, 202
Dudley, M., 14
Durnovo, L., 13

Earth, divisions of, 192
Easter, 46
Eber, 146
Eden, variant form of, 185
Edna, Nahor's wife, 34
Ēganyan, Ō., 101, 122, 127, 178, 204, 237, 239
Egypt, 19, 33–37, 65–66, 81, 113–14, 121, 124, 128, 195
Eliestros, son of Abraham, 125
Eliezer, 126
Elišē, 81
Emovr, 69
Enoch, 146
    confused with Enosh, 146
Enosh
    confused with Enoch, 146
Ephron, field of, 71
Ephron the Hittite, 44, 69, 116, 212
Ervine, R. R., 125
Esau, 74–76, 82, 163
    character of, 82
    garment, leather, 75
    grudge against Jacob, 76
Esdras apocalypses, 4
Eshel, E., 35, 192
Eucharist, 9, 11, 90, 99, 165, 170, 232
Euphrates, 77
Europe, 192
Eusebius of Emesa, 12
Eve, 37
    buried in grotto, 98

Exodus, 35, 78
Eynde, van den, C., 41

Fabricius, J., 42
Face, transformation of, 175
Festivals, of the Old Testament, 84
Firestone, R., 46–48, 66, 91, 231
Flood, 34, 52–53, 147
Four kings, 44, 92, 196
Fragrance, 203
Fringhian, F., 213
Früchtel, L., 10
Fruitfulness of flocks and births, 74

Gabriel (archangel), 46, 48
Gad, 76, 82
Gafni, I., 12
Galata, 78
Genesis, 78
    Armenian commentaries on, 18
Gerar, city, 24, 67
Gergerites, 74
Gergeshites, 85
Gomorreans, 48
Ginzberg, Louis, 9, 42
God
    discovery of, 18
    forgotten, 7, 146, 193, 223
    as hunter, 91
    incarnation of, 198
    visibility of, 198
God / Christ, eating, 118
God heals Abimelech's house, 68
Golgotha, 11–13, 17, 90, 94, 99–100, 212, 239
    Aqedah at, 120
    meaning of, 94, 98
Gomorrah, 37, 92
Grapes, 123
    Melchizedek offers to Abraham, 94
Great Thursday, 197
Greenfield, J. C., 35
Gregory of Xlat', 206
Grigor Narekac'i, 12, 17
Grigor of Tat'ew, 12, 239
Grypeou, E., 3, 46, 47

Haase, F., 42
Haelewyck, J.-C., 10, 24, 66, 82
Hagar, 90, 115, 165, 177, 205, 211
    Pharaoh gives to Sarah, 66, 115
Hagiography, 54
Haig, 193
Ham, 45
    seizes Palestine, 195
Hamor, sons of, 212
Haran (place), 19–20, 34, 43–44, 65, 69, 76–77, 81–82, 113, 194, 206, 210
Harl, M., 68
Hay, D. M., 9
Hayrapetian, Sh., 98–99
Hebron, 44, 195–96
    cave in, 69, 212
Hell, 2
Hezekiah, 37
High pillars, 195
Hillel, V., 79, 96, 181–83
Hittites, 85
Hivites, 85
Holy places, identification of, 161
Holy Week, 46
Homiletic passage, 200, 203, 230
Homosexuality, 48
Horeb, 163
House of idols, 43

Ibn 'Abbas, 91
Idol worship, 53, 193
Idols
    fall into mud, 238
    impotence of, 112
Illumination, 193
Invocation, magical, 83
Isaac, passim
    30 years old, 120
    beautiful on birth, 230
    Binding of. See Aqedah
    Birth of, 90, 127–28, 160, 174, 202, 211
    circumcision of, 67
    handsome, 174
    laid upon millstone, 120
    meaning of name, 68
    named at divine command, 202

sacrifice of, 54, 212
sacrifice of, and Christ's crucifixion, 212
story of, 237
type of Christ, 11, 13, 69, 90, 99–100
type of Christ's Passion, 241
virtues of, 160
Isaiah, 37
Isca (Ēskʻa, Iska), wife of Abraham, 65, 194
is Sarai, 65
Ishmael, 24, 82, 115, 125, 165, 177, 212
birth of, 66, 102, 211
circumcision of, 67
descendants of, 15
meaning of, 57, 66
Ishmaelites, 126
Ishodad of Merv, 41, 45
Islam, 3
Issachar, 76, 82
Istanbul, Armenian Patriarchate of, 78

Jacob, 33, 35, 74–77, 82, 163, 177, 213, 238
descendants of, 76, 82
dream of, 82
wrestles with the angel, 77
Jacob of Edessa, 43
Jared, 146
Jebusites, 85
mountains of, 212
Jeffreys, M., 19, 41, 97, 126
Jerusalem, 11, 98, 163, 175, 232
Abraham's city, 115
origin of name of, 98
Jochebed, 35, 238
John the Baptist, 238
Jordan, river, 50, 77
Joseph, 42, 76–77, 82, 100
buried in Shechem, 69
story of, 83
Judah, 76, 82

Kʻēosēyan, Y., 98–99
Kainan, 146
Kaxatʻam, wife of Levi, 35
Kenan b. Enosh, 193

Kessler, E., 1–2, 9, 12–13, 67, 90, 120
Keturah or Ketur(a), 70, 82, 126
Kévorkian, R., 101
Khachikyan, L., 17, 20, 24, 70, 179, 199–203
Kister, M., 42
Kiwleserean, B., 78
Knife, 231
Kohath, 33, 35, 238
Korah, 11
Kulik, A., 14

Laban, 76, 77, 82
Lamech, 146
Land, promise of, 195
Law
of forefathers, 146
forgotten, 2
second, 7
Łazinyan, A. A., 242
Leah, 35, 76, 82
Lebanon, forests of, 98–99
Leslau, W., 91
Levi, 33, 35, 76, 82, 238
Licht, J., 204
Light, pillar of, 162, 175
Lint, Th. M. van, 23, 86, 89, 91–92, 171, 182, 186, 198, 201–202, 227
Lipscomb, W. L., 30, 32, 237
Lists, 29
chronological, 29
Lot, 14, 37, 41, 44, 48–50, 92, 119, 156–59, 194, 196, 205, 210–11
daughters of, 15, 48–50
hospitality of, 14, 49, 157, 170, 172, 228–29
righteous, 54, 156
story of, 23
wife of, 49, 158–59, 171
wife of, compared with Sarah, 158
wife of, doubts of, 158, 229
wife of, petrified, 93, 159, 229
wife of, turned into salt, 171
Lot and Abraham, separation of, 195–96
Lowin, S. L., 42, 46
Luminaries, recognition of God through, 1
Lybia, 192

INDEX OF NAMES AND SELECT SUBJECTS

Machpelah, Cave of, 116
Mahalael, 146
Malk'atu, Abraham's mother, 23
Malxasean, S., 171, 236, 238
Mamray, see Mamrē
Mamrē, 6–7, 12–13, 44–46, 151–54, 160, 172
   black, 21, 45
   blessing of, 117
   character of, 21, 160
   field of, royal seat, 199
   hospitality of, 116–17, 151–52, 196, 225
   oak of, 22, 45–46, 69, 195–97, 241
   oak of, surpasses Eden, 199
   oak staff and oak of, 13–14, 45
   oak staff of, 45, 117, 118, 152
   philanthropy of, 45
   and sheep turn white, 117
   story of, 17, 21–22, 36, 44–46, 48, 89, 102, 116–18, 128, 151, 196–97, 242
   whitened, 152–53, 169, 197, 226
Marrow, 14, 121
Martirosyan, A., 101
Mary, Virgin, 23
Mastema, 18, 19, 204
Mat'evosyan, A., 7, 29
Matenadaran mss
   M0605, 83
   M0640, 206
   M2188, 83
   M2679, 192
   M4618, 37
   M4818, 13–14
   M6897, 83
Mathews, E. G., 7, 9, 15, 66, 68–70, 90, 119
Mathews, T., 114
Maundy Thursday, 46
Measure by measure, 202
Mécérian, J., 206
Medan, 82
Medieval grammatical forms, 179
Meillet, A., 24
Melchi. *See also* Melk'i, 97
Melchizedek, 3, 6–7, 12, 74, 90, 94, 99–100, 121, 162, 165, 175, 239
   anoints Abraham, 196
   ascetic, 4, 11, 33
   expatiation on, 8, 11, 14, 16
   in forest, 9
   genealogy of, 94, 97, 176
   gives Abraham bread and wine, 10
   God ordains, 94
   importance for Christians, 8
   king, 196
   king of Saɫim, 44
   meets Abraham, 9
   oracular function, 8, 70
   origins of, 239
   praises God, 91
   priestly function, 162, 165, 175, 177, 232–33
   recognizes God, 10–11, 164, 176, 193, 233
   snatched away by angel, 239
   story of, 10–12, 16–17, 91, 94, 128, 162–65, 175–77, 233–34
   type of Christ, 9, 177, 234
   wild man, 9, 163, 175
Mēlik'sēt'. *See* Melchizedek
Melk'a, wife of Nahor, 65
Melk'i, 11, 94, 97, 176, 232
   father of Melchizedek, 239
Melk'ised. *See* Melchizedek, 232
Mesopotamia, 194
Mesrob II, Patriarch of Constantinople, 78
Methuselah, 146
Michael (archangel), 46–47
Michael the Syrian, 35, 42–43, 64, 70, 81, 114, 163, 194
Midian, 82
Milchah (Meɫk'ea), 34
Milchah III, 35
Milk, 200
Misplacement of pages, 54
Moabites, 15
Molitor, J., 86
Monorhyme, 89
Moreh, oak of, 195
Moriah, 13
Moses, 29, 33, 35, 83, 238
   angels surround, 83
   prayer of, 84
Mount Adam, 156
Mount of Olives, 11, 17, 90–91, 94, 98, 242

INDEX OF NAMES AND SELECT SUBJECTS

Mount Sodom, 12, 156
Mount Tabor, 239
Mount Zion, 90, 100
Movsēs Xorenacʻi, 29, 32, 82
Mule, breeding of, 8, 43, 56, 65, 89, 125, 194
Muradyan, G., 101, 238
Murdoch, B. O., 100
MX. *See* Movsēs Xorenacʻi, 29
Myron, 14

Nahor, 32, 34, 43, 65, 81, 82, 119, 146, 194, 209
Naphtali, 76, 82
Napier, A. S., 100
New Israel, 15
Nicea, Council of, 92
Nimrod, 64
Ninos, 34
Noachic laws, 146
Noah, 12, 146, 192, 209, 223
    death of, 146

Oak staff becomes tree. *See* Mamrē, 226–27
Oak tree, 22, 165, 169, 195
Obscene deeds, 237
Offerings, types of, 85
Oil
    of anointment, 78
    of joy, 14
    sweet, 14, 119, 121
Onomastic traditions, 94
Orlov, A. A., 11, 175
Orthographic variants, 102–104
Oxford, Bodleian Arm ms f11, 94

Pʻilon Tirakacʻi, 29, 70, 192
Pahl, city, 82
Palestine, 81
    meaning of, 94, 97
Palhavounis, 82
Papazian, Michael, 17, 20, 24, 70, 179, 199–203
Parthians, 82
Peleg, 32, 146
Perezites, 85
Persians, 125

Petit, F, 12, 69, 70, 90
Petros, 125
Petrosyan, E., 18
Pharaoh, 24, 36, 44, 65, 67, 83, 90, 124, 149, 150, 205, 211
    affliction of, 66
    dream of, 115
    gifts to Abraham, 210
    pays indemnity of Abraham, 195
Philistines, 74
Philo, opposes astrology, 42
Piovanelli, P., 8
Place of the covenant, 161, 231
Poetic retelling, 86
Prayer, thrice daily, 46, 197
Priest, consecration of, 98
Promise of land, missing, 52
Prophecy, 6
Prophets, 172
Pseudo-Eupolemus, 42

Quinn, E. C., 100

R. Ḥiyya, 47
R. Nehemia, 45
Rachel, 76, 82
Ram, 13, 23, 69, 91, 99–100, 121, 161, 175, 212, 232
Raphael (archangel), 46
Ravens, 6–7, 18–19, 36, 89, 102, 113, 123, 127, 147–48, 193, 206
    story of, 18, 64, 209–10, 223
Rebecca. *See* Rebekah
Rebekah, 6, 7, 35, 69, 74, 75, 82
    consults Melchizedek, 70
Reu, 29, 32, 34, 146
Reuben, 76, 82
Rood Tree, 94, 99–100
Rowel, G., 14

Sabek, Story of, 44
Sabek, Tree of, 10, 23, 57, 69, 91, 100, 161, 175, 206, 212, 232
    Aqedah at, 120
Sacred places and sacred acts, 99
Sacrifices, series of, 232
Sacrificial beast, perfect, 91
Sahak Mrut, 46

Sahak. *See* Isaac
Sała I, 97
Sała II, mother of Melchizedek, 239
Sałim, 94, 97, 176, 232
Sałim, King, built Jerusalem, 163
Salt, pillar of, 49
Samaria, 43, 195
Šamiram, 34
Samuēl Karmǰajorecʻi, 1, 17, 241
Sanders, E. P., 47, 200
Sarah, passim
    appearance of, 150
    beauty of, 65, 114
    is Isca, 57
    laughter of, 22, 47–48, 118–19, 156, 170, 201, 228
    married to Abraham, 147
    no recourse to charms, 201
    untested, 202
    virtue of, 201
Sarah and Pharaoh, story of, 65–68, 74, 114–15, 149–50, 196, 206, 210, 224–25
Sarai. *See* Sarah
Satan, 13, 19, 22, 36, 46, 52, 135, 154
    blocks the way, 22, 52, 154–55, 169, 197, 204, 227
    wiles of, 195
Satran, David, 11
Sayatʻ Nova, 186
Scholasticism
    Armenian, 21
    texts, 29, 78
Scott, J. M., 192
Sea, 158
    blackened, 159
Sēdēk, 94, 97–98
    anointing of, 98
Seed plough, 18
Sekʻim. *See* Shechem, 195
Sela. *See also* Sała, 146
Semiramis, 34
Serug, 32, 34, 146
Servitude
    400 years, 119
    430 years, 35
    440 years, 119, 170
    460 years, 22, 156, 170, 228

Seth, 146
Sethites, lived on mountains, 98
Seven peoples, 85
Seven trials of Abraham, 90
Shechem, 69, 195, 212
    identified as Hebron, 57
Shelah, 97
Shem b. Noah, 9, 29, 94, 97–98, 146, 209
    guarded by angels, 98
    sons of, 98
Shulman, David, 3
Simeon, 82
Simon, 76
Slaves, black, 45
Smbat, 13
Sodom, 14, 24, 37, 42, 44, 49, 92, 103, 128, 159, 172, 196
    burning of, 49, 50, 93, 125, 159
    destruction of, 229–30
    and Gomorrah, 54
    mountain of, 170
    story of, 92, 119, 156–59, 170–71, 228–30
Sodomites, 48, 158–59, 211
    five kingdoms of, 196
Solomon, 125, 193
Sorcery, 194
Sovē. *See* Shuah, 82
Spring, at foot of oak tree, 152
Spurling, H., 1, 46, 47
Staff, 13
    fiery, 225
Stählin, O., 10
Stepʻanos Siwnecʻi, 22, 47
Steudel, A., 9
Stone, M. E., passim
Stone, N., 11
Stordalen, T., 99
Story of Moses, 146
Story of Noah, 146
Story of Terah, 127
Stromateis, 10
Sud, river, 113
Sur (Sor), river, 113
Sword, fiery, 115
Syria, 77
Syrians, 34

INDEX OF NAMES AND SELECT SUBJECTS

T'amrazian, H., 37
Table, cruciform, 169
Temple, Abraham burns, 5
Ten Commandments, 84
Ten Plagues, 83
Ten Trials of Abraham, 6, 16, 21, 90, 204–6, 211
Ter-Stépanian, A., 18, 101
Ter-Vardanian, G., 37
Terah, 20, 23, 32, 34, 36, 41, 43, 44, 65, 81, 89, 114, 123, 125, 146–48, 194, 209, 236
    death of, 43, 195
    goes to Canaan, 18–19
    idol maker, 112, 223
    idolater, 147, 193, 206, 223
    idolatrous temple, 57, 194, 210
    sons of, 64
Text, displacement of, 59–60
Textual clusters, 6
Textual relationships, 3
Theological discussion, 197–99
Thierry, J.-M., 213
Thirteen *middot,* 84
Thirty
    Adam created at, 97
    auspicious age, 97
Thomsen, P., 46
Thomson, R. W., 20, 29, 32, 34, 82
Three hundred and eighteen men, 10, 92, 99, 196
Three men, 3–4, 10, 13–14, 22, 89, 99, 103, 118, 155, 169, 197–98, 227, 241
    Christian interpretation of, 48
    eating of, 200, 241
    identity of, 46, 47
    wondrous discourse of, 155, 170
Tiran *vardapet,* 42, 69, 70, 83
Tithe, 9
Tower of Babel, 33, 41
Traditions, interrelations of, 6
Tree of Joseph, 94
Tree of Sabek, 94, 120, 161
Tree of Sēdēk, 94, 99–100
Tromp, Johannes, 3
Tuffin, P., 10, 19, 41–42, 66, 177, 195
Turks, 82

Twelve Patriarchs, 177
Twelve tongues, 192
Typological exegesis, 23, 54
Typology, 90

Undying worms, 193
Ur, 41, 43, 194, 206, 210
Ura, Reu's wife, 34

van Rompay, L., 12, 70
VanderKam, J. C., 30
Vardan Arewelc'i, 18
Vardan Aygekc'i, 98–99
Vardanyan, Edda, 213
Venice Mekhitarist ms V290, 36
Venison, 75
Vine, 94, 99
Vosté, J.-M., 41

Wahlgren, S., 41
Walraff, M., 13, 171, 195
Weitenberg, J. J. S., 12, 70
Well of Vision, 82
Wells, 82–83
Wieck, R. S., 114
Wilkinson, J., 46
World tree, 99
Wutz, F. X., 97

Xač'ik'yan. *See* Khachikyan, L.
Xač'atryan, P. M., 242

Yasif, E., 112
Yektan, 82
Yezbok (Ishbak), 82
Yovasap' (poet) 86
Yovasap' Sebastac'i, 86

Zakaria Catholicos, 1, 4, 16, 46, 100
Zebulun, 76, 82
Zechariah, 48, 202
Zekiyan, B. L., 17
Zemran, 82
Zeyt'unyan, A., 36–37, 76, 122, 127, 178
Zilpah, 82
Zion, 212
Zmrut, Sarah's mother, 23